YELLOWSTONE & GRAND TETON
NATIONAL PARKS

BRADLEY MAYHEW

ANDREW DEAN NYSTROM

AMY MARR

LONELY PLANET PUBLICATIONS
Melbourne · Oakland · London · Paris

Yellowstone & Grand Teton National Parks
1st edition – April 2003

Published by
Lonely Planet Publications Pty Ltd ABN 36 005 607 983
90 Maribyrnong St, Footscray, Victoria 3011, Australia

Lonely Planet Offices
Australia Locked Bag 1, Footscray, Victoria 3011
USA 150 Linden St, Oakland, CA 94607
UK 10a Spring Place, London NW5 3BH
France 1 rue du Dahomey, 75011 Paris

Photographs
Many of the images in this guide are available for licensing from
Lonely Planet Images.
W www.lonelyplanetimages.com

Front cover photograph
Elk on the banks of the Madison River,
Yellowstone National Park (Kraig Lieb/Lonely Planet Images)

ISBN 1 74104 116 3

text & maps © Lonely Planet Publications Pty Ltd 2003
photos © photographers as indicated 2003

Printed through Colorcraft Ltd, Hong Kong
Printed in China

YELLOWSTONE & GRAND TETON CONTENTS

THE AUTHORS

Bradley Mayhew

Bradley started traveling in China, Tibet, and northern Pakistan while studying Chinese at Oxford University. Since then he's written or co-authored Lonely Planet guides to *South-West China*, *Shanghai*, *Tibet*, *Mongolia*, and *Central Asia*, and has lectured to the Royal Geographical Society on Central Asia. A hopeless nomad, he now lives in Billings, Montana, from where he regularly tries in vain to get a decent flight connection to Asia.

Andrew Dean Nystrom

Born a mile high in Colorado, Andrew has many fond memories of visiting Yellowstone and Grand Teton with his family as a child. Trained as a geographer at the University of California, Berkeley, he volunteered for the National Park Service's Yellowstone Center for Resources as a thermal inventory researcher during the summer of 2002. While researching this book, he hiked hundreds of backcountry miles and tested the soakability of many hot pots. He's also contributed text and images to Lonely Planet's *Mexico*, *San Francisco*, and *USA* books, Fodor's guides to Mexico and California, and is the author of *Las Vegas Condensed*. He was last seen shipping out from the Falkland Islands for Antarctica in search of more hot springs and wildlife.

Amy Marr

Boston-born Amy's first camping trip was to Yellowstone when she was two. Her inaugural night in a tent was interrupted by a mama bear and her cubs pawing through the family cooler. After studying at Williams College and in Italy, she worked as a business writer and PR director before leading biking and hiking trips. In 1998 she moved to Santa Fe, where she managed *Outside Online*. Now a freelance writer and editor, she is firmly rooted in Marin County, CA, but still exhibits signs of restlessness, which she tempers with a healthy regimen of Mt Tam biking and hiking, and cooking for large groups of friends.

From the Authors

Bradley Mayhew Thanks to Andrew for his input and to Mariah and Kathleen for their guidance and above all patience on this book. This wasn't an easy project for all concerned and I appreciate the slack you cut me… repeatedly. Thanks to John and Sharon for the map, the ice cooler, and the truck that got me started in the first place. Above all thanks and love to my wife Kelli, who saw me disappear off to the park two days after our wedding and then return a couple of months later to work nights for a month in a mad rush to get the manuscript finished. This book would not have been finished without your patience and support. Thank you.

Andrew Dean Nystrom Many thanks to everyone at the Yellowstone Center for Resources, Spatial Analysis Center, and NPS Research Library. Special thanks to Anne Beausang, Tim Cahill, Liz Cleveland, Don George, Carrie Guiles, Charless and Marjorie Fowlkes, Christie Hendrix, John Hurst, Janet Lewis, Dan Mahoney, Malcolm Margolin, Steve Miller, Tanner Raymer, Anne Rodman, Shannon Savage, Jim Sinclair for the fishing lessons, and park historian Lee Whittlesey. At Lonely Planet, special thanks to Paul Carlstroem, Kate Hoffman, Kathleen Munnelly, and co-author Bradley Mayhew.

Amy Marr A warm thanks to my co-author Andrew, coordinating author Bradley, and project manager Kathleen for her unfailing support and excitement. Appreciation and thanks to Pete Wheelan and Kate Hoffman for including me in this project. Thank yous and love to my home team posse for keeping me well-fed and very happy – I miss you when I'm on the road. A special grazie to Stephanie and Katie, my two best vado pazzo cohorts, for the always-good vibes from NM. Lastly, a huge, gracious thanks to my parents, for the early introduction to national parks and adventure. You are both shining examples of steadfast love, enthusiasm, integrity, and kindness.

THIS BOOK

The first edition of *Yellowstone & Grand Teton National Parks* was researched and written by Bradley Mayhew, Andrew Dean Nystrom, and Amy Marr. Coordinating author Bradley Mayhew researched and wrote the majority of the book. Andrew Dean Nystrom researched and wrote the Ecosystem and History chapters, hiking in Yellowstone, and the Jackson and Jackson Hole sections. Amy Marr contributed the "Surfing the Web" section. Acclaimed travel journalist Tim Cahill graciously contributed the stirring preface.

From the Publisher

Yellowstone & Grand Teton National Parks was produced in Lonely Planet's Oakland office under the leadership of US Publisher Mariah Bear, and would not have been possible without her wisdom, wit, enthusiasm, and unwavering dedication. She has our heartfelt appreciation. Much praise is also due Kate Hoffman, who developed the National Parks series, devised the structure for the launch titles and commissioned and briefed this book. Kathleen Munnelly served as project manager and developmental editor.

Wade "Old Faithful" Fox was the main editor on the book, and David "Teton" Lauterborn pitched in with final edits and proofreading. Intrepid cartographers Bart "Lewis" Wright and Annette "Clark" Olson from Fineline Maps charted each geyser and peak in the parks and beyond. Ken DellaPenta indexed the book.

Design Manager Ruth Askevold created the magnificent template and cover, while Candice Jacobus designed the gorgeous color wraps and worked wonders with the layout. Hayden Foell drew the cute critters and majestic trees that grace the wildlife gallery.

Kudos to Glenn Beanland and the rest of the Lonely Planet Images crew, who worked so hard to find such charismatic megafauna. The historic photographs in this book appear courtesy of the National Park Service Historic Photograph Collection and the Denver Public Library.

Andreas Schueller provided invaluable technical assistance in translating tricky code. Amy Willis cheerfully helped research the illustrations.

Special thanks to Lonely Planet's Travel Editor Don George, who put us in touch with Tim Cahill and provided valuable guidance throughout production.

Thanks also to Lindsay Brown, who supplied us with material from *Hiking in the Rocky Mountains*; and to Global Publisher Simon Westcott for supporting the series.

ACKNOWLEDGEMENTS

Grateful acknowledgement is made to the National Park Service and to the Denver Public Library for use of their historic photographs.

Foreword

ABOUT LONELY PLANET GUIDEBOOKS

Although inclusion in a guidebook usually implies a recommendation, we cannot list every good place. Exclusion does not necessarily imply criticism. In fact, there are a number of reasons why we might exclude a place – sometimes it is simply inappropriate to encourage an influx of travelers.

The story begins with a classic travel adventure: Tony and Maureen Wheeler's 1972 journey across Europe and Asia to Australia. There was no useful information about the overland trail then, so Tony and Maureen published the first Lonely Planet guidebook to meet a growing need.

From a kitchen table, Lonely Planet has grown to become the largest independent travel publisher in the world, with offices in Melbourne (Australia), Oakland (USA), London (UK) and Paris (France).

Today Lonely Planet guidebooks cover the globe. There is an ever-growing list of books and information in a variety of media. Some things haven't changed. The main aim is still to make it possible for adventurous travelers to get out there – to explore and better understand the world.

At Lonely Planet we believe travelers can make a positive contribution to the countries they visit – if they respect their host communities and spend their money wisely. Since 1986 a percentage of the income from each book has been donated to aid projects and human rights campaigns, and, more recently, to wildlife conservation.

UPDATES & READER FEEDBACK

Things change – prices go up, schedules change, good places go bad and bad places go bankrupt. Nothing stays the same. So, if you find things better or worse, recently opened or long-since closed, please tell us and help make the next edition even more accurate and useful.

Lonely Planet thoroughly updates each guidebook as often as possible – usually every two years, although for some destinations the gap can be longer. Between editions, up-to-date information is available in our free, quarterly *Planet Talk* newsletter and monthly email bulletin *Comet*. The *Upgrades* section of our website (W www.lonelyplanet.com) is also regularly updated by Lonely Planet authors, and the site's *Scoop* section covers news and current affairs relevant to travelers. Lastly, the *Thorn Tree* bulletin board and *Postcards* section carry unverified, but fascinating, reports from travelers.

Tell us about it! We genuinely value your feedback. A well-traveled team at Lonely Planet reads and acknowledges every email and letter we receive and ensures that every morsel of information finds its way to the relevant authors, editors and cartographers.

Everyone who writes to us will find their name listed in the next edition of the appropriate guidebook and will receive the latest issue of *Comet* or *Planet Talk*. The very best contributions will be rewarded with a free guidebook.

We may edit, reproduce and incorporate your comments in Lonely Planet products such as guidebooks, websites and digital products, so let us know if you don't want your comments reproduced or your name acknowledged.

How to contact Lonely Planet:
Online: e talk2us@lonelyplanet.com.au, W www.lonelyplanet.com
Australia: Locked Bag 1, Footscray, Victoria 3011
UK: 10a Spring Place, London NW5 3BH
USA: 150 Linden St, Oakland, CA 94607

PREFACE

by TIM CAHILL

I think Yellowstone Park and its environs are the best place to live on earth. That is what I thought 25 years ago when I moved to a small town near the north entrance to the park, and it is what I think now.

I have had some difficulty verbally expressing this enthusiasm in anything less than a full-blown filibuster. Indeed, I can vividly recall a conversation I had a few years ago with a tourist gassing up his car at a local gas station. "I got my family with me," the man said. He motioned to his car. I noticed the out-of-state plates, the woman sitting patiently in the front seat, the two kids bouncing around in the back. "So," the guy said, "how far away is this park?"

"About 50 miles."

I believe the man fancied himself a canny traveler and not the kind of sap who'd visit a place simply because it was the world's first national park or because it was the beating heart of the largest intact temperate zone ecosystem on Earth.

"Is it worth the drive?"

This utterance challenged the assertion that there are no stupid questions. I took a deep breath. It was necessary to expound on the Park for a great long period of time while the woman in the car became considerably less patient and the kids careened around in the back like a pair of pinballs in urgent play. I told the man that Yellowstone contained more geysers than anyplace on earth and that they sprayed up and sideways and off at oblique angles and that they sometimes sounded like huge toilets in full flush and that these sounds would make his kids laugh. I hit heavy on the concept of charismatic megafauna and said that he and his family would certainly see dozens of huge and majestic elk; that they would encounter any number of bison, which are the largest land animal in North America. Bison and elk sightings, I said, were guaranteed, and it was more than likely they'd see pronghorn and coyotes and bald eagles. There was also a good chance they'd see wolves, and if they didn't see them, they might hear the eerie choruses of howls that always send shivers up my back. It was possible they'd spot black or grizzly bears, moose, otters, or beavers.

Additionally, there were large dumb trout in the rivers, and these rivers ran through meadows alive with more wildflowers than there were stars in the sky, or so it sometimes seemed to me. In places the land was bent and folded and shattered with the geologic evidence of an immense volcanic eruption that rocked the earth 600,000 years ago. Indeed, volcanic eruptions had created petrified forest upon petrified forest in various parts of the park and its environs. The best part of it was that you could walk to many of these places. There were nice family-length walks in the park, as well as full on backcountry expedition type hikes. There were mountains to climb, rock walls to scale, and waterfalls to admire just about anywhere you'd care to look. And, oh yeah, this time of year, you might see a few mountain bluebirds. I like mountain bluebirds. I like magpies and ravens and ospreys as well.

The man drove off in the direction of the park. I found myself exhausted and realized that I couldn't very well advise every single traveler who passes through my town. Which is why I welcome and recommend this book, a lively, well-written, and comprehensive guide to the best place on Earth, all done up in the accessible and authoritative Lonely Planet manner. It is the only book on the area some visitors will ever need, and it is just the first of many that others will eventually buy. These latter are the folks who will come back year after year because they realize, as I do, that this is simply the best place on Earth.

A final note: I ran into the family I'd counseled some days later. They were eating at a local restaurant, and the guy thanked me for my advice. He said that Yellowstone was worth the drive.

Tim Cahill is the acclaimed author of Hold the Enlightenment, Pass the Butterworms *and four other travel books. He is a founding editor of and monthly columnist for* Outside *magazine and has also written for* Rolling Stone, Esquire, *and the* New York Times Book Review.

There's nowhere in the world quite like Yellowstone. From its raging geysers to its free-roaming herds of bison, the land stands as one last remaining pocket of a wild, primeval America. As the world's oldest national park and part of the world's largest intact temperate mountain ecosystem, Yellowstone has become synonymous with environmental protection worldwide. Here you will find the country's largest elk herds, the continent's largest wild bison herd, and the world's densest collection of geysers and fossilized forests, set in a land roamed by wolves, grizzlies, lynx, moose, and antelope.

INTRODUCTION

The park is probably most famous for its geysers and hot springs – nature's crowd pleasers – whose magical explosions and graceful beauty still capture the visitor's imagination as they did 150 years ago. The blast of hot steam followed by cold air, the stench of rotten eggs, and the belching sound of a hot spring is best enjoyed in Yellowstone. The park's highways traverse these geysers, through meadows and forests, past roadside wildlife and campsites aromatic with pine needles and family campfires.

Each region of the park boasts its own character. To the northwest, Mammoth offers ornate terraces and colorful pools. Roosevelt is a wilder land of wolves and bison. Canyon holds one of the park's great draws in the Grand Canyon of the Yellowstone. Farther south, Yellowstone Lake is a huge wilderness of water that shelters the park's most remote reaches. Geyser holds the majority of the park's geothermal wonders.

South of Yellowstone is Grand Teton National Park, probably the most famous natural skyline in the United States, whose mountains have launched a million SUVs. These vertical peaks, reflected in a string of gorgeous glacial lakes, come closest to most people's picture-postcard image of alpine splendor and will send a shiver of excitement down the spine of even the least vertically inclined.

Opportunities to venture into the backcountry abound in both parks, whether on foot, horseback, boat, ski, or snowshoe. Buckle up and climb the Tetons, canoe around Shoshone Lake, mountain bike to the summit of Mt Washburn, or hike for days through the remote backcountry – the choice is yours.

In few other places is raw nature so accessible. In Yellowstone even the most sedentary couch potato can be at eye level with a mountain peak or hike around a glacial lake. Drive the Beartooth Highway, the northeast gateway to the park, and you'll find yourself at 10,000ft without even unbuckling your seatbelt. Only around Old Faithful does the wilderness give way in places to theme park chaos. Elsewhere, it's easier than you would imagine to lose the crowds. Park the car and head off down a trail, if only for a mile or two, and the park will reveal its true beauty.

Yellowstone's wonder doesn't diminish at its boundaries. The two parks and their surrounding six national forests and three national wildlife refuges together form a larger, interconnected area, six times the size of Yellowstone, called the Greater Yellowstone Ecosystem. Here you'll find the blue-ribbon trout streams and hiking routes of the Gallatin and Madison Rivers, the awesome 10,000ft-high Beartooth Plateau, and the broad Shoshone National Forest, which encompasses one of the largest tracts of wilderness in the Lower 48.

Created by the Yellowstone Act (1872) as a "public park or pleasuring-ground for the benefit and enjoyment of the people," Yellowstone now attracts up to 30,000 visitors daily, and more than three million visitors annually. Debate rages over how best to manage this influx. Ironically, the park's great appeal threatens to destroy the very features that attract such numbers.

Yellowstone is many things to many people: a natural Eden, a paradise lost, an extreme sports playground, or the world's biggest petting zoo. But all pigeonholing falls short. Yellowstone has a depth and breadth of beauty that requires repeated visits to fully appreciate its complexities and wonder.

Despite all the controversies, the traffic jams, and the crowds, Yellowstone and Grand Teton still deliver. Watch a moose trawl for food in a secluded pond, hike to magnificent Teton views, fish for trout under a golden sunset, and reinvigorate yourself in two of America's greatest natural wonders.

Using this Guidebook

The core of this book is the Yellowstone National Park chapter, which covers everything you'll need to know once you're in the park. The coverage is divided into six main regions, each of which has an overview of sightseeing, hiking, biking, and boating options in that region. You'll find similar coverage in the Grand Teton chapter.

The Highlights chapter offers an introduction to the parks' best sightseeing options. The Activities chapter gives an overview and basic tips on outdoor fun, from hiking to fishing. Planning is one chapter to read before you go; it details practical information such as how to get to the parks, what to bring, and how to avoid the worst of the crowds. Gateway Towns gives you the lowdown on hubs from which to tour the parks. Places to Stay and Places to Eat list a host of accommodation and dining options in and around the parks.

Greater Yellowstone takes you on a tour of the surrounding sights and national forests of the Yellowstone ecosystem, either for those who have time to explore these gems in detail or for those who are simply traveling through these corridors to or from the parks. The Excursions chapter suggests a couple of detours worth including in your itinerary if you have plenty of time.

Much of Yellowstone's fascination lies out of view, either deep underground or deep in the backcountry. To bone up on Yellowstone's true wonders, read the Geology, Ecosystem, and History chapters.

Yellowstone & Grand Teton National Parks

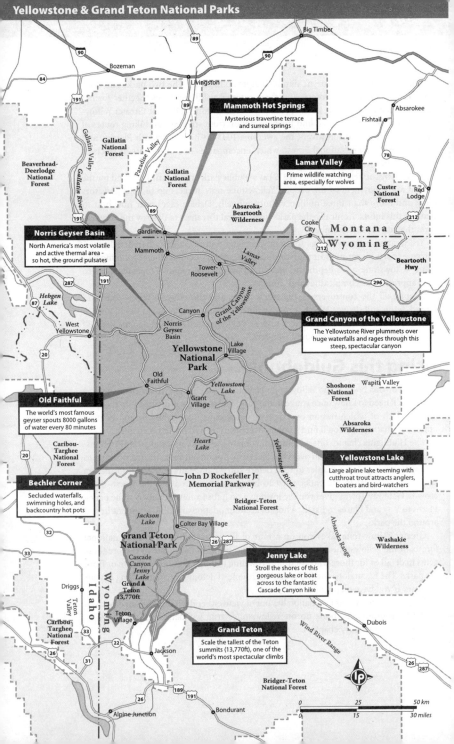

Mammoth Hot Springs
Mysterious travertine terrace and surreal springs

Lamar Valley
Prime wildlife watching area, especially for wolves

Norris Geyser Basin
North America's most volatile and active thermal area - so hot, the ground pulsates

Grand Canyon of the Yellowstone
The Yellowstone River plummets over huge waterfalls and rages through this steep, spectacular canyon

Old Faithful
The world's most famous geyser spouts 8000 gallons of water every 80 minutes

Yellowstone Lake
Large alpine lake teeming with cutthroat trout attracts anglers, boaters and bird-watchers

Bechler Corner
Secluded waterfalls, swimming holes, and backcountry hot pots

Jenny Lake
Stroll the shores of this gorgeous lake or boat across to the fantastic Cascade Canyon hike

Grand Teton
Scale the tallest of the Teton summits (13,770ft), one of the world's most spectacular climbs

Elemental, primeval, and awesomely beautiful, thermal features like Clepsydra Geyser (below, photo: Carol Polich) make Yellowstone a place like nowhere else on earth.

YELLOWSTONE & GRAND TETON
HIGHLIGHTS

Yellowstone and Grand Teton National Parks offer such a wonderful breadth of pleasures that each person's highlights will be unique. It may be the first time you saw a moose or went camping with the kids, the bison herd that passed a few feet from your car, or the thrilling sight of a geyser in action.

Immerse yourself in the parks - take a ranger hike, watch wolves in the Lamar Valley, bike up Mt Washburn, explore a self-guided trail around a homesteader's cabin, or mosey on down a backwoods path on horseback.

No matter what, one trip won't be enough. Read about Yellowstone, learn about its ecology and animals, appreciate its startling geology, and it will reward you for a lifetime. For an overview of the best of the parks and some suggested itineraries, read on…

GRAND CANYON The awe-inspiring Grand Canyon of the Yellowstone is a must-see. Its scenic overlooks are accessible by car, but only hardy hikers can reach the canyon floor.
[Photo: Andrew Brownbill]

WILDFLOWERS The spectacular wildflowers of Grand Teton National Park, like these Butter and Eggs, bloom in mid-summer. [Photo: John Elk III]

FLY FISHING Anglers ply the Yellowstone River, ranked as one of the nation's finest blue-ribbon rivers (along with Montana's Madison and Gallatin Rivers, also in the region). [Photo: John Elk III]

MORMON ROW The superbly photogenic barns of Mormon Row still stand as a testament to Jackson Hole's first settlers, with the Tetons as an impressive backdrop. [Photo: John Elk III]

YELLOWSTONE & GRAND TETON
HIGHLIGHTS

BLACK BEAR Smaller and less aggressive than grizzlies, black bears are often seen around Tower and Mammoth. [Photo: Carol Polich]

MORNING GLORY POOL Located in the Upper Geyser Basin, this is one of Yellowstone's most colorful thermal features. [Photo: Andrew Brownbill]

YELLOWSTONE'S GEYSERS Pink Cone Geyser in the Lower Geyser Basin is one of dozens of smaller geysers that erupt regularly throughout the day. [Photo: Carol Polich]

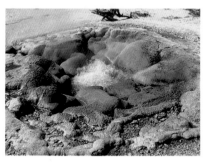

BUBBLING SPRING A small spring in the Midway Geyser Basin, dubbed "Hell's Half Acre" by Rudyard Kipling. [Photo: Donald C. & Priscilla Alexander Eastman]

BLACK SAND BASIN Winter visitors stroll the boardwalk over the hot springs of the Black Sand Basin, one mile northwest of Old Faithful. [Photo: Stephen Saks]

THE TETONS A winter sunrise illuminates America's most famous natural skyline, the magnificent Tetons. [Photo: Cheyenne Rouse]

YELLOWSTONE & GRAND TETON
HIGHLIGHTS

MUD POTS The colorful Fountain Paint Pot in winter.
[Photo: Carol Polich]

ELK Two elk lock antlers in the snow at the National Elk Refuge.
[Photo: Lee Foster]

GRAND PRISMATIC SPRING Brightly colored Grand Prismatic Spring in the Midway Geyser Basin is Yellowstone National Park's largest hot spring. [Photo: John Elk III]

YELLOWSTONE & GRAND TETON
HIGHLIGHTS

OLD FAITHFUL INN The world's largest log building, the rustic Old Faithful Inn, was built by Robert Reamer between 1903-04. [Photo: John Elk III]

OLD FAITHFUL The world's favorite geyser erupts before a Yellowstone setting sun. [Photo: Morgan Konn]

PETRIFIED FOREST Yellowstone's many petrified trees were buried in ash more than 50 million years ago. [Photo: Andrew Dean Nystrom]

BIGHORN SHEEP Rocky Mountain bighorns are commonly spotted in the Yellowstone region, particularly around Mt Washburn. [Photo: Carol Polich]

MAMMOTH HOT SPRINGS These ornate travertine terraces are made of limestone deposits and can grow up to an inch per day, although Minerva Spring, pictured, is now inactive. [Photo: Carol Polich]

ALPINE MEADOWS Summer brings a riot of wildflowers to alpine meadows throughout the Greater Yellowstone region. [Photo: Carol Polich]

HIKING A family enjoys a day hike in Grand Teton National Park. [Photo: Cheyenne Rouse]

BISON Yellowstone's magnificent bison are among the USA's last free-roaming herds. [Photo: Carol Polich]

With so much to see and do in Yellowstone and Grand Teton, the real question is where to begin. This chapter suggests some options, though no matter which attractions and activities you choose as your focus, you really can't go wrong.

HIGHLIGHTS

The golden rule when planning your vacation is to avoid being too ambitious. Don't try to cover the entire region in one military-style maneuver. If you have only a short time, then choose one area of the parks to explore. Don't be afraid to leave some things out – you'll have an excuse to return! Yellowstone and Grand Teton are places that reward many visits at different times of the year.

Suggested Itineraries

The following itineraries are designed to get you started, but they're not meant to be prescriptive – there's no "right way" to explore the parks. Beyond this, the best advice you'll hear is to slow down and to get out of the car. As remarkably accessible as Yellowstone's beauty is by car, you'll only come to grips with the park on foot. As John Muir once said, "Nothing can be done well at a speed of 40 miles a day. The multitude of mixed, novel impressions rapidly piled on one another make only a dreamy, bewildering, swirling blur, most of which is unrememberable."

ONE DAY

To take in **Yellowstone** in a day, start out early, stay late, and take in Old Faithful (p 112), Grand Prismatic Spring (p 114), and Canyon Junction (p 90). The exact itinerary depends on from which direction you're entering and leaving the park, but you can manage either the south loop or north loop in a day; to attempt both is overly ambitious. Try to arrange some wildlife viewing, either first thing in the morning or just before dusk, and take one short hike, perhaps the Yellowstone River Picnic Area (p 87) or Mystic Falls (p 120) trails.

If you have just a day in **Grand Teton**, make a beeline for Jenny Lake (139) as early as possible to get the best light on the Tetons. Take a walk along Leigh Lake (p 138) or the ferry to Inspiration Point and hike up Cascade Canyon (p 140). Break for lunch at Signal Mountain (p 135) or Colter Bay (p 134), where you can take a boat out for an hour. Make predusk wildlife viewing a priority at either Swan Lake (p 134), near Colter Bay, or Oxbow Bend (p 135). If you are day-tripping from Jackson, return south down Hwy 191.

THREE DAYS

This is enough time for a speedy Billings to Jackson run; over the Beartooth Hwy (Hwy 212), through Canyon and Geyser Countries, down to Grand Teton and Jackson. See p 209 for details.

From the north you could do a loop from Bozeman (p 221), taking in Paradise Valley (p 207), Mammoth (p 77), and Old Faithful (p 112) and then heading to Lake (p 97), Canyon (p 90), Roosevelt (p 85) and back either up Paradise Valley or (given another day) over the Beartooth Hwy (p 209). You could do a similar "lollipop loop" from the south starting at Jackson (p 66).

FIVE DAYS

An extra two days is enough time to add a day hike or overnight backpacking trip, perhaps Grand Teton's Paintbrush Divide (p 146).

From Billings or Bozeman, head down to Red Lodge (p 224) and spend a night on the Beartooth Plateau (p 209). Continue through the park, heading south down one side of the Grand Loop Rd (p 74) past Canyon and Lake, to Grand Teton for a day and then return back up the other side of the loop, visiting Old Faithful and Mammoth.

ONE WEEK

A good schedule in this case is two days in Grand Teton, four days in Yellowstone, and one day in one of the corridors into the park. In Yellowstone you'd be able to take in Canyon, Geyser, Mammoth, and Lake, as well as a day hike and some time exploring the Beartooth Hwy.

If you are heading back up to Yellowstone from Grand Teton, make a loop trip by heading west over Teton Pass and then back north up Idaho's Teton Valley (p 218) from Jackson.

MORE THAN ONE WEEK

Now you can really explore the Greater Yellowstone Ecosystem. Spend a day or two hiking outside the park, in the Beartooth Plateau (p 209), Gallatin Valley (p 204), or Hebgen Lake (p 200) regions. Take a horseback or backpacking route such as the Teton Crest Trail (p 147) and make a side trip to Cody (p 225), Bozeman (p 221), or Jackson (p 66). Explore the different regions of the park, with a day or two in each, and savor the time.

Driving Tours

There's hardly a mile of highway in the Greater Yellowstone region that can't be called scenic. These are drives to be savored, not sped through at 75mph.

You just can't go wrong on Yellowstone's main **Grand Loop Rd**. Views are always great, whether from Dunraven Pass, alongside Yellowstone Lake and the Madison River, or across open valley. The road crosses the Continental Divide three times between Old Faithful and the south entrance.

The most dramatic drive in the region is probably the 65mi **Beartooth Hwy** from Red Lodge to Cooke City. Journalist Charles Kuralt ranked the Beartooth Hwy the "Number One Scenic Highway in America." Much of the drive climbs above 10,000ft, passing countless lakes and views of the Absaroka Range. This road connects with the park's scenic northeast entrance road from Cooke City to Tower-Roosevelt Junction.

If you don't agree with Kuralt, then try Teddy Roosevelt, who dubbed the Wapiti Valley from Cody to Yellowstone's east entrance "the most scenic 52 miles in the

United States." Now called the **Buffalo Bill Scenic Hwy** (Hwy 14/16/20), it's certainly a grand route, from the semi-deserts of Wyoming, through badlands-style eroded volcanic cliffs, and finally up into lovely alpine scenery, all the way hugging the scenic North Fork of the Shoshone River.

An excellent add-on to a Beartooth Hwy drive is the **Chief Joseph Scenic Hwy** (Hwy 296), which connects Cody to the Beartooth Plateau over Dead Indian Pass and the dramatic Clark's Fork junction. For the premier drive into or out of Yellowstone, combine the Beartooth Hwy, the Chief Joseph Scenic Hwy, and the Buffalo Bill Scenic Hwy into one 180mi viewfest.

OFF THE BEATEN TRACK

Shhh … don't tell anyone about these six seldom-visited sights:

✔ **Shoshone Geyser Basin**, Geyser Country – Hike or bike to catch a backcountry eruption

✔ **Imperial Geyser**, Geyser Country – Lose the crowds just 10 minutes past popular Fairy Falls

✔ Upper Geyser Basin by **full moon** – Geyser eruptions seem even eerier

✔ **Bechler Corner** and **Grassy Lake Rd** – The bone-crushing drive deters most visitors

✔ **Fossil Forest Hike**, Roosevelt Country – An unmarked turnoff and path leads up to fine views

✔ **Shadow Mountain**, Grand Teton – A rough drive or mountain bike ride to Teton views

If you are headed north out of the park, you can't beat the subtle beauty of **Paradise Valley** (Hwy 89). The valley's ranches glow golden at sunset.

For one-way scenic overlooks, the two top choices are Grand Teton's **Signal Mountain Rd**, which offers fine views of the Tetons, or **Sawtell Peak Rd** in Idaho's Island Park, which promises panoramic views over Henry's Lake, Island Park, and southeast Yellowstone, as far as the west side of the Tetons. Arguably the best roadside views of the Tetons come from the top of **Shadow Mountain** (8299ft), on the east edge of Grand Teton National Park, but it's a rough drive to the top.

Inside Grand Teton National Park, **Teton Park Rd** (the park's "inner road") offers the best roadside views of the Tetons. The short one-way **Jenny Lake Scenic Dr** takes you to a good overlook of the lake and views up dramatic Cascade Canyon.

If you have time for a half-day excursion from Grand Teton, it's well worth driving east from Moran Junction along Hwy 26 to **Togwotee Pass**, where the views

OUR FAVORITE HIKES

✔ **Cascade and Paintbrush Canyons**, Grand Teton

✔ **Teton Crest Trail**, Grand Teton

✔ **Mt Washburn**, Yellowstone

✔ **Black Canyon of the Yellowstone**

✔ **Two Ocean Lake**, Grand Teton

✔ **Bechler River**, Yellowstone

✔ **Avalanche Peak**, Yellowstone

✔ **Leigh Lake**, Grand Teton

✔ **Fossil Forest**, Yellowstone

west to the Tetons are excellent. From the pass continue on to lovely Brooks Lake. Togwotee Pass also makes a particularly spectacular entry into the park.

This road is actually part of the crescent-shaped Wyoming Centennial Scenic Byway, from Dubois to Grand Teton and then southeast from Jackson to Pinedale.

Watching Wildlife

Yellowstone's megafauna is one of its greatest attractions, for young and old alike. **Bison** never fail to impress, and you'll cherish the first time you see a **moose** grazing a lakebed. Fewer things will get your heart pumping faster than a **bear** sighting.

If you are serious about spotting wildlife, then invest in some good binoculars; if you are really serious, get a spotting scope. A good-quality telephoto camera lens can also work quite well.

The different seasons each offer their own highlights; spotted **wapiti calves** and baby bison are a cute draw in late spring, and the fall rut brings the echo of bugling **elk** across the park. In general, spring and fall are the best times to view wildlife. In summer you need to head out around dawn and dusk, as most animals withdraw to forests to avoid the midday heat. Always pack a drink and a snack for yourself, in case you come across something exciting.

The park's northeastern Lamar Valley has been dubbed the "Serengeti of North America" for its large herds of bison, elk, and the occasional **grizzly** or **coyote**. The valley is by far the best place to spot **wolves**, particularly in spring. If you are interested in wolves, get a copy of the park's wolf observation sheet, which differentiates the various packs and individual members. It's posted at campgrounds

TOP WINTER ACTIVITIES

✔ Join a ranger-led **snowshoe hike** at Old Faithful or Grand Teton's Moose Visitor Center

✔ Take a **sleigh ride** in Jackson's National Elk Refuge

✔ Snowshoe, ski, or snowmobile to a **forestry cabin** with a group of friends

✔ Mush! Take a half-day **dog-sledding trip**

✔ Ski or snowshoe out to frozen **Mystic Falls**, west of the Upper Geyser Basin

at Pebble and Slough Creeks, which make the best wolf-watching bases.

The central Hayden Valley is the other main wildlife-watching area, and its pullouts can get crowded with spotters around dusk. The valley is a good place to view large predators like wolves and grizzlies, especially in spring, when thawing winter carcasses offer almost guaranteed sightings. Coyotes, elk, and bison are all common. The tree line is a good place to scan for wildlife. The more you know about animals' habitat and habits, the more likely you are to catch a glimpse of them.

If all else fails, you are guaranteed a grizzly sighting at West Yellowstone's Grizzly & Wolf Discovery Center.

Follow the proper etiquette when watching wildlife:

• Animals have the right of way; allow animals (generally bison) to cross the road freely and in their own time.

- Don't chase animals.
- If you cause an animal to move, you are too close.
- Never position yourself between an animal and its young.
- It's illegal to move closer than 100yd from bears or 25yd from all other animals.
- Don't feed the animals!

For a much more detailed discussion of wildlife, including specific information on many of the plants, birds and mammals found in this region and the environment that supports them, see the Greater Yellowstone Ecosystem chapter (p 249).

Geology

Yellowstone is one of the most geologically breathtaking and unique places in the world. The more you learn about it, the more interesting it becomes. See the Geology chapter (p 242) for an introduction to the subject and a list of the top 10 geologic "must-sees."

Geysers are the Yellowstone show headliners, exploding into the air like the chime of the earth's underground alarm clock. The **mud pots** are its comedians, gasping and burping from various corners of the park. **Hot springs** proffer a more graceful and ephemeral beauty.

The park's geysers are concentrated in its Upper and Lower Geyser Basins, and there are dozens to choose from. Our recommendation is to spend half a day seeing the highlights of Upper and Midway Geyser Basins, including Old Faithful and Grand Prismatic Spring, and then take a hike or bike ride to a more remote backcountry gusher like Imperial Geyser or Lone Star Geyser.

> ## YELLOWSTONE'S TOP THERMAL FEATURES
>
> ✔ **Grand Prismatic Spring**, Midway Geyser Basin
> ✔ **Old Faithful**, Upper Geyser Basin
> ✔ **Echinus Geyser**, Norris Geyser Basin
> ✔ **Porcelain Basin**, Norris Geyser Basin
> ✔ **Mammoth Terraces**, Mammoth
>
>

The other main groupings of thermal features are found at Norris and Mammoth Junctions, both of which are well worth a couple of hours. Mud Volcano, south of Canyon Junction, and West Thumb Geyser Basin, on Yellowstone Lake's southwest shore, come lower down the totem pole.

Relaxing

What with a tight itinerary, traffic jams, full parking lots, full restaurants, and full campgrounds, a trip around Yellowstone can leave you with the last thing you want – more stress. Pack that book you never got around to reading and reserve at least some time out from sightseeing.

Hiking is one of the most relaxing activities, forcing you to slow your pace and clear your mind. Picnic areas are good places for some time out, and they are almost always in scenic areas.

You'll find a few nice **beaches**, particularly Sedge Bay on Yellowstone Lake and Leigh Lake in Grand Teton, which are fine spots to spend a lazy afternoon. A few hours in the hot springs of Chico or Boiling River will wash away the long drive. If you've got the money, pamper yourself in the spas at Chico or Teton Valley.

SOAKING

Yellowstone has a long history of soaking, but today there are only a couple of places where swimming is tacitly allowed (though not advertised), principally the **Boiling River** just north of Mammoth and the **Firehole River** in Geyser Country.

The rule is that you can't swim in hot springs, but you can swim where hot springs empty into a nonthermal river. Prime backcountry soaks are the reward for hiking the four-day Bechler River Trail (p 125). Other backcountry soaks are whispered about furtively in local bars; try these at your own risk.

It's important to realize the inherent dangers in hot spring soaking. See "Getting in Hot Water" in the Planning chapter (p 53).

Some other great spots for a soak include Granite Hot Springs southeast of Jackson, Huckleberry Springs near Flagg Ranch on the Rockefeller Parkway, and Chico Hot Springs, a swimming pool in a fine Victorian inn in Paradise Valley. In Grand Teton, String Lake is a popular place for a warm-weather dip.

Cool Stuff for Kids

A trip to a national park promises the classic family vacation. Camping under a starry sky, fishing for cutthroat trout, and toasting marshmallows over a hot campfire are rites of passage children will remember all their lives.

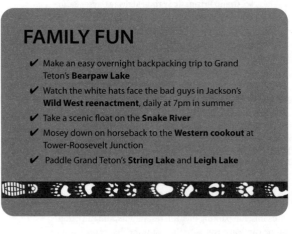

FAMILY FUN

✔ Make an easy overnight backpacking trip to Grand Teton's **Bearpaw Lake**

✔ Watch the white hats face the bad guys in Jackson's **Wild West reenactment**, daily at 7pm in summer

✔ Take a scenic float on the **Snake River**

✔ Mosey down on horseback to the **Western cookout** at Tower-Roosevelt Junction

✔ Paddle Grand Teton's **String Lake** and **Leigh Lake**

Some park **hikes** are perfect for families. See the "Best Hikes for Little Legs" boxed text (p 36) in the Activities chapter for some suggestions. Kids love splashing about in the warm water springs of Boiling and Firehole Rivers or the tiny beaches at **Leigh Lake**, so bring swimsuits and towels. Visitor centers stock a wide range of children's activity books and games, including child-oriented wildlife-spotting guides.

Outside the parks, kids will enjoy the interactive exhibits of the **Draper Museum** at Cody (part of the Buffalo Bill Historic Center), as well as the huge dinosaur skeletons at Bozeman's **Museum of the Rockies**. Kids just love getting splashed (and preferably doused) in water, whether it's standing next to **Echinus Geyser** or floating in a white-water raft.

NPS PHOTOGRAPHS

If you love the great outdoors, the Yellowstone region is as good as it gets. Whether it be hiking, biking, climbing, camping, fishing, rafting, kayaking, or even hot-air ballooning, there is no shortage of ways to commune with nature.

ACTIVITIES

This chapter provides introductory information and an overview of activities that are possible in Greater Yellowstone. See the entries under separate park regions for more details, specific park regulations, and trip ideas.

Hiking & Backpacking

There is no better way to escape the crowds and appreciate the region's unique beauty – alpine vistas, cascading waterfalls, up close wildlife, and hyperactive thermal areas – than on the trail.

Yellowstone National Park is blessed with 92 official trailheads, leading to more than 900mi of maintained trails and 300 designated backcountry campsites. There are thousands more miles of unmapped, untamed trails pioneered by animals. National Park Service (NPS) statistics indicate that each year less than 1% of the park's visitors apply for a backcountry permit and that 90% never even make it off a boardwalk.

At higher elevations, trails are often snow-covered until late July. August and September are the driest months, and May and June are the wettest. Low elevation trails may harbor ticks from mid-March to mid-July, so wear insect repellent on your pants, ankles, and cuffs. Mosquitoes are most intense in June and July, petering out by mid-August. September is an excellent month for hiking. Note that trails can close without warning at any time due to fire or bear activity.

Grand Teton National Park has 200mi of hiking trails and some of the most sublime alpine scenery in the country. Obtain the NPS brochures *Day Hikes* or *Backcountry Camping* to plan your hike. Higher elevations often remain snow-covered until late July, and high passes such as Paintbrush Divide and Hurricane Pass remain under snow as late as mid-August.

Backcountry permits are required for overnight trips in Grand Teton. Popular campsites like Bradley Lake, Surprise Lake, Upper Paintbrush, Holly Lake, Phelps Lake, Cascade Canyon, Marion Lake, and Leigh Lake fill up fast, so plan in advance or keep your itinerary flexible.

DIFFICULTY LEVEL

You'll find hikes suitable for everyone from the novice to the pro in Greater Yellowstone. We have graded the major trail descriptions in the parks to help you gauge which hike is right for you:

Easy: These gentle hikes are mostly flat with clear trails. Good for families.

Moderate: Hikes with limited elevation gain or distances over 5mi.

Difficult: Expect significant elevation gain, for which you need to be in decent shape. Trails might be indistinct in places. Only experienced hikers should attempt a very strenuous hike.

The duration for hikes listed in this guide refers to walking time only and doesn't include breaks.

DAY HIKES

Almost every part of the Greater Yellowstone region offers outstanding hiking. Don't overlook the longer trails – you can fashion short day hikes by following the first couple miles of a longer trail.

Travelers with little hiking experience will appreciate the national parks' well-marked and well-maintained trails, often with rest room facilities at either end. Some less-frequented trails are not maintained. In some forested areas these trails may be marked by a series of blazed trees; on rocky moraines look for cairns. No permits are required for day hikes.

If you're worried about hiking by yourself, try a ranger-led hike. Yellowstone's Ranger Adventure Hikes are an excellent way to take in a ranger's enthusiasm and expertise. See p 37 for details.

The Hole Hiking Experience (☎ 866-733-4453; www.holehike.com) offers privately guided hikes and snowshoe trips in Jackson Hole and the Teton Valley.

BACKCOUNTRY HIKES

To really escape the crowds, head into the more remote backcountry. Overnight trips in the two national parks require backcountry permits, available from visitor centers or ranger stations.

Backpacking trips can be as easy or challenging as you like. Backcountry campsites like those at Yellowstone's Ribbon Lake or Grand Teton's Leigh and Bearpaw Lakes are less than two hours' hike from the trailhead. Hone your backcountry skills on an easy overnight trip before heading deeper into the wilderness.

Longer backpacking trips in the region are often done as horse pack trips (see p 30). A new variation on this theme is the llama pack trip, which substitutes these more docile South American animals for the less predictable horse. **Lone Mountain Ranch** (☎ 800-514-4644) at Big Sky operates four- to six-day llama treks into Yellowstone or the Spanish Peaks area for around $200 per person per day.

The 150mi **Howard Eaton Trail**, named for a famous Bighorn Mountain guide, is Yellowstone's longest trail. The remote southwest wilderness offers some interesting hiking and kayaking combinations.

Outside the parks, the eastern Absaroka Range of Shoshone National Forest is the wildest and most inaccessible wilderness in Greater Yellowstone (and its prime grizzly habitat) and offers some fine extended backcountry hikes into Yellowstone. These remote wildernesses are generally visited by horse packers, as distances are large, the terrain is rugged, and trails are seldom used. Hunters frequent these areas in late September and early October, so wear orange clothes and expect dispersed sites to fill up.

NAME	TYPE	LOCATION (STARTING)	DISTANCE (R/T)	DURATION	CHALLENGE	ELEVATION CHANGE	FEATURES	FACILITIES	DESCRIPTION	PAGE
Avalanche Peak Loop	Day Hike	Lake Country	4mi	3.5-5hrs	moderate-difficult	2100ft			A quick but steep alpine ascent with superb views.	104
Beaver Ponds Trail	Day Hike	Mammoth Country	5mi	2.5 hrs	easy-moderate	350ft			Short loop trail good for spotting moose.	84
Bechler Meadows & Bechler Falls	Day Hike	Bechler Corner	8mi	2.5-3.5 hrs	easy	negligible			Late-season loop around the famous waterfall wonderland.	124
Bechler River Trail	Overnight	Bechler Corner	28mi	4 days	moderate	1100ft, 800ft descent			Waterfalls, wild berries, wildlife, and springs you can soak in.	125
Black Canyon of the Yellowstone	Overnight	Mammoth Country	18.5mi (one-way)	1-2 days	easy-moderate	1250ft descent			Rewarding route exploring Yellowstone River's thundering rapids.	82
Bunsen Peak & Osprey Falls	Day Hike	Mammoth Country	4.25mi	2.5-3.5 hrs	moderate	1300ft (2100ft w/ side trip)			A quick, rewarding, non-technical ascent with an optional waterfall.	81
Electric Peak	Overnight	Mammoth Country	20mi	1-2 days	difficult	3700ft			Challenging route to rocky summit with amazing views.	84
Elephant Back Mt Loop	Day Hike	Lake Country	3.5mi	1.5-2 hrs	easy	800ft			Good, easy family hike to an overlook of Yellowstone Lake.	105
Fairy Falls & Twin Buttes	Day Hike	Geyser Country	6mi	3-4 hrs	easy	negligible			Easy hike to an enchanting waterfall and seldom-seen geysers.	119
Fossil Forest Trail	Day Hike	Roosevelt Country	3-4mi	2.5-3.5 hrs	moderate-difficult	800ft			Demanding hike rewards with excellent views, wildlife, petrified trees, and wildflowers in July.	88
Heart Lake & Mt Sheridan	Overnight	Lake Country	16mi	1-2 days	easy-moderate	345ft (3145ft w/ side trip)			Varied hike to a wildlife-rich lake and interesting thermal area.	101
Lone Star Geyser & Shoshone Lake	Day Hike	Geyser Country	4.8mi	1.5-2.5 hrs	easy	400ft			Popular flat hike or bike ride to an isolated, very predicable geyser.	121
Mary Mountain Trail	Day Hike	Canyon Country	20mi	1 day	moderate-difficult	500-900ft			A wildlife-rich traverse of the seldom-seen Central Plateau.	95
Mt Washburn & Sevenmile Hole	Day Hike	Canyon Country	11.4mi (one-way)	5-7 hrs	moderate	1500ft			Endless panoramas, hot springs, waterfalls, and Grand Canyon views.	93
Mystic Falls & Biscuit Basin Loop	Day Hike	Geyser Country	3mi	1.5-2 hrs	easy	700ft			Easy loop hike to Yellowstone's most accessible backcountry cascade.	120
Pelican Valley Loop	Day Hike	Lake Country	16mi	6-8 hrs	moderate	negligible			Flat loop through prime grizzly bear, bison, and wolf habitat.	103
Yellowstone River Picnic Area Trail	Day Hike	Roosevelt Country	4mi	1.5-2 hrs	easy	800ft			Easy jaunt with unobstructed views down into the Grand Canyon of the Yellowstone.	87

All hikes have trailhead parking.

Views   Wildlife Watching   Fishing   Great for Families   Thermal Features   Waterfalls   Bicycles   Restroom   Ranger Station   Drinking Water   Picnic Sites   Backcountry Campsite

RESPONSIBLE BACKCOUNTRY USE

Yellowstone's backcountry environments are fragile and cannot support careless activity, especially in the wake of increased visitation. A hiker's aim should be to "leave no trace." See the website W www.lnt.org for more advice.

Hiking

To prevent further erosion, always stay on the trail and don't make your own shortcuts, especially when switchbacking uphill. Stay in the middle of the trail even when it's muddy – this will prevent the mud patch from spreading.

Campsites

To preserve the environment, use old campsites instead of clearing new ones. Camp at least 200ft from the nearest lake, river, or stream. Different hiking parties often have to share a common camping area. In such cases, pitch your tent a respectful distance from others and avoid intrusive noise.

Campfires

For many hikers, sitting around a fire is almost synonymous with a wilderness experience; however, campfires cause major environmental degradation in heavily used backcountry areas. Campfires are now restricted in many parts of Yellowstone, Grand Teton, and surrounding national forests. During a long dry spell, a local campfire ban may be imposed on public lands. If there already is a fire ring, use only dead and downed wood.

We recommend that all hikers carry and use a lightweight stove. If you do light a fire, keep it at least 9ft away from flammable material (including grass and wood), watch it at all times, and douse it thoroughly with water or dirt before going to sleep or leaving the site – always be sure it is fully out.

Water & Toilets

Water contaminated by careless or irresponsible hikers is a common cause of illness in the backcountry. Always use toilets established at trailheads, campsites, or along trails, regardless of how smelly they are. Where no toilet exists, bury human waste in a 6-inch-deep "cathole" at least 300ft from the nearest lake or watercourse. Pack out toilet paper in a sealed plastic bag.

Avoid using soaps and detergents – sand or a kitchen scourer will clean your pots remarkably well. In high altitude lakes even biodegradable soap may not degrade. Tip dishwater far from streams and remove residue food (it may attract bears) with a small basin or strainer.

Access

Access to some hikes outside the national parks is via private property, which may extend well beyond the trailhead. Roads or trails through freehold land are not automatically a right of way, and the goodwill of local landholders depends on the continuing cooperation of all visitors. Please do not camp (or collect firewood) on private land without permission, and leave stock gates as you find them.

SAFETY

The major forces to be reckoned with while hiking and camping are the elements and your own frame of mind. Be prepared for Yellowstone's unpredictable weather – you may go to bed under a clear sky and wake up under two feet of snow, even in mid-August. Afternoon

HIKING IN GRAND TETON

NAME	TYPE	LOCATION (STARTING)	DISTANCE (R/T)	DURATION	CHALLENGE	ELEVATION CHANGE	FEATURES	FACILITIES	DESCRIPTION	PAGE
Avalanche Canyon & Lake Taminah	Day Hike	Central Tetons	11mi	6-7 hrs	difficult	2300ft			This lightly-traveled valley is for experienced hikers only.	144
Death Canyon	Day Hike	Central Tetons	8-10mi	5 hrs	moderate	1360ft			Towering cliffs, lovely forest, and prime moose habitat make this one of the parks' most varied hikes.	145
Garnet Canyon	Day or Overnight Hike	Central Tetons	12mi	9 hrs	very difficult	4800ft			High-altitude hike into the heart of the Tetons blurs the line between hiking & climbing.	143
Hermitage Point	Day Hike	Colter Bay	9.2mi	4 hrs	Easy	negligible			Flat hike past two lakes with lots of wildlife and the option of a shorter 3mi trail.	136
Lake Solitude	Day Hike	Central Tetons	14.4mi w/boat shuttle; 18.4mi without	6-7 hrs	moderate	2240ft			The most popular and scenic hike in the park, with breathtaking views of the central Tetons.	141
Leigh Lake & Bearpaw Lake	Day Hike	Central Tetons	7.4mi	3.5 hrs	easy	negligible			Stunning lakeshore views of Mt Moran, with shorter options for a good family hike.	141
Marion Lake & Death Canyon	Overnight	Central Tetons	18mi (or 23mi loop)	2 days	moderate	600ft, 4800ft descent			A high-altitude, mainly downhill, hike with mountaintop views.	148
Paintbrush Divide Loop	Overnight	Central Tetons	17.8mi	2-3 days	moderate	3775ft			Two high-altitude lakes linked by a high pass makes this a classic hike. Stunning views of the central Teton summits.	146
Surprise & Ampitheater Lakes	Day Hike	Central Tetons	9.6mi	5-6 hrs	difficult	3000ft			Tough hike to alpine lakes carved high into a rocky cirque.	142
Taggart & Bradley Lakes	Day Hike	Central Tetons	5.9mi	3 hrs	easy	560ft			Easy loop provides fine views of the Tetons.	144
Teton Crest Trail	Overnight	Central Tetons	39.9mi	4-5 days	moderate-difficult	6000ft			An exhilarating high-level route through the wild heart of the Tetons, offering superb views.	147
Two Ocean Lake & Grand View Point	Day Hike	Colter Bay	6.4mi	3.5 hrs	easy-moderate	400ft			Lovely lakeside walk in a quiet corner of the park, with optional uphill detour to a viewpoint.	136

All hikes have trailhead parking.

Views · Wildlife Watching · Great for Families · Rock Climbing · Restroom · Ranger Station · Drinking Water · Picnic Sites · Store · Boat Shuttle · Canoeing · Backcountry Campsite

weather is particularly volatile in the Tetons. Check the latest weather forecast before setting off, and keep a careful watch on the weather.

All hikers (even day hikers) should carry a raincoat or poncho, water purifier and water bottle, some food, a hat, sunscreen, and insect repellent. Longer hikes require a basic first-aid kit, an accurate topographical map, a compass, and whistle. If you sweat a lot, take an extra shirt, or you'll quickly get very cold when you reach your destination.

Carrying and using a topographic map will greatly increase the safety of your hike and become more important the farther you venture into the backcountry. Allow more than enough time to complete each leg of the hike before nightfall, especially late in the season when days are shorter.

River crossings are potentially dangerous – check current flows and crossings with a ranger office. In spring and early summer, cross in morning, as afternoon flows are higher. At deeper crossings, stand sideways as you cross, use a stick or pole, and undo the waist and chest straps of your backpack in case you fall. Groups should hold hands or interlock arms.

EXTREME SPORTS

Need an adrenalin fix? Live dangerously with the following five:

✔ **Parasail** off Rendezvous peak
✔ **Raft** the white water of the Yellowstone, Snake, or Gallatin Rivers
✔ **Mountain bike** down from the ski lifts at Big Sky, Jackson Snow Mountain, or Grand Targhee in Teton Valley
✔ Learn the ropes on a **mountaineering course** halfway up Grand Teton.
✔ Take a **glider trip** over the Tetons from Driggs, Idaho

If bouldering or hiking downhill, avoid sprains, especially at the end of the day when you're tired. In the wilderness a small injury like a sprain or bad blister can quickly snowball into a real emergency.

Highest safety measures suggest never hiking alone, but regardless, the most important thing is to always let someone know where you are going and how long you plan to be gone. Use sign-in boards at trailheads or ranger stations. Travelers who are looking for hiking companions can inquire or post notices at ranger stations, outdoor equipment stores, campgrounds, and hostels. Don't rely on your cell phone for emergency contact, as coverage is spotty in Yellowstone.

People with little hiking or backpacking experience should not attempt to do too much, too soon. Know your limitations, know the route you are going to take, and pace yourself accordingly.

Rock Climbing & Mountaineering

American mountaineering was born in the Tetons (Paul Petzoldt built the country's first guiding school here in 1929), and they remain among America's premier climbing areas. Excellent short routes abound, as well as the classic longer summits like Grand Teton, Mt Moran, and Mt Owen along famous routes like the Upper Exum Ridge and Owen-Spalding route. The best season for climbing is mid-July through August.

Exum Mountain Guides (☎ 307-733-2297; Ⓦ *www.exumguides.com*) at Jenny Lake or **Jackson Hole Mountain Guides** (☎ 307-733-4979, 800-239-7642; Ⓦ *www.jhmg.com*) in Jackson both offer guided climbs. Both claim that after passing a two-day climbing course ($165), even novices should be able to summit Grand Teton on a guided climb ($350 to $400 per person). The most popular climbs are day-long climbs of South (12,514ft) and Middle Teton (12,804ft) and two-day ascents of Grand Teton (13,770ft).

The Way-Wired Mountaineer website (Ⓦ *www.way-wired.com*) is a good resource for both climbing and skiing in Grand Teton.

The South Fork of the Shoshone River, 40mi southwest of Cody, has the region's best **ice climbing** November to April. For details contact the climbers' nerve center **Bison Willy's Bunkhouse** (☎ 307-587-0629; Ⓦ *www.bisonwillys.com*).

Road & Mountain Biking

Bicycling is possible year-round, but late April to October is when the park's roads, which range from 5300ft to 8860ft, are usually snow-free.

Cyclists may ride on all public roads and a few designated service roads but are not allowed on any trails or backcountry areas. Most park roads are rough and narrow and do not have shoulders: expect careless drivers with one eye on the bison and another on the elk. Snowbanks cover many roadsides through June, making cycling more challenging.

A map in the *Bicycling in Yellowstone National Park* brochure shows suggested routes, such as the 3mi unpaved climb from the Chittenden Rd trailhead to Mt Washburn's summit (10,243ft). Some information is available on the park's website.

Bicycle repairs, parts, and rentals are not available inside the park; it's typically 20 to 30mi between services.

On the plus side, a limited number of campsites are reserved for hikers and cyclists at almost all campgrounds in Yellowstone National Park.

Among the recommended rides in Grand Teton National Park are the wide-shouldered Teton Park Rd from Moose north to Jackson Lake Junction, the Mormon Row/Kelly Loop via Antelope Flats Rd, and the Shadow Mountain mountain bike trail. Teton Park Rd is open to pedestrians, cyclists, and in-line skaters only (no motorized vehicles) throughout April.

TOP FIVE BIKE TRIPS

Wave good-bye to the RVs on these prime biking routes:

✔ **Mt Washburn** – strenuous uphill along a former service road

✔ **Lone Star Geyser** – Flat ride to a backcountry geyser

✔ **Shadow Mountain** – Strenuous climb but uncontested views of the Tetons

✔ **Antelope Flats** – Stunning views of Mormon Row and bison

✔ **Paradise Valley** – Get off the highways on the Old Gardiner Rd or East Valley Rd

Teton Mountain Bike Tours (☎ 307-733-0712; Ⓦ *www.tetonmtbike.com*) offers guided mountain bike tours of Grand Teton and Yellowstone. Half-day tours cost around $50 and include transportation, bike hire, and helmet. **Backroads** (☎ 800-462-2848; Ⓦ *www.backroads.com; 801 Cedar St, Berkeley, CA 94710-1800*) leads organized bike vacations with camping and inn options ($1000 to $2000).

ACTIVITIES

Outside the park, bikes are restricted from entering designated wilderness areas, but may otherwise ride on national forest trails. Trail etiquette requires that cyclists yield to other users. Helmets should always be worn to reduce the risk of head injury, but they are not mandated by law.

Outside the parks, Big Sky and Grand Targhee offer lift-serviced trails, and West Yellowstone has an excellent network of trails both in and outside Yellowstone National Park. There are also good single tracks in the Absaroka and Gallatin Ranges, accessible from Paradise Valley. Bozeman is the state's mountain-biking hub, largely due to its young and fearless population. Jackson is the major hub for rides around Jackson Hole.

Horseback Riding & Pack Trips

Given Wyoming and Montana's cowboy heritage, moseying down the trail is naturally a very popular summer activity throughout the Yellowstone region – usually, but by no means always, associated with guest (dude) ranches. Visitors enjoying guest-ranch vacations will often enjoy unlimited access to riding and may even join in cattle drives à la *City Slickers*.

More casual riders will find horseback riding an expensive activity, as visitors during the short summer tourist season end up paying for the cost of feeding these hay burners over the winter: Rates for recreational horseback riding start around $15 to $25 an hour, $60 to $70 for a half day and $75 to $130 for a full day. Guided trips usually require a minimum of two persons. Backcountry pack trips, again with a guide, cost upward of $100 per person per day and usually involve some related activity, such as fly-fishing.

Experienced riders may want to let the owners know, or you may be saddled with an excessively docile stable nag.

In Yellowstone Park there are corrals at Mammoth, Roosevelt, and Canyon Junction. Grand Teton has rides from Jackson Lake Lodge and Colter Bay. Ranches in the Wapiti and Gallatin Valleys operate horse rides for nonguests.

The following organizations provide contact information for all of their state's licensed outfitters:

Montana Outfitters & Guides Association (☎ *406-449-3578;* Ⓦ *www.moga-montana.org*), 2 North Last Chance Gulch, PO Box 1248, Helena, MT 59624

Wyoming Outfitters & Guides Association (☎ *307-527-7453;* Ⓦ *www.wyoga.or*g), 1716 8th St, Cody

Idaho Outfitters & Guides Association (☎ *208-342-1919, 800-494-3246;* Ⓦ *www.ioga.or*g), 711 N 5th St, Box 95, Boise, ID 83701

Rafting

Commercial outfitters in Grand Teton and outside the parks provide white-water experiences ranging from inexpensive half-day trips to overnight and multiple-day expeditions. More sedate float or tube trips are also available.

White-water trips run the Yellowstone River in Paradise Valley from Gardiner, the Gallatin River from bases near Big Sky, the Snake River between Hoback Junction and Alpine south of Jackson, and the Shoshone River west of Cody. The Yellowstone River is the longest free-flowing river in the country.

Scenic floats through Grand Teton National Park down the Snake River are popular with families. Wildlife viewing is best at dusk and dawn

White-water trips take place in either large rafts seating 12 or more people, or smaller rafts seating six; the latter are more interesting and exciting because the ride over the rapids can be rougher and because everyone participates in rowing. Full-day trips usually run anywhere from $50 to $90 depending on where you are, and overnight trips can cost $100 to $200.

While white-water trips are not without danger, and it's not unusual for participants to fall out of the raft in rough water, serious injuries are rare, and the vast majority of trips are without incident. All trip participants are required to wear US Coast Guard–approved life jackets, and even nonswimmers are welcome. All trips have at least one river guide trained in lifesaving techniques.

River classifications can vary over the course of the year, depending on the water level. Higher water levels, usually associated with spring runoff, can make a river trip more difficult.

Canoeing & Kayaking

Yellowstone offers some exciting opportunities for paddlers, whether it be relaxing family paddles or multiday backcountry trips to remote lakeside campsites. Waterborne travel offers yet another perspective on the park's breadth of beauty.

Shoshone Lake, the largest backcountry lake in the Lower 48 is the most popular destination. Access is up the Lewis River Channel and offers the chance to visit the remote Shoshone Geyser Basin. Huge Yellowstone Lake offers access to the park's remotest reaches, where boaters can combine a water trip with a hike into the park's rarely visited southeast corner.

Grand Teton's Jackson Lake offers breathtakingly scenic backcountry trips, with several islands to explore and more hiking add-ons in the little-visited northwest corner. Novice and family paddlers will love String, Leigh, and Lewis Lakes. Early morning paddles on Two Ocean Lake can't be beaten for peaceful wildlife watching.

Canoes are available for rent in Grand Teton, but you won't get very far, as renters can only paddle within the bay. For longer trips you are better off renting from outdoor shops such as Dornan's at Moose.

Day-only paddling on the Snake River ranges from novice to experienced and offers good wildlife watching.

Fishing

The Yellowstone region boasts some of the best fly-fishing in America, and the sport is taken very seriously, particularly in Montana. In the mid-1990s the sport got a major image makeover through Robert Redford's movie *A River Runs Through It*, set on Montana's Blackfoot River and filmed on the Gallatin and Madison Rivers.

Seven pan-fryable species swim Yellowstone's waters: cutthroat, rainbow, brown, brook, and lake (Mackinaw) trout; Arctic grayling; and mountain whitefish. The park alone boasts more than 400 fishable waters.

Yellowstone's fishing season runs from Saturday of Memorial Day weekend to the first Sunday in November, except Yellowstone Lake, which opens June 15. Bait angling is generally prohibited. Make sure to pick up a copy of the relevant state or park fishing regulations. Catch and release is standard practice in many areas and has played a major part in boosting fish stocks.

The park's best fishing streams are the Gibbon, Madison, and Yellowstone Rivers, though you can't really go wrong anywhere. Slough Creek has gained a reputation as angling heaven. The Madison, Gibbon, and Firehole Rivers in Yellowstone are fly-fishing only.

In Grand Teton National Park, Leigh and Jenny Lakes both offer good fishing and are stocked with lake, brown, brook, and Snake River cutthroat trout. Generally the best fishing is in spring and fall. One of the best fishing spots is on the Snake River just below the Jackson Lake dam (there is parking on both sides of the river). Ice fishing is growing in popularity.

Outside the park, the Madison is probably the region's most famous river, though it's also the busiest, especially during the early July salmon fly hatch. The Henry's Fork of the Snake River in Island Park is another prime spot.

All the region's prime fishing areas have a good stock of fishing stores, which volunteer tips on where to fish and what flies to pack and offer equipment, guides, and float trips. Some have websites that post fishing reports. Fly "afishionados" will want to pay a visit to Livingston's **Fly-fishing Museum**.

FISHING LICENSES

Outside the parks, Wyoming generally offers year-round fishing. Fishing licenses cost $10 a day ($3 for Wyoming residents) or $65 a year ($15 for Wyoming residents). For details contact the **Wyoming Game & Fish Dept** (☎ 307-777-4600; W http://gf.state.wy.us/).

To get a Montana fishing license, you must first have a $7 conservation license – good for the rest of your life and available where fishing licenses are sold. A seasonal license costs $60 for nonresidents and is good for one year; a two-day stamp costs $15. For more information contact the Bozeman section of **Montana Fish, Wildlife & Parks** (☎ 406-994-4042, 24-hr information 406-994-5700; W www.fwp.state.mt.us/; 1400 South 19th, Bozeman, MT 59718).

Local vendors and the **Idaho Dept of Fish & Game** (☎ 208-334-3700; W www.state.id.us/fishgame) issue fishing licenses. A license costs $10.50 for the first day and $4 for additional consecutive days; for the full season it costs $74.50 ($23.50 for Idaho residents).

Winter Sports

Winter is an increasingly popular time to visit Yellowstone, though the 140,000 winter visitors in 2001–02 remains a fraction of summer visitation. The winter sports season generally runs from the end of November to April, depending on weather, though February and March generally offer the best conditions.

Most park trails are not groomed, but unplowed roads and trails are open for cross-country skiing. Some roads are groomed for snowmobiles and other snow vehicles. Backcountry trips require extra caution, as streams and geothermal areas can be hidden by snow: Carry a map and compass when you venture off designated trails or roads.

In Grand Teton National Park, the **Moose Visitor Center** is the focus of winter activity and the place to get information on ski trail, weather, road, and avalanche conditions. All park campgrounds are closed in winter, but there is limited tent camping and RV parking ($5) near the Colter Bay Visitor Center. Teton Park Rd is plowed from Jackson Lake Junction to Signal Mountain Resort and from Moose to the Taggart Lake Trailhead.

Jackson and **Big Sky** are two of the Rockies' most popular ski destinations, equipped with the latest in chair-lift technology, snow-grooming systems, and facilities.

Ski areas are generally well equipped with places to stay, places to eat, shops, entertainment venues, child-care facilities (both on and off the mountain), and transportation. At major ski areas, lift tickets cost anywhere from $35 to $65 for a full day or about half that for a half day (usually starting at 1pm). Three-day or weeklong lift passes are more economical, especially if they do not need to be used on consecutive days. Equipment rentals are available at or near even the smallest ski areas.

There are also ample opportunities for cross-country and backcountry skiing, which offers an alternative to snowmobile use.

Many places specialize in winter activities and offer weekend or weeklong packages that include lodging, meals, and equipment rental. More than a dozen outfitters offer ski trips, and another 20 outfitters rent snowmobiles and offer guided tours. West Yellowstone is the major base for organized winter activities into Yellowstone.

One fun trip is to take a **snowcoach** to the Old Faithful Snow Lodge and spend a few days skiing around geyser basins, the Grand Canyon of the Yellowstone, and up Mt Washburn. For nonskiers there are **scenic chairlifts** at Grand Targhee and Big Sky.

INFORMATION

Get the *Montana Winter Guide* from the Montana tourist board (see p 44) or go to the website W www.wintermt.com.

The West Yellowstone Chamber of Commerce offers a free *Winter Guide to Yellowstone Country* map, which details snowmobiling routes for a hundred miles or so. Most national forests supply free winter-use travel maps.

For information on snow and avalanche conditions in Bridger-Teton National Forest contact the **Backcountry Avalanche Hazard & Weather Forecast** (*recorded information* ☎ 307-733-2664; W *www.jhavalanche.org*).

Mountain Weather (W *www.mountainweather.com*) presents Jackson Hole snow and weather reports and links to other resorts and webcams at Grand Targhee.

DOWNHILL SKIING & SNOWBOARDING

Greater Yellowstone has some of the Rockies' premier ski runs. **Jackson Hole Mountain Resort** in Teton Village is the largest resort in Wyoming, offering a variety of world-class skiing. Other nearby resorts include the **Snow King Resort** in Jackson and **Grand Targhee Ski & Summer Resort** in Alta.

Big Sky is Montana's premier resort, 33mi south of Bozeman. With a gondola, nine chairlifts, 80mi of runs, 4180ft of vertical drop, and ever-increasing resort developments at the foot of the slopes, Big Sky beats Montana's other ski hills hands down.

Red Lodge Mountain is increasing in popularity; besides being next to a fun party town, it has a good network of nearby cross-country trails. Most resorts offer a full range of other winter sports, including introductory snowboarding lessons.

CROSS-COUNTRY & BACKCOUNTRY SKIING

Nordic, or cross-country, skiing offers a chance to exercise, experience natural beauty at close quarters, and save a few dollars on a downhill lift ticket. The national park and forest services maintain summer hiking trails as cross-country trails during the winter, offering great opportunities to experience wilderness areas that teem with people in the summer.

The relatively new sport of backcountry skiing finds its roots in its Nordic cousin. The difference lies in the equipment and the terrain. Special telemark bindings, boots, and skis now allow winter skiers not only to travel cross-country but also to tackle steep slopes or bowls that lie along their paths. This is one of the most difficult types of skiing to learn, and the best place for a first try is at a ski resort or local snow slopes – *not* deep in the wilderness.

NPS, USFS, BLM, and private lands support hundreds of miles of cross-country trails. Although many resorts offer cross-country facilities adjacent to alpine slopes, most Nordic skiers prefer to avoid the downhill crowds by visiting dedicated Nordic areas and backcountry trails.

The best of these are **Rendezvous Cross-Country Ski Trails** in West Yellowstone, with 18.5mi of dedicated groomed Nordic paths (Rendezvous is the winter training ground for the US Nordic team).

West Yellowstone is also the jumping-off point for access to the cross-country trails in Yellowstone's extreme northwest corner. The Fawn and Bighorn Pass Trails connect to form a loop of around 10mi through elk wintering areas.

In Grand Teton, winter backcountry trails are marked with orange flags. Trails are not machine groomed but are well used and so normally well packed down. Avalanches are a major hazard in the canyons and upper areas of the Tetons. Good skiing routes include the 5mi up Signal Mountain Rd, the trail from the Taggart Lake parking area to the Jenny Lake overlook, and the uphill route up and around Two Ocean Lake.

Lone Mountain Ranch at Big Sky has 46.5mi of privately groomed trails, and nearby Mountain Meadows Guest Ranch has a further 15.5mi. Red Lodge Nordic Ski Center has 9mi of trails.

One great trip is the ski run from Wind River Lake at Togwotee Pass to Brooks Lake Lodge for lunch. Bear Creek Rd, starting from Jardine (5mi from Gardiner), has 6.5mi of occasionally groomed trail.

SNOWSHOEING

In Yellowstone and elsewhere you can generally snowshoe anywhere there's a trail – the problem is getting to the trailhead. Try not to mark groomed cross-country trails with your shoes, though – stay a few paces from any groomed areas. You can access trails from the Mammoth–Cooke City road all winter, and ski shuttles run to several snow-bound parts of the park from Mammoth and Old Faithful. Most resorts and hotels rent snowshoes.

Rangers lead snowshoe hikes from West Yellowstone's **Riverside trail** (BYO snowshoes) and Grand Teton's **Moose Visitor Center** (snowshoes provided). Lone Mountain Ranch at Big Sky has three special snowshoe trails.

SNOWMOBILING

The future of this controversial sport in Yellowstone and Grand Teton National Parks remains to be determined, but even if snowmobiles are eventually banned from the parks, the surrounding national forests offer hundreds of miles of trails to explore.

West Yellowstone is the much touted "snowmobile capital of the world." Each March the town hosts the World Snowmobile Expo. You can also legally drive snowmobiles in town. West Yellowstone and the neighboring Island Park region of Idaho offer more than 1000mi of snowmobile trails, mostly in Targhee National Forest. The popular

SNOWMOBILE WARS

The National Park Service has had to contend with ever-increasing winter use since Yellowstone was opened to snowmobiles in the early 1960s. Up to 1600 snowmobiles a day now pass through Yellowstone and Grand Teton, and pollution levels from emissions at peak times have been measured as being greater than the pollution levels in Los Angeles.

In 2000 the NPS decided to phase out recreational snowmobile and snowplane use by winter of 2003-04, to be replaced by a more sustainable (and NPS-managed) mass-transit snowcoach system.

The Snowmobilers Manufacturing Association, backed by the snowmobile-dependent economies of gateway towns like West Yellowstone, promptly launched a lawsuit. The lawsuit claimed that the NPS had failed to take into account the new cleaner and quieter four-stroke engines, which are more akin to cars than the old roaring two-stroke vehicles.

The Bush administration settled the lawsuit by reversing the planned phase out, and in November 2002 announced that snowmobile entry into the parks would be capped at 1100 machines each day (higher than average levels but less than peak visitation). Only four-stroke engines would be allowed.

Despite the ruling, the issue is far from settled. Four environmental groups promptly filed suit to block the new proposal and return to the planned phase out. Recent calls by environmentalists to ban all winter road grooming (which would eliminate {all} motorized oversnow travel in the park) has upped the ante even further. Meanwhile, many snowmobiling supporters are unhappy with the caps, which they maintain are unnecessary. With such strong feelings on both sides of the issue, it is almost certain that the controversy will continue.

34mi Two Top Mountain Loop was the country's first National Recreational Snowmobile Trail. The Yellowstone region is so important to snowmobiling that the Polaris Frontier model was specifically designed for the park and is only available here.

Flagg Ranch is the southern snowmobiling gateway to Yellowstone and Grassy Lake Rd. The Togwotee Pass area is another favorite. The 360mi Continental Divide Snowmobile Trail connects Dubois to Togwotee Pass, Grand Teton, and Yellowstone. For trail conditions call ☎ 307-739-3612. For general Wyoming snowmobile trail conditions call ☎ 800-225-5996. Wyoming State has excellent snowmobiling information at W http://wyotrails.state.wy.us/snow.

Speed limits are generally 45mph. Snowmobiles are not allowed in any wilderness areas. If you are new to snowmobiling, bear in mind that it's much more comfortable to ride solo than to double up. When renting, check the cost of clothing rental, insurance, and whether the first tank of gas is free. Backrests and heated handgrips are desirable extras.

SNOWCOACH TOURS

Snowcoaches are the future of winter travel in Yellowstone. Pioneered in Canada, they are essentially converted vans on snow tracks.

Several companies in West Yellowstone offer full-day snowcoach trips into the park, to either Canyon or Old Faithful.

DOGSLEDDING

Winter activities don't get more romantic than this. Several companies offer day and half-day trips ($125/85 per adult/child under 10) by paw power.

Companies include **Klondike Dreams** *(☎ 800-561-0815, 406-646-4988;* **W** *www.klondikedreams.com)* in West Yellowstone and **Spirit of the North** *(☎ 406-682-7994;* **W** *www.huskypower.com)* in Big Sky.

In Dubois, **Continental Divide Dogsled Adventures** *(☎ 800-531-MUSH;* **W** *www.dogsledadventures.com)* runs day trips in the Togwotee area to Brooks Lake Lodge, plus overnight trips in yurts (Central Asian–style circular tents).

Fun for the Kids

Hiking, paddling, rafting, fishing, and horseback riding are all activities you can share with your kids, offering an opportunity for families to bond, share time, and have some fun.

Don't be overly ambitious when planning activities with your children. Let them set the pace, and realize early on that you're not likely to make it to the top of Grand Teton on this trip. Try to pick a route that offers a shortcut back if necessary. Have a firm destination, like a lake or falls, as kids like to know when they've arrived and how far is left to go. Fit your kids out in a mini backpack (with snacks and a packed lunch) and a small hiking stick to help them feel part of the expedition. Watch out particularly for dehydration, sunburn, and mosquitoes. Never underestimate the misery of a thirsty, sunburned, bitten, and exhausted child with a 3mi hike still ahead.

BEST HIKES FOR LITTLE LEGS

If you're hiking with young children, try the following destinations, all within 2mi of a road:

✔ **Wraith Falls**, on the Mammoth-Tower/Roosevelt road

✔ **Ribbon Lake**, near the Grand Canyon of the Yellowstone

✔ **String** and **Leigh Lake**, in Grand Teton National Park

✔ **Natural Bridge**, near Bridge Bay

✔ **Mystic Falls**, Upper Geyser Basin

✔ **Artist Paint Pot**, near Norris Junction

✔ **Storm Point Nature Trail**, on the north side of Lake Yellowstone

In general children must be at least eight years old for horseback riding (and at least 4ft tall) and six years old for scenic floats.

Yellowstone National Park runs the **Junior Ranger Program**, which encourages children to learn about the park by attending a ranger talk and other activities. *The Nature Paper*, which has questions, games, and places for rangers to verify that the child has attended a talk, costs $3 and takes two days to complete. At the end, your child will receive a junior ranger badge. The program is aimed at five- to 12-year-olds and runs June to Labor Day. Grand Teton has a similar **Young Naturalist** program ($1).

There are several ranger-led activities aimed at families, including two-hour activity afternoons for eight- to 12-year-olds at Madison three times a week. Rangers also give short talks aimed at children in the Mammoth (in the afternoon) and Old Faithful (in the morning) Visitor Centers. Several campgrounds run family-oriented campfire lectures in the early evenings.

Xanterra runs **Yellowstone Buddies** at Old Faithful Inn, an interpretive program around Old Faithful for six- to 11-year-olds. The cost is $22 for a three-hour morning with lunch or $15 for a two-hour evening. It's held Monday to Thursday from July until mid-August. The **Yellowstone Association** *(☎ 307-344-2289;* W *www.yellowstone association.org)* offers year-round programs aimed at families with children eight to 12.

From June to mid-August rangers in Grand Teton National Park lead daily **Young Naturalist** hikes at 1:30pm from either the Jenny Lake or Colter Bay Visitor Centers (three times a week from Jenny Lake, four times from Colter Bay). The 2mi walks take 1.5 hours, so be back promptly to pick up little Jimmy. Numbers are limited to 12, so make reservations at visitor centers.

Joining a Group

Joining a group is an excellent way to explore the parks, especially if you're traveling on your own. Group activities provide knowledge and insight for both first-time visitors and those seeking to learn something new. They can also be a great opportunity to make friends and have fun.

MEETING THE RANGERS

Yellowstone has more than 4000 excellent ranger-led programs a year, from slide shows and talks to free hikes and even canoe trips. Campfire talks are held nightly at all campground auditoriums. For times and locations, see the park newspaper, *Yellowstone Today*. Programs generally kick in around June and peter out after Labor Day. They are free of charge.

Ranger Adventure Hikes are a recent innovation – a more challenging fee-based program of day hikes that depart from Old Faithful and Mammoth daily (except Sunday) at 8am from mid-June to the end of August. Hikes range from the easy hike to Lone Star Geyser to the strenuous hike up to Snow Pass. Destinations include Shoshone Lake, Mallard Lake, and less-visited sites like Pocket Basin and Temple Mountain. Tickets should be purchased in advance at visitor centers and cost $15 for adults and $5 for children aged seven to 15.

Grand Teton has a similar program of events and talks, though on a smaller scale. Campfire talks and slide shows are held most evenings at the major campgrounds, including Flagg Ranch on the Rockefeller Parkway. For a program and schedule see the bulletin boards at visitor centers or the park paper, the *Teewinot*. It's well worth trying to catch a couple of these programs.

Between early June and early September there are free ranger-led hikes at Jenny Lake, Colter Bay, Taggart Lake, and String Lake.

TAKING AN ORGANIZED TOUR

Park concessionaires run most activities inside the parks. In Yellowstone, **Xanterra** operates everything, from stagecoach rides to wildlife watching tours and lake cruises – for details see p 76. In general prices are reasonable, though they can quickly mount up for families. Xanterra also has a range of general sightseeing tours, which are worth considering if you only have a day in the park.

Science & Nature

The parks' ranger talks and hikes include such topics such as geology, wildlife, fish management, and wildflowers and are always accessible. Attractions such as the

Draper Museum of Natural History in Cody and the **Grizzly & Wolf Discovery Center** in West Yellowstone teach visitors through exhibits, talks, and videos.

The **Yellowstone Association** (☎ 307-344-2294; W www.yellowstoneassociation.org) runs a range of wildlife-watching courses and offers private, six-hour morning or evening wildlife-watching tours ($165 for up to four people), during which a naturalist joins you in your vehicle.

Teton Science School (☎ 888-945-3567, 307-733-2623; W www.wildlife expeditions.org) has half-day ($85), full-day ($145), and multiday wildlife-viewing trips to Teton and Yellowstone in a safari-style SUV. Group size is limited to six.

Off the Beaten Path (☎ 800-445-2995; W www.offthebeatenpath.com) in Bozeman, runs wildlife safaris throughout the region, as does **Yellowstone Safari Co** (☎ 406-586-1155; web www.yellowstonesafari.com), also in Bozeman.

Photography

From late June to late August, Kodak sponsors free daily photography walks of the park's most popular sights, as well as illustrated talks on taking photographs in Yellowstone and a twice-weekly photography walk for kids and their parents along Yellowstone Lake. See the park newspaper for schedules.

Xanterra offers daily photo "safaris" from Old Faithful and Lake Hotel. Tickets cost $40/16 for adults/children under 16.

The **Yellowstone Institute** (☎ 307-344-2294; W www.yellowstoneassociation.org/institute) offers four- to five-day nature photography courses ($235) several times a year.

Taking a Class

Established in 1907, the nonprofit **Yellowstone Institute** (☎ 307-344-2294; W www.yellowstoneassociation.org/institute; PO Box 117, Yellowstone National Park, WY 82190) is an educational field program offering one- to five-day outdoor courses in the humanities and cultural and natural history. The institute's headquarters are at the historic Buffalo Ranch, where most courses are held from late May to late September (some in January and February). Courses start at $50 to $60 per day, excluding food and accommodations. Buffalo Ranch's self-catering log-cabin bunkhouses cost $20 per person. Ask for a summer or winter catalog.

Courses range from identifying mammal tracks and wild edible plants to geology and historical topics. They also run backpacking and horse pack trips, kayaking, fly-fishing, and backcountry courses. "Lodging and Learning Programs" are four- to five-day packages that include food and park accommodations. These are particularly popular in winter.

The highly regarded **Teton Science School** (☎ 307-733-4765/3; W www.teton science.org) in Kelly offers lectures ($5) and natural-history seminars (from $50 per day) for children and adults. It also houses the free Murie Natural History Museum; call for an appointment to visit.

AMK Ranch (☎ 307-543-2463) near Leek's Marina is the site of a combined University of Wyoming and NPS research center. Talks are held at 6:30pm in the Berol Lodge every Thursday from mid-June to early August on all things historical and biological (most but not all on the Yellowstone ecosystem). Come at 5:30pm for the pre-talk barbecue ($4).

Targhee Institute (☎ *307-353-2233*) at Grand Targhee Ski & Summer Resort runs activity and educational programs for adults over 50 in association with **Elderhostel** (☎ *877-426-8056; 11 Ave de Lafayette, Boston MA 02111-1746*).

Working & Volunteering

The main Yellowstone Concessionaire, **Xanterra** *(human resources ☎ 307-344-5324, 24-hr application request line 307-344-5627,* W *www.yellowstonejobs.com for online applications)*, employs 3000 people in summer and 300 in winter, who do everything from making beds to making soup. Pay starts at about $6 per hour. Employee housing and food cost around $70 per week (RV sites $30 to $40 per week). Apply in December for summer jobs and in August/September for winter positions. It helps if you are available for the entire season.

For job opportunities with Grand Teton Lodge Company call ☎ 800-350-2068.

TOP PHOTO OPS

✔ **Schwabacher Landing**, Grand Teton

✔ **Oxbow Bend**, Grand Teton

✔ **Mormon Row**, southeast Grand Teton

✔ **Artist Point**, Grand Canyon of the Yellowstone

✔ **Grand Prismatic Spring**, Midway Geyser Basin

Yellowstone Park Medical Services *(☎ 800-654-9447 ext 462; 707 Sheridan Ave, Cody, WY 82414)* fills a small number of professional and nonprofessional positions at its park medical clinics.

Occasional seasonal jobs (for US citizens only) are available with the National Park Service, but these are hard to come by; check for openings at W www.sep.nps.gov.

The National Park Service runs a volunteer program. See the website W www.nps.gov/volunteer for details. The forest service accepts a wider range of volunteers, from trail maintenance to campground hosts, and normally supplies board and a subsistence wage. See the website at W www.fs.fed.us/r4/volunteer/index.html.

So, you've finally decided to take that long overdue Yellowstone vacation – cascading waterfalls, roaming bison, exploding geysers … oh yes, and three million other tourists. If you are reading this section for the first time in your RV halfway to Wyoming, then pull over, read the highlights chapter, come up with a rough itinerary, and book some accommodations. Even the most nonchalant, laid-back traveler will find that a small amount of planning greases the wheels of Yellowstone travel.

PLANNING THE TRIP

Some ultra-organized travelers book their accommodations a year in advance. Others just turn up at the park, grab a first come, first served campsite, and base themselves there for a week. The deciding factor is how flexible you can be. If your deadlines are tight (and most people's are), then book at least a few nights' accommodations well in advance. There's nothing worse than driving around, tired and cranky, looking for the park's only vacant campsite, only to face a 40mi drive back out of the park.

If you're planning to take one of the most popular backpacking routes, consider booking your backcountry sites by April. Even park activities like horseback riding and cookouts should be reserved a couple days in advance. The golden rule is, the more specific a plan you have, the earlier you need to book. The more interesting and upscale accommodation options (such as the yurts at Harriman State Park or the cabins at Jackson Lake Lodge) start taking bookings in November for the following year.

So if you've promised your kids a hike with a llama, or your sweetie a secluded lakeshore cabin, then preplan and prebook, as there are simply too many other visitors to leave things to chance.

If you've decided to just drive into the wild blue yonder, that can work too, but you'll have to opt for remote campsites in secluded areas and more time in the surrounding national forests. And these just may end up being the highlights of your trip.

When to Go

For most travelers, the Yellowstone region is a summer destination, when the weather is most forgiving and there are more services. But the area offers draws in any season. Winter promises special activities and is becoming increasingly popular.

SEASONAL HIGHS & LOWS

The weather is notoriously unpredictable in the Rockies. Freak storms can bring snow in high summer, and chinook winds can temporarily raise temperatures by 25°F in midwinter. Annual rainfall has more to do with park topography than seasonal variations, ranging from 10 inches in the north to about 80 inches in the southwest.

Spring

Average high temperatures in April and May range from 40°F to 50°F, with low temperatures ranging from 0°F to -20°F. In late May and June average high temperatures are from 60°F to 70°F. Snow lingers into April and May.

May and June are usually quite rainy, and this, combined with snowmelt, means that spring rivers and waterfalls are at their peak. This is a good time for wildlife viewing, but many hiking trails are boggy, and there is still snow at higher elevations. In June wildflowers start to bloom at lower elevations.

Summer

It starts to feel like summer in the Rocky Mountains around June, and the warm weather lasts until about mid-September. High temperatures at lower elevations are usually around 70°F and occasionally reach 80°F, with nighttime lows ranging from 40°F to 30°F. Temperatures are 10°F to 20°F cooler at high elevations and at least 10°F higher down on the plains around Cody and Billings.

July and August are the driest months, but afternoon thunderstorms are common, especially in the Tetons, which create their very own microclimate.

As visitor numbers peak, moose and elk retreat into the backcountry to avoid both the heat and the tourists. Mosquito season kicks in until mid-August. Daylight remains until about 9:30pm, allowing ample time for late-afternoon and evening excursions. August is a prime hiking month, when wildflowers are in full bloom at higher altitudes.

Fall

The weather becomes increasingly unreliable into fall. While winter weather doesn't usually settle in until late November, snowstorms can start hitting the mountain areas as early as September, and snow starts piling up by mid-October.

Average high temperatures are 40°F to 60°F, with low temperatures ranging from 20°F to 0°F. Lower elevations outside the park are often still warm into October.

September is a good month to visit. Elks bugle during the fall rut, and the aspens and cottonwoods turn golden, especially in Grand Teton, which boasts more impressive fall colors than Yellowstone. Nights can be cold if you are camping, but you should be able to negotiate off-season discounts at many hotels. Hiking and fishing are excellent. On the downside, ranger programs start to peter out after Labor Day, campsites start to close some of their services in September, and the days begin getting shorter.

Winter

The park's winter season generally runs from late November to March. High temperatures average 0°F, but occasionally rise to 20°F, with low temperatures ranging from 0°F to subzero. Occasionally a warm, westerly chinook wind blows in over the Rockies and raises winter high temperatures to 40°F, melting the snowpack. More often the wind-chill factor intensifies because of cold winter winds. The average winter snowfall is 150 inches, with 200 to 400 inches at higher elevations.

PARK OPENING DATES

Yellowstone

Yellowstone's opening schedule is fiendishly complicated. The north entrance at Gardiner is open year-round, as is the north road from Gardiner to Cooke City via Mammoth and Tower-Roosevelt Junction.

The first roads to open, in mid-April, are the West Entrance Rd and the following sections of the Grand Loop Rd: Mammoth Hot Springs to Norris Junction, Norris Junction to Madison Junction, and Madison Junction to Old Faithful. The south and east entrances, the Grand Loop Rd over Craig Pass (8262ft) between West Thumb Junction and Old Faithful, and the East Entrance Rd typically open in early May. The Grand Loop Rd between Tower and Canyon Junctions over Dunraven Pass (8859ft) is the last to open, usually by Memorial Day.

Once open, entrances stay open 24 hours. Roads sometimes have limited open hours when affected by road reconstruction. To check road conditions, call the park at ☎ 307-344-7381 or see the Planning a Visit section of the park website (🆆 www.nps.gov/yell).

All park roads close on the first Monday in November, except for the Gardiner–Cooke City road. The Beartooth Hwy (Hwy 212) between Red Lodge and Cooke City is blocked by snow from mid-October to around Memorial Day.

Entrances open to snow vehicles (snowmobiles) from the third Wednesday in December through mid-March, when spring plowing starts. Roads out of Norris are the first to close. All roads are closed again by the second Monday in March, except for the Gardiner–Cooke City road, which is open all winter.

Grand Teton

Grand Teton National Park is open year-round, though some roads and most services close in winter.

In winter you can drive along US 26/89/191 to Flagg Ranch but no farther. Teton Park Rd is closed to motorized vehicles from Taggart Lake Trailhead to Signal Mountain from November 1 to May 1, as is the unpaved portion of the Moose-Wilson road inside the park. Grassy Lake Rd is closed by snow from mid-November to late May.

COPING WITH THE CROWDS

Come July, Yellowstone braces for the summer tourist invasion. If you are traveling during this peak season, be prepared to share the park's wonders, as well as its campgrounds, parking spots, and hiking trails. It may not be quite the wilderness experience you were hoping for.

Traveling in the off-season offers many rewards; you don't have to contend with crowded roads, shops or visitor centers, and places to stay offer more affordable rates. The downside is that tours and guided activities have limited schedules, restaurants are sometimes shut for the season, and campgrounds become unreliable. The best off-season time is just after Labor Day, from the middle of September through October, as the weather usually stays warm and services aren't yet totally shut down. The campgrounds are also quieter, as most kids have gone back to school.

If you have to travel in July and August, don't panic, it's still surprisingly easy to avoid the worst of the mayhem. You'll lose 90% of the tourists simply by walking a mile from the road.

The second golden rule is to do what the other park animals do; get up early, rest at lunchtime, and stay out late. Be at the trailhead at 8am for the best light, the fewest tourists, and the most parking spaces. Get active during the hour just before sunset; the land basks in gorgeous light, the tourists are rushing back to set up their campsites, and the wildlife is back out again.

To avoid the worst of the cafeteria lines, get used to eating meals outside of set times. Have lunch at 2pm and you are guaranteed a seat. Bear in mind that roads are generally busiest between 11am and 3pm.

Finally, if it gets too much, head out of the park. While the Gallatin National Forest may not sound as sexy as Yellowstone National Park, the hikes are just as superb and the mountains just as breathtaking as they are over the border – and you'll probably have the trail to yourself.

SPECIAL EVENTS

The National Park Service rarely lets its hair down, but there are some excellent events in the surrounding communities that are well worth attending.

One oddity is Yellowstone's **Christmas in August** (August 25), which dates back to the turn of the last century, when a freak August snowstorm stranded a group of visitors in the Upper Geyser Basin. Old Faithful Inn is decked out with Christmas decorations and carol singers. It's all a bit surreal.

In Yellowstone's gateway communities, rodeo is the major cultural event of the year. Cody's nightly summer rodeo is well worth attending (and better than the twice-weekly fairground affairs held in Jackson). The **Cody Stampede** is the region's biggest July 4 weekend rodeo, but there are also smaller rodeos at this time in Livingston and Red Lodge. More rodeos pull into Gardiner in mid-June and West Yellowstone in mid-August.

Yellowstone's history of "mountain man rendezvous" resulted from trade and social interactions between trappers, settlers, and Native Americans in the mid-19th century. The get-togethers gave lonely trappers the chance

---

GETTING HITCHED

Thinking of getting married in the region? Following is a list of scenic sites to tie the knot, with excellent catering. You certainly won't have far to travel for your honeymoon!

- ✔ The lovely, classic **English-style church** at Mammoth
- ✔ **Church of the Transfiguration** at Moose, a tiny chapel with huge Teton views
- ✔ The gazebo or riverside site at **Red Lodge Chapel**, in full view of the Beartooth Mountains

---

to revive social connections, let their hair down, and spend a little money. Reenactments are held in late July at Red Lodge's **Mountain Man Rendezvous** and West Yellowstone's **Burnt Hole Rendezvous** in August. The latter is a reenactment of the 1859 gathering and includes tomahawk throwing competitions, black-powder marksmanship contests, and lots of teepees. Nearby Pinedale's **Green River Rendezvous** is one of the biggest, held in late July.

The region's Native American culture is celebrated in the **Annual Plains Indian Powwow**, held in mid-June at Cody's Buffalo Bill Historic Center; July's **Native American Festival Show & Dance** in Teton Village; and the **Crow Fair** in the Crow Agency, west of Billings, on the third weekend in August, which features Native American dances, rodeo, and snacks.

Music lovers can choose between Cody's **Yellowstone Jazz Festival** or the excellent **Grand Teton Classical Music Festival** in Teton Village, both in July, or the regionally famed **Targhee Bluegrass Festival**, held in August at Grand Targhee Ski Resort in Idaho's Teton Valley.

Gathering Information

The **National Park Service** *(NPS;* W *www.nps.gov)*, an agency of the Dept of the Interior, administers Yellowstone, Grand Teton, and the Rockefeller Parkway.

For Yellowstone information, call ☎ 307-344-7381, visit the website at W www.nps .gov/yell, or write to the National Park Service, Visitor Services Office, Box 168, Yellowstone National Park, WY 82190.

For information on activities, camping, and accommodations in Yellowstone, contact **Xanterra Parks & Resorts** *(*☎ *307-344-7311;* W *www.travelyellowstone.com; Reservations Dept, Box 165, Yellowstone National Park, WY 82190-0165)*.

For Grand Teton information, call ☎ 307-739-3300, visit the website at W www .nps.gov/grte, or write to PO Drawer 170, Moose, WY 83012.

USEFUL ORGANIZATIONS

The nonprofit **Yellowstone Association** *(*☎ *307-344-2293;* W *www.yellowstone association.org)* supports educational, historical, and scientific programs via the Yellowstone Institute. Annual memberships start at $30.

Yellowstone Park Foundation *(*☎ *406-586-6303,* W *www.ypf.org)* is dedicated to funding park projects such as wolf monitoring, trail upkeep, and the proposed new visitor center at Old Faithful. Send tax-deductible contributions to the Yellowstone Park Foundation, 222 E Main, Suite 301, Bozeman, MT 59715, or support the park by signing up for a Yellowstone Park Visa card through US Bank, which donates a percentage of every purchase to the foundation.

Grand Teton National Park Foundation *(*☎ *307-732-0629;* W *www.gtnpf.org; PO Box 249, Moose, WY 83012)* is that park's equivalent organization. Profits from Grand Teton Bottled Water, on sale throughout the region, go to the foundation. Another noble organization is the **Grand Teton Natural History Association** *(*☎ *307-739-3606;* W *www.grandtetonpark.org; PO Box 170, Moose, WY 83012)*, which supports educational and scientific programs in Grand Teton through book sales and membership dues.

The **Greater Yellowstone Coalition** *(*☎ *406-586-1593;* W *www.greateryellowstone.org)* monitors environmental issues in areas around the park and offers educational backcountry trips year-round (the winter wolf-watching trip is said to be superb).

Volunteer with **Buffalo Field Campaign** *(*☎ *406-646-0070;* W *www.wildrockies .org/buffalo; PO Box 957, West Yellowstone, MT 59758)* and you get to patrol for Yellowstone bison that wander out of national park boundaries onto private land in search of food during winter. Bring your own personal gear; food and lodging are provided.

State Tourist Offices

Montana's statewide tourist board, **Travel Montana** *(*☎ *406-841-2870, 800-VISIT-MT;* W *www.visitmt.com; 301 S Park Ave, PO Box 200533, Helena, MT 59620)* offers free publications, including the *Montana Vacation Guide, Montana Winter Guide*, and *Yellowstone County*. The website is particularly useful.

The **Wyoming Division of Tourism** (☎ 307-777-7777, 800-225-5996; Ⓦ www.wyomingtourism.org) produces the very helpful seasonal *Wyoming Vacation Guide*, which includes a state highway map and a winter guide. The website is useful, as is Ⓦ www.state.wy.us.

The **Idaho Travel Council** (☎ 208-334-2470, 800-635-7820; Ⓦ www.visitid.org; 700 W State St, Boise) supplies the *Official Idaho State Travel Guide*, the useful *Idaho RV & Campground Directory*, and either a summer or winter activity package.

Reservations Agencies

Most of the gateway towns surrounding the parks offer agencies that will gladly help you book your entire vacation, from car rental to hotel rooms and excursions – for a fee of course. You won't save any money, but they can be a useful one-stop shop:

Do Jackson Hole (☎ 800-500-3654, 307-739-1500, Ⓦ www.dojacksonhole.com)
  PO Box 9221, S Hwy 89, Jackson
Cody Area Reservations (☎ 888-468-6996, 307-587-0200)
Jackson Hole Central Reservations (☎ 800-443-6931, 307-733-4005,
  Ⓦ www.jacksonholeresort.com) 140 E Broadway, Jackson, WY
West Yellowstone Central Reservations (☎ 888-646-7077, 406-646-7077,
  Ⓦ www.yellowstonereservation.com) 211 Yellowstone Ave, West Yellowstone, MT 59758
Yellowstone Vacations (☎ 800-426-7669, 406-646-9564)

SUGGESTED READING

Intimate explorations of the Yellowstone region's rich realm of plants, animals, habitats, and seasonal intricacies are available in books like *Greater Yellowstone*, by Rick Reese, and *Yellowstone: A Visitor's Companion*, by George Wuerthner. *Wildlife Watchers Guide: Yellowstone and Grand Teton*, by Todd Wilkinson and Michael Francis, is a popular guide to the animals you'll encounter in the parks. *Windows into the Earth*, by Robert B Smith and Lee J Siegel, is an always-accessible and well-illustrated examination of the geology behind (and beneath) Yellowstone and Grand Teton.

For a historical chronicle of the park's original inhabitants, try *Indians in Yellowstone National Park*, by Joel C Janetski. *Downriver: A Yellowstone Journey*, by Dean Krakel, is a literate travelogue that traces the ecology and history of the Yellowstone River.

For travel with an environmental slant, *Walking Down the Wild: A Journey Through the Yellowstone Rockies*, by Gary Ferguson, is one naturalist's account of his 500mi trek through the Greater Yellowstone region. *Teewinot*, by Jack Turner, is a climber's ode to the Tetons. It will get you as close to the Teton peaks and their changing seasons as most ever get.

Death in Yellowstone, by Lee Whittlesey, the park's archivist, is a morbidly fascinating chronicle of "accidents and foolhardiness" in the park over the last century or more.

A River Runs Through It, by Norman Maclean, is mandatory reading for armchair anglers. The namesake movie was filmed in the region.

For broader coverage of the tri-state area (plus Colorado), check out Lonely Planet's *Rocky Mountains* guide.

Hiking Guides

If you have extended time or are able to make repeated visits to the parks, it's worth investing in a specialist trail guidebook. Lonely Planet's *Hiking in the Rocky Mountains* details hikes in Greater Yellowstone and many other locations throughout the Rockies.

SURFING THE NET

Online you can research specific hikes, find average temperatures and summer crowd counts, book hotel rooms, make campground reservations, buy wilderness maps, or anything else you may need.

This section offers a roundup of the top sites for the Greater Yellowstone area. For other specific websites, see the relevant sections of this guide or the appendix. Some of the best sites belong to the state tourist offices (see p 44) and the neighboring national forests (see p 201).

Lonely Planet's own website (W www.lonelyplanet.com) also makes a great resource; it's home to the Thorn Tree bulletin board, where you can ask fellow travelers for their tips and share your own when you get back.

GENERAL PARKS INFORMATION

W www.nps.gov/yell/
The official Yellowstone National Park website should be your first port of call for everything from bear updates to backcountry permit requirements. There are downloadable trip planners, an interactive park map, and a helpful list of outfitters within the park. Best of all, you can download current issues of *Yellowstone Today* for a rundown of daily programs and schedules.

W www.nps.gov/grte/
The official Grand Teton National Park site offers similar information and resources.

W www.americanparknetwork.com
Order free park guides to Yellowstone and Grand Teton from the **American Park Network**.

W www.travelyellowstone.com
The online home for Yellowstone's concession services group (Xanterra Parks & Resorts), which oversees all lodging, restaurants, stores, tours, activities, and transportation within Yellowstone.

W www.yellowstoneassociation.org
The Yellowstone Association site features class listings, membership news, and Yellowstone's primary online shopping site, which sells books, videos, and other gear. Members receive a 15% discount on book sales, the profits from which support the parks.

W www.grandtetonpark.org
The Grand Teton Natural History Association operates this site, with an online bookstore and membership information.

W www.yellowstoneparknet.com
Claiming to promote the "Yellowstone lifestyle," this detail-rich site has a snappy grid organization and covers both the park and surrounding communities, though many of the "hot sites" feel like paid advertising. This site also owns W www.parkreservations.com, which covers lodging and activity reservations for Yellowstone and other national parks.

W www.yellowstone-natl-park.com
Every so often a personal website morphs into a reputable source for public

information. Such is the case with Yellowstone fan John Uhler's site, which offers extensive information on park lodging and activities.

W www.yellowstonepark.com
The *Yellowstone Journal* (☎ 307-332-2323, 800-656-8762) is an independent, tourist-oriented publication that provides useful information on the park's wildlife and ecology. Its site features monthly news, decent links, and lots of interactive polls and trivia.

W www.yellowstone.net/newspaper
Browsing the *Yellowstone Net News* is a good way to survey the scene from a safe distance.

W www.yellowstone-reservations.com/
Not the prettiest site and a bit cumbersome to navigate, this is still a good one-stop source for booking online lodging as well as activity-specific reservations. This is merely a reservation service, not the authorized concessionaire of Yellowstone, so there may be additional booking fees.

W www.yellowstonegifts.com
The park's official online gift store features adventure planners, some apparel, and the National Park version of Monopoly.

SPECIAL INTEREST

W www.yellowstonenationalpark.com
This attractive and easy-to-navigate site is a consortium of sorts, featuring authors' new works on Yellowstone, photography, and excellent camping and hiking information (with trail descriptions).

W www.gorp.com
The extensive Great Outdoor Recreation Pages (GORP) are an excellent general resource on outdoor activities, both in the parks and beyond.

W http://volcanoes.usgs.gov/yvo/
Interested in Yellowstone's geological wonders? Take a gander at this site for monthly data on in-park activity and FAQs.

W www.geyserstudy.org/geyser_main.htm
Features the daily temperature and time at Old Faithful and excellent in-depth information and maps on Yellowstone's many thermal attractions.

W www.aqd.nps.gov/grd/parks/yell/
A good online primer for Yellowstone geology. Not-too-wordy field notes, a geologic time scale, and a comprehensive glossary of terms are bonuses.

W www.his.state.mt.us/
The online home of the Montana Historical Society, which houses the premier collection of Yellowstone photographs from 1872 through the 1920s, most left by F Jay Haynes, the park's first official photographer.

W www.fws.gov
The Fish & Wildlife Service provides information about fishing regulations and viewing local wildlife.

— **Amy Marr**

Hiking Grand Teton National Park and *Hiking Yellowstone National Park*, both by Bill Schneider, are also good resources. *Yellowstone Trails: A Hiking Guide*, by Mark C Marschall, is another good companion, as is the detailed and compact *Exploring the Yellowstone Backcountry*, by Orville E Bach.

Moving outside the parks, *Jackson Hole Hikes*, by Rebecca Woods, is an excellent guide, which covers the Targhee, Towotee, Gros Ventre, and Teton regions. *Targhee Trails*, by the same author, concentrates on hikes west of the Tetons. *Hiking the Beartooths*, by Bill Schneider, is an excellent resource to one of Greater Yellowstone's prime hiking spots.

MAPS

The National Park Service hands out good park maps at the entrance stations, but these are intended only for general orientation. A good topographic map is essential for any hiking trip. National Geographic's *Trails Illustrated* and **Earthwalk Press** both offer pre-folded, waterproof maps of Yellowstone and Grand Teton, with 80ft contour intervals.

Trails Illustrated's *Yellowstone National Park* has a scale of 1:168,500. Separate smaller scale maps (1:83,333) cover Mammoth Hot Springs, Old Faithful, the Tower/ Canyon area and Yellowstone Lake. They also produce a 1:78,000 *Grand Teton National Park* map), with a 1:24,000 inset of the Grand Teton climbing area.

Earthwalk produces a 1:106,250 *Hiking Map & Guide: Yellowstone National Park* and a 1:72,500 *Hiking Map & Guide, Grand Teton National Park*, with 1:48,000 blow-ups of the popular central regions.

Getting to backcountry trailheads outside the parks can be a trying tangle of switchback roads and unmarked forest service roads. If you are going to be hiking outside the park, get a topographic map or a USGS map of the area.

USGS Maps

The United States Geological Survey (USGS) publishes detailed 1:24,000 topographic maps, known as "quads," covering the entire Greater Yellowstone region. Due to their large scale, quads reproduce topographic detail quite accurately, but having to use numerous maps – especially for longer hiking routes – is cumbersome and expensive. Also, many quads have not been revised for decades, so infrastructure such as trails, roads or buildings may be shown incorrectly.

To order a USGS map index and price list, phone ☎ 888-ASK-USGS (275-8747), visit the USGS website at Ⓦ http://mapping.usgs.gov, or write to USGS Information Services, Box 25286, Denver Federal Center, Denver, CO 80225.

USFS ranger district offices, park visitor centers, and outdoor stores in regional towns usually sell hiking maps and some USGS quads.

CD-ROMs

CD-ROMs containing hundreds of digitized USGS 1:24,000 quads and 1:100,000 topographic maps that cover entire states are widely available from around $50. Trails Illustrated's *National Parks of the USA* ($30) focuses on 15 parks, including Yellowstone, Grand Teton, and Glacier, and will work out elevation profiles for chosen trails and print custom topo maps. It's also GPS compatible.

Companies like **iGage** *(Ⓦ www.igage.com)* and **Maptech** *(Ⓦ www.maptech.com)* also sell software that allows hikers using a GPS receiver (see GPS, later) to plot their exact route on their computers.

What's It Going to Cost?

The cost of your Yellowstone vacation will be largely decided by whether you spend your nights round the campground fire or at the lobby bar. Campsites inside the parks range from $10 to $15, and you can prepare your own food for a song, especially if you stock up on supplies outside the park. Outside the parks, many national forests even offer free dispersed camping. RV sites cost around $30 with hookups.

Once you've paid your park entry fee ($10-20), all sights inside the park are free, as are most ranger programs. There's no charge to hike or for backcountry permits. The entry fee for Yellowstone also covers Grand Teton. The pass is valid for seven days, so keep your receipt for reentry.

Costs rise faster than the Tetons as soon as you check into the park's hotels. The cheapest cabins in Yellowstone start at around $55, and most hotel rooms start at $90. You can shave a bit off this by staying outside the parks in the gateway towns, but even here you're going to have to shell out $70 for even a budget motel room in summer. Restaurants aren't a bad value in the park, and you can eat fairly well from $10 per head per meal.

PETS IN THE PARK

Tight restrictions on pets in Yellowstone and Grand Teton National Parks mean you're probably better off leaving Fido at home. Pets must be on a leash at all times and are not allowed on any boardwalks, backcountry trails, or more than 100ft from roads or paved paths. Pets are allowed in Yellowstone's cabins, but not in the hotel. Dogs are allowed in most campgrounds. It's illegal to leave any pet unattended in the parks. Needless to say, you will have to clean up after your pet.

Transportation costs aren't bad if you have your own vehicle (though gas is 15% pricier in the park than elsewhere in Wyoming and Montana) but car rental (and especially RV hire) will chew up a significant chunk of your vacation budget.

Activities can also mount up – a Wild West cookout for a family of four will set you back more than $100 for two hours of fun. On the bright side, you can hike for days for little more than the cost of a few granola bars.

Bear in mind that tipping (around 10-15%) is generally expected on horse-packing and rafting trips and stays at dude ranches.

Accommodation tax ranges from 4% to 8% and varies from county to county, even inside the park. Sales tax is 4% in Wyoming (plus up to 2% county tax) and 5% in Idaho. There is no statewide sales tax in Montana.

NATIONAL PARKS PASSES

You can purchase any of several types of passes that grant unlimited access to national parks. The passes admit a private vehicle and its passengers, or the pass holder, spouse, and children, at parks where per-person fees are imposed. You'll need a photo ID to use the pass.

An annual pass for Grand Teton and Yellowstone National Parks costs $40. An annual **National Parks Pass** costs $50 and is available at any fee-charging national park. You can also apply online at W www.nationalparks.org.

✔ WHAT TO PACK

When choosing your clothes, remember that heavy denim jeans take forever to dry. Sturdy cotton or canvas pants are good for hiking through brush, and cotton or nylon sweats are comfortable to wear around camp or at night. You'll need a wool or fleece sweater at any time of the year.

Layering is essential. Be prepared for changeable weather, including flash thunderstorms and frosts even in the middle of summer. Base layers of synthetic fabrics (not cotton) are most effective in wicking moisture from the body.

If you forget that special widget for your stove, don't panic – excellent outdoor gear and clothing is available at reasonable prices throughout the region, especially in Cody, Jackson, and Bozeman.

The following is meant to be a general guideline. Know yourself and what special things you may need on the trail:

✔ Boots – Light to medium are recommended for day hikes, while sturdy boots are necessary for extended trips with a heavy pack. Most important, they should be well broken-in and have a good heel. Waterproof boots are preferable in spring and early summer.

✔ Alternative footwear – Flip-flops, sandals, or running shoes are best for wearing around camp and crossing streams.

✔ Rain gear – Light, breathable, and waterproof is the ideal combination. Check for sealed seams and contoured hoods that won't obscure your vision.

✔ Hat – Wool or fleece is best for cold weather, and a cotton hat with a brim is good for sun protection (baseball caps will leave you with sunburned ears).

✔ Bandana or handkerchief – This is your best bet for a runny nose, dirty face, picnic lunch, and a flag.

✔ First-aid kit – Include self-adhesive bandages, disinfectant, antibiotic salve or cream, gauze, small scissors, and tweezers.

✔ Camera and binoculars – Don't forget extra film and a spare camera battery.

✔ Small towel

✔ Sundries – toilet paper, sealable plastic bags, insect repellent, flashlight, sunscreen, lip balm, moleskin for foot blisters, and sunglasses.

If you are camping, also consider the following items:

✔ Stove – Lightweight and easy to operate is ideal. Most outdoors stores sell and rent propane or butane stoves. Multi-fuel stoves are versatile but need pumping, priming, and lots of cleaning.

✔ Water purifier – Either tablets such as Potablae Aqua or Aquamira, liquid iodine, or a filter; water can be purified by boiling it for at least 10 minutes.

✔ Waterproof matches or lighter

✔ Sleeping bag – Goose-down bags are warm, lightweight, and compact but useless if they get wet. Synthetic bags are cheaper and better in the wet, but they are bulky, unless you get a compression sack.

✔ Sleeping pad – A blow-up mat like a Therm-A-Rest makes a huge difference to comfort and heat loss.

✔ A fold-up chair and a gas lamp are useful for park campgrounds.

A **Golden Eagle Hologram** (which you affix to your pass) costs an additional $15 and extends access into sites administered by the US Fish & Wildlife Service, the Forest Service and the Bureau of Land Management.

Golden Age Passports carry a onetime fee of $10 and allow US residents 62 years and older (and accompanying passengers in a private vehicle) unlimited entry to all sites in the national park system, with 50% discounts on camping and other fees. **Golden Access Passports** are free and offer the same benefits to US residents who are blind or permanently disabled.

Bringing the Kids

Yellowstone offers the quintessential family vacation, and the NPS looks after its young visitors well. There are plenty of kids' activities, and most restaurants offer kids' menus. Children under 12 stay free in park accommodations.

There are plenty of activities to keep children amused, from horseback riding to white-water rafting. For tips on hiking with your kids and a rundown of the best family hikes, see the Activities chapter (p 36).

KEEPING IT FUN

Active, adventurous, and environmentally aware parents are often eager to have their kids develop similar interests, but be careful not to turn the fun stuff into a chore. Confiscating Gameboys at the park gate is one thing, but don't make your kids memorize 80 types of rock before they can go toast their marshmallows.

Keep the kids in mind as you plan your itinerary. Even better, include them in the trip planning from the get-go. If they've helped to work out where the family is going, they'll be more interested when they arrive, or so the theory goes. For information, advice, and anecdotes, check out Lonely Planet's *Travel With Children*, by Cathy Lanigan.

Don't drive all day; break up car time with ice cream stops, hikes, picnics, and the like. Visitor centers have lots of child-orientated exhibits and can divert kids' attention though children's books, coloring books, and jigsaw puzzles while you furtively check out the hiking books.

Mix up natural scenery with the contrasting attractions of towns like West Yellowstone and Jackson. Spend some time at places that both kids and adults can enjoy, such as the Draper Museum of Natural History in the Buffalo Bill Historical Center in Cody, the Rendezvous Aerial Tram in Teton Village, or the alpine slide at Jackson's Snow King resort.

Both parks operate activities aimed at kids and their parents, and these can be a good way for families to learn together. Junior ranger programs are a particularly good way to spark the minds of young kids. See the Activities chapter (p 36) for details.

KEEPING IT SAFE

When hiking with children, make sure they carry a flashlight and whistle and know what to do if they get lost. Some families carry small walkie-talkies so they can keep track of everyone during hikes or visits to busy visitor centers.

Watch for dehydration, sunburn, mosquito bites, even a simple chill – children lose heat much faster than adults. Be particularly careful of children if you stop by the roadside to watch wildlife; everyone involved is likely to be watching the bison instead of the traffic.

Be extra vigilant at overviews like the Grand Canyon of the Yellowstone or the Yellowstone River Picnic Area hike, as some areas have no guardrails and sheer drops of several hundred feet. Thermal areas are another potential danger, as kids often don't comprehend just how hot the water is. More than one child has been burned while testing the waters of a hot spring.

Health & Safety

For suggestions on how to hike safely, see the Activities chapter (p 26).

DISABLED TRAVELERS

Yellowstone has many accessible boardwalks and trails and several wheelchair-accessible backcountry campsites, including Goose Lake in Geyser Country and Ice Lake on the Norris-Canyon road, which is half a mile from the trailhead and has a wheelchair-accessible vault toilet. The pamphlet *Visitor Guide to Accessible Features in Yellowstone National Park* is available online at the park website or by writing to the Park Accessibility Coordinator, PO Box 168, Yellowstone National Park, WY 82190-0168.

Wheelchair accessible trails in Grand Teton include the 6-mile paved trail along String Lake. Accessible accommodations are available at several campsites and all lodging facilities. For more details contact the Accessibility Coordinator, Grand Teton National Park, PO Drawer 170, Moose, WY 83012.

Deaf visitors can get information at TDD ☎ 307-344-2386 (Yellowstone) or TDD ☎ 307-739-3400 (Grand Teton).

Access Tours *(☎ 307-733-6664; Box 2985 Jackson, WY 83001)* runs tours in Grand Teton and Yellowstone for those with physical disabilities.

EMERGENCIES

In an emergency of any sort dial ☎ 911. If you need to contact friends or family, emergency messages can be posted at the park's entry stations and visitor centers.

WATER PURIFICATION

As a rule, don't drink any snowmelt, stream, lake, or ground water without boiling it for at least 10 minutes, filtering it with a filter at 0.5 microns or smaller, or treating with water tablets. What you want to avoid is *Giardia lamblia*, a microscopic waterborne parasite that causes intestinal disorders, with symptoms such as chronic diarrhea, bloating, and appalling gas. Treatment requires a course of antibiotics. Iodine will not destroy *Giardia*.

ALTITUDE SICKNESS

In the thinner atmosphere of the Rockies, lack of oxygen may cause headaches, nausea, nosebleeds, shortness of breath, physical weakness, and other symptoms. These can lead to serious consequences, especially if combined with heat exhaustion, sunburn, or hypothermia. Most people adjust to altitude within a few hours or days, but you need to be careful (especially with children) when driving and overnighting on the Beartooth Plateau, where altitudes reach 10,000ft. In mild cases of altitude sickness, everyday painkillers such as aspirin may relieve discomfort. If symptoms persist, descend to lower elevations.

HYPOTHERMIA

Temperatures in the mountains can quickly drop from balmy to below freezing. A sudden downpour and high winds can also rapidly lower your body temperature.

Symptoms of hypothermia include shivering, loss of coordination, slurred speech, and disorientation or confusion. These can be accompanied by exhaustion, numbness (particularly in toes and fingers), irrational or violent behavior, lethargy, dizzy spells, muscle cramps, and bursts of energy.

To treat early stages of hypothermia, get victims out of the wind or rain, remove any wet clothing, and replace it with dry, warm clothing. Give them hot liquids – not alcohol – and high-calorie, easily digestible food like granola bars, trail mix, energy bars/drinks, or chocolate. In advanced stages, it may be necessary to place victims in warm sleeping bags and get in with them. If possible, place the victim near a fire or in a warm (not hot) bath. Do *not* rub a victim's skin.

SUNBURN

You face a greater risk from sun exposure when hiking at high elevations. Sunburn is possible on hazy or cloudy days and even when it snows. Use sunscreen and lip moisturizer with UV-A and UV-B protection and an SPF of 30 or greater. Reapply it throughout the day. Wear a wide-brimmed hat and sunglasses and consider tying a bandanna around your neck for extra protection.

Dangers & Annoyances

ROAD ACCIDENTS

Rubbernecking while watching wildlife is a common cause of traffic jams. This and high speeds are the main causes of the more than 600 annual vehicular accidents in Yellowstone. Pull completely off the road if you absolutely must get that rutting elk snapshot, and stick to the speed limits (generally 45mph). About 90 animals a year are killed by vehicles in Yellowstone, so go slow.

GETTING IN HOT WATER

You'll see plenty of signs warning you to stay on existing boardwalks and maintain a safe distance from all geothermal features. Thin crusts can break, giving way to boiling water. Even warm springs can be dangerous; temperatures often fluctuate, sometimes dramatically, so what is safe one day may not be safe the next. About 20 people have died in Yellowstone's hot springs since the 1880s; some have backed into hot springs while taking photos, and more than one pet has jumped gleefully into a boiling pool. In winter 1996–97 a young bison fell into Blue Star Spring near Old Faithful and was killed, causing the pool to smell like beef soup for days.

The park service warns that spring waters can cause a rash and that thermophilic amoebas in the water can transmit amoebic meningitis (though there has apparently never been a recorded case of this). If you do swim in any of the areas mentioned in this guide, keep your head above the surface and don't take in any water.

BEAR NECESSITIES

Travelers in the Yellowstone region need to be bear aware, whether camping in a developed site or hiking in the backcountry.

It's helpful to learn the difference between grizzly bears and black bears, since the two model different behaviors (adult grizzlies, for example, can't climb trees very well, but black bears can). You can't rely on color alone – black bears also come in various shades of brown, and some grizzly bears look almost black. Instead, look for the distinguishing hump on the grizzly's shoulder as well as long claws and the wide, dish-shaped face. Grizzlies have rounded ears and tend to be quite a bit bigger than black bears.

Bears live a sedentary life and will typically avoid contact if given sufficient warning of an approaching individual. The main causes of human-bear conflict include the animal's instinctual protection of its young, the presence of food, and surprise encounters. To learn more about the habits of bears, see p 253 of the Ecosystem chapter.

BEARS & FOOD

Bears are obsessed with food and rarely "unlearn" lessons acquired in finding it. In the past, Yellowstone's bears were regularly fed (often as a spectacle for tourists) and allowed to pick over garbage dumps. Conditioned to associate humans with food, large numbers of these so-called "habituated" bears harassed picnickers or aggressively raided camps. Nowadays, even mildly troublesome bears are usually destroyed. Don't let your carelessness result in the death of one of these magnificent creatures.

Bears don't see well, but they do have an extremely keen sense of smell and are attracted not just to food but to other fragrant items such as toothpaste, lotions, perfumes and deodorants. Developed campgrounds provide bear-resistant metal boxes, but in other areas campers should always lock their food out of sight within the car. *Never* store or eat food in your tent, and don't sleep in the clothes you wore while fishing or cooking.

Bear holdup
in Yellowstone, 1958

NPS PHOTOGRAPHS

All backcountry campers must hang food and scented items such as garbage, toothpaste, soap, or sunscreen at least 12ft above the ground and 200ft from their tents. Carry a robust stuff-sack attached to a 50ft length of rope for this purpose. First weight the sack with a rock and throw it over a high, sturdy limb at least 4ft from the tree trunk. Gently lower the sack to the ground with the rope, stash *everything* that might be attractive to bears, then pull the sack back up close to the tree limb. Finally, tie off the end of the rope to another trunk or tree limb well out of the way. Backcountry campgrounds in Yellowstone and Grand Teton invariably supply a food pole, which simplifies the food hanging process.

BEAR ENCOUNTERS

Statistically speaking, there is less than one bear attack a year in Yellowstone. Take precautions and it won't be you.

Your best defenses against surprising a bear are to remain alert, avoid hiking at night (when bears feed), and be careful when traveling upwind near streams or where visibility is obstructed. Check current bear activity with rangers before setting off. Bear management areas at Mt Washburn and around Yellowstone Lake are closed to visitors in early summer. Several trails are also closed in early summer, including the those to Riddle, Heart, and Mary Lakes.

Bells have been a favorite noisemaking deterrent for years, but rangers warn that most bells are too soft and high-pitched. The human voice is effective (show tunes seem to work especially well), though you may irritate fellow hikers if you're too loud.

There are several defensive strategies to employ, but no guarantees, if you do encounter a bear. If the bear doesn't see you, move a safe distance downwind and make noise to alert it to your presence. If the bear sees you, slowly back out of its path, avoiding eye contact, speak softly and wave your hands above your head slowly. Never turn your back on a bear and never kneel down.

Sows with cubs are particularly dangerous, and you should make every effort to avoid placing yourself between a sow and her young. A sow may clack her jaws, lower her head, and shake it as a warning before she charges.

If a bear does charge, do not run (bears can sprint up to 40mph for short distances) and do not scream (that may frighten the bear, making it more aggressive). Bluff charges are common. Drop to the ground, crouch face down into a ball, and play dead, covering the back of your neck with your hands and your chest and stomach with your knees. Do not resist the bear's inquisitive pawing – it may get bored and go away. Climbing a tree is one option, but only if you have time to climb at least 15ft.

If a bear attacks you in your tent at night, you're likely dealing with a predatory bear that perceives you as a food source. In this extremely rare scenario you should fight back aggressively with anything you can find; don't play dead.

PEPPER SPRAYS

Pepper sprays are deterrents that contain the severe irritant oleoresin capsaicin. Their effectiveness in deterring aggressive bears is a matter of debate, but many backcountry travelers now carry pepper spray as a last line of defense. It can be particularly useful in the extremely unlikely event you're attacked in your tent at night.

Rangers recommend a minimum size of 7.9oz (225g), and a concentration of 1.4% to 1.8% capsaicin, such as sprays manufactured by the Bozeman company UDAP (W www.udap.com). These are widely available in backpacking stores around Yellowstone and cost around $40. The spray can reach up to 30ft but is less effective in windy conditions. Pepper spray must be carried within immediate reach – not buried in your pack. For the best results, wait until the bear is 15ft away (gulp) and try to spray downwind; in several documented cases, victims of bear attacks have blinded themselves with their own pepper spray.

Carrying pepper spray is not a substitute for vigilance or other safety precautions. Remember also that pepper spray does *not* work like bug repellent – it may actually *attract* bears if sprayed on tents or packs.

BEARS & WOMEN

While it has not been proven that bears show an affinity for menstruating women, more than one woman has been attacked by a bear during her menstrual cycle. If you have your period while hiking in bear country, be sure to carry plenty of tampons (pads are not recommended) and sealable plastic bags in which to dispose of them. If you accidentally bleed on clothing or gear, wash it out immediately. Women who have a heavy menstrual flow may want to schedule their trip for before or after their period.

SNAGS

Burned in the 1988 and 2000 fires, tens of thousands of dead trees, or "snags," remain standing, posing a threat to oblivious hikers. Avoid leaning against damaged trees, and watch and listen for falling timber when hiking through burned areas, especially if it's windy.

LIGHTNING

Getting struck by lightning in one of Yellowstone's (and especially Grand Teton's) afternoon storms is a real possibility. If you do get caught out during a lightning storm, steer clear of exposed ridges, open areas, lone trees, the base of cliffs, and shallow caves or depressions. Move away from bodies of water or beaches. If camping, sit on a foam mattress in a crouched position, your arms around your knees.

FIRE

Fire danger in the Rockies varies from year to year but is often extreme in July and August. Local park and USFS offices can advise hikers about forest fires, and fire warnings are usually posted at wilderness access points. Always check with a ranger station or visitor center before embarking on a hike. For fire updates contact the parks at ☎ 307-739-3300 or check out their websites. Alternatively, contact the **National Interagency Fire Center** (☎ *208-387-5050;* W *www.nifc.gov*).

WILDLIFE

Most problems in Yellowstone stem from inappropriate visitor behavior around wildlife. Some folks don't realize that all of Yellowstone's animals are wild and potentially dangerous. Mom says: Do not harass, feed, or approach wildlife. Stay at least 100yd away from bears and at least 25yd away from other wildlife; it's illegal to approach any closer.

The wise learn to recognize bear habitat and exercise extreme caution – every year grizzlies maul a few visitors. (See "Bear Necessities" p 54.) Bison, which can weigh 2000lb and sprint at 30mph, actually injure (gore) more visitors than do bears. Read *Death in Yellowstone*, by park archivist Lee Whittlesey, for all the gory details.

Moose can also be surprisingly aggressive, particularly mothers protecting their young. There are no poisonous snakes in Yellowstone.

INSECTS

Mosquitoes can be a major irritant in early and midsummer (until around mid-August), so remember to carry mosquito repellent. The most effective sprays contain DEET (the higher the percentage of DEET the more effective the spray). DEET is powerful stuff and should be kept away from plastics. Citronella is a kinder (to the skin at least) alternative.

Getting There

The main gateways (and airports) nearest to Yellowstone National Park are Jackson (56mi), Cody (52mi), Bozeman (65mi), Billings (129mi), and Idaho Falls (107mi). Depending on your direction of travel, it may be cheaper to land in Salt Lake City (390mi) or Denver (563mi) and rent a car there.

AIR

Jackson Hole Airport, 8.5mi from Jackson, is definitely the closest airport to Grand Teton National Park – in fact, it's 4mi *inside* the park. There are frequent flights between Jackson Hole and Salt Lake City (Delta/SkyWest), Denver (United), and Chicago (American Airlines). Inquire about possible future nonstop service to New York City. If you are flying into Jackson, get a seat on the right side of the plane, as these normally offer the best views.

AMERICA'S MOST SCENIC AIRPORT

Jackson Hole Airport abounds in controversy. Not only is it the only US airport inside a national park, but it also has one of the shortest commercial runways in the nation. Planes periodically overshoot the tarmac. Things bog down further during the comings and goings of Air Force Two, which shuttles Dick Cheney to his vacation home here.

Boosters want the runway extended, but airport expansion is currently restricted under a 50-year agreement signed by the airport and NPS in 1983. Recent moves by local Jackson businesses to subsidize (and thus guarantee) flights from busy airports like Chicago, New York, and Atlanta will only aggravate the problem. One option is to move the airport to Idaho Falls, 100mi away.

In the meantime, put your seat in its upright and locked position and enjoy your free scenic view of Grand Teton National Park.

West Yellowstone has the closest airport to Yellowstone National Park, with three daily summer flights (June through September) to and from Salt Lake City (SkyWest, with connections on Delta).

Billings' **Logan International Airport** (W *www.flybillings.com*) has connections to and from Salt Lake City (Delta Airlines), Denver (Continental and United Airlines), Minneapolis (Northwest Airlines), and Seattle (Alaska Air).

Bozeman's **Gallatin Field** airport (W *www.gallatinfield.com*) has flights to and from Denver (United), Detroit (Northwest), Minneapolis (Northwest), Salt Lake City (Delta), and Seattle (Horizon).

Cody's **Yellowstone Regional Airport** (W *www.flyyra.com*) has flights to and from Salt Lake City (SkyWest) and Denver (Great Lakes Aviation).

Idaho Falls' recently renovated **Fanning Field Municipal Airport** has flights to and from Boise (Horizon), Salt Lake City (SkyWest-Delta), and Seattle. Private planes can land at several small airstrips, including Driggs and Mission Field, east of Livingston.

CAR

It's almost impossible to visit Yellowstone without your own vehicle. There's no public transportation of any kind inside the park and only minimal transportation in the gateway corridors. What's surprising is that despite the volume of traffic trundling through the park, there appears to be little movement in the direction of a mass transit system inside the park.

Car Rental

Car rental rates in the towns around Yellowstone vary considerably throughout the year, with summer weekends bringing the highest rates. See the individual towns in the Gateway Towns and Excursions chapters for car rental company contact details.

Jackson, Billings, Bozeman, and Cody have the best selection of rental companies and thus slightly lower rates. All the airports have car rentals. The major companies are **Hertz** (Ⓦ www.hertz.com), **Avis** (Ⓦ www.avis.com), **Thrifty** (Ⓦ www.thrifty.com), and **National** (Ⓦ www.nationalcar.com).

RV Rental

Renting an RV can seem an attractive proposition (think of all the money you save in accommodations), but it's not necessarily a cheap option. RVs only get about nine miles to the gallon, so gas is likely to be a significant additional expenditure. You need to reserve RV rentals well in advance in summer.

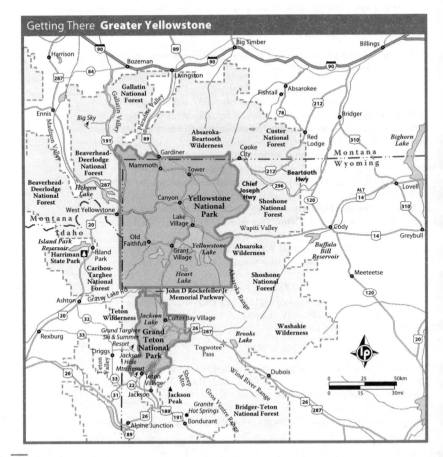

Getting There **Greater Yellowstone**

Cruise America (☎ 480-464-7300, fax 480-464-7321; Ⓦ www.cruiseamerica.com; 11 W Hampton Ave, Mesa, AZ 85210) rents a range of RVs through local dealers in Salt Lake City and Jackson. There's a three-day minimum rental. High-season rates last from mid-June to mid-August. A seven-night rental (1000mi included) costs from $875 for the smallest RV in the off-season to $1500 for the largest RV in high season. Harley-style Honda motorbikes are also available from $100 per day.

Driving

If your vision of driving around Yellowstone is of an open road and Steppenwolf blasting on the stereo, then brace yourself for a crushing blow. At peak times expect to be part of a snaking line of vehicles stuck behind a lumbering RV as it wheezes over the Continental Divide. And if anyone gets even the slightest whiff of a bison or moose, expect the traffic to grind to a halt. It pays not to be in a hurry inside the park.

Practice courteous driving etiquette. If you're driving a slow vehicle, use the numerous pullouts to let faster traffic pass. If you don't want your open driver's side door torn off by a passing bus, pull fully off the road when watching wildlife. Wildlife always has the right of way. If you're in a group, swap drivers periodically so everyone has time to fully enjoy the views.

Gas prices inside the park are about 15% higher than elsewhere in Wyoming and Montana. Prices rise as you get closer to the park, peaking at Red Lodge and Cooke City.

Speed limits in the park are generally 45mph, dropping to 25mph or less at popular pullouts or junctions. Hwy 191 in Grand Teton National Park has a limit of 55mph. Roads outside the park generally have limits between 55 and 65mph, with highways up to 65 or 75mph.

On motorcycles, helmets are required for anyone under 18 in Montana and Idaho or under 19 in Wyoming.

Road Conditions

Yellowstone's roads are sorely in need of repair, and there's always one section of the Grand Loop under construction, causing delays of up to an hour. Sometimes sections of road are closed between certain hours; see the parks' newspapers or websites for current road conditions.

Perched on the parks' boundaries, four towns serve as visitor hubs, where you can stock up on groceries, fill up your car with gas, check email, and bed down for the night.

GATEWAY TOWNS

South of Grand Teton, only Jackson ranks as a destination in its own right, followed distantly by West Yellowstone. To the north, Gardiner is the oldest gateway to Yellowstone. To the northeast is Cooke City, the most isolated and rustic of the four gateways, with fewer visitors and less obvious tourist trappings. It's many visitors' favorite for these very reasons.

For details about accommodations and dining options in these towns, check out the Places to Stay (p 174) and Places to Eat (p 191) chapters.

West Yellowstone
MAP 16
TEL 406 • POP 1222 • ELEVATION 6600FT

The small, tourism-based town of West Yellowstone, Montana, is well equipped to lodge, feed, and briefly entertain visitors headed to Yellowstone National Park, a quarter mile from the town center. The town itself has expanded rapidly in recent years and now boasts more manmade "attractions" than Yellowstone's two other gateway towns combined. Families will find plenty of diversions.

What West Yellowstone residents find most redeeming is that outside the park, within a bike ride, ski, or long run from town, open wilderness abounds and is often uncrowded, even at the height of tourist season. The town bustles during the high seasons (June to September and mid-December to mid-March) and resembles a ghost town other times of the year.

Most locals fought against the NPS' proposed ban on snowmobiling in Yellowstone National Park (see the "Snowmobile Wars" boxed text on p 35), and some are still not happy with the limits imposed in November 2002. Unrestricted snowmobiling continues outside the park, and West Yellowstone will doubtless remain its hub, as well as a launching pad for snowcoach and ski tours.

HISTORY

In 1908 the town of Riverside opened a post office at the end of the Union Pacific Railroad track. The following year Dick Murray opened Murray's Yellowstone Hotel (still standing as the Madison Motel), and Sam and Ida Eagle opened a general store on Yellowstone Ave (still in operation as Eagle's Store). Thus Yellowstone (renamed the same year) began welcoming travelers. The Union Pacific complex, consisting of the depot, a dining hall (or "beanery"), and lodge, was the hub of activity and the community's major employer.

Yellowstone National Park's popularity brought enough visitors to support service businesses alongside Union Pacific, and with the growth of automobile travel, independent operations soon overshadowed the railroads. In 1920 the community changed its name to West Yellowstone to define itself geographically and avoid confusion between the town and the park.

ORIENTATION & INFORMATION

US 191 (from Bozeman) and US 287 (from Ennis) meet 8mi north and run through town as Canyon St (West Yellowstone's main drag) then turn east at Yellowstone Ave to enter the park. US 20 heads west into Idaho.

West Yellowstone's **Chamber of Commerce Information Center** (☎ *406-646-7701,* Ⓦ *www.westyellowstonechamber.com; Canyon St),* one block south of Yellowstone Ave, has a Yellowstone National Park information desk and brochures with discount coupons for local attractions.

The **Gallatin National Forest Service Headquarters** (☎ *406-646-7369)* is on Canyon St, two blocks north of Firehole Ave.

Canyon Street Laundry *(312 Canyon St; open 7am-10pm)* has coin-operated machines, drop-off service, and slightly rundown public showers ($2 for 6 minutes).

Tiny **West Yellowstone Public Library** (☎ *406-6469017; 220 Yellowstone Ave; closed Sun and Mon)* has free Internet service (30 minutes maximum). It gets booked up quickly, so phone ahead to reserve time. Alternatively, purchase Internet access for $5 per hour at either **West Yellowstone Web Works** *(27 Geyser)* or The Madison Hotel.

For topo maps, natural history guides, and a good general selection of books (particularly on women in the West), stop at the **Book Peddler** (☎ *406-646-9358; 106 Canyon St; open 8am-10pm in summer).* There's also an espresso bar with pastries and a few lunch items.

Eagle's Store & Tackle (☎ *406-646-9300; W Yellowstone Ave)* sells backpacking supplies.

THINGS TO SEE & DO

At 9:30am daily the chamber of commerce presents a discussion on things to do in Yellowstone. Rangers offer talks daily at 2pm at either the Grizzly & Wolf Discovery Center or Museum of the Yellowstone. There are also twice weekly ranger-led slide shows at 8pm at the Grizzly & Wolf Discovery Center. In winter, rangers lead snowshoe hikes along the Riverside trail. Bring your own snowshoes.

Five bears (Kodiak and grizzly) and nine gray wolves are kept in a pseudo-natural setting at the **Grizzly & Wolf Discovery Center** (☎ *406-646-7001;* Ⓦ *www.gizzlydiscoveryctr.com; admission $8.50, children aged 5-12 $4; open daily 8am-dusk)* in Grizzly Park. Why keep live animals in captivity a quarter mile from one of the largest natural habitats in the Lower 48? The concept is to educate travelers about the nature of bears and wolves, while protecting "problem bears" – repeat offenders of garbage bin raids or harmful encounters with people. The center is now not-for-profit, having been bought out by employees and locals in 1999.

The twice-daily wolf feedings (sorry, "enrichment") are worth catching. There are also kids' programs and naturalist presentations, while movies are shown on request.

Next door, the **Yellowstone IMAX Theater** (☎ 406-646-4100; admission $8; hourly showings 9am-9pm May-Sep, 1pm-9pm Oct-Apr) may be the only way for summer travelers to see Yellowstone in the winter or without crowds – all on a screen six stories high. Films rotate, but *Yellowstone* and *Bears* are always showing.

The **Museum of the Yellowstone** (☎ 406-646-1100; 124 Yellowstone Ave; admission $6/4; open 9am-9pm, mid-May-mid-Oct), housed in the 1909 Union Pacific railroad depot, was revamped in 2002 and now explores the history of visitors to Yellowstone, with an emphasis on early stagecoach and rail travel. There are also displays on the 1988 fires, wildlife, and earthquakes. Still, it's hard to justify the high price tag.

It's worth a (free) visit to the wonderfully preserved 1903 **Oregon Short Line Rail Car** in the Holiday Inn.

The **Playmill Theater** (☎ 406-646-7757; W www.playmill.com; 29 Madison Ave; tickets $11/9; open Memorial Day-Labor Day) is a local institution and has been churning out light musicals, melodramas, and comedies for 40 years. Reserve your tickets in advance.

ACTIVITIES

West Yellowstone is host to a range of cultural and sporting events, from summer rodeo and mountain man rendezvous to the Spam Cup, a series of ski races in which the lucky winner receives a free can of Spam.

Summer

Both the Rendezvous and Riverside trail systems (see Winter) offer great **mountain biking** and **trail running** when the snow melts.

Free Heel and Wheel (☎ 406-646-7744; W www.freeheelandwheel.com; 40 Yellowstone Ave) is the place to stop for maps, mountain bike rentals ($20 to $35 per day), ski ($15 to $25) and snowshoe ($15) rentals, friendly trail advice, and free group activities (trail runs, mountain bike rides, etc) five days a week.

Yellowstone Bicycles (☎ 406-646-7815; 132 Madison Ave) rents bikes from $20 a day, including recumbents, which are best described as a La-Z-Boy on wheels.

Bud Lilly's Trout Shop (☎ 406-646-7801; W www.budlillys.com; 39 Madison Ave) rents fishing equipment and offers one-day float and walk trips from $175 per person. **Arrick's Fly Shop** (☎ 406-646-7290; W www.arricks.com; 37 Canyon St), **Jacklins** (☎ 406-6467336; W www.jacklinsflyshop.com; 105 Yellowstone Ave), and **Madison River Outfitters** (406-646-9644; W www.madisonriveroutfitters.com; 117 Canyon St) are all good places for fishing information, equipment, and guides.

Nine miles from West Yellowstone, **Parade Rest Ranch** (☎ 406-646-7217; W www.paraderestranch.com) offers horseback rides from one to four hours ($30 to $65 per person, no rides Sunday), including sunset rides and corral rides for kids under seven. They also offer Western cookouts overlooking Hebgen Lake on Monday and Friday evenings ($24 to $29).

Winter

In November the 30mi of groomed skiing and skating trails in the **Rendezvous Trail System** are training ground for US Olympic cross-country ski teams. Trails are groomed November through March, and there are kids' loops. In March the Rendezvous Marathon Ski Race draws hundreds of skiers.

Less developed and more scenic are the **Riverside Trails**, which start on the east side of Boundary St between Madison Ave and Firehole Ave. The main trail cuts through 1.5 miles of fir and pine and emerges amid old NPS roads and other trails alongside the Madison River.

Many of the town's hotels rent their own snowmobiles and offer winter lodging and rental packages. Two of the many snowmobile rental agencies are **Rendezvous Snowmobile Rentals** (☎ 406-646-9564; W *www.yellowstonevacations.com; 415 Yellowstone Ave*) and **Two Top Snowmobile Rentals** (☎ 406-646-7802; W *www.twotopsnowmobile.com; 646 Gibbon Ave*). Agencies rent snowmobiles for $100 to $139 per day.

If you've always wanted to stand behind a pack of huskies and cry out, "Mush!" **Klondike Dreams** (☎ 406-646-4988) runs half-day ($125, three hours) and full-day ($165 to $200 per person, six hours) dog-sledding trips in the Gallatin Forest southeast of Hebgen Lake. They also offer sled shuttles to the forestry cabins at Basin and Beaver Creeks.

ORGANIZED TOURS

Gray Line Tours (☎ 406-646-9374, 800-523-3102; *555 Yellowstone Ave*) runs eight-hour bus tours of the park daily in the summer for $42 per person.

In winter **Yellowstone Alpen Guides** (☎ 800-858-3502, 406-646-9591; W *www.yellowstoneguides.com; PO Box 518, 537 Yellowstone Ave*) runs 10-person snowcoach tours to Old Faithful ($87 per person) and Canyon ($97). Tours depart daily mid-December through mid-March. They provide a picnic lunch and stop at the more famous geyser basins for short walking tours. Guided or independent skiing and snowshoeing options are also available, as are summer van tours of the park and multiday tours.

Snowcoach Yellowstone (☎ 800-426-7669; W *www.snowcoachyellowstone.com; 201 Canyon St*) also run full-day guided snowcoach tours of the park for $84 ($64 children under 13).

Skiers and snowboarders shouldn't miss a backcountry trip with **Hellroaring Ski Adventures** (☎ 406-646-4571; W *www.skihellroaring.com*). For $80 to $175 per person (depending on the number in your group), you get a shuttle, guide, meals (take off $25 if you supply your own food), avalanche rescue equipment, climbing skins, hut accommodations, and some fine terrain in the Centennial Mountains. Hut rental, for a minimum of four experienced people, costs $25 per person per night.

GETTING THERE & AWAY

Greyhound buses to/from Bozeman and Idaho Falls stop at the Western Union office (☎ 406-646-1111; *126 Electric St*), also the home of **Yellowstone Taxi** (☎ 406-646-1111).

Budget (☎ 406-646-7882, *131 Dunraven St and Yellowstone Airport*) and **Big Sky Car Rentals** (☎ 800-426-7669; *415 Yellowstone Ave*) offer car rental from $45 a day.

Gardiner
MAP 14
TEL 406 • POP 120 • ELEVATION 5134FT

A quintessential gateway town founded and fed on tourism, Gardiner, Montana, is the only entrance to Yellowstone National Park open to automobile traffic year-round. Park St is the dividing line between Park County and Yellowstone National Park, and Mammoth Hot Springs is 5mi south.

The town is named after Johnston Gardiner, an early trapper. Gardiner only made it onto the map in the 1880s when the Northern Pacific Railroad unveiled its Park Branch Line from Livingston to nearby Cinnabar. Stagecoaches ferried passengers on the last leg of the journey to the park, and Gardiner grew as a transit stop.

The only real point of interest here, aside from the abundant food and lodging, is the Roosevelt Arch, dedicated by Teddy Roosevelt himself in 1903. The town is friendly though, and it makes a good base from which to explore the northern reaches of the park.

ORIENTATION & INFORMATION

Gardiner is 53mi south of Livingston via US 89, which is known as Scott St where it parallels the Yellowstone River and 2nd St where it turns south to cross the river.

The Yellowstone River, which flows east to west through town, divides Gardiner into two distinct sections: the older grid to the south, bordering the national park, and the newer strip along Scott St, where most tourist services now operate.

The **chamber of commerce** (☎ 406-848-7971; W www.gardinerchamber.com; 220 W Park St) is helpful and also runs an information kiosk at the corner of 3rd and Park Sts.

The **Gallatin National Forest Gardiner District Office** (☎ 406-848-7375; 805 Scott St; closed weekends) provides maps and hiking information.

First National Park Bank on Scott St has an ATM. The nearest medical facility is the **Mammoth Clinic**, 5mi south in Yellowstone National Park.

The **Flying Pig Camping Store** (☎ 406-848-7510) stocks all kinds of gear (including bear pepper spray) and offers Internet access ($6 per hour). The nearby **Silvertip Bookstore** (☎ 406-848-2225) has espresso, smoothies and Internet access, in addition to a stock of local interest books. Both places are open until 9pm in summer.

Public showers are available at Yellowstone RV Park ($4).

The rodeo pulls into town five times during the summer.

ACTIVITIES

On the Yellowstone River, **river rafting** trips run through the Class II to III rapids of Yankee Jim Canyon, one of Montana's more famous white-water spots. The **Yellowstone Raft Company** (☎ 406-848-7777; W www.yellowstoneraft.com; 406 Scott St) runs half-day white-water trips for $31/21 adults/children, full-day for $66/46 including lunch. They also have half-day kayaking lessons on the river for $69.

Wild West Whitewater Rafting (☎ 406-848-2252; W www.wildwestrafting.com) does similar floats, as well as gentler scenic floats in the upper Paradise Valley. **Montana Whitewater** (☎ 800-586-4465; W www.montanawhitewater.com; 403 Scott St) rents canoes and float tubes in addition to raft trips on the Yellowstone and Gallatin.

Several outfitters run **fishing** trips, **horseback riding**, and pack trips into Yellowstone and other nearby mountain areas, including **Wilderness Connection** (☎ 406-848-7287), **Hell's A-Roarin' Outfitters** (☎ 406-848-7578), **Rendezvous Outfitters** (☎ 406-848-7710), and **North Yellowstone Outfitters** (☎ 406-848-7651). Rides start at around $25 per hour, $65 per half day, and $100 per full day.

Parks' Fly Shop (☎ 406-848-7314), on 2nd St between Stone and Main Sts, publishes an angler's map of Yellowstone National Park and surrounding areas. Float trips are around $115 per person (including lunch and equipment), less with three or more people. In winter the action switches to cross-country ski rental.

For back road biking routes north of Gardiner see the Paradise Valley section in the Greater Yellowstone chapter (p 208). For the backdoor route into Yellowstone Park see the Mountain Biking section of Mammoth Country in the Experiencing Yellowstone chapter (p 85).

ORGANIZED TOURS

The park concessionaire, **Xanterra** (☎ *307-344-7901)*, runs daily tours of Yellowstone, taking in all the major sights in about 10 hours. Tours leave from Gardiner. Tickets costs $42 or $20 for children aged 12 to 16 (children under 12 are free).

Cooke City
MAP 13
TEL 406 • POP 85 • ELEVATION 7600FT

Set between two forested ridges of the Beartooth Mountains, this one-street Montana town (population 85 in winter, 350 in summer) on the northeast edge of Yellowstone gets a steady flow of summer visitors en route between the scenic splendors of the Beartooth Highway and the national park. There's not much here in the way of shops, sights, or even trailheads, but the isolated town has a backwoods feel that's more laid-back and less commercial than the park's other gateway towns and a year-round population that's as rugged as the surrounding peaks.

Cooke City's isolation is due to geography and the lack of a railroad link. Citizens lobbied to bring the railroad to the mining town, even going so far as to rename the town in 1880 after a bigwig in the Northern Pacific Railroad (the town's original name was Shoo-Fly), but even this blatant flattery failed to overcome hard economics.

In winter the road from Yellowstone is only plowed as far as Cooke City, so visitors – mostly backcountry skiers and snowmobilers – tend to check in and stay awhile.

INFORMATION

The **chamber of commerce** (☎ *406-838-2495;* [W] *www.cookecitychamber.com)* should be of some help, provided anyone is there. The Cooke City General Store sells topographic maps. Internet access is an outrageous $1 per five minutes in the Sinclair gas station in the center of town.

The tiny **Cooke City Bike Shack** (☎ *406-838-2412)* is a good stop for anyone who wants to hike, bike, or ski in the immediate area. They have a good inventory of equipment (from freeze-dried food to pepper spray) and maps, and the owner is a longtime local who is tremendously helpful with trail suggestions.

In a vehicular emergency contact AAA-endorsed **Bearclaw Mountain Recovery** (☎ *406-838-2040)*. Gas prices are the highest in the Yellowstone region, but there's not a whole lot you can do about it.

THINGS TO SEE & DO

Sightseers are going to be stumped in Cooke City. The historic **Cooke City General Store** is a fun browse and has some interesting history on the walls. They also have a good supply of groceries, beer, and wine. Kids will like the animal exhibits in the **Yellowstone Trading Post**, next to the Beartooth Café.

AROUND COOKE CITY

The network of mining roads northeast of Cooke City offers opportunities to get off the beaten track. About 1.5mi east of Cooke City, near Colter campground, the unpaved Lulu Pass–Goose Lake Rd leads north to Fisher Creek. After 1.5mi is the **Aero Lakes Trailhead**, which offers a fine day hike to Lady of the Lake (3mi round-trip) and to Lower Aero Lake (11mi round-trip).

A little farther up the track is the very rough, high-clearance vehicle only Goose Lake Track (#3230), which leads up to scenic Mud, Round, and Long Lakes. The road is so bad that it's probably easier to just park and walk.

The road enters the Absaroka-Beartooth Wilderness after about 5.5mi, and all vehicles must stop at the boundary. From here it's 4mi, past Goose Lake, to **Grasshopper Glacier**. The glacier takes its name from the millions of now extinct grasshoppers entombed in the ice after a freak snowstorm froze a swarm. Recent thawing has exposed and decomposed many of the grasshoppers, so check with a ranger station to see what's left before making the long trip. July and August are really the only months to attempt a visit.

In winter the above-mentioned tracks are popular with snowmobilers and Nordic skiers. There are several snowmobile rental outfits in town (which switch to ATV rentals in summer). Cooke City Bike Shack can arrange one-way snowmobile shuttle drops for skiers.

Grasshopper Glacier takes its name from the millions of now extinct grasshoppers entombed in the ice.

Jackson
MAP 18
TEL 307 • POP 8647 • ELEVATION 6234FT

After a week in the woods, Jackson Hole's historic heart can easily induce sensory overload. Die-hard Wyomingites disparage it as a tourist enclave where rhinestone cowboys and jet-setting celebs frequent fancy restaurants, rapacious realtors push overpriced timeshares, and fatuous shoppers swarm kitschy boutiques. The rapidly growing town suffers from Wyoming's worst traffic and a growing rift between the rich and working class. However, Jackson also supports a vigorous cultural life and, with its busy airport, is a major gateway to Grand Teton and Yellowstone National Parks.

ORIENTATION & INFORMATION

The town of Jackson marks the intersection of Hwy 22 (heading west to Teton Pass) and US 26/89/191. The main drag follows east-west Broadway into downtown, where it turns north onto Cache St at the town square, the heart of the pedestrian-oriented commercial district. The exclusive community of Wilson is on Hwy 22, 5mi west of Jackson, just west of the junction with Hwy 390 (Moose-Wilson Rd), which leads north 7mi to Teton Village.

The helpful, grass-roofed **Jackson Hole & Greater Yellowstone Visitor Center** (☎ 307-733-3316; **W** *www.jacksonhole chamber.com; 532 N Cache St; open 8am-7pm daily in summer,*

8am–5pm in winter) provides rest rooms, an ATM, and a courtesy phone for free local calls. The chamber's new one-stop **Do Jackson Hole Visitor Information Center** *(☎ 307-739-1500, 866-500-3654;* Ⓦ *www.dojacksonhole.com)* is off US 26/89/191 next to Albertson's on the south end of town.

The **Bridger-Teton National Forest Headquarters** *(☎ 307-739-5500)* and **Jackson Ranger District** *(☎ 307-739-5400;* Ⓦ *www.fs.fed.us/btnf; 340 N Cache St; open 8am–4:30pm Mon-Fri)* are side-by-side. The **Wyoming Game & Fish Department** *(☎ 307-733-2321; 420 N Cache St; open 8am–5pm Mon-Fri)* is close by.

Bank of Jackson Hole ATMs are at 990 W Broadway and at the corner of Broadway and Cache.

Tune to 90.3 FM (NPR), 93.3 (KJAX), or 96.9 (KMTN) for the local lowdown.

Free newspapers include the *Jackson Hole Daily* (liberal) and the *Daily Guide* (conservative). **Valley Bookstore** *(☎ 307-733-4533, 800-647-4111; 125 N Cache St in Gaslight Alley)* is the best in town.

Clean up for a song at **Soap Opera Laundromat** *(☎ 307-733-5584; 850 W Broadway)*.

The region's primary hospital is at **St John's Medical Center** *(☎ 307-733-3636; 625 E Broadway)*.

THINGS TO SEE & DO

The **Jackson Hole Museum** *(☎ 307-733-2414; 105 N Glenwood St; adult/senior/child/family $3/2/1/6; open 9:30am–6pm Mon-Sat, 10am–5pm Sun, late May–early Oct)* explores local lore from hunter-gatherers to the present epoch. One-hour Jackson walking tours depart 10am Tuesday, Thursday, Friday, and Saturday.

The **Jackson Hole Historical Society & Museum** *(☎ 307-733-9605; 105 Mercill Ave; admission free; open 8am–5pm Mon-Fri June–Sept)* focuses on Plains Indians, early Jackson Hole settlement, and the creation of Grand Teton National Park. It also maintains an extensive research library.

Three miles north of town on the west side of US 26/89/191, the **National Museum of Wildlife Art** *(☎ 307-733-5771; 2820 Rungius Rd; adult/child/family $6/5/14; open 8am–5pm daily in summer, 9am–5pm daily in winter, 9am–5pm Mon-Sat and 1-5pm Sun in spring and fall)* fills 12 galleries with works by important American outdoor sculptors and painters, including George Catlin, Albert Bierstadt, and Carl Rungius. The 51,000-sq-ft Arizona sandstone facility blends into the landscape overlooking the National Elk Refuge. The on-site **Rising Sage Cafe** *(☎ 307-733-8649)* is superb.

About 7000 Rocky Mountain "welfare" elk (and a few hungry wolves) winter at the 25,000-acre **National Elk Refuge** *(☎ 307-733-9212; admission free)*, northeast of Jackson via Elk Refuge Rd, an extension of E Broadway. When snow covers the native grasses October through May, the elk are fed alfalfa hay pellets. The refuge offers one-hour winter sleigh rides ($15/11/free adults/children/children under five), departing from the National Museum of Wildlife Art mid-December through early April. Just north of the refuge is the **Jackson National Fish Hatchery** *(☎ 307-733-2510; 1500 Fish Hatchery Rd; admission free)*; open for tours 8am to 4pm daily.

ACTIVITIES

Jackson is all about getting outside and working up a sweat, no matter what the season. Following are a few options, which are only limited by your lack of gear or imagination. The shops listed are great places to fill in the gaps with rentals and trip suggestions.

Jackson Hole's Gros Ventre Mountains offer superb day hikes with expansive views and wildlife, including treks to **Sheep Mountain** and **Jackson Peak**. Call ☎ 307-690-5646 for details about car shuttles.

Mountain Biking

Teton Cycle Works *(☎ 307-733-4386; 175 N Glenwood St)* is a superb full-service shop with knowledgeable staff and rentals. **Hoback Sports** *(☎ 307-733-5335; 40 S Millward St)* has a good map of area bike trails.

Popular rides include **Cache Creek**, southeast of Jackson into the Gros Ventre; **Game Creek**, along USFS Rd 30455 east off US 26/89/191 south of Jackson; and **Spring Gulch Rd**, west of and parallel to US 26/89/191 between Hwy 22 and Gros Ventre Junction. Hard-core riders should try **Old Pass Rd**, the old route over Teton Pass, south of Hwy 22.

Rock Climbing & Mountaineering

For instruction and guided climbs, contact **Exum Mountain Guides** *(☎ 307-733-2297; W www.exumguides.com)* or **Jackson Hole Mountain Guides & Climbing School** *(☎ 307-733-4979, 800-239-7642; W www.jhmg.com; 165 N Glenwood St)*. Exum runs climbing schools in Grand Teton National Park and at the upper cliffs at the Jackson Hole Mountain Resort, accessed by the aerial tram.

Singles seeking climbing partners swear by the bulletin board at **Teton Mountaineering** *(☎ 307-733-3595; 170 N Cache St)*, which stocks a good range of books and outdoor gear. **Teton Rock Gym** *(☎ 307-733-0707; 1116 Maple Way)* offers a wide variety of indoor sport climbs ($15 per day).

White-Water Rafting & Floating

Rafting is popular through the **Class III Snake River canyon**, south of Jackson along US 89/26 between Hoback Junction and Alpine. Ospreys and eagles nest in trees along the river, and wildlife viewing is possible. Half-day trips (from $35) put in at West Table Creek; they take out at Sheep Gulch (8mi). Full-day trips (from $60) put in at Pritchard Creek, upstream from West Table Creek, take a break at Pine Creek campsite, and take out at Sheep Gulch (16mi). The rafting season runs May to Labor Day. It gets crowded on the river in July and August; reserve ahead. Rates typically include transportation to and from Jackson.

Half-day **scenic float trips** (from $40/30 adults/children) on a 13mi section of the swift-flowing Snake River put in south of Grand Teton National Park and take out north of Hoback Junction, passing through the bird- and wildlife-rich Jackson Hole wetlands.

Reputable Jackson-based outfitters include:

Barker-Ewing River Trips *(☎ 307-733-1000, 800-448-4202; W www.barker-ewing.com; 45 W Broadway)*

Dave Hansen Whitewater *(☎ 307-733-6295, 800-732-6295; W www.davehansenwhitewater.com; 515 N Cache St)*

Jackson Hole Whitewater *(☎ 307-733-1007, 800-700-7238; W www.jhwhitewater.com; 650 W Broadway)*

Lewis & Clark River Expeditions *(☎ 307-733-4022, 800-824-5375; W www.lewisandclarkexpeds.com; 335 N Cache St)*

Sands Wild Water River Trips *(☎ 307-733-4410, 800-358-8184; W www.sandswhitewater.com; 110 W Broadway)*

Canoeing & Kayaking

Rendezvous River Sports & Jackson Hole Kayak School (☎ *307-733-2471, 800-733-2471;* W *www.jhkayakschool.com; 225 N Cache St)* and **Snake River Kayak & Canoe School** (☎ *307-733-9999, 800-529-2501;* W *www.snakeriverkayak.com; 365 N Cache St)* both offer hourly instruction. For rig rentals try **Leisure Sports** (☎ *307-733-3040; 1075 S US 89).*

Reel & Fly-Fishing

Native whitefish and cutthroat, as well as lake and brown trout abound in most area waterways. Fishing is subject to Wyoming state regulations. Licenses are available for purchase at outdoor shops and visitor centers.

Horseback Riding

In Jackson, trail rides depart from **Snow King Stables** (☎ *307-733-5781),* behind Snow King Resort. **Bar-T-5 Corral** (☎ 307-733-5386, 800-772-5386; 812 Cache Creek Dr) leads guided rides east of Jackson in the Cache Creek drainage. **A-OK Corral** (☎ *307-733-6556; 9550 S Henry Rd),* on US 26/189/191 just north of Hoback Junction, offers guided rides and full-day excursions. All three offer cookouts and evening excursions.

Other Summer Activities

Scenic 20-minute rides up the **Snow King Chairlift** ($8/6/5) at Snow King Resort offer views from 7751ft of five mountain ranges. Tickets with lunch at Panorama House, the restaurant at the top, cost $12. When you hike to the summit, a chairlift ride down costs only $1. The lift operates 9am to 6pm daily mid-May to early September, with extended summer hours.

The resort's meandering 2500ft **Alpine Slide** (☎ *307-733-7680)* is open late May to mid-September. Other diversions include **indoor ice skating** and **alpine golf**.

Jackson Hole Paragliding (☎ *307-739-2626, 690-8726)* offers tandem rides from several local peaks (no experience necessary) starting at $150 for half-hour flights. **Rainbow Balloon Flights** (☎ *307-733-0470, 800-378-0470)* and **Wyoming Balloon Co** (☎ *307-739-0900; 450 E Sagebrush)* offer hour-long flights over the Tetons if you can afford the $175 per person fee. The season runs from early June to mid-September. Balloon flights are dependent upon the weather.

Jackson Hole Golf & Tennis Club (☎ *307-733-3111; 6mi north of Jackson; green fees $35-145, club rental $45)* has a Robert Trent Jones Jr-designed course, ranked as the best in Wyoming. You'll also find a good restaurant, a swimming pool, and tennis courts.

Skiing & Snowboarding

The local favorite ski hill is the year-round 400-acre **Snow King Resort** (☎ *307-733-5200, 800-522-5464;* W *www.snowking.com; 400 E Snow King Ave),* on the south edge of town at a base elevation of 6237ft.

Three lifts serve various downhill ski and snowboard runs with a maximum vertical drop of 1571ft (15% beginner, 25% intermediate, 60% advanced). Full-day lift tickets are $32/22 adults/children, while half-day tickets (good after 1pm) are $20/14. The ski season runs Thanksgiving to March. Night skiing (Monday to Saturday 4:30 to 8:30pm) is popular. This north-facing slope catches less snow than other resorts but is well suited for children and families.

The best values are packages such as the **Ski All Three** deal ($199 to $299 depending on dates), which includes three night's lodging, daily breakfast, two full-day lift tickets good at Snow King, Jackson Hole Mountain Resort, and Grand Targhee, and transfers to and from the airport and between the ski hills.

See the Jackson Hole section in the Greater Yellowstone chapter (p 216) for details on nearby ski areas.

ENTERTAINMENT

The free weekly *Jackson Hole Weekend Guide* appears Friday and reviews local entertainment options, as does the *Stepping Out* insert.

Jackson's nightlife landmark is the touristy **Million Dollar Cowboy Bar** (☎ 307-733-2207; 25 N Cache St). Also facing the town square, **The Rancher** pool hall (☎ 307-733-3886; 20 E Broadway) is a local happy-hour favorite.

The homebrew is better than the pub grub at the **Snake River Brewing Co** (☎ 307-739-2337; 265 S Millward St). The **Virginian Saloon** (☎ 307-733-2792; 750 W Broadway) has a daily happy hour (4pm to 7pm) and a big-screen TV.

Snow King Resort's popular **Shady Lady Saloon** (☎ 307-733-5200) features live jazz during the high season.

Wilson's **Stagecoach Bar** (☎ 307-733-4407; 5755 W Hwy 22) is worth the short drive: "Mon-day" means reggae; Thursday is disco night; and every Sunday the famous (and aging – they've been playing here for more than 30 years) Stagecoach Band plays country and western favorites until 10pm. Herb tokers and cowpokes mingle here like no other place in the West.

Local theater troupes stage Broadway-style musical comedies and dinner at the **Jackson Hole Playhouse** (☎ 307-733-6994; 145 W Deloney Ave) and **Main Stage Theatre** (☎ 307-733-3670; cnr Broadway and Cache Dr).

The 1941 sandstone **Teton Theatre** (120 N Cache Dr) is the best place to catch a flick; ring the **Jackson Movieline** (☎ 307-733-4939) for a rundown of what's showing at all three of Jackson's movie houses.

SPECIAL EVENTS

Jackson hosts many annual events. Check local newspaper listings to see what's on. The **ElkFest & Antler Auction** takes place every May around the town square. The **Teton County Fair** takes over the Teton County Fairgrounds (Snow King Ave and Flat Creek Rd) in late July. Also held at the fairgrounds, the **Jackson Hole Rodeo** (☎ 307-733-2805) saddles up at 8pm Wednesdays and Saturdays June through August. September's **Jackson Hole Fall Arts Festival** features live auctions, artist talks, and samples of local chef's culinary wizardry.

GETTING THERE & AWAY

The busy **Jackson Hole Airport** (☎ 307-733-7682, 733-5454 paging) is 7mi north of Jackson off US 26/89/191, within Grand Teton National Park. Airport expansion is a hot topic, but is currently restricted due to a 50-year agreement signed by the airport and National Park Service in 1983 (see the "America's Most Scenic Airport" boxed text, p 57). A shuttle between downtown and the airport runs $12/20 one-way/round-trip, or $20/35 per person to Teton Village.

Alltrans' Jackson Hole Express (☎ 307-733-1719, 800-652-9510; Ⓦ *www.jacksonholebus.com*) shuttles daily between the Salt Lake City airport and Jackson ($54/98 one-way/round-trip, 4.5hrs), via Idaho Falls ($31/52 one-way/round-trip, 2.25hrs); reservations are recommended. Pickup is at the Exxon/Jackson Hole Country Store, on the corner of South Park Loop Rd and Broadway, across the street from the Movie Works Plaza, just south of the US 26/89/191 and Hwy 22 junction. Idaho Falls–based **CART** *(☎ 208-354-2240)* offers bus service between Jackson and Idaho Falls via Teton Valley.

Jackson is bisected by US 26/89/191, 4mi south of the south entrance to Grand Teton National Park. US 26/89/191 leads north to Moran Junction (31mi), where US 89/191/287 continues north to Yellowstone's South Entrance (57mi). US 26 heads east over Togwotee Pass (9658ft) to Riverton (168mi) via Dubois and the Wind River Indian Reservation, and south to Alpine (35mi) at the Wyoming-Idaho state line. US 89 leads north through Grand Teton and Yellowstone National Parks to Gardiner and southwest to Salt Lake City (270mi). US 191 goes south to Hoback Junction (12mi) and Rock Springs (178mi) on I-80.

GETTING AROUND

Southern Teton Area Rapid Transit *(START;* ☎ *307-733-4521)* runs a free around-town shuttle and two routes (Red Line and Workers' Special) between Jackson and Teton Village. One-way fares are free within town limits and $1 to $2 outside of town; exact change is required. Check maps and timetables posted at stops for current routes and schedules.

Car rental agencies **Alamo** *(☎ 307-733-0671, 800-327-9633)*, **Avis** *(☎ 307-733-3422, 800-331-1212)*, **Budget** *(☎ 307-733-2206, 800-527-0700)*, and **Hertz** *(☎ 307-733-2272, 800-654-3131)* all have locations at the Jackson airport. In town are **Eagle Rent-A-Car/Cruise America RV Rentals** *(☎ 307-739-9999, 800-582-2128; 345 N Cache St)*, **National** *(☎ 307-733-0735, 800-227-7368; 345 W Broadway)*, **Rent-A-Wreck** *(☎ 307-733-5014; 1050 US 89 S)*, and **Thrifty** *(☎ 307-739-9300, 800-367-2277; 220 N Millward St)*.

Call **A-1** *(☎ 307-690-3900)*, **All-Star** *(☎ 307-733-2888, 800-378-2944)*, **Alltrans** *(☎ 307-733-3135, 800-443-6133)*, or **Buckboard** *(☎ 307-733-1112, 877-791-0211)* for a taxi.

NPS PHOTOGRAPHS

Yellowstone National Park is the crown jewel of the Greater Yellowstone Ecosystem and the destination of nearly every visitor to the region. More than three million people a year are drawn to its fantastic geysers, waterfalls, canyons, wildlife, and lakes. A journey to the park isn't just a vacation, it's a modern pilgrimage to one of America's most admirable and enduring national landmarks.

EXPERIENCING
YELLOWSTONE

Yellowstone offers several distinct regions, and it's worth investing time to visit at least a couple to get a feel for the park's diversity. The two greatest draws are the Grand Canyon of the Yellowstone (Canyon Country) and the geysers around Old Faithful (Geyser Country), followed by the geothermal terraces at Mammoth (Mammoth Country), vast Yellowstone Lake (Lake Country), and wildlife-rich Lamar Valley (Roosevelt Country).

Your interests will dictate how you spend your time in the park. All areas offer superb fishing, hiking, and wildlife watching. Whichever you choose, reserve a little free time. The crowds and traffic will seem twice as bad if you're in a rush, and you'll appreciate the extra time if you have a surprise encounter with a moose or bison.

Yellowstone's spectacular roadside sights are reward enough, but your fondest memories may well be the precious moments of calm and beauty at the beginning and end of each day. From geysers and gorges to golden lakeshore sunsets or dawn mists rising over a steaming geyser basin, Yellowstone's beauty is both spectacular and subtle.

When You Arrive

When the park is open (early May to early November and late December to mid-March), all park entrances are open 24 hours daily. Entry reservations are not necessary, but a park entrance permit is. Permits, available at all five park entrance stations (credit cards accepted) and valid for seven days for both Yellowstone and Grand Teton National Parks, cost $20 per private (noncommercial) vehicle, $15 per person for individuals entering by motorcycle or snowmobile, and $10 per person for individuals entering by bicycle, skis, or on foot. Keep the entrance fee receipt for reentry to the park. An annual Yellowstone and Grand Teton National Parks pass costs $40 for vehicles, bicyclists, and snowmobiles. For more details on park passes see the Planning chapter.

Park admission is free on August 25, the anniversary of the founding of the National Park Service (NPS).

Upon entry, visitors receive a free map and copy of the park's seasonal newspaper, *Yellowstone Today*, with a useful orientation map and schedule of ranger-led activities, special events, exhibits, and educational activities.

ORIENTATION

Seven distinct regions comprise the 3472 sq mi park (starting clockwise from the north): Mammoth, Roosevelt, Canyon, Lake, and Geyser Countries; the Norris area; and remote Bechler Corner in the extreme southwest.

A clockwise drive from the North Entrance begins at Mammoth Hot Springs in the dry, low-elevation northwest corner of the park. East of here is Tower-Roosevelt Junction. Farther east is Roosevelt Country, the wildest part of the park accessible by road and home to wolves and bison in the Lamar Valley. From Tower-Roosevelt Junction the highway heads south past Mt Washburn (10,243ft), over Dunraven Pass (8859ft), to Canyon Junction. Dunraven Pass offers awesome views of the Absaroka and Teton Ranges and the Grand Canyon of the Yellowstone.

Continue south along the Yellowstone River through wildlife-rich Hayden Valley to Fishing Bridge Junction (7792ft). This is Lake Country, dominated by the watery wilderness of Yellowstone Lake.

The Grand Loop Rd skirts the lake's northwest shore to West Thumb Junction, then heads west over Craig Pass (8262ft) to Old Faithful in the heart of Geyser Country, home to the park's richest collection of geothermal features. South of here is remote Shoshone Lake.

Turning north from Old Faithful, the Grand Loop Rd follows Firehole River past several beautiful geyser basins to Madison Junction (6806ft) and the popular fly-fishing stretches of the Madison and Gibbon Rivers. From here a road leads west out of the park to the gateway town of West Yellowstone. The Grand Loop Rd continues northeast up the Gibbon River canyon to Norris Junction, home to the park's second most impressive collection of geysers. From here the road heads past views of the Gallatin Range, back to Mammoth Hot Springs.

The Bechler Corner region, in the far southwest, is only accessible by road from Ashton, Idaho, or by a four-day hike from the Old Faithful region.

Entrance Stations

The park has five entrance stations. The historic arched **North Entrance Station** (5314ft), on US 89 near Gardiner, Montana, is the only one open year-round. The other four are typically open from early May to late October, weather permitting: the **North-east Entrance** (7365ft), on US 212 near Cooke City, Montana; the **East Entrance** (6951ft), on US 14/16/20 at the head of the Wapiti Valley; the **South Entrance** (6886ft), on US 89/191/287 north of Grand Teton National Park; and the **West Entrance** (6667ft), on US 20/191/287 near West Yellowstone, Montana. Notice boards at entrances indicate which campgrounds are full or closed.

Major Roads

Conceived by Lt Daniel C Kingman in 1886 and named by writer Harry W Frantz in 1923, the 142mi, figure-eight **Grand Loop Rd** passes most of the park's major attractions. The 12mi Norris-Canyon road links Norris and Canyon Junctions, dividing the Grand Loop Rd into two shorter loops: the 96mi Lower (South) Loop and the 70mi Upper (North) Loop.

INFORMATION

Yellowstone National Park headquarters (☎ 307-344-7381; W www.nps .gov/yell; open 9am-6pm daily) is at Fort Yellowstone in Mammoth Hot Springs. Most of the park's brochures are downloadable from its website.

Yellowstone's visitor centers and information stations are usually open 9am to 6pm daily, with extended hours from 8am to 8pm in summer. Most are closed or open reduced hours Labor Day to Memorial Day; the Albright Visitor Center in Mammoth is open year-round, and the Old Faithful Visitor Center is open in winter. Check the park newspaper for current hours of operation. The visitor centers and information stations are:

Albright Visitor Center, Mammoth (☎ 307-344-2263) – Open year-round, with videos and displays on park history.

Canyon Visitor Center (☎ 307-242-2550) – Open late May to early October, with a backcountry office and displays on bison.

Fishing Bridge Visitor Center (☎ 307-242-2450) – Open late May to late September, with bird exhibits.

Grant Village Visitor Center (☎ 307-242-2650) – Open late May to late September, with exhibits on wildfires.

Old Faithful Visitor Center (☎ 307-545-2750) – Open late May to early November, and mid-December to mid-March, with videos and geyser predictions.

Madison Information Station – Open late May to early October.

West Thumb Information Station – Open late May to late September.

There are **ranger stations** (open 8am to 5pm) at Grant Village, Lake Village, Bechler, Tower-Roosevelt Junction, Old Faithful, Lamar Valley, and the west and south entrances.

Bookstores

The nonprofit **Yellowstone Association** (☎ 307-344-2293; W www.yellow stoneassociation.org) operates bookstores (usually open 9am to 5pm) at the park's visitor centers, information stations, and at Norris Geyser Basin. Hiking maps and guidebooks are usually available.

The park produces a series of informative pamphlets (50¢) on Yellowstone's main attractions; these are available at visitor centers and in weatherproof boxes at the sites.

Policies & Regulations

It is illegal to collect plants, flowers, rocks, petrified wood, or antlers in Yellowstone. Firearms are prohibited in the park. Swimming in water of entirely thermal origin is prohibited.

BACKCOUNTRY PERMITS

A free backcountry-use permit, available at visitor centers and ranger stations, is required for all overnight backcountry trips. The backcountry-use permit is site and date specific and states the campsite where you must overnight. Outside of summer call ☎ 307-344-7381 for details on getting your permit. Send for (or download from the park website) the very useful Backcountry Trip Planner, which lists all campsites.

About half the backcountry sites can be reserved by mail; a $20 reservation fee applies regardless of the number of nights. Booking starts on April 1, when all existing reservations are dealt with at random. Reservations can be made in person or through the mail to Backcountry Office, PO Box 168, Yellowstone National Park, WY 82190. Applications must be on a Trip Planner Worksheet, available with the Backcountry Trip Planner on the NPS website (in the publications sections) or by contacting the **central backcountry office** (☎ *307-344-2160;* ⓔ *yell_bco@nps.gov).* Send the nonrefundable cash, check, or money order with booking. You will receive a confirmation notice, which must be taken to a backcountry office to exchange for a permit not more than 48 hours before your trip but before 10am on the day of your trip departure.

The remaining backcountry-use permits are issued no more than 48 hours in advance on a first come, first served walk-in basis. There are backcountry offices at the Canyon and Mammoth visitor centers and at ranger stations at Grant Village, Lake Village, Bechler, Tower-Roosevelt Junction, Old Faithful, and the West and South Entrances.

HORSE PACKING

Horse-packing parties must obtain a backcountry-use permit for overnight trips. A horse-use permit is also required for day trips. Both are available at most ranger stations. The *Horse Packing in Yellowstone* pamphlet lists regulations. Pack animals include horses, burros, mules, ponies, and llamas.

Some backcountry trails are closed to stock, and those that are open may be temporarily closed in spring and early summer due to wet conditions. Overnight pack trips are not allowed until July 1. Stock can only be kept at designated campsites. Hay is not permitted at the trailhead or in the backcountry.

FISHING

The useful *Fishing Regulations* pamphlet details the park's complex rules and regulations. The fishing season usually runs from the Saturday of Memorial Day weekend to the first Sunday in November, except for streams that flow into Yellowstone Lake and some tributaries of the Yellowstone River, which open July 15. Other rivers are permanently closed to fishing, including the Hayden Valley stretch of the Yellowstone River; others may close during the season due to bear activity.

Cutthroat trout, grayling, and mountain whitefish are native to the park and are catch-and-release in all park waters. Some areas (such as the Gibbon River below Gibbon Falls) are open to fly-fishing only. Lead weights are prohibited; only nontoxic alternatives are sanctioned.

A Yellowstone Park (not a Wyoming state) fishing permit is required for anglers age 16 and older. These cost $10 for 10 days or $20 for the year; nonfee permits are required for anglers ages 12 to 15. Permits are available from ranger stations, visitor centers, and Hamilton stores. A boating permit is required for float tubes, which are allowed only on the Lewis River between Lewis and Shoshone Lakes.

BOATING

Boating is permitted May 1 to November 1, although some areas may close during the season. Motorized vessels are allowed only on Lewis Lake and parts of Yellowstone Lake. Sylvan, Eleanor, and Twin Lakes and Beach Springs Lagoon are closed to boating. All streams in the park and the Yellowstone River are also closed to boating, except on the Lewis River between Lewis and Shoshone Lakes, where hand-propelled vessels are allowed. Launching is permitted only at Bridge Bay, Grant Village (opens mid-June), and Lewis Lake. Hand-carried vessels may launch at Sedge Bay. Study the *Boating Regulations* pamphlet before embarking.

A boating permit is required for all vessels, including float tubes. Permits for motorized vessels cost $10 per week or $20 per year and are available from Canyon Visitor Center, Bridge Bay Marina, Grant Village Visitor Center, Lake Ranger Station, Lewis Lake Ranger Station, and the South Entrance. Permits for nonmotorized vessels cost $5 per week or $10 per year and are available from the above-mentioned offices, as well as the Albright and Mammoth Visitor Centers, Old Faithful Backcountry Office, Northeast Entrance, and Bechler Ranger Station.

Unpredictable weather and high wind on Yellowstone Lake's open water can easily capsize a small vessel: Be cautious and remember that hypothermia sets in quickly in the lake's 45°F waters. The best place for information is the Backcountry Ranger Station by the Conoco at Grant Village.

Waterskiing and Jet Skis are prohibited. Personal flotation devices (PFDs) are required for all craft.

For more boating details see p 30.

Getting Around

Unless you're part of a guided bus tour, the only way to get around is to drive. There is no public transportation within Yellowstone National Park, except for a few ski drop services during winter.

DRIVING

The speed limit in most of the park is 45mph, dropping to 25mph in busy turnouts or junctions.

Gas and diesel are available at most junctions. Stations at Old Faithful and Canyon are open whenever the park is open to vehicles. The Roosevelt station closes at the beginning of September, Fishing Bridge in mid-September, Grant Village at the end of September, and Mammoth in early October. After regular station hours, gas is often available for an extra charge of between $15 and $35.

Towing and repair services and basic car parts are available at Conoco stations at Old Faithful (late April–early November), Grant Village (late May-mid-September), Fishing Bridge (late May–early September), and Canyon (after hours gas ☎ 344-7381, breakdown service ☎ 242-7644l; May-Sep).

Dial ☎ 307-344-2114 to check road and weather conditions prior to your visit, as road construction, rock or mudslides, and snow can close park entrances and roads at any time. See the Planning chapter (p 42) for details on road opening and closing schedules.

ORGANIZED TOURS

Xanterra *(☎ 307-344-7311)* runs a slew of daily tours, all of which offer discounts for children aged 12 to 16 and are free for kids under 12. The ambitious 10-hour **Yellowstone**

in a Day *(Jun–late Sep)* departs from Gardiner ($42/20 adults/children 12 to 16) or Mammoth Hot Springs ($40/19).

The eight-hour **Washburn Expedition** *(mid-June–late Sep)* departs Bridge Bay Campground, Lake Yellowstone Hotel, and Fishing Bridge RV Park ($34/16) or Canyon Lodge ($28/16) and takes in the upper loop, including Mammoth and Norris. Also eight hours, the **Circle of Fire** *($38/17; mid-May–mid-Oct)* departs Old Faithful Inn, Grant Village, Lake Yellowstone Hotel, Fishing Bridge RV Park, and Canyon Lodge and takes in the lower loop, including the geyser basins and Canyon.

Less-grueling three- to four-hour Lamar Valley **wildlife excursions** *(mid-June–mid-Aug; $30/13, $24/11 from Canyon)* depart at about 4pm from four locations (Bridge Bay Campground, Lake Yellowstone Hotel, Fishing Bridge RV Park, and Canyon Lodge).

Two-hour **sunset tours** *($17/8.50; weekdays mid-June–mid-Sep)* on a 1937 touring bus run from Lake Yellowstone Hotel and Fishing Bridge RV Park along Lake Yellowstone's north shore to Butte Overlook. Two-hour twilight tours of **Hayden Valley** *($14/8; mid-June–mid-Aug)* run from Canyon Lodge. **Photo safaris** *($40)* depart daily from Lake Yellowstone Hotel and Old Faithful Inn.

The following independent outfitters offer similar tours at slightly higher rates:

Buffalo Bus Co (☎ 406-646-9353, 800-426-7669; Ⓦ *www.yellowstonevacations.com/buffalo.htm*)
   415 Yellowstone Ave, West Yellowstone, MT

Gray Line of Yellowstone (☎ 307-733-4325, 800-443-6133 in summer, 406-646-9374,
   800-523-3102 in winter; Ⓦ www.graylinejh.com) 1580 W Martin Lane, Jackson

Greyhound Bus Lines (Ⓦ www.greyhound.com), Bozeman (☎ 406-587-3110), Livingston
   (☎ 406-222-2231), Idaho Falls (☎ 208-522-0912), West Yellowstone (☎ 406-646-7666)

MAMMOTH COUNTRY
Map 5

Mammoth Country is renowned for its graceful geothermal terraces, numerous elk, and the towering Gallatin Range to the northwest. As the lowest and driest region of the park, it's also the warmest and a major base for winter activities.

The region's Northern Range is an important wintering area for wildlife. Some 15,000 elk winter here, attracted by the lower temperatures and lack of snow on many south-facing slopes (due to the sun and prevailing wind). The poorly aerated and drained soil supports scant vegetation, creating "dry desert" conditions and raising concerns about whether the land can support the elk population.

ORIENTATION

For visitors (and most elk) the focal point of the Mammoth region is Mammoth Junction, 5mi south of the

HIGHLIGHTS

Don't Miss: Lower Terrace of Mammoth Hot Springs and winter wildlife

Family Fun: Easy hike to Wraith Falls

Activity: Take a plunge in the warm waters of Boiling River

Wildlife: Elk at Mammoth, wildfowl at Blacktail Ponds, moose at Willow Park

Off the Beaten Track: Bike the Old Gardiner Rd or hike down to Osprey Falls

park entrance, which contains the region's main services. Just south of the junction is Mammoth Hot Springs, the main thermal attraction in the area. From here roads go south to Norris (21mi) and east to Tower-Roosevelt Junction (18mi).

MAMMOTH

Mammoth Junction (6239ft) is on a plateau above Mammoth Campground. Surrounding the campuslike historic and administrative heart of the park is a hotel, restaurant, store, gas station, and the Albright Visitor Center (Horace Albright was the Yellowstone's first park service superintendent and later director of the NPS). Elk regularly graze on the manicured lawns, bringing traffic to a standstill, and the sounds of bugling elk echo around the region in fall.

Fort Yellowstone

Mammoth Hot Springs was known as Fort Yellowstone from 1886 to 1918, when the US Army managed the park. The **Mammoth Visitor Center Museum** *(☎ 307-344-2263)* was formerly the army's bachelor quarters, but now features 19th-century watercolors by Thomas Moran (1837–1926) and black-and-white photographs by William Henry Jackson, both of whom accompanied the 1871 Hayden expedition. There are also displays on the park's early visitors, lots of stuffed animals, and a 20-minute video on the establishment of the park.

If you're particularly interested in park history, pick up the *Fort Yellowstone Historic District Tour Guide* brochure for a self-guided tour of the fort's original buildings. The tour takes in the former jail (under renovation), barracks, granary, and stables, most of which have been converted to employee residences. Pop into the lovely English-style church (1913), which features stained glass windows that depict Old Faithful and Yellowstone Falls. Rangers lead 75-minute history walks three times weekly, departing from the visitor center at 9am.

Mammoth Hot Springs

The imposing Lower and Upper Terraces of Mammoth Hot Springs are the product of dissolved subterranean limestone (itself originally deposited by ancient seas), which is continually deposited as the spring waters cool on contact with air. As guidebooks love to say, the mountain is in effect turning itself inside out. The terraces owe their colors to the bacteria and algae that flourish in the warm waters. See the Geology chapter (p 245) for more details.

Two hours' worth of boardwalks wend their way around the Lower Terraces and connect to the Upper Terraces Loop. The rutting Rocky Mountain elk that sometimes lounge on Opal Terrace are a favorite photo opportunity.

Surreal **Palette Springs** and sulfur-yellow **Canary Springs** are the most beautiful sites, but thermal activity is constantly in flux, so check the current state of play at the visitor center. The famous ornate travertine formations that characterize **Minerva Spring** are now inactive. At the bottom of the terraces, by the parking area, is the phallic, dormant 36ft-tall hot spring cone called **Liberty Cap**, apparently named after hats worn during the French Revolution.

A less stimulating 1.5mi paved one-way road loops counterclockwise around the Upper Terraces; no vehicles longer than 25ft are permitted. The overlook affords impressive views of the Lower Terraces and Fort Yellowstone.

Ninety-minute ranger walks leave from the Upper Terraces parking lot daily at 5pm.

Boiling River

One of the few places where you can take a soak in Yellowstone, Boiling River is one of the best. See p 53 for the dangers of soaking in hot springs.

The turnoff to the parking area is along the Montana-Wyoming border, by a sign that marks the 45th parallel (halfway between the equator and the North Pole). A trail leads .5mi (about 15 minutes) along the river to a point where an underground boiling river surfaces from below a limestone overhang. There are several pools along the riverside.

TRUMAN EVERTS

Everts Ridge, northwest of Mammoth, is named after Truman Everts, a member of the 1870 Washburn-Langford-Doane expedition and a notable early tourist disaster story.

Separated from his group near Yellowstone Lake in September 1870, Everts soon lost his bearings and promptly broke his glasses. Then his horse bolted, taking all Everts' equipment with it save for a penknife and pair of opera glasses. He kept warm at night by sleeping by hot springs near Heart Lake until he ended up badly burning himself.

After 37 days lost in the wilderness, Everts was finally discovered, shoeless, frostbitten, emaciated, delirious, and raving like a madman … but alive.

Bring a towel and flip-flops. The only changing area is the vault toilet at the parking lot. Swimming is allowed only during daylight hours, and food, pets, alcohol, and nudity are prohibited. The pools are closed during high river levels (most commonly in spring).

MAMMOTH TO TOWER

The 18mi road to Tower-Roosevelt Junction heads east from Mammoth over the Gardner River Bridge, where the Gardner River meets the Yellowstone River. By the roadside just over 2mi from Mammoth is pretty **Undine Falls**.

The easy 1mi round-trip walk to **Wraith Falls** is a good family hike through pretty meadows and fire burn patches. The trail begins at the pullout east of Lava Creek Picnic Area, 5mi from Mammoth, and follows Lupine Creek for 15 minutes to the base of a 79ft cascade.

Just past Blacktail Ponds is **Blacktail Trailhead**, which leads down into the Black Canyon of the Yellowstone and Gardiner.

Young children might enjoy the **Children's Fire Trail**, a .66mi boardwalk through fire burns that was funded in part from children's donations.

The 7mi **Blacktail Plateau Dr** detours off the main highway to offer glimpses of gorgeous summer wildflowers (June and July) and golden fall colors (September). RVs and trailers are not allowed down the rough, unpaved road.

If you continue east on the main Grand Loop Rd, you'll pass **Phantom Lake** (which has normally dried up by July) and a **scenic overview** of Hellroaring Mountain, Garnet Hill, and the Yellowstone River and Hellroaring Creek valleys.

THE BANNOCK TRAIL

The Blacktail Plateau Dr follows part of the Bannock Trail, a hunting route taken by Bannock Indians in the mid-19th century. The trail continued through the Roosevelt region to Soda Butte Creek before leaving what is now the park at its northeast corner.

A couple of miles farther is the **Hellroaring Trailhead**, popular with horse trips. Half a mile past here, **Floating Island Lake** is dense with vegetation, making it a good place to view birds.

Just before you pull into Tower-Roosevelt Junction is the turnoff to the heavily visited **Petrified Tree** (no RVs or trailers). The tree is worth a quick look if haven't seen a petrified tree before, but the parking lot can be cramped and busy.

MAMMOTH TO NORRIS

Past Mammoth's Upper Terraces the road enters a jumbled landscape of **hoodoos**, formed when a travertine terrace slipped down the hillside, breaking into fragments. The road rises to the Golden Gate, formed from cooled ash flows, and Bunsen Peak (8564ft), a plug of solidified magma that formed inside a long since eroded volcanic cone. The hiking and biking trail heads off around Bunsen Peak. Farther along on the right, **Swan Lake** offers good bird watching and views of the Gallatins.

Two miles farther, turn off for the **Sheepeater Cliffs**, an amazing collection of half-million-year-old hexagonal basalt columns, stacked like building blocks. You'll find a scenic picnic area and walks along the river to more formations. The Sheepeaters, also known as the Tukudika, were a subtribe of the Shoshone and the park's earliest year-round inhabitants.

The road passes Indian Creek Campground, **Willow Park** (a good place to look for moose), and Appolinaris Spring, once a popular stagecoach stop in the 1880s for parched travelers headed to Norris.

Obsidian Cliff exposes the interior of a 180,000-year-old lava flow. Rapid cooling prevented the formation of crystals and fused the lava into this form of glass. Obsidian, used for spearheads and arrowheads, was widely traded by Native Americans and was one of the major reasons early peoples visited the Yellowstone region. The park service was forced to remove the cliffside trails due to pilfering of the obsidian – leave it alone!

Roaring Mountain is a huge bleached hillside pockmarked with hissing fumaroles. During a period of increased activity around the turn of the last century, visitors could hear the fumaroles from more than 4mi away. Across the road you'll find a forest naturally reseeded after fires.

From here the road passes North and South Twin Lakes (the latter of which, though small, offers peaceful canoeing) and descends to beautiful **Nymph Lake**. The lake's bubbling pools, bleached white shoreline, and steaming geysers and the nearby overview of the geyser basin lend the area a powerfully primeval air, something out of the landscapes of Tolkien or the age of the dinosaurs. The road quickly descends into the Norris basin.

HIKING & BACKPACKING

Hikes in the relatively low-elevation area around the park's north entrance highlight scenic canyons, panoramic peaks, and numerous lakes, streams, and waterfalls, all under the backdrop of the Gallatin Range. This is one of the park's hottest regions in summer, so consider hiking later in the season or outside of midday.

BUNSEN PEAK & OSPREY FALLS
Distance: 4.25mi round-trip
Duration: 2.5-3.5 hours
Challenge: Moderate
Elevation Change: 1300ft (2100ft with side trip)

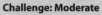

Bunsen Peak is a popular family day hike, with an optional descent to the base of seldom-visited Osprey Falls. The most direct route, **Bunsen Peak Trail**, climbs east out of Swan Lake Flats and Gardners Hole to the exposed summit of Bunsen Peak (8564ft), with outstanding panoramas of the Gallatin Range, Blacktail Deer Plateau, and the Black Canyon of the Yellowstone 3000ft below. Return by the same route or descend via the gentler east slope to the Osprey Falls Trail, which drops 800ft into Sheepeater Canyon. Bunsen Peak was named by the 1872 Hayden Survey for German scientist Robert Wilhelm Eberhard von Bunsen (after whom the Bunsen burner was also named), whose pioneering theories about the inner workings of Icelandic geysers influenced early Yellowstone hydrothermal research. Bunsen Peak's trails (especially along the south slope) are free of snow much earlier than those on most other peaks in the park and thus can be negotiated as early as May with some mild glissading. Snowfields, however, remain through June. Be prepared for frequent afternoon thunderstorms, which bring fierce winds and lightning year-round.

From the Mammoth Visitor Center, head 4.5mi south on Grand Loop Rd, cross the Golden Gate Bridge, and turn left into the unpaved parking area on the east side of the road, just beyond the Rustic Falls turnout. The Glen Creek Trailhead (1K3) is directly across the road.

From 7250ft, the well-trodden single-track dirt trail begins behind a barricade on the left (north) side of unpaved **Bunsen Peak Rd**. The trail gradually climbs through sagebrush interspersed with wildflowers, then enters a heavily burned Douglas fir and lodgepole pine mosaic. Here the trail quickly begins a series of switchbacks, where you may spot bighorn sheep and catch a glimpse of the **Mammoth Hot Springs Terraces**. Beyond the Cathedral Rock outcrop, the exposed dome-shaped peak comes into view.

Radio communications equipment marks the first of three small summits. Continue east along the loose talus ridge to the exposed easternmost summit for the best panoramas. Electric Peak (10,992ft) looms largest to the northwest, marking the park's northern boundary, with the Absaroka Range and impressive Black Canyon of the Yellowstone to the northeast.

Either retrace your steps down the west slope or wind around the peak to descend the east slope (see side trip) to the Osprey Falls Trail.

Side Trip: Osprey Falls & Sheepeater Canyon (2.5-4 hours, 6.6mi round-trip, 800ft ascent) This hike can be done separately from the Bunsen Peak Trailhead or as part of a day hike to the summit. The rough trail descends Sheepeater Canyon to the Gardner River and approaches the base of the impressive, seldom-seen 150ft Osprey Falls. In the early morning and evening, hikers often spot wildlife (elk, bison, waterfowl) in the meadows and ponds of Gardners Hole, near the parking area.

The trail, an abandoned dirt road, begins 3.2mi beyond the barricade on Grand Loop Rd, nearly opposite the Bunsen Peak trail junction. It rapidly descends 800ft from the canyon rim in a bit more than .5mi via a series of narrow, rocky switchbacks to the base of the falls. You're more likely to see marmots or water ouzels in the canyon than the namesake bighorn sheep or osprey, which now prefer to nest along the Yellowstone River. Retrace your steps out of the canyon and return to the trailhead via Bunsen Peak Rd.

BLACK CANYON OF THE YELLOWSTONE
Distance: 18.5mi one-way
Duration: 1-2 days
Challenge: Easy-moderate
Elevation Change: 1250ft descent

Despite its lack of thermal activity, the Black Canyon is one of Yellowstone's classic hikes. The route is approached as a day hike from either end or as a moderate overnight trip, preferably starting from the uphill end to take advantage of the 1250ft descent. From about .5mi down the unpaved Hellroaring gravel pit service road, the route goes downstream through a little-visited valley, where the Yellowstone River alternately meanders, surges into rapids, and plunges over waterfalls.

You may extend the trip to 22mi by starting from the Tower Junction Trailhead (2K2) or shorten it to a more manageable 12.1mi day hike by starting at Blacktail Deer Creek Trailhead (1N5), 6.8mi east of Mammoth. There are 18 backcountry campsites near or along the route, so a number of overnight trip variations are possible. The 10 riverside sites from 1R2 to 1Y1 are all excellent choices, though none allow campfires – site 1Y7

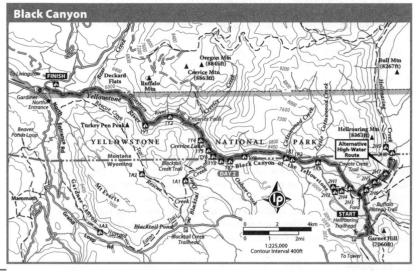

(roughly halfway) is the suggested stopping point. Avid anglers often spend a week along the trail when the hatch is on.

This route traverses the lowest elevations of any trail in the park and should be free of snow by early June. The Hellroaring Creek ford can be dangerous in anything but low water. The section near Gardiner crosses steep and eroded slopes that are slippery during spring runoff. The meadows at the start of the route, with thigh-high grasses in places, offer haven to a range of insects, including ticks. Bring bug spray, long pants, and patience.

The Hellroaring Trailhead (2K8) turnoff is 3.5mi west of Tower and 14.5mi east of Mammoth, off the Mammoth-Tower road. Follow the gravel service road .5mi north to the parking area.

In Gardiner the trail ends behind the private Rocky Mountain Campground, on the first road heading east from town on the north side of the Yellowstone River bridge. The trail is not posted from the road, and there's no parking at the campground, but campground staff can advise on suitable parking nearby.

Day 1: Hellroaring Trailhead to Campsite 1Y7 (3.5-4.5 hours, 9mi, 800ft descent) The trail begins by descending 700ft (via switchbacks) during the first mile through scattered trees to a sturdy metal suspension bridge that spans a gorge above the mighty Yellowstone River. This first impressive encounter with the river is also the last for 2.5 hours. The trail heads north into rolling sagebrush lowlands for .4mi to **Hellroaring Junction**. The tricky Hellroaring Creek ford is often waist-deep until August and should only be attempted in low water. Alternatively, use the Hellroaring stock bridge 1.5mi upstream and add 3mi to your total distance.

Beyond the ford, a short, steep 400ft climb leads up to a good canyon overlook. The long, gradual descent passes Little Cottonwood Creek (and campsite 1R3), the Wyoming-Montana border (and campsite 1R2), then, .1mi farther, Cottonwood Creek (and campsite 1R1), en route to the north bank of the Yellowstone, which is calm and green at this stage. Riverside campsite 1Y9 is an easy 1.6mi downstream, just over three hours from the trailhead, with campsites 1Y7 and 1Y5 .6mi and 1.4mi farther downstream. No wood fires are allowed at any of these sites.

Day 2: Campsite 1Y7 to Gardiner (4-5 hours, 9.5mi, 200ft descent) After a flat stretch along the riverbank, the trail continues with a short climb to another suspension bridge, at the Blacktail Deer Creek Trail junction. Do not cross here, but descend through pine trees to the deep, green oval of **Crevice Lake**, 1.4mi northwest of 1Y7. The pines shade the lakeshore as far as the footbridge over Crevice Creek.

Past campsite 1Y4, the Yellowstone changes character again as it enters a small canyon. The trail climbs high above the canyon, weaving through a boulder field. Switchbacks descend to an overlook of the short but impressive 15ft **Knowles Falls**. A section of flat bank then leads to more continuous rapids, where the trail is forced to make a steep climb over a rocky shoulder as the river thunders along below a steep cliff.

Scattered pines lead down to the riverbank again, before the trail negotiates a rock outcrop via a narrow ledge just past campsite 1Y2. From here it's a gentle climb away from the river past campsite 1Y1 and several park boundary posts.

The trail's anticlimactic homestretch undulates along the dry slopes of Deckard Flats, crossing **Bear Creek** on a wooden footbridge. Steep hillsides force the path to contour along a sometimes narrow ledge that is slippery when wet. The town of **Gardiner** and the Yellowstone-Gardner River confluence eventually come into view around a right-hand bend in the river. Note: The last .5mi of trail crosses private land.

BEAVER PONDS TRAIL
Distance: 5mi
Duration: 2.5 hours
Challenge: Easy-moderate
Elevation Change: 350ft

This 5mi loop with gentle climbs and considerable wildlife begins between Liberty Cap and a private house next to the bus parking lot. The trail ascends 350ft through the fir and spruce forests along Clematis Creek and in 2.5mi reaches beaver ponds amid meadows, where beavers and moose emerge in the mornings and evenings. The trail is clearly signposted except for one junction. After the first .5mi, as you switchback uphill, take the left path – this leads to a signed junction to the Beaver Ponds Loop (left to the Sepulcher Mountain Trail). As the path flattens, it passes the cables of a hilltop radio transmitter and a 4WD service track before descending to the first of several beaver-dammed ponds. This is a good place to spot moose. There are fine views of Sepulcher Mountain in the background. From the ponds, hike back through the sagebrush plateau until you reach a ridge with views over Mammoth.

ELECTRIC PEAK
Distance: 20mi round-trip
Duration: 1-2 days
Challenge: Difficult
Elevation Change: 3700ft

One of the higher summits in the park, **Electric Peak** (10,992ft) overlooks the town of Gardiner. The summit is reached via a 4mi spur trail off the Sportsman Lake Trail, 5.8mi north of the Glen Creek Trailhead (itself roughly 4mi south of Mammoth on the Grand Loop Rd), or hike directly from Mammoth via Snow Pass. Both routes are strenuous and involve almost 3000ft of ascent along the mountain's rocky south spur, requiring some minor scrambling. There are no really dangerous drop-offs except for the summit itself. Although Electric Peak is sometimes climbed as a long day hike, it's better to book campsite 1G3 or 1G4 and take two days. Trails Illustrated's 1:83,333 map No 303 *Mammoth Hot Springs* covers the route. Otherwise, use three USGS 1:24,000 quads: *Mammoth, Quadrant Mountain, and Electric Peak.*

An alternative to ascending Electric Peak is to branch off north to Cache Lake 2mi before the turnoff to Electric Peak. There are good views of Electric Peak from the lake. This makes a 10mi round-trip hike from Glen Creek Trailhead.

Other Hikes

There are several other cardio hikes in the Mammoth area. West of Mammoth is **Sepulcher Mountain** (9652ft). The loop hike via **Howard Eaton Trail** climbs 3400ft to its summit and returns via Snow Pass (11mi).

Alternatively, the 19mi trail to **Mount Holmes** (10,336ft) begins south of Indian Creek at Willow Flats Picnic Area and heads west to the summit. It's a long day hike with an elevation gain of 3000ft. Alternatively, make camp at 1C4 or 1C3 and take radial hikes to the peak and nearby Grizzly and Trilobite Lakes.

Three longer east-west backpacking routes begin west of Mammoth and lead to US 191 in Montana: The 19.5mi **Bighorn Pass Trail** begins from Indian Creek Campground, and the 21mi **Fawn Pass Trail** and 23mi **Sportsman Lake Trail** to its north both begin at Glen Creek Trailhead south of Mammoth.

An appealing longer hike is the 12.5mi **Blacktail Deer Creek Trail**, 7mi east of Mammoth. It descends 1100ft from the trailhead north into the Black Canyon of the Yellowstone to join the Black Canyon of the Yellowstone hike (see Hiking earlier). After crossing the river, it continues downstream (northwest) to Gardiner, Montana, necessitating a vehicle shuttle.

MOUNTAIN BIKING

The **Old Gardiner Rd** between Mammoth and Gardiner was the late-19th-century stagecoach route into the park. After an initial uphill the dirt road then descends 1000ft in 5mi. It's not a stunning ride but does offer a rare opportunity to bike in peace inside the park. You'll have to arrange a car shuttle or face a long uphill back. From Gardiner you can continue along dirt roads up into Paradise Valley (see p 207 in the Greater Yellowstone chapter). From May to October the road is open to motorized traffic (no RVs or trailers) one-way to Gardiner.

Now closed to motor vehicles, six-mile **Bunsen Peak Rd** is a dirt road popular among bikers. Probably the best option is to combine the bike ride with a hike to Osprey Falls (p 81). To do this, park your bike at a rack by the trailhead, about 3mi into the ride. From here it's best to return the way you came. It's possible to continue to Mammoth, but you'll have to arrange a car shuttle. Biking up the main road isn't much fun due to the gradient, traffic, and lack of a bicycle lane.

Unpaved **Blacktail Plateau Dr** offers a challenging ride, though there can be a fair amount of vehicle traffic.

ROOSEVELT COUNTRY
Map 3

President Theodore Roosevelt visited this area in the park's northeast corner in 1903 and established the rustic Roosevelt Lodge near Tower-Roosevelt Junction in 1906. Visitors seeking a real Wild West experience can still find it here. Fossil forests, the commanding Lamar River Valley and its tributary trout streams, and the Absaroka Range's craggy peaks are the highlights in this remote, scenic, and undeveloped region.

The Northeast Entrance Rd passes through the Lamar Valley from Cooke City to meet the Grand Loop Rd at Tower-Roosevelt Junction (6270ft), which then leads west to Mammoth Hot Springs and south to Tower Fall and Canyon Junction. Tower Ranger Station is just west of Tower-Roosevelt Junction. The Lamar Ranger Station is at Buffalo Ranch, just off the Northeast Entrance Rd.

NORTHEAST ENTRANCE TO TOWER-ROOSEVELT

A couple of miles inside the northeast entrance the road enters Wyoming and follows Soda Butte Creek, offering fine views of Barronette Peak (10,404ft) to the west. Near Pebble Creek Campground at tiny Icebox Canyon, the lovely valley opens up. Southeast is a ridgeline known as the Thunderer (10,554ft), after the frequent storms that gather here.

Two miles past Pebble Creek is an unmarked turnout for the easy .5mi walk through fir forest and summer wildflowers to **Trout Lake**, named after its abundant cutthroats. Farther along the road watch for the whitish-yellow travertine cone of **Soda Butte**, the only thermal feature in this part of the park.

The road now joins the mixed sage and grasslands of the **Lamar Valley**, one of the parks premier wildlife viewing areas. The roadside turnouts between Pebble and Slough (pronounced slew) Creek Campgrounds are the park's prime wolf-watching spots. The Druid pack (named after nearby Druid Peak) frequents the area. Check out the wolf-watching leaflets at the two campgrounds for information on the park's various packs. Both elk and bison also make the broad Lamar Valley their winter range, occupying separate ecological niches. Coyotes, pronghorns, and bears also reside here.

About 6mi before Tower-Roosevelt Junction a dirt road turns off north to Slough Creek Campground, offering fishing and hiking access. Farther along the main road are several glacial lakes, which are periodically closed to protect nesting trumpeter swans. Several turnouts offer good viewing from a distance. Just before Tower the road passes the Yellowstone Picnic Area and bridges the Yellowstone River. For details on the Mammoth to Tower road see p 79.

Calcite Springs Overlook

This worthwhile overlook 1.5mi south of Tower-Roosevelt Junction offers vertiginous views of a section of the Grand Canyon of the Yellowstone known as The Narrows. A short trail leads to views north of the gorge's sulfuric yellows and smoking sides. On the far side of the canyon, look for vertical basalt columns, part of a 25ft-deep lava flow that covered the area 1.3 million years ago. Below the basalt are glacial deposits; above the basalt are layers of volcanic ash. There is another area of basalt columns by the roadside, farther along the main road. You'll find dramatic (and crowd-free) views of Calcite Springs and The Narrows from the Yellowstone River Picnic Area Trail (see below).

Tower Fall

Two and a half miles south of Tower-Roosevelt Junction, Tower Creek plunges over 132ft Tower Fall before joining the Yellowstone River. The fall gets its name from the pinnacle-like volcanic breccia towers that rise around the fall like a demonic fortress, earning the nickname "Devil's Den." Landscape painter Thomas Moran created one of his most famous paintings here.

From a scenic overlook 450ft past the Hamilton store, a 1mi round-trip trail descends 200 vertical feet to the base of the falls for the best views. Stop for well-deserved ice cream at the top on the way back.

Tower Fall Campground is just across the road from the parking area.

TOWER TO CANYON

The Grand Loop Rd starts to climb from Tower Fall on its way to Dunraven Pass (8859ft). East of the road along Antelope Creek is prime grizzly habitat, closed to visitors.

Branching off to the left just before the pass, Chittenden Rd is a popular hiking and mountain biking trail to the summit of **Mt Washburn** (10,243ft). A second, hiking-only trail leads to the peak from Dunraven Pass. See p 93 for details of the hike to Mt Washburn and p 97 for details of the bike route.

Dunraven Pass is named after the British Earl of Dunraven, whose park travelogue brought Yellowstone to the attention of European travelers. Just below the pass is the **Washburn Hot Springs Overlook**, where an interpretive sign describes the hot springs and the surrounding Yellowstone caldera. For a closer view of springs, take the Mt Washburn and Sevenmile Hole hike described in the Canyon Country section (p 93).

HIKING & BACKPACKING

Hikes in this region lead to petrified forests, meadows of wildflowers, and excellent places to spot bison and bighorn sheep.

YELLOWSTONE RIVER PICNIC AREA TRAIL
Distance: 4mi round-trip or loop
Duration: 1.5-2 hours
Challenge: Easy
Elevation Change: 800ft

Popular with picnicking families, this easy, scenic stroll offers occasional glimpses of osprey and bighorn sheep – bring your binoculars. To get to the trailhead, take the Northeast Entrance Rd across the bridge from Tower-Roosevelt to the signed picnic area parking lot, 1.5mi east of the junction.

Several unofficial dirt trails climb the steep slopes behind the pit toilets east of the picnic area. The official (signed) trail ascends a few hundred feet to the rim of the **Black Canyon**, then traces the canyon's north rim for a couple of miles, providing unobscured views down to the Yellowstone River and north beyond rolling ridges to the peaks of the Absaroka Range.

The trail stays in open country on the ridgeline 800ft above the canyon floor for the entire route. You can often smell sulfur emanating from the Calcite Springs thermal area across the canyon. Bighorn sheep sometimes wander through **The Narrows** in the shadow of basalt columns at Overhanging Cliff. The trail abruptly ends at a bald hilltop lookout and three-way junction with the **Specimen Ridge Trail**. Below you is the site of the Bannock Indian ford, used by the Bannock during their annual hunting trips across the park. Retrace your steps, or follow the Specimen Ridge Trail downhill to the road and return to the picnic area. Before reaching the road, watch carefully for the final left turn, otherwise you'll have to hike along the road, an unpleasant end to a lovely hike.

FOSSIL FOREST TRAIL
Distance: 3-4mi
Duration: 2.5-3.5 hours
Challenge: Moderate-difficult
Elevation Change: 800ft

A must for amateur geologists, this unmaintained trail sees few hikers, though you may hear howling wolves in the early morning. The trailhead isn't marked, so be sure not to confuse it with the Specimen Ridge Trail farther west. From Tower-Roosevelt Junction take the Northeast Entrance Rd east for 4mi. The pullout is on the south side of the road 1mi southwest of the turnoff to Slough Creek Campground. There is no water along the trail.

The hike leads to one of several patches of petrified forest scattered along Specimen Ridge, thought to hold the word's largest collection of petrified trees. These forests were buried in ash around 50 million years ago; see the Geology chapter (p 246) for more on petrified trees.

Please don't pocket any of the petrified wood here or elsewhere in the park. If you are desperate for a petrified wood souvenir, then get a permit from the Gallatin National Forest Gardiner Ranger Station and head to Tom Miner Basin in Paradise Valley (see the Greater Yellowstone chapter, p 207).

From the unmarked trailhead the fairly clear path starts off following a dirt track and then veers right and heads up the hillside for 45 minutes, through wildflowers and two small patches of forest to two isolated petrified tree stumps. From here it's all uphill, curving first to the left and then right. Follow the ridgeline up to a cairn, where a side path offers an alternate route down to the main loop road. The main trail continues up a ridge and then branches right on a subtrail, skirting and then traversing a small patch of forest to the stump of a petrified giant redwood. Below the huge stump are two thinner but taller upright trees. Dozens of trees lie scattered along the forested slopes.

Cut across to the main trail and continue 30 minutes uphill along the ridge to the summit of Specimen Ridge, marked by a cairn and flagpole. There are wonderful views from here of bison herds in the valley below, birds of prey riding the thermals, and the Grand Canyon of the Yellowstone River in the distance. Return the way you came – the views west are stunning.

Other Hikes

The 4mi **Lost Lake Loop** trail begins behind Roosevelt Lodge (take the right fork), climbing about 300ft past Lost Lake en route to a petrified tree, from which the trail descends to the Tower Ranger Station. Another option is to head up to **Lost Creek Falls**, either by taking the left branch at the initial fork behind Roosevelt Lodge or by taking the right branch and then taking a left just before Lost Lake.

From the stagecoach road just north of Tower-Roosevelt Junction, the 7.5mi **Garnet Hill Trail** is an easy three-hour loop north of the Grand Loop Rd. The trail heads northwest along Elk Creek and then loops around Garnet Hill to return to Roosevelt Lodge. For an extension, take a left at the Garnet Hill junction, a right to cross the suspension bridge over the Yellowstone River, then drop down to Hellroaring Creek (add 2.5mi). You can also reach the trail from Hellroaring Trailhead, 3.5mi west of Tower-Roosevelt Junction.

The **Slough Creek Trail**, which begins .5mi before Slough Creek Campground, is a pleasant overnight hike along a popular fishing stream. It's possible to head east up Elk Tongue Creek, cross Bliss Pass (8mi from the trailhead), and descend Pebble Creek to the namesake campground for a total hike of 21mi. Bliss Pass may be snowbound until mid-July, and fording Pebble Creek can be tricky early in the season. This is a popular horse trail. The first part of the hike follows a historic wagon trail still used by the Silver Tip Ranch; though it lies just outside the north boundary, the trail is only accessible from the park.

If you're only up for a day hike, try the first part of the Slough Creek Trail. Head uphill past the patrol cabin to where the trail rejoins the river at the first meadow (4mi round-trip), or continue to the second meadow or nearby McBride Lake (cross Slough Creek) for a 6mi round-trip hike. Be sure to take the right branch at the junction with the Buffalo Plateau Trail. There's also some nice hiking along the fishing trails that head up Slough Creek from the campground.

Pebble Creek Trail to Warm Creek Trailhead (3K4) is a scenic 12mi hike. The trail heads up Pebble Creek for 10mi through areas of burns and wildflowers, crosses a pass, then drops down to the Warm Creek Trailhead and a nearby picnic area on the Grand Loop Rd.

Specimen Ridge Trail is a popular but long 19mi hike up and along the ridge, past Amethyst Mountain, then down into the Lamar Valley. Check with rangers beforehand that the Lamar River ford is traversable.

An extensive trail network branches off the upper Lamar Valley from the Lamar Valley Trailhead (3K1), 4.7mi southwest of Pebble Creek Campground. The main trail is the **Lamar River Trail**. Other trails lead off this one, heading west after 1.4mi to join the Specimen Ridge Trail, east to Cache Creek after 3.1mi, or east to Miller Creek after 9.3mi. The Miller Creek Trail eventually climbs up either Bootjack Gap or the sculptured peaks of the Hoodoo Basin for an ambitious multiday hike into the Sunlight Basin of Shoshone National Forest. The main trail continues south along the Lamar River, ultimately leading toward Wyoming's Wapiti Valley via the Frost Lake Trail.

OTHER ACTIVITIES

The park concessionaire, Xanterra, operates all activities listed below. Reservations are recommended and can be made by phone (☎ 307-344-7311) or at activities booths at most hotels.

Daily **stagecoach rides** ($7/6 adults/children under 11) depart from Roosevelt Lodge from early June to early September.

Old West cookouts are a fun family trip, either on horseback (one-hour trips $43/33, two-hour trips $53/33) or by horse-drawn wagon ($32/20 per person); reservations are required. Trips depart in the late afternoon and travel to the former site of Uncle John Yancey's Hotel, one of the park's earliest accommodations, for a gut-busting chow-down of steak and beans accompanied by campfire music.

Corrals next to Roosevelt Lodge offer one-/two-hour **trail rides** for $25/37, three times a day. Two-hour rides run just once a day, so reserve ahead.

CANYON COUNTRY
Map 4

The Canyon area is the second most heavily visited part of the park after Old Faithful, due largely to the scenic grandeur of the Grand Canyon of the Yellowstone, but also because of the junction's central location and its concentration of visitor services.

The Grand Canyon of the Yellowstone is the star of the show. A series of scenic overlooks and a network of trails along the canyon's rims and interiors highlight its beauty from a dozen angles. The park's most impressive panoramas extend north from Canyon Junction (7918ft) to Tower-Roosevelt Junction. Mud Volcano is Canyon Country's primary geothermal area.

HIGHLIGHTS

Don't Miss: Grand Canyon, Lower Falls

Best Wildlife: Hayden Valley for bison, coyotes, and bears; ospreys in canyon

Best Views: Artist Point, Brink of the Upper Falls

Family Fun: Day hike to Ribbon Lake, or make it an easy overnight camping trip

Best Activity: Hike or mountain bike to Mt Washburn

ORIENTATION & INFORMATION

Canyon Village and Canyon Ranger Station lie just east of Canyon Junction along North Rim Dr. Canyon Village has a hotel and an activities center, plus three restaurants, a general store, an outdoor gear store (with one-hour film processing), and an ATM. The campground has showers (7am to 1:30pm and 3pm to 9:30pm), laundry (7am to 9pm), and an ice machine.

Canyon Visitor Center is worth a visit for its bison exhibit. Look for the Far Side card and the amazing period picture of buffalo skulls. You won't be able to peel your eyes away from a ghoulishly entertaining video of tourists over the years being attacked by bison. There are plans to build a permanent geology exhibit at the center.

GRAND CANYON OF THE YELLOWSTONE

After its gentle ride north from Yellowstone Lake through the Hayden Valley, the Yellowstone River suddenly plummets over first Upper Falls (109ft) and then Lower Falls (308ft) before raging through the 1000ft-deep Grand Canyon of the Yellowstone. More than 4000ft wide at the top, the canyon snakes for 20mi as far as The Narrows near Tower-Roosevelt Junction. The only way to reach the canyon floor is via the Sevenmile Hole Trail (see p 95).

Much of the canyon's beauty comes from its depth of colors, a byproduct of iron oxidization in the rock (the canyon is in effect rusting) and not as many assume from sulfur. Whiffs of steam still rise from vents in the canyon wall. See the Geology chapter (p 246) for information on how the canyon was formed.

The Lower Falls are twice the height of Niagara and are most impressive in the spring (least impressive in the fall). The falls boast an eye-catching green notch at a point where the water is deep and less turbulent. Bring binoculars to spot ospreys that nest in the canyon from late April till early September.

Rangers lead hikes daily at 9am from the parking lot above Uncle Tom's trailhead and give short talks four times a day (10am for kids) at Artist Point.

North Rim

Three popular scenic overlooks line the 2.5mi North Rim Dr (one-way beyond Canyon Village): Inspiration, Grandview, and Lookout Points.

Most visitors drive between the viewpoints, but you can also hike and bike along the **North Rim Trail**. The trail parallels the road from Inspiration Point to the Upper Falls Overlook (2.5mi) and then continues .75mi farther to Chittenden Bridge on South Rim Dr, where it links up with the South Rim Trail. The only disadvantage to this route is that it's one-way, so you'll have to either retrace your steps or arrange a designated automobile driver (or DAD) to pick you up.

The one-way drive turns off the main road near Canyon Campground. Take a left to reach busy **Inspiration Point**. Just before Inspiration Point is a huge granite boulder scooped up from the Beartooth Mountains by a glacier and deposited here 80,000 years ago. The **Glacier Boulder Trail** starts here for the 5mi to Sevenmile Hole (see p 95). An easy one-hour round-trip hike takes you along this trail through lovely forest to views of **Silver Cord Cascade**, the park's highest falls.

The one-way road continues to **Grandview Point** and then **Lookout Point**. Lookout Point offers the best views of the Lower Falls, while an adjacent .5mi trail drops 500ft to Red Rock for even closer views. Half a mile beyond Lookout Point, a steep .75mi trail descends 600ft to the **Brink of the Lower Falls**, for close-up views of the tumbling white water. Heading back up isn't half as much fun as going down.

The **Upper Falls Viewpoint** is also accessible by road: The turnoff is south of Canyon Junction and Cascade Creek on the main Grand Loop Rd to Fishing Bridge.

South Rim

South Rim Dr passes the Wapiti Trailhead en route to the canyon's most spectacular overlook, at Artist Point. The 3.25mi **South Rim Trail** follows the canyon rim from Chittenden Bridge to Point Sublime via Artist Point.

Uncle Tom's Trail, which begins near the Upper Falls Viewpoint, is a steep route that descends 500ft to the base of the Lower Falls. The trail was constructed in 1898 by early park entrepreneur Uncle Tom Richardson, who would lead tourists across the river and down a series of trails and rope ladders for views of the falls and a picnic lunch. Clear Lake Trail heads from the parking lot across South Rim Dr.

Artist Point was not, as many people assume, named for the spot where Thomas Moran sketched his famous landscape of the falls. It was actually named by a park photographer for its superlative scenic views.

From Artist Point a trail leads 1mi to **Point Sublime**. The second half of this trail was closed at last check due to erosion, so check with the visitor center to see if it has

YELLOW STONE

The name "Yellowstone" was not inspired by the Technicolor walls of the Grand Canyon, but rather the yellowish-tan bluffs near the confluence of the Yellowstone and Missouri Rivers in western North Dakota. In 1798, British fur trader David Thompson anglicized the phrase "R. des roches Jaunes," which was used on a French map to describe the area near the Mandan villages of the upper Missouri. The French had for their part simply (mis)translated the Minetaree Indian name for the river.

since reopened. Even if closed, it's still worth going partway past Artist Point for great views of the canyon walls. The 4mi (two-hour) round-trip hike to Ribbon Lake (see p 96) branches off from here.

CANYON TO LAKE

South of Canyon Junction, the Grand Loop Rd winds down 16mi to Lake Yellowstone via the Hayden Valley and Mud Volcano.

Hayden Valley

The Yellowstone River is broad and shallow as it meanders through the vast grasslands of Hayden Valley. This former lakebed was formed in the last ice age when a glacial outburst flooded the valley, turning the region into an arm of Yellowstone Lake. The fine silt-and-clay soil prevents water from percolating into the ground, making the area marshy and impermeable to most trees. This supports the rich shrubs and grasses favored by bison.

Hayden Valley is one of the park's premier **wildlife viewing** areas. With patience you're likely to see coyotes, springtime grizzlies, elk and lots of bison. Bird watching is equally good, including white pelicans and trumpeter swans, sandhill cranes (also at Alum Creek), ospreys, and bald eagles. There are popular viewing areas 1mi north of Sulfur Cauldron and 1.5mi north of Trail Creek. Set up your spotting scope early, as pullouts fill with cars an hour or two before dusk.

Rangers lead midweek walks in the Hayden Valley three times a week at 7am.

Mud Volcano

One of the park's most geologically volatile regions, this thermal area 10mi south of Canyon Junction and 6mi north of Fishing Bridge Junction contains an assortment of mud pots and other gurgling sulfurous pits. It's also a favorite grazing ground for bison and elk. The nearby Sour Creek resurgent dome superheats the mud volcanoes. During a series of earthquakes in 1979 the mud pots developed enough heat and gases to literally cook lodgepole pines and grasses on neighboring hillsides. One mud pot was recently discovered under the parking lot after part of the tarmac peeled away.

Mud Volcano itself has not erupted since the 1871 US Geological Survey (USGS) expedition first encountered it. A crater is all that remains of the original cone. **Dragon's Mouth Spring** lies just out of sight and is constantly in flux. In 1999 the pool cooled and its color changed from green to white.

The easiest way to see the other sights is to follow the boardwalk (there are some steps) clockwise, past Mud Geyser and up Cooking Hillside. Halfway up, **Churning Cauldron** is a favorite. The dark colors of this and other pots are due to the presence of iron sulfides.

Black Dragon's Cauldron appeared in 1948 in a crack in the earth and has since moved south along the crack to produce an elliptical pool. Nearby **Sour Lake** is as acidic as battery acid. **Sulfur Cauldron**, just a few hundred yards north, by a pullout in the road, is one of the most acidic springs in the park, at pH 1.3. Other thermal areas, visible across the Yellowstone River, can only be reached by hiking the Howard Eaton Trail.

Rangers lead hikes daily at 1pm to **The Gumper**, a huge seething mud pot off the boardwalk behind Sour Lake. Visitors are not allowed to leave the boardwalk unguided.

HIKING & BACKPACKING

Though the surrounding backcountry draws far less attention than does the Grand Canyon of the Yellowstone, it is every bit as interesting. Abundant wildlife, good camping, mesmerizing cascades, and great vistas await.

MT WASHBURN & SEVENMILE HOLE

Distance: 11.4mi one-way
Duration: 5-7 hours
Challenge: Moderate
Elevation Change: 1500ft

Mt Washburn (10,243ft) is all that remains of a volcano that erupted some 640,000 years ago, forming the vast Yellowstone caldera (see the Geology chapter, p 242). A popular, short out-and-back hike (6mi, about four hours) climbs to the fire lookout tower on Mt Washburn's summit, which overlooks the caldera to its south. A rewarding side trip leads down to Sevenmile Hole and offers a rare chance to access the impressive Grand Canyon of the Yellowstone. The hike is easily done in reverse, though doing so adds 850ft of ascent.

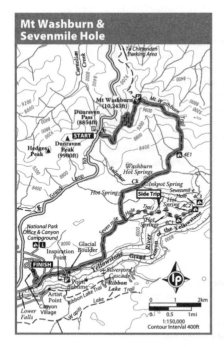

Mt Washburn & Sevenmile Hole

The Washburn Bear Management Area, immediately east of the trail on the mountain's east slope, is closed annually August 1 to November 10 and open May 10 to July 31 only by special permit from the Tower Ranger Station – avoid wandering off-trail. Snow often obstructs the Dunraven Pass approach through the end of June. The Chittenden approach retains snow a bit longer, but snowfields on both trails can be negotiated with basic route-finding skills. Wildflower displays in July and August are legendary. Keep in mind that grizzlies flock to Mount Washburn's east slopes in large numbers during August and September in search of ripening whitebark pine nuts. Frequent afternoon thunderstorms bring fierce winds and lightning – note the lightning rods on the lookout tower.

Use the south side of Trails Illustrated's 1:83,333 map No 304 *Tower/Canyon*. Two USGS 1:24,000 quads also cover the route: *Canyon Village* and *Mount Washburn*. The suggested route starts from Dunraven Pass (8859ft) on the Grand Loop Rd, 4.8mi north of Canyon and 14.2mi south of Tower. Alternatively, begin from the larger Chittenden parking area (4.9mi north of the pass), from which a marginally steeper hike joins the main route described below.

The wide trail (along a rough, disused road) makes a comfortable, steady ascent through a forest of subalpine firs to a minor gap. Continue northeast up broad switchbacks, then follow a narrow ridge past a few stunted whitebark pines to the gravel Chittenden Rd at the Mt Washburn Trail junction. The road curves to the left after a few minutes and emerges at the three-story fire-lookout tower, about two hours (2.5mi) from the trailhead. From the viewing platform and ground-level public observation room (with sheltered pit toilets, a calling-card-only pay phone, and a public 20x Zeiss telescope) enjoy majestic panoramas (when the weather is clear) across the Yellowstone caldera south to the Tetons and north to the Beartooths. Keep your eyes peeled for marmots and bighorn sheep basking near the summit.

The **Mt Washburn Trail** drops southeast along an undulating ridge past alpine wildflower meadows. After dipping through a saddle to another little gap at the tree line, bear right and descend 2.6mi from the summit through small clearings to **Washburn Meadow** and campsite 4E1 (campfires allowed). Keep your wits about you – this is prime grizzly habitat.

The trail descends southwest through boggy grassland grazed by elk and deer to **Washburn Hot Springs**, a small field of boiling mud pots (including the plopping black Inkpot) and hissing fumaroles. Proceed past more small thermal areas to the Sevenmile Hole Trail junction, 2.9mi from campsite 4E1.

Turning right, the trail is broader and leads along the north rim of the 1200ft-deep **Grand Canyon of the Yellowstone**, passing through lodgepole forest carpeted with fragrant, low-lying grouseberry shrubs. The views are increasingly spectacular as you pass the unsigned overlook of long, thin **Silver Cord Cascade**, which drops nearly 1000ft to the canyon floor. The amazing Technicolor columns of the canyon's eroding sides stretch another 1mi to the Glacial Boulder Trailhead. Canyon Village is 1.5mi west along paved Inspiration Point road.

Side Trip: Sevenmile Hole (3-5 hours, 5.2mi round-trip, 1400ft descent/ ascent) Sevenmile Hole is a minor hydrothermal area at the bottom of the Grand Canyon of the Yellowstone. Unattended food must be out of reach of bears – hang (don't dump) your pack at the junction. Fishers who frequently make the hike claim it feels like "five miles in, seven miles out." When the hatch is on, the hole is a very popular overnight destination.

The steep trail switchbacks down through Douglas firs, passing a 10ft-high geyser cone before arriving at another, mostly dormant thermal area. Weave amid the bubbling pools and small geysers past campsite 4C1, then cross a small thermal stream to campsite 4C2 beside the Yellowstone River. Large springs emerge from the reddish chalky cliffs on the river's east bank. To reach campsite 4C3, ford narrow Sulphur Creek, then follow the riverbank past a tiny hot pool. Stock animals and wood fires are not allowed at any of the campsites.

An alternative route to Sevenmile Hole leaves from the Glacial Boulder Trailhead just before Inspiration Point. This out-and-back hike is 11mi round-trip and drops 1400ft in 1.5mi; as always, the hard part is the return trip.

MARY MOUNTAIN TRAIL
Distance: 20mi
Duration: 1 (long) day
Challenge: Moderate-difficult
Elevation Change: 500-900ft, depending on trailhead

Since overnight camping is forbidden along this popular east-west wildlife migration corridor, hikers explore the route from either end as an out-and-back jaunt. The most interesting sections are the first 4mi from either trailhead.

The trail's west half (from Nez Percé Trailhead to Mary Lake) is closed annually for bear management from March 10 to the Friday of Memorial Day weekend (late May); travel on the east half of the trail is allowed year-round.

Trees are scarce in Hayden Valley, and as bison are desperate for scratching posts, you're as likely to stumble over trail signposts as find them upright. Bison, wolves, and grizzlies use the corridor to migrate between meadows, thus route-finding is further complicated by numerous divergent animal trails. Carry a map and compass and yield the trail to wildlife without exception – especially during the fall bison rutting season.

Use two Trails Illustrated 1:83,333 maps, No 302 *Old Faithful* and No 305 *Yellowstone Lake*, which cover all but the easternmost tenth of the trail, or three USGS 1:24,000 quads – *Lower Geyser Basin, Mary Lake,* and *Crystal Falls* – for more detailed coverage.

Mary Lake is approximately halfway (10mi) from either trailhead. Hiking east from Hayden Valley (the route described here) avoids nearly 1000ft of ascent.

The east trailhead is off the Grand Loop Rd, 4.5mi south of Canyon, .25mi north of Alum Creek, and 11.5mi north of Lake Village. The west trailhead is also off the Grand Loop Rd, just south of Nez Percé Creek, 6.5mi south of Madison Junction and 9.5mi north of Old Faithful.

The trail's east half traces the north bank of thermally active **Alum Creek**, winding along the forested edge of Hayden Valley through perennially marshy sagebrush-grassland meadows – favored bison and grizzly habitat. The often-unblazed trail crosses several marshy seeps over 4mi before entering the **Violet Creek** thermal area, a popular day-hike destination.

After an easy ford of Violet Creek, you'll climb 400ft to the **Central Plateau**. You'll pass numerous bison wallows and the sulfurous gas vents near **Highland Hot Springs**, reached after 9mi and an easy ford of upper Alum Creek. One mile farther along the old Mary Mountain stagecoach road, the trail emerges from a monotonous lodgepole pine alley to the west shore of 20-acre **Mary Lake**, a fine (fishless) spot for a quick dip on a hot summer day.

Past the faintly signed **Plateau Trail** junction (see Alternate Route) and Mary Lake Patrol Cabin, the slippery, gravel trail descends 900ft via switchbacks to the head of Nez Percé Creek at the boggy Cowan Creek meadow crossing. The trail continues due west through meadows and dense stands of unburned lodgepole pines, crossing the creek several times.

Beyond the log crossing of Magpie Creek, the final 4mi of the trail gently descends into the hydrothermally riddled Culex Basin, switching to the south bank of the creek (good fishing for rainbow and brown trout) after a final ford 2mi from the trailhead. The final stretch passes through more prime open bison habitat near perpetually percolating Morning Mist Springs, at the base of the conspicuous **Porcupine Hills**. Hikers routinely spot bison and their calves here from late April through early June.

Alternate Route: Cygnet Lakes/Plateau Trail to Mary Lake (6-8 hours, 16mi round-trip, 360ft ascent) The north-south Plateau Trail (not shown on most maps) traverses the mixed burned forest of the seldom-visited **Central Plateau**. Start from the Cygnet Lakes Trailhead (halfway between 4K2 and 4K3), on the south side of the Canyon-Norris road, 6.5mi east of Norris Junction and 5.5mi west of Canyon Junction. It joins the Mary Mountain Trail at Mary Lake. Though the trail is only officially maintained up to the meadows at Cygnet Lakes, hikers claim it's often in better shape than the plateau portions of the Mary Mountain Trail.

Other Hikes

Southeast of the South Rim, two trails meander through meadows and forests and past several small lakes. From Artist Point take the trail toward Point Sublime, turn off halfway past Lily Pad Lake and then branch left and descend to **Ribbon Lake** (2 hours round-trip), where there's a good chance of spotting moose. For a close-up view of **Silver Cord Cascade**, continue on the path to the canyon rim, then head left along the canyon wall to the small falls. A faint path connects to the main trail at a small footbridge. Head back the way you came. Two nice backcountry sites by the lake make for an easy overnighter less than 2mi from the trailhead (4R1 is right on the lake; 4R2 is on the main trail and less private). Mosquitoes can be a problem here before mid-August. Instead of branching left to Ribbon Lake after Lily Pad Lake, you can take the right fork to Clear Lake, fed by hot springs. An alternative route is the **Clear Lake Trail**, which begins at the parking lot near Upper Falls Viewpoint.

The easy 4.4mi round-trip **Cascade Lake Trail** begins from the picnic area of the same name on the Grand Loop Rd, 1.5mi north of Canyon Junction. For a more strenuous hike (6mi round-trip), take the right fork just before Cascade Lake (about 2.5mi from the trailhead), which leads up through meadows and whitebark pines to **Observation Peak** (9397ft). You'll climb about 1400ft.

From Cascade Lake you can continue west onto the Solfatara Plateau to join the **Grebe Lake Trail**, which passes Grebe and Wolf Lakes; these are also accessible from trailheads on the Norris-Canyon road. This is a popular area for easy overnight hikes, with campsites at all four lakes (Cascade, Grebe, Wolf, and Ice) and even atop Observation Peak. Grebe Lake offers the nicest campsites. The trails can be wet and buggy mid-June to mid-July.

MOUNTAIN BIKING

Chittenden Rd to **Mt Washburn** is open to bikers and offers a heart-pumping round trip of around three hours. It's a strenuous 3mi up, but the descent is great fun. Watch out for hikers and other bikers on the downhill run, as there are several blind corners.

LAKE COUNTRY
Map 2

Yellowstone Lake (7733ft), the centerpiece of Lake Country, is one of the world's largest alpine lakes and home to the country's largest inland population of cutthroat trout. The Yellowstone River flows north from the lake through the Hayden Valley to the Grand Canyon of the Yellowstone. In the mountains south of Yellowstone Lake, the mighty Snake River begins its long journey through Wyoming and Idaho to Oregon and the Columbia River. The alpine Absaroka Range rises dramatically east and southeast of the lake, marking the border of the park's remote and pristine Thorofare region.

ORIENTATION & INFORMATION

A 22mi section of the Grand Loop Rd hugs Yellowstone Lake's shoreline between Fishing Bridge Junction to the north and West Thumb Junction to the west. There are visitor centers and convenience stores at Fishing Bridge, Bridge Bay, and Grant Village. Grant Village and Lake Village offer the most visitor services, including dining.

HIGHLIGHTS

YELLOWSTONE LAKE

Boasting a surface area of 136 sq mi and 110mi of shoreline, Yellowstone Lake has drawn visitors for millennia; artifacts found along the lakeshore date back 12,000 years. Though its average depth is 140ft (maximum 390ft), the lake remains frozen almost half the year, from January to late May/early June.

You'll find excellent fishing and boating, and the lake is also prime bird and wildlife habitat. Visitors can watch native cutthroat trout spawn in June and July from both Fishing Bridge and LeHardy's Rapids, 3mi north of the bridge. Spawning grounds like this are important food sources for grizzlies, and several areas around the lakeshore are closed during spring and early summer. For details on fishing and boating options see the Fishing and Boating entries later in this section.

Thermal activity rings the lake, and in cold weather the steaming thermal areas blur into the water. For details on the fascinating geology of the lake see p 245.

Rangers lead tours of Yellowstone Lake's shoreline daily from Fishing Bridge.

LeHardy's Rapids

Named after Paul LeHardy, an early topographer whose rafting expedition came to an abrupt end here in 1873, these rapids formally mark the end of Yellowstone Lake. Boardwalks lead down to the rapids, whose steplike cascades were created by rock uplift.

Fishing Bridge

There has been a bridge at Fishing Bridge since 1902, but the bridge was closed to fishing in 1973 to protect spawning cutthroat trout (they just love the gravelly bottom), thus benefiting resident grizzlies. The **visitor center** was built here in 1931 as an information station for the first automobile tourists. The center contains displays on local birdlife (look for the great skulls on the candelabra).

Lake Village

Lake Village's Lake Hotel (1891) is the oldest operating hotel in the park. Robert Reamer (who also designed the Old Faithful Inn) rebuilt the hotel in 1903, adding ionic columns and false balconies. Once called the Lake Colonial Hotel, it still maintains a Southern colonial feel. It's one of the most stylish spots in the park, especially when classical concerts are held in the sunroom, and it's a great place for a drink on a rainy day or after a sunset lakeside stroll. Summer weekday tours of the hotel are given at 5:30pm.

You'll find several spots to picnic and/or fish between Lake Village and West Thumb. Near Bridge Bay, **Gull Point Dr** is a scenic picnic spot and popular fishing area.

West Thumb Geyser Basin

West Thumb is a small volcanic caldera spawned some 150,000 years ago inside the much larger Yellowstone caldera. Waters from Yellowstone Lake filled the crater, creating West Thumb Bay, a circular inlet on the lake's west end. The geyser basin still pours more than 3000 gallons of hot water per day into the lake.

Although West Thumb is not one of Yellowstone's prime thermal sites, the .5mi shoreline boardwalk loop (with a shorter inner loop) passes more than a dozen geothermal features. Many smaller thermal areas surround West Thumb, such as the roadside Pumice Point and Potts Hot Spring Basin.

At famous **Fishing Cone**, anglers used the infamous "hook 'n' cook" method to prepare their catch, dropping fish into the boiling water while still on the line. Fluctuating lake levels in spring and early summer sometimes submerge the cone. Lakeshore Geyser is similarly underwater early in the year.

Abyss Pool is one of the park's deepest springs. Nearby **Black Pool** is one of the prettiest, though it's now completely clear after years of supporting black thermophiles. **Thumb Paint Pots** are struggling to regain the energy that once catapulted boiling mud 25ft into the air.

Rangers lead a 2mi "Summer of Fire" walk daily at 8am in July and August to explore the effects of 1988's fires on the region. Reservations are required (call ☎ 307-242-2650 or stop by Grant Visitor Center), and tours depart from the Lake Overlook Trailhead at the parking lot. There are also twice-daily tours (90 minutes) of the geyser basin, departing at 10am and 4pm from mid-June to early September (no reservations required). The West Thumb Ranger Station is an original, dating from 1925. It serves as a summer bookstore and winter warming hut.

GRANT VILLAGE TO SOUTH ENTRANCE

Grant Village is a sterile scar of blockhouses and tourist facilities named after Ulysses S Grant, the president who established Yellowstone National Park in 1872.

The **visitor center** offers an exhibit on fire and an hourly 20-minute video entitled *Ten Years After the Fire*. There are short ranger talks on the back porch at 11:30am, 2:30pm, and 7:30pm. The evening talk is aimed at children.

From Grant Village the road climbs to the **Continental Divide** (7988ft) and drops into a burn area, past several trailheads. **Lewis Lake**, the third largest in the park, comes into view here, and several lakeview pullouts offer good picnic sites. For boaters, Lewis Lake is the gateway to remote Shoshone Lake.

South of the lake is 30ft **Lewis Falls**, which always seems to be jammed with traffic. Walk a little way along north side for the best views or along the south side for the closest access. If the weather gods are smiling, you should catch your first glimpse of the Tetons to the south.

To the west the Pitchstone Trailhead cuts over the pitchstone (ash tuft) plateau to Grassy Lake Rd. The roadside meadows in this area are excellent places to spot moose.

A major burn area signals the start of **Lewis Canyon**. There are lots of pullouts along the roadside, but the southernmost offers the best views. The canyon walls are volcanic rock that dates from an eruption 70,000 years ago.

Just before the South Entrance, a small pullout beside a bridge offers access to small Moose Falls and Crawfish Creek.

The entrance station is adjacent to the Snake River Picnic Area. From here it's 18mi to Colter Bay and 43mi to Moose Visitor Center, both in Grand Teton

National Park. For details of the trip south see the John D Rockefeller Jr Memorial Parkway entry (p 150) in the Grand Teton chapter.

FISHING BRIDGE TO EAST ENTRANCE

Off the lake's northeast shore is Pelican Valley, one of the park's prime grizzly habitats. At Pelican Creek Bridge, 1mi east of Fishing Bridge Visitor Center, you'll find an easy 1mi loop trail through lodgepole forest and across wetlands. Keep an eye out for moose. The lakeside ponds south of the highway promise good bird watching.

Storm Point, 1.5mi farther east, juts into the north end of the lake. The 2mi **Storm Point Trail** begins near Indian Pond, which was formed by a giant steam (not lava) explosion. The walk offers excellent habitat diversity, including meadows, shoreline, and old forest. This loop trail is also a good place to look for bison, moose, marmots, and waterfowl. Rangers lead walks here daily at 11am. The trail is closed in late spring and early summer due to bear activity; at other times keep your eyes open around dusk and dawn. Just east of Storm Point a dirt road branches north to the Pelican Valley Trailhead (see p 103).

Like West Thumb, crater-shaped **Mary Bay** is the result of a thermal explosion. Both Mary Bay and neighboring Sedge Bay are peppered with underwater thermal areas, of which roiling **Steamboat Point** is the most obvious. **Sedge Bay** beach is a launching point for canoe or kayak trips south along the lake's east shoreline. Bird watchers flock to the bay's southeast corner.

As the East Entrance Road turns away from the lake, a mile-long paved road (no buses or trailers) branches north to the **Lake Butte Overlook**, which offers grand views of Yellowstone Lake and makes an intrepid winter ski-skating site. Farther east is the less impressive Yellowstone Lake Overview.

The main road gradually climbs up the west slope of the Absaroka Range past lovely **Sylvan Lake** (with a picnic area and catch-and-release fishing), Eleanor Lake, and the Avalanche Peak Trailhead (see p 104). The road peaks at the slide area of **Sylvan Pass** (8530ft), dominated by 10,238ft Top Notch Peak to the south. East of the pass the landscape quickly turns more rugged and impressive, and the high barren walls of Mt Langford (10,774ft) and Plenty Coups Peak (10,937ft) rise to the south. Middle Creek parallels the road to the south, offering several good fishing spots.

The park's East Entrance marks the boundary between Yellowstone National Park and Shoshone National Forest. The road beyond leads to Cody via the Wapiti Valley. For details about the Buffalo Bill Scenic Byway, see the Greater Yellowstone chapter (p 212).

HIKING & BACKPACKING

Boating, fishing, and watching wildlife are the most popular activities in this region. The following hikes either put you in a position to do one of these activities (away from the crowds) or lead you to grand overviews of the area.

HEART LAKE & MT SHERIDAN
Distance: 16mi round-trip
Duration: 1-2 days
Challenge: Easy-moderate
Elevation Change: 345ft (3145ft with side trip)

Although the 1988 fires devastated several sections of the shoreline, 2160-acre Heart Lake retains much of its charm. Extending from its northwest shore is an extensive thermal field, which includes boiling hot pots and a large geyser. The lake's tranquil waters are a rich habitat for waterfowl, and there are plentiful stocks of cutthroat and elusive but record-setting lake (Mackinaw) trout.

Mt Sheridan (10,308ft), the highest summit in the Red Mountains, rises from the lake's west shore and provides a wonderful panorama. Although very fit people do hike to Heart Lake and climb Mt Sheridan in a long, uncomplicated day hike, it's much more enjoyable to spend a night (or two) along the lakeshore.

The trail to Heart Lake is closed to all travel from April 1 to June 30 due to high bear activity – confirm current regulations with a backcountry office. All west shore campsites have a two-night limit from July 1 to September 1. Heavy snow persists along the trail up to Mt Sheridan until mid-July or later. It's worth noting that Heart Lake is prime grizzly habitat and that there's often little water available along the trail leading to the lake.

Use the south side of Trails Illustrated's 1:83,333 map No 305 *Yellowstone Lake*. Two 1:24,000 USGS maps also cover the route: *Heart Lake* and *Mount Sheridan*. The trailhead is 5.3mi south of Grant Village and 16.7mi north of the South Entrance, off South Entrance Rd. There's a toilet at the trailhead.

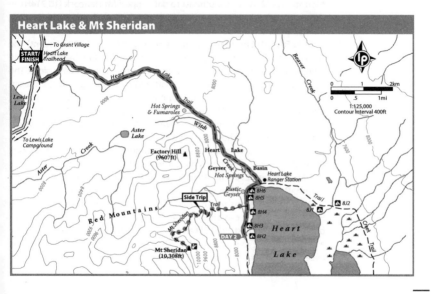

Day 1: Heart Lake Trailhead to Heart Lake (3-5 hours, 8mi, 345ft ascent) Follow the sandy, mostly single-track trail southeast through lodgepole forest severely affected by the 1988 fires. After a few miles the trail rises slightly over a minor watershed to the first group of smoking fumaroles at the north foot of bald-topped **Factory Hill** (9607ft), 1.5-2 hours from the trailhead. From here you get your first view of the lake, 2mi farther downhill.

Wind your way down into the intensely active **Heart Lake Geyser Basin** past numerous spurting springs and boiling pools, most of which are a short way off to the right. The trail crosses and recrosses warm Witch Creek to reach the Heart Lake patrol cabin, just off the lake's north shore (7450ft). The log cabin operates as a staffed summertime ranger station and is a good place to inquire about fishing conditions. Trail Creek Trail departs left (east) around the lake's northeast shore, a popular jumping-off point for stock users bound for the Thorofare region.

Heart Lake Trail continues right, first following the gray sand beach to cross the Witch Creek inlet on a log bridge, then tracing the lake's west shore to reach campsite 8H6. This is the first of five sites along the unburned strip of firs and spruces fringing the shoreline. Follow the steam along a often-overgrown trail along the tree line behind 8H6 to another fascinating thermal area. Here, azure Columbia Pool awaits and Rustic Geyser spouts up to 50ft at irregular intervals, while other springs bubble up into large calcified bathtubs.

The main trail continues past campsite 8H5 to junction with the Mt Sheridan Trail, then proceeds about another mile south past campsites 8H4 and 8H3 to 8H2; only 8H2 and 8H3 allow campfires.

There are good views across the 180ft-deep lake east to Overlook Mountain (9321ft) and southeast to flat-topped Mt Hancock (10,214ft). In the evenings, pairs of grebes often dive and court each other with mellow, lilting voices.

Side Trip: Mt Sheridan (4-6 hours, 6mi round-trip, 2800ft ascent) The Mt Sheridan Trail cuts briefly over open meadows before beginning a spiraling ascent along a steep spur largely covered by whitebark pines. The spur leads into a saddle amid wind-battered firs. Continue left (southeast) up the narrowing tundra ridge over old snowdrifts to reach the 10,308ft talus-covered summit. The fire lookout (staffed in summer but otherwise locked) covers a complete panorama, encompassing the Pitchstone Plateau to the west, Shoshone Lake to the northwest, Yellowstone Lake to the northeast and the jagged Tetons to the south. Snowdrifts often persist through mid-July, and there's no water available along the trail.

Day 2: Heart Lake to Heart Lake Trailhead (3-5 hours, 8mi, 680ft ascent) Retrace your Day 1 steps back to the Heart Lake Trailhead.

Alternative Campsites There are six additional campsites surrounding Heart Lake: 8J1 (two-night limit) and 8J2 (two-night limit, stock parties only) on its northeast side, 8J4 and 8J6 on the southeast shore, 8J3 nearby along Surprise Creek, and 8H1 at the lake's southwest corner. All sites except 8H1 allow campfires.

Rangers recommend a minimum party of four hikers for this popular lollipop loop. Backcountry camping is not allowed anywhere in the valley. Heat is an issue, since there's no shade along the trail. Hiking in the morning or late afternoon on overcast, rainy, or even snowy days offers the best chance to catch a glimpse of charismatic wildlife.

Due to heavy grizzly bear activity, Pelican Valley is subject to annual closure from April 1 to July 3 and is open for day use only (9am to 7pm) from July 4 to November 10. The July 4 opening is typically the busiest day in the valley, when animals are likely to be most skittish. Off-trail travel is prohibited on the first 2.5mi of the trail year-round.

The trailhead is at a gravel parking lot on the east end of an old service road, off the north side of the East Entrance Rd, 3.5mi east of Fishing Bridge and 23.5mi west of the East Entrance. The lot is across the road from the trailhead for Storm Point and Indian (ex-Squaw) Pond. Use the north side of Trails Illustrated's 1:83,333 map No 305 *Lake Yellowstone*.

The Pelican Valley Trail follows the abandoned Turbid Lake service road due east for a few minutes, then veers north along the forest edge to an overlook, which provides the first sight of the Pelican Creek drainage, a couple of miles from the trailhead. The trail descends through open meadow to the valley floor, passing through several boggy sections. Near the poorly signed Turbid Lake Trail junction, scan the forest edge (and trail) for signs of coyotes, bison, elk, and grizzlies.

A mile farther the trail passes the rickety remains of the **Pelican Creek Bridge**, near which you may spot cutthroat trout. Make the easy ford and climb a terrace for 1.5mi to the bridge over Astringent Creek, just before another junction. The marshy area around a group of thermal springs just south of the trail is another good place to watch for wildlife. Continue east along the forest edge, scanning the clover patches for bear scat.

Follow the old service road northeast for 1.5mi to another easy ford of Pelican Creek and the Upper Pelican Creek Trail junction. Stay in the meadows to the right for .33mi to the Pelican Cone Trail junction, where a small stream provides the valley's best drinking water. The now ill-defined trail cuts south away from the valley edge, crossing rolling meadows to a ford of **Raven Creek**, which requires a bit of careful searching to find a shallow spot – there are plenty of waist-deep swimming holes here.

Beyond Raven Creek, the poorly defined trail heads southeast through sagebrush-interspersed meadows. Where the trail passes a sulfurous-smelling pond to the right, scan the forest edge to the left with binoculars for the denning Mollie's (ex-Crystal Creek) pack of wolves, though they're seldom seen during daylight hours.

The trail passes through a dormant thermal area, then a patch of unburned forest and over some rolling sagebrush hills to the Pelican Springs Patrol Cabin and the Mist Creek Pass Trail junction. From here, it's a well-defined, undulating 5mi back to the Pelican Bridge junction along the forested south edge of the valley.

AVALANCHE PEAK LOOP
Distance: 4mi
Duration: 3.5-5 hours
Challenge: Moderate-difficult
Elevation Change: 2100ft

This unrelenting ascent (and descent) is not recommended for those with weak knees. The peak of the subalpine wildflower bloom coincides with late-spring snowmelt. Several species of high alpine butterfly are best spotted in midsummer. No matter what the season, pack your hiking poles and a jacket for protection against gusty winds and afternoon thundershowers. Snowfields persist above the tree line through mid-July, even on the trail's south-facing slopes.

The trailhead lies off the East Entrance Rd .5mi west of Sylvan Pass, 19mi east of Fishing Bridge Junction, and 8mi west of the park's East Entrance. The paved parking area is on the south side of the road, near the picnic area at the west end of Eleanor Lake. Use the north side of Trails Illustrated's 1:83,333 map No 305 *Yellowstone Lake*.

From the signed trailhead (8466ft), the infrequently blazed but well-maintained (by Sierra Club volunteers) trail climbs steeply through lush, unburned spruce and fir forest along a small unnamed stream. Thirty minutes from the road the trail crosses the stream and traverses west across an old avalanche chute, then east again into mature whitebark pine forest. Signs mark revegetation areas where an abandoned trail used to climb straight up the chutes.

A little over a mile from the road the trail levels out and emerges at the base of a huge amphitheater-like bowl. Here, the signed third revegetation area marks a junction, from which a steeper, more exposed route heads off to the left (west) and a more gradual unmaintained route veers off to the right around the back side of the bowl. The main trail to the left climbs along open talus slopes to arrive at the mountain's south ridge.

Pause before the final, windy ascent to enjoy the views south across the Absaroka Range and Lake Yellowstone. The true summit (10,566ft), with panoramic views extending north to the Beartooths and south to the Tetons, lies to the northeast along the narrow ridge beyond a series of talus wind shelters. After a scenic picnic lunch, either retrace your steps or follow a precipitous, unstable talus trail down the east arm of the peak to the saddle shared with jagged **Hoyt Peak** (10,506ft), which straddles the Shoshone National Forest boundary. Descend through a series of sparsely forested rolling hills to rejoin the main trail at the foot of the bowl.

ELEPHANT BACK MOUNTAIN LOOP
Distance: 3.5mi
Duration: 1.5-2 hours
Challenge: Easy
Elevation Change: 800ft

This popular 800ft ascent is a great family picnic option and is a favored destination of Lake Hotel guests. The trailhead is 1mi south of Fishing Bridge Junction and .5mi north of the Lake Village turnoff on the Grand Loop Rd. It's a .25mi one-way walk from the Lake Hotel through the woods past Section J of the hotel's cabins. Use the north side of Trails Illustrated's 1:83,333 map No 305 *Yellowstone Lake*.

The beginning of this lollipop loop trail parallels Grand Loop Rd for a hundred yards, then abruptly ducks into the forest. A few minutes from the road it passes the old Lake Village waterworks, then crosses beneath a power line and begins a steady climb. The forest floor here is thick with wild-flowers, wild berries, and fungi. Watch for deer and moose. After passing through 1mi of unburned lodgepole pines, the trail reaches a junction.

Both trails lead to the panoramic overlook (8600ft) of Yellowstone Lake and Stevenson Island, Pelican Valley and the Absaroka Range. The trail to the left (.8mi) is somewhat steeper, while the trail to the right (.9mi) is gentler. Hike up the steep one and back down the easier one for an easy-on-the-knees loop. The wooden benches in a clearing at the top are a favorite picnic spot. Pelican Valley's meadows lie to the left, Stevenson Island sits in the lake straight ahead, and the Absaroka Range outlines the horizon for as far as the eye can see.

Other Hikes

A section of the 150mi **Howard Eaton Trail** follows the Yellowstone River north from the parking lot east of Fishing Bridge for 3.5mi to LeHardy's Rapids. You could continue to Artist Point in Canyon for a 15.5mi shuttle hike, past thermal features, but the trail is not maintained and for experienced hikers only. This is prime grizzly habitat, so consult with rangers.

The 3mi (1.5 hour) round-trip **Natural Bridge Trail** starts at the Bridge Bay Marina parking lot. The trail heads toward the campground, swings left to join the bike trail, then continues right for 1mi along the former road. Bridge Creek carved out the rhyolite cliffs to create the bridge 50ft above the creek. You can hike to the top but not across the bridge (an early park superintendent actually wanted to build a road across the bridge). The trail is closed from late spring to early summer due to bear activity.

Two short hikes leave from the parking lot of the West Thumb Geyser Basin. The 2mi round-trip **Yellowstone Lake Overlook Trail** climbs 400ft through meadows to outstanding views of the lake and the Absaroka Range. The trailhead is on the south side of the parking lot (on the right as you drive in). On the other side of the lot is the shorter 1mi **Duck Lake Trail** trailhead. The trail bears scars from the 1988 fires and offers views of Yellowstone Lake.

South of Grant Village, marshy meadows surround **Riddle Lake**, a favorite of moose. The trailhead is off the South Entrance Rd 3mi south of Grant Village, just south of the Continental Divide sign. The 5mi round-trip trail traverses the Continental Divide and drops down to the lake. The trail is closed April 30 through July 15 due to bear activity.

Shoshone/Dogshead Trailhead offers two ways of getting to Shoshone Lake. Popular with anglers, the 6.5mi **Shoshone Lake (Lewis River Channel) Trail** follows the north shore of Lewis Lake, along the Lewis River Channel, to Shoshone Lake. You can return the same way or come back along the shorter (4.7mi) forested **Dogshead Trail**.

BIKING

An excellent family biking trail follows an old paved service road 1.5mi to **Natural Bridge**, joining the hiking trail en route. The road starts opposite the northbound turnoff to Gull Point Dr, just south of the Bridge Bay turnoff, but there's no parking here.

BOATING

Yellowstone Lake

Yellowstone Lake is ideal for extended kayak, boat, and sailboat exploration, but it's important to recognize the dangers before you plan a trip. Water temperatures are very cold, averaging only 45°F in the summer. More than 100 people have died in the park's lakes and streams. Moreover, sudden winds can quickly churn up 3ft to 5ft waves, so plan to do your paddling in early morning and late afternoon and avoid open-water crossings. Prevailing winds are from the southwest, so if you're headed south, you'll need to set off around dawn.

The **backcountry ranger office** (☎ *307-242-2609; open 8am-5pm)* by the Conoco station at Grant Village is an excellent resource. Ask for the folder *Backcountry Campsites on Yellowstone Lake*, which describes all lakeshore campsites in detail, with GPS coordinates, photos, and their mileage from the nearest boat put-ins. Some sites have restrictions on docking, hiking, etc. You may also need fishing, boating, and backcountry permits (all lake campsites require a backcountry permit).

From Grant Bay the closest campsites are at Breeze Bay (8 to 10mi away), some of which are for first- and last-night use only. The canoe and kayak put-in near Trail Creek Patrol Cabin at Sedge Bay (Trailhead 5K4) is the closest point from which to access the lake's southeast arm (21mi), from which you can hike to the park's remote reaches.

There are docks around the lake at Wolf Bay, Eagle Bay, and Plover Point, plus several anchor-only sites, including two at Frank Island. Grant Village has a new marina, down the road opposite the Conoco station.

Bridge Bay marina (☎ *307-242-3880; open 8am-8pm)* offers dock slip rentals ($12 to $16 per night) and hourly rowboat ($7.50 per hour or $34 per day) and outboard ($30 per hour) rentals. No advance reservations are accepted.

One-hour **sightseeing cruises** *($9.25/5 adults/children)* around Stevenson Island on north Yellowstone Lake operate at least five times daily from June to mid-September.

Boating Regulations The speed limit on the main lake is 45mph. The limit on the south arms is 5mph, while the southernmost inlets are closed to motorboats. Frank Island and the south end of Stevenson Island are closed May 15 to August 15 to protect nesting ospreys and bald eagles. There is a .5mi closure around Molly Island to protect breeding pelicans. The south and east shorelines of the lake are off-limits May 15 to July 14 to prevent bear disturbance.

Landing is not allowed on the thermally affected shore between Little Thumb Creek and the south end of the West Thumb thermal area.

Shoshone Lake

The largest backcountry lake in the Lower 48, Shoshone Lake is only open to hikers and hand-propelled boats. One-third of all of Yellowstone's backcountry use takes place along its shores. You'll find plenty of opportunities for extended hiking and kayak trips.

Boat access is up the channel from Lewis Lake. From mid-July to August the channel requires portage of up to 1mi in cold water (bring appropriate footwear), though in spring you can often paddle all the way up.

Of the 20 lakeshore campsites, 13 sites are reserved for boaters, five for hikers, and three are shared. All have pit toilets. Rangers claim the nicest campsites are 8Q4, 8R4, and 8R1. Wood fires are not allowed along the lakeshore.

Most boaters make their first camp on the south shore (campsites nearest to the channel are reserved for first- and last-night use only). If you need to cross the lake, do so early in the morning and at the narrows in the center of the lake. The lake is icebound until mid-June, when flooding is possible at shoreline campsites. Backcountry boating campsites at Shoshone Lake cannot be reserved before July 1 or 15, depending on the site.

For information on one possible hike to Shoshone Lake see the Lone Star Geyser & Shoshone Lake hike (p 121).

FISHING

Yellowstone Lake is stocked with cutthroat trout, longnose dace, redside shiners, long-nose suckers, and lake chub. Illegally introduced lake trout are rapidly upsetting the lake's ecosystem.

LAKE TROUT

Rangers fear that illegally introduced lake (or Mackinaw) trout, which have no natural predators, could upset the ecological balance of Yellowstone Lake. Yellowstone's native cutthroat trout have evolved in isolation and lack the ability to compete with lake trout. This could have worrying effects on the ecological balance, impacting bear, osprey, and otter populations, which depend on cutthroat trout as a major food source.

In an attempt to redress the situation, catch-and-release fishing regulations were introduced in 1998. Before July 15, all cutthroats must be released. After July 15 you can keep two cutthroats a day as long as they are less than 13 inches. Park rangers request that you keep all lake trout and inform a ranger where you caught them.

Fishing is not allowed on Pelican Creek from its outlet 2mi upstream or on the Yellowstone River from .25mi upstream of Fishing Bridge to its outflow from Yellowstone Lake. Hayden Valley is closed to fishing except for two short catch-and-release stretches.

Popular shore or float-fishing spots include Gull Point, Sand Point Picnic Area, Sedge Bay, Mary Bay, and Steamboat Point.

Bridge Bay marina runs guided Yellowstone Lake **fishing trips** ($55 to $72 per hour with a two-hour minimum, up to six anglers) from mid-June to mid-September. These boats require reservations (☎ 307-344-7311). Prices include three rods and reels. There's a tackle shop at the marina, and the office is a good place for fishing information. The marina area is closed to fishing.

NORRIS
Map 4

The Norris area was a former US Army outpost. The historic log Norris Soldier Station (1908) houses the **Museum of the National Park Ranger** *(☎ 307-344-7353; open 9am-6pm, end May-end Sep)*, often staffed by retired NPS employees. The museum's exhibits detail the evolution of the ranger profession from its military origins, including a fun mock-up of an old ranger cabin. Norris is named after Philetus W Norris, the park's second superintendent.

The Gibbon River flows through meadows in front of the building, making it a pleasant place to look for wildlife. Norris campground is right next door.

HIGHLIGHTS

Don't Miss: Porcelain Basin, Echinus Geyser

Wildlife: Elk Park for, well … elk

Family Fun: Artist Paint Pots

Off the Beaten Track: Monument Geyser Basin

ORIENTATION & INFORMATION

Norris sits at the junction of roads from Madison (14mi), Canyon (12mi), and Mammoth (21mi) Junctions. There's not much in the way of facilities here – bring water, as the stuff in the campground spigots is putrid. North of the junction is Norris Campground; west is Norris Geyser Basin, with busy bathrooms, an information station, and a bookstore. A 1mi trail connects the basin and the campground.

NORRIS GEYSER BASIN

North and west of Norris Junction, the Norris Geyser Basin is North America's most volatile and oldest continuously active geothermal area (in existence for some 115,000 years). It's also the site of Yellowstone's hottest recorded temperatures, as three intersecting faults underlain by magma come within 2mi of the surface. Barely 1000ft below the surface, scientific instruments have recorded temperatures as high as 459°F.

Norris' geothermal features change seasonally: Clear pools transform into spouting geysers or mud pots and vice versa. Thermal activity is also affected by mysterious disturbances, which generally last only a few days before things revert to "normal."

Norris Geyser Basin features two distinct areas: Porcelain Basin and Back Basin. Overlooking Porcelain Basin is the **Norris Museum** *(☎ 307-344-2812; open 8am-7pm* *late May–end Sep, 9am–6pm end Sep–mid-Oct)*, which opened as the park's first in 1930. A board gives the time of Echinus Geyser's last eruption, as well as weather forecasts. Ranger-led 90-minute walking tours of the basin leave the museum three times daily. The area's only bathrooms are in the parking lot. The parking area and toilets can get very crowded, so try to schedule a visit early or late in the day.

Porcelain Basin

One mile of boardwalks loop through open Porcelain Basin, the park's hottest exposed basin. (The name comes from the area's milky deposits.) The ground actually pulsates here in places. Check out the views from **Porcelain Terrace Overlook**, near the Norris Museum. Trails descend from the museum, branching left past **Crackling Lake** and the **Whale's Mouth**, a gaping blue hot spring, to the swirling waters of **Whirligig Geyser**. This geyser became dramatically acidic in 2000, creating many of the stunning colors in its drainage channels. Nearby **Constant Geyser** erupts frequently. You'll also find several vents, including Hurricane Vent and **Black Growler Steam Vent**, the latter of which has moved several times in recent years.

Up a side path, **Congress Pool** appeared in 1891, the year scientists convened in Yellowstone for a geologic congress.

Back Basin

Two miles of boardwalks and gentle trails snake through forested Back Basin. Here **Steamboat Geyser**, the world's tallest active geyser, infrequently skyrockets up to 400ft. The geyser was quiet for most of the 1990s but erupted twice in 2002. Nearby Cistern Spring is linked to the geyser through underground channels and empties for a day or two following Steamboat's eruptions. The spring is slowly drowning its surroundings in geyserite deposits.

Dramatic **Echinus Geyser** (e-**ki**-nus), the park's largest acidic geyser, erupts regularly (currently every two hours), with spouts reaching up to 60ft and sometimes continuing for more than an hour. You can get closer to the action here than at almost any of the park's other geysers, and if you sit in the grandstand, you may well get wet during an eruption (kids love it). The water air-cools to safe temperatures and isn't that acidic (pH 3.5, like vinegar or lemon juice) but will harm glasses and camera lenses. Eruption times are calculated by the museum to within an hour. Furious bubbling signals an imminent eruption. Echinus is named for its spiny geyserite deposits (echinoderms include sea urchins), characteristic of acidic solutions.

After deposits sealed its vent, **Porkchop Geyser** violently erupted in 1989, blowing huge lumps of geyserite 200ft into the air. Nearby **Pearl Geyser** is one of the park's prettiest. Punsters love the British pronunciation of Veteran Geyser – "Veteran Geezer." Minute Geyser is a victim of early visitor vandalism and sadly no longer erupts every 60 seconds.

NORRIS TO MADISON JUNCTION

Just over 3mi from Norris Junction, by a turnout past Elk Park, are the easily missed **Chocolate Pots**, a brown-tinged hot spring.

Just under 5mi south of Norris Junction an easy 1mi trail leads through burned forest to the fun mud pots and springs of **Artist Paint Pots**.

The road crosses the Gibbon River three times, past several roadside hot springs. **Gibbon Falls** is one of the park's prettiest falls, though parking can be a real pain.

For the best views of the falls you'll have to descend to the river along an anglers path. The falls flow over the rhyolite remnants of the Yellowstone caldera (see the Geology chapter, p 242).

NORRIS TO CANYON

The 12mi Norris-Canyon road connects the two parts of the Grand Loop Rd across the cooled lava flows of the Solfatara Plateau. About 2mi into the drive a one-way side road branches off past **Virginia Cascade**, which like Gibbon Falls lies on the caldera boundary. One story goes that the superintendent wanted to name the falls after his wife, Virginia, but the NPS was against naming park features after living people, so they compromised by naming the fall after the state of Virginia (wink, nod).

Back on the main road a small boardwalk trail marks the spot where a freak tornado ripped through the plateau in 1984. This was also the spot of the fiercest of 1988's wildfires.

Ice Lake Trail leads .5mi to the namesake lake, with one handicapped-accessible backcountry site. Trails continue northeast along the border of a major burn area to Wolf Lake (3mi) and Grebe Lake (another 1.5mi). For more details see p 97.

Farther down the Norris-Canyon road, you'll pass the **Cygnet Lakes** (see p 96) and Cascade Creek Trailhead, which offers an alternative route through burned forest to Grebe Lake.

HIKING

The **Monument Geyser Basin Trail** leads up to some fairly remote thermal features. The dormant cones are among the park's tallest, and you're likely to have them all to yourself. There's not much thermal action, but it's a nice cardio hike. The trail follows the Gibbon River for .5mi, then heads uphill for another .5mi, offering fine views of Gibbon Meadows en route. Budget around 45 minutes up, half an hour down, and 30 minutes to explore.

The **Solfatara Creek Trail** offers a shuttle hike that starts or ends at Norris Campground (Loop C). The 6.5mi one-way hike passes through some small thermal areas and the nearby Lake of the Woods, but the trail can be faint in places. Just before Madison Junction (14mi from Norris) is the trailhead for the hike up to Purple Mountain.

GEYSER COUNTRY
Map 6

Geyser Country holds the park's most spectacular geothermal features, which are concentrated in several adjacent basins. The Firehole River and its tributaries flow through the area, feeding 21 of the park's 110 waterfalls. The Firehole and Madison Rivers offer superb fly-fishing, and the meadows along them support large wildlife populations.

Budget at least half a day here to see Old Faithful, and a whole day to see all the geyser basins. If time is tight, concentrate on Upper and Midway Geyser Basins and skip Biscuit and Black Sand Basins.

The most famous geysers always attract a crowd, but sometimes it's the smaller features that are the most interesting. The smaller geysers make up for their lack of size with great names, such as North Goggles, Little Squirt, Gizmo, Spanker, Spasmodic, Slurper, and Bulger (aliases the seven dwarfs might adopt to form a criminal gang).

Historian Daniel Boorstin has suggested that Yellowstone Park's enormous appeal is "due to the fact that its natural phenomena, which erupt on schedule, come closest to the artificiality of 'regular' tourist performances." So grab some popcorn and check estimated show times on the visitor center board.

HIGHLIGHTS

Don't Miss: Upper Geyser Basin, Grand Prismatic Spring

Family Fun: Belching mud pots, swimming in the Firehole River

Off the Beaten Track: Imperial Geyser, Shoshone Lake hiking

Best Activity: Cycle to Lone Star Geyser, fly-fish the Gibbon and Madison Rivers

ORIENTATION & INFORMATION

The Old Faithful area boasts a visitor center, two gas stations, three hotels, and several general stores, including the original 1897 knotty pine Hamilton Store, the oldest structure still in use in the park. The combined ranger station, backcountry office, and clinic are set back from the main parking area, across the west parking lot from the visitor center.

Public showers are available in the reception area at Old Faithful Lodge between 6:30am and 11pm. There are no campgrounds in the Old Faithful area.

UPPER GEYSER BASIN

This heavily visited basin holds 180 of the park's 200 to 250 geysers, one of the world's greatest concentrations of geysers, the most famous being geriatric **Old Faithful**. Boardwalks, footpaths, and a cycling path along the Firehole River link the five distinct geyser groups, the farthest of which is only 1.5mi from Old Faithful.

The **Old Faithful Visitor Center** *(open late Apr–early Nov and mid-Dec–mid-Mar)* offers a bookstore and information booth and shows films 30 minutes before and 10 minutes after an eruption of Old Faithful. Rangers give a geology talk outside the visitor center three times a day and offer an evening presentation at 8pm. There's a short talk for kids at 10am. Daily geology walks depart at 10am from Castle Geyser and at 6pm from the visitor center.

The best loop around the Upper Geyser Basin follows the paved road one way and the boardwalk the other for a total of 3mi. To this you can add a small hike up to Observation Point for views over the basin. There is a smaller loop around Geyser Hill, but you'll miss many of the best geysers if you only take this loop.

You can combine the central geyser loop with surrounding thermal areas by hiking out to Biscuit and Black Sand Basins or biking past many of the geysers to Biscuit Basin and back.

✔ TIP

The first thing to do when you arrive at Old Faithful is to check the predicted geyser eruption times at the visitor center and then plan your route around these. Predictions are made for the region's six main geysers – Old Faithful, Grand, Castle, Riverside, Daisy, and Great Fountain – and these are also posted at Old Faithful Lodge, Old Faithful Inn, and the Madison Information Station.

Remember, though, that geysers rarely erupt on schedule, so take some snacks and sunblock for the wait. There's always something erupting in upper Geyser Basin, and if you're really lucky, you'll catch a biggie like Beehive or Daisy.

For a pre- or post-geyser overview of the entire basin, follow a branch trail a couple hundred feet to Observation Point. From here you can descend to Solitary Geyser to rejoin the boardwalk for a 1.1mi loop.

Solitary Geyser started off as a hot spring until it was diverted into a swimming pool in the 1940s (the pool was dismantled in 1950). The lowering of the water level in the geyser triggered eruptions that continue to this day, even though water levels have returned to normal. Small eruptions occur every four to eight minutes.

Old Faithful

Erupting every 80 minutes or so to impatient (preliminary hand clapping is not uncommon) visitors' delight, Old Faithful (named by the Washburn Expedition in 1870) spouts some 8000 gallons of water up to 180ft in the air, though the last time we checked, the old salt was in need of a dose of Viagra. Water temperature is normally 204°F and the steam is about 350°F.

Though neither the tallest nor most predictable geyser in the park, Old Faithful is considered the tallest predictable geyser. The average time between shows is 79 minutes, though this has historically varied between 45 and 110 minutes.

Scientists have worked out that the length of time until the next eruption is mathematically linked to the duration of the last eruption. A two-minute eruption takes 55 minutes to recover; a 4.5-minute eruption takes 90 minutes. Rangers correctly predict eruptions to within 10 minutes about 90% of the time. And no, Old Faithful has never erupted on the hour.

After years of studying the geyser, we have our own method of calculating exactly when an eruption of Old Faithful is imminent. Just count the number of bored people seated around the geyser – the number of tourists is inversely proportional to the amount of time left until the next eruption.

Geyser Hill

Not far from Old Faithful is the unmarked **Chinese Spring**, named after a Chinese laundry that once operated here. Dirty clothes were put into the spring along with soap, and the owners waited for the clothes to fly out, apparently clean, in an induced eruption. Don't try a repeat performance, unless you want a citation.

Consistent seepage from **Giantess Geyser** and **Vault Geyser** have created geyserite terraces that look like scaled relief maps. Giantess springs to life between two and six times a year, though when active, the geyser erupts twice hourly for up to 40 hours. The surrounding area shakes from underground steam explosions just before it erupts. Vault Geyser was inactive for a decade until bursting back into life in 1998.

Doublet Pool is known for its deep blue color, scalloped geyserite border, and the occasional thumping that emanates from collapsing steam and gas bubbles deep underground. **Aurum Geyser** resembles a human ear in outline and is thought somehow to be connected to water deposits in the meadow behind the geyser.

The **Lion Geyser** group is a gathering of four interconnected geysers (two lions and two cubs) whose eruptions are preceded by a roar, hence the name. **Heart Spring** is said to resemble the shape of a human heart.

Beehive Geyser erupts twice a day, up to 190ft through its 4ft-high nozzle. Beehive has an "indicator," a smaller vent, which when active signals the main eruption.

Erupting every 20 minutes, **Plume** is one of the easiest geysers to catch. It's also one of basin's youngest geysers, created by a steam explosion in 1922. Interestingly, its eruptions seem to have different phases at night and day. Nearby **Anemone Geyser** erupts every 15 minutes or so.

The Main Loop

Along the tarmac trail west of the Old Faithful Inn is **Castle Geyser**, whose huge cone, resembling a bleached sandcastle, attests to its status as the oldest geyser in the region. Castle goes off every 12 hours or so; the water eruption is followed by a noisy 30-minute steam phase, as the heat and steam energy long outlast the water supply. Nearby **Crested Pool** is almost constantly boiling. This is one of the best places to get views of the basin.

The predictable **Daisy Geyser** lets loose at an angle up to 75ft every 90 to 135 minutes, except when nearby Splendid Geyser erupts. Splendid is one of the largest in the region but erupts irregularly – apparently sometimes triggered by a change in atmospheric pressure, which slightly reduces the pool's boiling point. Neighboring **Comet Geyser** is constantly splashing. All three geysers are linked underground.

Grotto erupts every 8 hours for up to 10 hours. The cone takes its weird shape from trees that have been encased in the geyserite. The picturesque **Riverside Geyser** puts on an amazing show when a 75ft column of water arcs over the Firehole River, often capped by a rainbow. Twenty-minute outpourings occur about every six hours; water spilling over the cone signals an imminent eruption.

A steamy favorite, well worth the walk, is beautiful **Morning Glory Pool**, named after the flower. Unfortunately, the pool is slowly changing temperature and, therefore, color, due to the tons of trash thrown into the pool by past visitors (the main access road to Old Faithful used to pass the pool). The refuse diminishes circulation and accelerates heat loss. As the pool cools, orange bacteria spreads from its sides, replacing the gorgeous blue tones.

From Morning Glory hardcore geyser gazers can follow a walking trail to several minor features such as **Artemisia Geyser**, named for its similarity to the color of sagebrush (*Artemisia*), and **Atomizer Geyser**, named for the large amounts of steam that follow its minor eruptions.

Back toward Old Faithful, a boardwalk branches off the cycle path to **Giant Geyser**, which produces stupendous 250ft eruptions but may be dormant for decades. It currently erupts every three to 10 days (with eruptions that last an hour), reaches heights of 180 to 250ft and expels more than a million gallons of hot water. The cessation of otherwise continuous **Bijou Geyser** nearby signals an imminent eruption of Giant Geyser.

The strikingly colorful **Chromatic Pool** and **Beauty Pool** are linked, so when one drops, the other rises.

Next is **Grand Geyser**, one of the world's tallest predictable geysers (150-180ft). It spews in bursts every eight to 12 hours and lasts about 12 minutes. It will often pause after nine minutes and then restart after a minute or so; the subsequent bursts are typically the most spectacular.

Sawmill Geyser is in eruption about 30% of the time, but its extents are highly variable. Water spins violently in its crater like a circular saw. Nearby **Spasmodic** is also in eruption a third of the time and erupts from more than 20 vents.

Old Faithful Inn

Seattle architect Robert C Reamer designed the enchanting Old Faithful Inn (1904), a national historic landmark and one of world's largest log buildings. The log rafters of its lobby rise nearly 90ft, and the chimney of the central fireplace (actually eight fireplaces combined) contains more than 500 tons of rock. It's definitely a worthwhile visit, even for nonguests. Be sure to check out the Crow's Nest, a wonderful top-floor balcony where musicians used to play for dancers below (it hasn't been used since 1959). The 2nd-floor observation deck provides views of Old Faithful geyser and is a popular place for a coffee.

Free 45-minute Historic Inn tours depart from the fireplace at 9:30am, 11am, 2pm, and 3:30pm.

BLACK SAND BASIN

This geyser basin, 1mi northwest of Old Faithful, has a few interesting features. The black sand is derived from volcanic glass (obsidian).

Cliff Geyser is named for the geyserite wall that separates the geyser from Iron Creek. **Emerald Pool** gets its pretty color from yellow bacteria that blend with blue reflected from the sky. **Rainbow Pool** is one of the most colorful in the park.

Unsigned **Handkerchief Pool** was once one of Yellowstone's most famous features. Visitors would place a handkerchief in the pool and watch it get sucked down and then spat out "clean." The pool stopped functioning in 1928, but has since restored itself. Today it's illegal to throw anything into any of Yellowstone's thermal features.

You can access Black Sand Basin by car or, better, by foot from Daisy Geyser. Rangers lead walks here daily at 1pm.

BISCUIT BASIN

Two miles farther north, Biscuit Basin was named for biscuitlike deposits that surrounded stunning **Sapphire Pool**, but these were destroyed during eruptions that followed the 1959 Hebgen earthquake.

The main features here are **Jewel Geyser**, which erupts every 10 minutes or so, and **Shell Geyser**, which is shaped like a clamshell.

A .5mi hiking and biking trail leads from across the highway to Upper Geyser Basin's Daisy Falls.

The Mystic Falls Trail starts here, offering two alternate hikes. There are free daily ranger-led hikes to the falls at 8am.

MIDWAY GEYSER BASIN

Five miles north of Old Faithful and 2mi south of the Firehole Lake Dr entrance is Midway Geyser Basin. The algae-tinged indigo waters of the 370ft-wide **Grand Prismatic Spring**, the park's largest and deepest (121ft) hot spring, are the key geothermal feature here. The spring drains into **Excelsior Pool**, a huge former geyser that blew itself out of existence in the 1880s. The pool continually discharges an amazing 4000 gallons of boiling water a *minute* into the Firehole River.

For the most dramatic photos of Grand Prismatic Spring, drive south to Fairy Falls Trailhead, walk for 1mi, and then take a faint path up the side of the fire-burned ridge (itself a lava deposit from the west rim of the caldera).

LOWER GEYSER BASIN

Separate roads access the three main sections of this sprawling thermal basin: the main Grand Loop Rd passes Fountain Paint Pot; Firehole Lake Dr loops off the main road to Great Fountain and other geysers; and Fountain Flat Dr offers access to hiking trails and minor thermal features.

Firehole Lake Drive

Firehole Lake Dr is a one-way 3mi road starting 2mi north of Midway Geyser Basin and about 1mi south of the Fountain Paint Pot parking lot. It passes several pretty pools and large geysers, including **Great Fountain Geyser**, which soars up to 200ft in a series of staccato bursts every 11 hours or so. Eruption times are predicted by the visitor center at Old Faithful to within a couple of hours, and you'll often find people waiting with a picnic lunch and a good book. Violent boiling in the crater signals an imminent eruption.

The nearby 30ft cone of **White Dome Geyser** usually erupts every half hour or so. **Pink Cone Geyser** gets its color from manganese dioxide deposits. A road was built right across the side of this cone in the 1930s.

Firehole Lake is a large hot spring ringed by several small geysers, including the raging waters of Artemisia Geyser and the sensuous smoothness of Young Hopeful. Across the road, **Hot Lake** offers more geysers and even a small cascade of boiling water on its edges. **Steady Geyser** is in continual eruption through one of two vents.

Fountain Paint Pot

Roughly midway between Madison Junction and Old Faithful, **Fountain Paint Pot Nature Trail** takes in four types of thermal features along a .5mi boardwalk loop, though none of the sights are all that spectacular. The area around the thermal features is slowly being drowned in deposits. Beyond, a grassy basin supports the park's largest bison herd.

The **mud pots** are the top-billed comedians of the show. Red Spouter is also interesting, since it acts like a muddy hot spring in early summer only to become a fumarole later in the year. Morning and Fountain Geysers are impressive but infrequent gushers.

Clepsydra Geyser has erupted almost constantly since the Hebgen Lake earthquake in 1959 (see p 202). The geyser was named Clepsydra (Greek for "water clock") at the time when it used to go off every three minutes on the button. Jelly Geyser does indeed look like an upside-down bowl of Jell-O.

For a map of Fountain Paint Pot and Firehole Lake Dr pick up the park service trail guide (50¢). Rangers lead tours here three times a week at 9am.

Fountain Flat Drive

This former freight road turns off the Grand Loop Rd at pleasant Nez Percé Picnic Area and continues for 1.5mi to a hiking and biking trailhead. Just beyond the parking lot is the **Ojo Caliente (Hot Water) Hot Springs**, which empty into the river. Just over the bridge are trails to Sentinel Meadows on the right and more thermal features on the left. From here the road is accessible to bikers and hikers all the way to Fairy Falls Trailhead. The trail is wheelchair accessible for 2.2mi to the Goose Lake (OD5) campsite.

FIREHOLE CANYON DR

The one-way Firehole Canyon Dr leaves the Grand Loop Rd just south of Madison Junction. The road passes 40ft-high **Firehole Falls** at the foot of towering dark rhyolite cliffs, but the main attraction here is the lukewarm **Firehole Swimming Area** *(no fee)*, one of the few locations in the park that's open for swimming. There's a toilet here but very limited parking.

YELLOWSTONE'S WINTER WONDERLAND

Winter is a magical time to visit Yellowstone. The falls turn to frozen curtains of ice, wildlife is easier to spot, the geysers are even taller and steamier than normal, and nearby trees ("ghost trees") are covered in frozen steam and snow. The warm thermal areas around Old Faithful, Norris, and Mammoth become winter refuges for elk and bison, and the thermally heated (and thus still flowing) rivers attract wildfowl.

The winter season runs from the third week of December to mid-March, and activity centers on Mammoth Hot Springs Hotel and Old Faithful Snow Lodge, the only two accommodations open in the park. Independent travel is more difficult in winter, and most people sign up for a lodging and activity package, which often works out cheaper than arranging everything yourself. The **Yellowstone Institute** *(☎ 307-344-2294; w www.yellowstoneassociation.org/institute)* runs excellent winter programs.

Accessing the park can be tricky. The only road open year-round is the northern Mammoth–Cooke City road via Tower-Roosevelt Junction, plus a small extension to Mammoth's Upper Terraces.

The long-term future of Yellowstone winter use lies in mass transit snowcoaches. During the season, Xanterra *(☎ 307-344-7311)* operates one-way snowcoach tours once a day between Old Faithful and Mammoth ($49), West Yellowstone ($46), and Flagg Ranch ($51). Most other snowcoach companies offer only round-trip day trips from West Yellowstone.

WINTER FACILITIES

Mammoth Hot Springs Hotel and Old Faithful Snow Lodge and their restaurants are the only places open, though there is limited (and very cold!) winter camping at Mammoth Campground and Old Faithful.

Both hotels rent snowshoes ($11 per day), cross-country skis ($14), snowmobiles ($165 per day), and winter attire, and they also offer skiing instruction. It's possible to rent a snowmobile in Mammoth and drop it off at Old Faithful (or vice versa) for no extra charge. After a day on a snowmobile you'll need a dip in Mammoth Hotel's hot tubs, which rent for $15 per hour.

There are no public accommodations in Canyon, but **Yellowstone Expeditions** *(☎ 800-728-9333; w www.yellowstoneexpeditions.com)* runs a winter yurt camp there for their cross-country ski and snowshoe tour clients. Four-day tours from West Yellowstone cost around $735 per person, including transportation, accommodations, food, and a guide.

Visitor centers at Old Faithful and Mammoth are open year-round. There are winter warming huts at Mammoth, Indian Creek, Old Faithful, West Thumb, Fishing Bridge, Madison, and Canyon; the latter two have fast food. All except Old Faithful are open 24 hours. You can get snowmobile fuel at Canyon, Old Faithful, and Mammoth, and possibly at Fishing Bridge (check at a ranger station).

ACTIVITIES

Once inside the park, use **skier shuttles** to get to and from trailheads, where you can take a trail or just ski back. Shuttles operate from Mammoth to Golden Gate and Indian Creek ($12 round-trip; 10 per day); from Mammoth to Tower Junction ($12.50; six per day) for the Blacktail Plateau, Lost Lake, and Tower Falls; and from Old Faithful to Fairy Falls and Divide Lookout (each $11).

Three-hour guided **snowshoe tours** ($22, $27 with shoe rental) depart from Mammoth (Sunday) and Old Faithful (Thursday and Sunday). Half-day guided **ski tours** ($35) leave at noon from Old Faithful to Fairy Falls (Saturday) and DeLacy Creek (Wednesday).

Combined **snowcoach and ski tours** run from both Mammoth and Old Faithful to Canyon ($99). Five times weekly there are full-day snowcoach tours to Canyon from Old Faithful ($97) and Mammoth ($92).

All backcountry trails are marked with orange markers, so you can ski most of the backcountry trails described under hiking. Upper and Midway Geyser Basins make for some fine ski trips. You can ski or snowshoe from Old Faithful to Black Sand or Biscuit Basins or to Lone Star Geyser. Frozen Fairy Falls is a popular ski day trip. In the Mammoth region it's possible to ski from Indian Creek Campground to Sheepeater Cliffs and then along a backcountry trail to Bunsen Peak Trail and back to Mammoth (5mi). In the park's northeast corner a popular ski trail parallels the northeast entrance road below Barronette Peak (10,404ft).

From West Yellowstone it's a 60mi round trip to Old Faithful and 90mi round trip to Canyon.

REGULATIONS

In November 2002 Yellowstone's winter-use controversy was (temporarily) put to rest when President Bush introduced a daily cap of 1100 snowmobiles allowed into the park, to take effect December 2003. At least 80% of these must be led by commercial guides, and only four-stroke machines will be allowed. A maximum of 550 snowmobilers per day will be allowed through the park's west entrance at West Yellowstone. The compromise seems, predictably enough, to have pleased no one (see the aside "Snowmobile Wars" on p 35). It would be wise to check current developments before heading out on a snowmobile vacation.

In a separate development, in winter 2002-03 snowmobiles were banned from all the park's side roads, including the Lake Butte Overlook, Firehole Canyon Dr, and a section of the Grand Loop Rd from Canyon to Tower. All other roads are groomed for oversnow travel. The Canyon to Washburn Hot Springs Overlook section of this road is open to Nordic skiers.

Snowmobile operators must carry a valid state driver's license. Noise levels must not exceed 78 decibels at a distance of 50ft during full acceleration. Off-road snowmobiling is prohibited.

SAFETY

There are obvious dangers involved in winter travel. Visitors (especially snowmobilers) should carry extra clothing, matches, a flashlight, a whistle, and backup food. Snowmobilers should also carry a toolkit. Avalanches are a particular danger at Sylvan Pass, between Wapiti and Yellowstone Lake, so don't dally here.

All winter visitors need to be particularly careful around thermal areas, as snow can mask potentially lethal pools. Don't approach wildlife during winter; any unnecessary movement will cost them calories they can ill afford.

MADISON TO WEST YELLOWSTONE

Madison Junction sits at the confluence of the Firehole, Madison, and Gibbon Rivers. Towering above the small information station is National Park Mountain, which commemorates the spot where the notion of preserving Yellowstone was first mentioned in 1870.

The Madison Valley is of interest mainly to anglers and wildlife watchers, though all will appreciate the sublime afternoon light and active herds of deer, elk, and bison. The 14mi road to West Yellowstone is one of the park's busiest corridors.

Two miles east of Madison, the Harlequin Lake Trailhead leads half a mile north to a pond. This is also a fine place to spot wildlife in the lovely valley to the south. From here the road threads between Mt Haynes on the left and Mt Jackson on the right, past several excellent fly-fishing spots, before the valley opens up to views of the distant Gallatin Range.

Four miles farther, Riverside Dr is a 1mi two-way road that's useful for fishing access and perhaps some family biking. Two Ribbons Trail is a .75mi wheelchair-accessible trail that offers a fairly dull loop or point-to-point stroll through some fire burns.

Shortly after you enter Montana, about 2mi before West Yellowstone, a side road to the north accesses several fishing spots.

OLD FAITHFUL TO WEST THUMB

Three miles into the 17mi drive between Old Faithful and West Thumb is **Kepler Cascades**, where a wooden platform offers fine views of the 125ft cascades. Just past the cascades turnout is the parking area for the hike or bike ride to **Lone Star Geyser**. The road climbs past Scaup Lake, the

REGENERATION – AFTER THE FIRE

Catastrophic wildfires swept across 1.4 million acres of the Greater Yellowstone Ecosystem in the summer of 1988 and torched one-third of Yellowstone National Park. More than 25,000 firefighters battled 51 fires during the driest summer in 112 years.

Fifteen years later, the aftermath of the fires is still very much in evidence. But scientific researchers have closely monitored the long-term effects and subsequent regeneration of the forests. Far from marking a disaster, many observers now describe the fires as a natural event heralding a new cycle of growth.

Many plants and trees depend on high temperatures to trigger the release of their seeds, and surveys estimated that there were as many as one million seeds per acre on the ground during the fall of 1988. It was also found that only 390 large mammals (less than 1% of the park's total) perished in the fires, the vast majority being elk. The year after the fires, populations of all grazing and browsing mammals flourished thanks to succulent new vegetative growth. Birds thrived on the increased numbers of insects living on dead wood. Ten years later grasses, wildflowers and shrubs were clear winners, aided by increased sunlight and soil nutrients.

For hikers, Yellowstone's scenery has been affected to a certain degree, but not all in a bad way and certainly not to the degree described by the media at the time. Wildflowers are blooming, many views are now unimpeded, and it's now easier to see the wildlife thanks to the burns and richer grazing.

Spring Creek Picnic Area, and the Divide Trailhead before reaching **Isa Lake** at Craig Pass 8261ft).

Craig Pass is an unassuming spot of deep significance. Lily-choked Isa Lake sits astride the Continental Divide and drains (or rather seeps) into both the Atlantic and Pacific drainages. The west side of the lake drains *east* year-round into the Firehole River, which flows into the Missouri and Mississippi before finally reaching the Atlantic; the east side (in spring only) flows *west* into the Snake and thus the Pacific Ocean. Imagine the water particles eagerly anticipating which trip they'll get to make.

From the pass, the road descends to the DeLacy Creek Picnic Area and Trailhead (see p 122) and shortly afterward offers tantalizing views of remote Shoshone Lake. From here the road ascends back across the Continental Divide (8391ft), before finally descending to excellent views of Yellowstone Lake and the turnoff to West Thumb (see the Lake Country section, p 97, for routes onward from here).

HIKING & BACKPACKING

The meandering Firehole River is the aquatic backbone of the park's most geothermally active region. Even the short hikes described below will get you away from the crowds at old Faithful to some spectacular backcountry waterfalls and geysers.

FAIRY FALLS & TWIN BUTTES
Distance: 6mi
Duration: 3-4 hours
Challenge: Easy
Elevation Change: Negligible

Fairy Falls (197ft) is one of the park's most accessible backcountry cascades. Tucked away in the northwest corner of the Midway Geyser Basin, the waterfall receives relatively few visitors, even though it's only a short jaunt from Old Faithful. Beyond Fairy Falls the lollipop loop trail continues to a hidden thermal area at the base of the Twin Buttes, two conspicuous bald hills severely charred in the 1988 fires. The geysers are undeveloped, and you're likely to have them to yourself – in stark contrast to the throngs around Grand Prismatic Spring.

The Fairy Falls (Steel Bridge) Trailhead is just west of the Grand Loop Rd, 1mi south of the Midway Geyser Basin turnoff and 4.5mi north of the Old Faithful overpass. Use the north side of Trails Illustrated's 1:83,333 map No 302 *Old Faithful*.

Cross the Firehole River on the silver trestle bridge, then head northwest along Fountain Flat Dr, which is now a wide gravel biking and hiking path. After 1mi you'll notice multicolored steam rising from **Grand Prismatic Spring** on the right. You can't reach the boardwalk from this trail, but you can scramble up the unofficial trails to your left for a fine bird's-eye view. Continue .33mi to a trail junction and turn left onto the narrower Fairy Creek Trail. The trail, which winds 1.6mi past campsite OD1 through lodgepole forest

Fairy Falls & Twin Buttes

burned in the 1988 fires, is uninteresting at first, but as you near Fairy Falls, you'll find a variety of lush foliage growing on the damp ground amid blackened stumps.

At 197ft, **Fairy Falls** is the park's seventh-highest waterfall, but the volume of water is hardly on a par with the falls on the Yellowstone River. Still, patterned streaks of white water blanket the dark lower rocks, and clumps of raspberries and fireweed flourish around a pretty pool, which makes for a fine swimming hole on a hot summer day.

After crossing a footbridge, the trail continues .7mi northwest toward the prominent **Twin Buttes** and conspicuous plumes of rising steam. Cross several marshy patches with the aid of log bridges and head for the closest plume emanating from **Spray Geyser**, erupting frequently to a height of 6 to 8ft. Return a little way along the trail, then continue west, following the outlet from **Imperial Geyser**, which is lined with orange algae. Imperial plays almost perpetually, projecting blasts of water up to 20ft into its large rainbow pool. If you care to climb onto the buttes, head across the open slopes behind Imperial Geyser. After discovering the collection of little pools hidden in a hollow between the two summits, you can continue to either summit without much difficulty. Views to the east encompass the Lower and Midway Geyser Basins, while to the west the trail-free Madison Plateau stretches off toward the park boundary. Retrace your steps to the Fairy Falls Trailhead.

MYSTIC FALLS & BISCUIT BASIN LOOP
Distance: 3mi loop
Duration: 1.5-2 hours
Challenge: Easy
Elevation Change: 700ft

The shorter, out-and-back option to the base of the falls is relatively flat and thus popular with families. Due to a lack of shade, the longer loop hike to the overlook is best done in the morning or late afternoon.

The Biscuit Basin turnoff is 2mi north of the Old Faithful overpass and 14mi south of Madison Junction, on the west side of Grand Loop Rd. Use the north side of Trails Illustrated's 1:83,333 map No 302 *Old Faithful*.

From the parking area, head west across the Firehole River bridge. Follow the Biscuit Basin boardwalk loop .33mi around to the left past several notable geysers and hot springs. Just west of Avoca Spring, the wide, sandy Mystic Falls Trail (blazed but unsigned) ducks into burned lodgepole forest dotted with wildflowers.

EXPERIENCING YELLOWSTONE

The undulating trail parallels, but does not cross, the **Little Firehole River**. Soon you'll reach the signed Summit Lake/Little Firehole Meadows junction. From here it's .7mi to the left on the most direct route to the falls, saving the longer overlook loop – visible on a cliff to the right – for the return trip. Heading upstream into the canyon, the path can be muddy where seeps cross the trail. After 10 to 15 minutes the trail arrives at the bottom of 70ft **Mystic Falls**, where orange hot spring bacterial seeps are in abundance. A series of switchbacks leads to the top of the falls.

Retrace your steps to complete this family-friendly hike. If you're fit or traveling without children, you can choose instead to complete the loop (which adds 1mi and a sweaty 500ft elevation gain) by continuing .5mi through more burned lodgepoles to the Fairy Creek\Little Firehole Meadows Trail junction. Turn right and descend to the **Biscuit Basin Overlook** for an expansive bird's-eye view of the Upper Geyser Basin and 1988 wildfire aftermath. Follow the switchbacks downhill to rejoin the Mystic Falls Trail, then retrace your steps to Biscuit Basin.

LONE STAR GEYSER & SHOSHONE LAKE
Distance: 4.8mi round-trip
Duration: 1.5-2.5 hours
Challenge: Easy
Elevation Change: 400ft

This paved hike is very popular with day hikers and cyclists, yet quite a contrast to the chaotic scene around Old Faithful. To completely avoid the crowds, pick up the **Howard Eaton Trail** (OK2) 1mi south of the Old Faithful overpass, an alternative (if longer and less interesting) route. The overnight side trip to Shoshone Lake explores the park's most popular backcountry body of water and an impressive geyser basin.

Lone Star erupts almost exactly every three hours, and it's definitely worth timing your visit. Check with Old Faithful Visitor Center for predicted eruption times. Grants Pass, between Lone Star and Shoshone Lake, isn't normally clear of snow until late June.

The suggested hike begins at the Lone Star Trailhead, 2.6mi (a 30-minute hike) south of the Old Faithful overpass off the Grand Loop Rd and 14.6mi northwest of West Thumb, just south of the Kepler Cascade turnout. The Kepler turnout is a more secure overnight parking spot, since it sees much more traffic. Use the north side of Trails Illustrated's 1:83,333 map No 302 *Old Faithful*. Two USGS quads also cover the route: *Old Faithful* and *Shoshone Geyser Basin*.

From the Lone Star Trailhead, immediately above **Kepler Cascades** (where the Firehole River speeds through a spectacular little gorge), take the old paved road (closed to cars) past a tiny weir that diverts water to Old Faithful village.

The road crosses the Firehole River bridge, heading upstream past the Spring Creek Trail junction (and a route diverging right) to end at the steep-sided, 9ft-tall **Lone Star Geyser** after an easy 2.4mi. This isolated geyser goes off for 2 to 30 minutes at intervals of almost exactly three hours, sending a jet of boiling water up to 45ft into the air. Check the NPS logbook near the footbridge to gauge exactly when the next eruption might occur (if you catch an eruption, fill in the log for future visitors). If you have some time to kill, consider following the first part of the side trip described below to check out thermal areas along the Firehole River.

Side Trip: Shoshone Lake & Shoshone Geyser Basin (1-2 days, 11.6mi round-trip, 400ft ascent) To explore overnight options, proceed past the geyser and turn left to head southwest past the least desirable campsite OA1 (campfires OK), recrossing the Firehole River on a footbridge after .3mi to intersect with the Shoshone Lake Trail, which leads 5.8mi south to the **Shoshone Geyser Basin**. The trail soon passes a small thermal field of scalding hot pools and hissing steam vents, the most attractive, off-trail campsite OA2 (campfires OK) in .4mi, and finally the best option for through-hikers, campsite OA3, in another .8mi.

Climb south over the broad rolling ridge to cross unsigned **Grants Pass** (8010ft), which marks the **Continental Divide**. The sandy trail heads down through superb stands of tall, old-growth Engelmann spruce and white-bark pine to reach the Bechler River Trail junction, 4.25mi from Lone Star Geyser. Inviting campsite 8G1 (no campfires) is a short way down the Shoshone Lake Trail, on a rise above the meadows framing **Shoshone Creek**, 2mi northwest of the impressive Shoshone Geyser Basin.

Alternative Campsites All of Shoshone Lake is a "no wood fire" area. There are a total of six mixed hiker- and boat-accessible campsites along the north and west shores of Shoshone Lake; 8R5 and 8T1 are by far the closest to the Shoshone Geyser Basin. The other four hiker-accessible campsites (8R4, 8R2, 8S3, and 8S2) are good options if you'd like to extend your trip and explore the lake. Thirteen exclusively boat-in sites along both the north and south shores offer those with floating transportation the option of spending weeks here.

Other Hikes

The **DeLacy Creek Trail** leads to Shoshone Lake, the park's largest back-country lake. The trailhead is on the Grand Loop Rd, east of Craig Pass near the DeLacy Creek Picnic Area, 9mi west of West Thumb Junction. The trail is 3mi one-way to the lake. It's possible to do a 28mi loop of the lake before returning to DeLacy Creek. Alternatively hike in to the lake via Lone Star Geyser and Grants Pass and then out along the north shore of Shoshone Lake to the DeLacy Creek Trail for a shuttle hike of around 22mi.

A possible day hike from Old Faithful is the 6.8mi round-trip **Mallard Lake Trail**, which climbs up the Mallard Lake resurgent dome (a bulge in the earth caused by a volcanic upsurge). The trail starts from behind the cabins of Old Faithful Lodge and crosses the Firehole River to climb through an area of fire burns.

Leaving from Old Faithful, rangers lead "Adventure Hikes" ($15) to Mallard Lake, Shoshone Lake, Lone Star Geyser, and others in the region. See the park newspaper for details.

BIKING

The former service road to **Lone Star Geyser** makes for a fine (and flat) 5mi round-trip bike ride, though you'll have to dismount for the last section to the actual geyser. Take a packed lunch for the geyser wait. Park in the Lone Star Geyser lot next to Kepler Cascades.

The 4mi-long gravel **Old Fountain Freight Rd** between Fountain Flat Dr and Fairy Falls Trailhead offers an opportunity to combine a bike ride with a hike to Fairy Falls. Park your bike at the trail junction 3mi from Fountain Flat Rd and then hike the 1.6mi to Fairy Falls. From Fairy Falls you can continue 2.6mi along the Grand Loop Rd to Biscuit Basin, where you'll find a bikeable trail to Daisy Geyser and Old Faithful.

Bikes are allowed on the road (not the boardwalk) between Old Faithful and Morning Glory Pool (1.3mi) and between Daisy Geyser and Biscuit Basin (1.3 mi). Inquire at the west gate about the bike trail that leads to the Madison River access road.

FISHING

The Madison and Gibbon Rivers offer some of the park's best and most scenic fly-fishing. The Firehole (between Biscuit and Midway Geyser basins), Madison, and Gibbon (downstream from Gibbon Falls) Rivers are open for fly-fishing only.

BECHLER CORNER
Map 1

Known for its numerous waterfalls and the park's highest rainfall, the remote Bechler (**Beck**-ler) region is largely the preserve of hardy backpackers, outfitters, and horseback riders who brave flooded streams, monster mosquitoes, and wet marshland to access beautiful backcountry and the park's largest waterfalls.

Visitors en route to a hike in the region or headed along Grassy Lake Rd to the John D Rockefeller Parkway might want to pay a visit to the Cave Falls cascades and swimming hole (see p 124). For details on Grassy Lake Rd and its day hikes to Beula Lake and Union Falls see the Greater Yellowstone chapter (p 220).

HIGHLIGHTS

Don't Miss: Cascade Corner, a wild area of the park that's largely inaccessible to vehicles.

Best Activity: The four day Bechler River Trail, on foot or, for tough nuts, winter skis.

Take it Easy: Soak it up in backcountry hot springs like Ferris Fork Swimming hole at Cave Falls.

ORIENTATION & INFORMATION

Bechler is accessed from either the Bechler Ranger Station or Cave Falls Trailhead, both off of Cave Falls Rd via US 20 from Ashton, Idaho, a minimum two-hour drive from West Yellowstone, Montana, via ID Hwy 47 and Marysville Rd. The only alternative approach is the brutal, unpaved Grassy Lake Rd/Reclamation Rd, from the turnoff just north of Flagg Ranch, part of John D Rockefeller Memorial Parkway, 2mi south of Yellowstone's South Entrance; allow at least two hours from Flagg Ranch.

HIKING & BACKPACKING

Though Bechler offers several day hikes, the region is best traversed as part of a longer backcountry trip. The area is popular with both backpackers and anglers, almost all of whom are seasoned Yellowstone travelers, and competition for backcountry campsites is fierce, even outside the high season of mid-July through August.

Campsites are not reservable in advance for camping dates prior to July 20. Sites may be available for in-person permits, depending on prevailing weather conditions. Mosquitoes are often brutal along the river until the end of July.

BECHLER MEADOWS & BECHLER FALLS
Distance: 8mi loop
Duration: 2.5-3.5 hours
Challenge: Easy
Elevation Change: Negligible

Bechler Meadows' extensive wetlands attract much wildlife (including grizzly and black bears) and several rare waterfowl, including gray owls and great blue herons. By starting out from the Cave Falls Trailhead or by taking the Bechler Falls side trip, you can add substantial cascades to the circuit's spectacular mix.

The suggested route avoids all fords, so there's no need to inquire about river levels before departing. Use the south side of Trails Illustrated's 1:83,333 map No 302 *Old Faithful*.

From Bechler Ranger Station, follow the Bechler Meadows Trail 3mi northeast past the Boundary Creek Trail junction through unburned lodgepole pine forest to the Bechler River/Rocky Ford cutoff junction.

Depending on the time of year – bugginess declines later in the season – you might make a short foray .5mi north across a wood-and-cable suspension bridge over Boundary Creek past campsite 9B1 into the expansive Bechler Meadows to look for rare waterfowl like sandhill cranes and furtive wildlife such as moose, or angle around the ford for rainbow trout. See the Bechler River Trail for a suggested one- to three-day extension.

Follow the cutoff southeast .7mi past campsite 9C1 to the wide Rocky Ford at the Bechler River Trail junction. Instead of fording the river, trace the river's west bank south for 2mi to the next junction, where a cutoff leads west 2mi through lush unburned forest back to the ranger station.

Side Trip: Bechler Falls & Cave Falls (30-45min, 1mi out-and-back, 0ft ascent) This rewarding out-and-back detour heads .5mi downstream from the Bechler River/Ranger Station cutoff to 15 to 30ft **Bechler Falls**, one of Bechler's widest and most voluminous waterfalls. From here you can either retrace your steps or opt instead to follow the riverbank trail .5mi east to the equally impressive 20ft **Cave Falls**, which is much wider than it is tall. Don't miss the swimming hole at the base of the falls.

BECHLER RIVER TRAIL
Distance: 28mi out-and-back
Duration: 4 days
Challenge: Moderate
Elevation Change: 1100ft (800ft descent)

Near the head of Bechler Canyon, the Ferris Fork side stream is home to several hidden waterfalls and one of the few legal backcountry hot pot soaks. The river is chock-full of rainbow trout and thus attracts many anglers.

While securing your permit at the backcountry office, ask about river ford and trail conditions – high water and swarms of bugs typically persist along this route through mid- to late July. All of the campsites mentioned here (except 9B9) limit stays to one night.

Use the south side of Trails Illustrated's 1:83,333 map No 302 *Old Faithful*. Three USGS 1:24:000 quads also cover the route: *Trischman Knob*, *Cave Falls*, and *Bechler Falls*.

Day 1: Bechler Ranger Station to Campsite 9B4 (3-4 hours, 6.5mi, 0ft ascent) See the beginning of the Bechler Meadows Trail description for directions from Bechler Ranger Station to Rocky Ford. This extremely wide crossing of the Bechler River is tricky even in low water after mid-July and may be impassable after heavy rains. The slightly shorter (but less interesting and often boggy) alternative is Bechler Meadows Trail, which requires a shorter, knee- to thigh-high ford near campsite 9B2 (no campfires).

Beyond the ford, the **Bechler River Trail** heads east past the **Mountain Ash Creek Trail** junction, then cuts north through forested patches and open grassy plains beside the meandering river to campsite 9B3, at the edge of a broad clearing 7mi from the trailhead. The recommended stop for the first night's stay is the semiprivate, hiker-only campsite 9B4 (no campfires), .5mi farther along at the mouth of **Bechler River Canyon**.

Day 2: Campsite 9B4 to Three River Junction (3.5-4.5 hours, 7.5mi, 600ft ascent) The trail continues to parallel the river, climbing through fir-spruce forest alternating with meadows fringed by birch and boulder fields choked with raspberries, thimbleberries, and huckleberries galore. After 1.8mi, a signed side trail descends 300yd to a scenic overlook of **Colonnade Falls**, where the Bechler plunges 85ft in two stages. The steepening trail soon passes damp campsite 9B5 to reach the spectacular **Iris Falls**, a 40ft-high curtain of water spraying thick rainbow-filled mist into the air.

The trail ascends through more old fir-spruce forest past gliding cataracts with picturesque islets and riverside campsite 9B6 to another major ford (a 50ft-wide waist-deep wade). Upstream, the trail sees many muddy moments as it crosses several cold minor side streams before trailside campsite 9B7. A mile upstream, just before campsite 9B8 (and a pit toilet), is the last, less-serious ford, below a patch of burned forest.

Another mile on, the trail passes several algae-rich thermal areas fringing **Three Rivers Meadow**, then passes inviting campsite 9B9 (no campfires, two-night limit), with a hiker-only site tucked away on the east side of the canyon near the base of a thundering waterfall that descends from

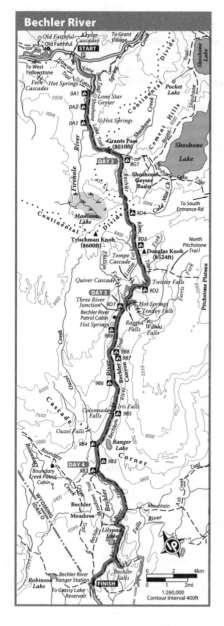

Bechler River

towering **Batchelder Column**. The **9B9 stock-only campsite** and an **NPS patrol cabin** lie across a bridge on the opposite riverbank.

It's worth the steep extra mile slog up out of the lovely river flats to the canyon's wild upper valley, where hidden campsite 9D1 (no campfires) awaits beyond a footbridge over the Bechler's **Ferris Fork**. The lovely site is perched on a peninsula near **Three River Junction**, overlooking the Gregg, Ferris, and Phillips Forks' tumbling confluence.

Day 3: Campsite 9D1 to Ferris Fork Hot Springs (3-4 hours, 4mi out-and-back, 500ft ascent) Since you've made it all this way, why not stay an extra day? When booking your trip, reserve another campsite in the 9B group and spend a day exploring the area around Three River Junction.

Beyond 9D1, the trail switches back uphill .5mi past 45ft **Ragged Falls** to an unsigned (but well-beaten) turnoff on the east side of the trail for **Ferris Fork Hot Springs**. The springs' submerged thermal source emanates from the middle of a 45ft-diameter, waist-deep soaking pool, where it mixes with chilly water from the stream's main channel, magically creating a legal five-star soak.

After checking out the interesting nearby thermal features, you might choose to bushwhack another .5-1.5mi upstream along the Ferris Fork to seek out a quintuplet of seldom-seen waterfalls: 33ft **Tendoy Falls**, 20ft **Gwinna Falls**, 35ft **Sluiceway Falls**, and 28ft **Wahhi Falls**.

Retrace your steps down into Bechler Canyon to your chosen 9B series campsite. If you're unable to reserve a campsite for the final night, it's a long but manageable 13.5mi descent back to the ranger station.

Day 4: Bechler River Canyon to Bechler Ranger Station (4-5 hours, 8-12mi, 800ft descent) Retrace your steps down the canyon to the **Bechler Ranger Station** via **Bechler Meadows Trail**, the most direct route, or the more scenic **Bechler River Trail**.

GROCERY STORES

Hamilton Stores at Canyon Junction, Bridge Bay, Fishing Bridge, Grant Village, Lake Yellowstone, Mammoth, and Tower-Roosevelt Junction carry basic groceries, plus limited camping and fishing supplies.

MONEY

There are 24-hour ATMs at Canyon Lodge, Canyon General Store, Fishing Bridge General Store, Grant Village General Store, Lake Yellowstone Hotel, Old Faithful Inn, Old Faithful General Store, Old Faithful Snow Lodge, Mammoth General Store, and Mammoth Hotel. The front desks of all park accommodations exchange foreign currency 8am to 5pm weekdays.

POST & COMMUNICATIONS

The only year-round **post office** is at Mammoth Hot Springs. Seasonal post offices are at Canyon, Lake, and Grant Villages and Old Faithful.

There is currently no public Internet access in the park. Most hotel rooms inside the park don't even have a telephone connection. You'll have to go to the towns that border the park for access.

Cell phone coverage is very patchy in the park. Bring yours along, but don't rely on it for emergency communications.

MEDICAL SERVICES

Yellowstone Park Medical Services operates three clinics:

Lake Hospital *(☎ 307-242-7241)* – Open 8:30am to 8:30pm daily, mid-May to mid-September, with a 24-hour emergency service

Mammoth Hot Springs Clinic *(☎ 307-344-7965)* – Open year-round 8:30am to 1pm and 2pm to 5pm weekdays except Wednesday afternoon

Old Faithful Clinic *(☎ 307-545-7325)* – Open 8:30am to 5pm daily, mid-May to mid-October

NPS emergency medical technicians and medics *(☎ 307-344-2132)* are on call 24 hours a day, year-round. First aid is available at visitor centers and ranger stations. In an emergency call ☎ 911. Emergency messages can be left on boards at park entrances and visitor centers.

SHOWERS & LAUNDRY

Canyon Village, Fishing Bridge RV Park, and Grant Village provide laundry and showers; Old Faithful Lodge and Roosevelt Lodge offer showers only; and Lake Lodge has laundry only. All facilities close in winter. Showers cost $3.

PHOTOGRAPHY

There are one-hour photo developing centers in Hamilton Stores at Canyon, Fishing Bridge, and Old Faithful.

The Teton Range's jagged "witch hat" spires comprise the centerpiece of spectacular Grand Teton National Park, attracting climbers from around the world. A row of twelve glacier-carved summits rises above 12,000ft with stunning abruptness, crowned by shark-tooth-shaped Grand Teton (13,770ft) and reflected in dozens of sublime glacial lakes.

EXPERIENCING
GRAND TETON

Grand Teton National Park lies just south of Yellowstone National Park and stretches 40mi along the compact, 15mi-wide range. On its west boundary the park merges with the Jedediah Smith Wilderness within Targhee National Forest. To the east is the Bridger-Teton National Forest. The abrupt east side of the Teton Range overlooks the Jackson Hole valley, where Jackson Lake catches the Snake River as it flows south from its source in Yellowstone National Park, while the gentler west side slopes toward Idaho's Teton Valley.

In many ways Grand Teton is a strange sort of park. Its main lake is dammed, there's a major airport within its borders, powerboats roar up and down Jackson Lake, hunters stalk elk within the park in autumn, and private homes and ranches dot the park landscape. These compromises were made to realize creation of the park back in 1950.

The park is dwarfed by Yellowstone, but this lends it a greater intimacy, allowing visitors to really get to know the area in a few days. Wherever you go in the park, the Tetons' splendor will continually draw your gaze. Lovers of alpine scenery will arguably find more to impress here than in Yellowstone.

Hikers, climbers, boaters, rafters, anglers, and other outdoor enthusiasts will find plenty to do. Specific hikes and detailed listings for other activities are found under respective areas of the park.

Note: The John D Rockefeller Jr Memorial Parkway is not strictly part of Grand Teton National Park but is administrated by the park, so we have generally listed it in this book under Grand Teton.

TETON NAMES

The park newspaper takes its name from the Shoshone name for the Teton range – the Teewinot, or "Many Peaks." The name Grand Tetons means "Large Teats" in French, which, as one author put it, is what happens when you let French fur trappers name a mountain range. The Snake gets its name from the local Shoshone, or Snake, Native American tribe.

Seeing the Sights

Must-sees include Jenny and Leigh Lakes. Take the ferry across Jenny Lake and walk at least partway up Cascade Canyon. Teton Park Rd is the park's most scenic drive, while Jenny Lake Scenic Dr is worth a detour. You'll find some of the best views of the Tetons from the top of Shadow Mountain, but it's a rough drive up a remote gravel road.

To get a feel for homesteader life, visit the Cunningham Cabin and Menor's Ferry. Amateur geologists should make a beeline for the Gros Ventre Slide, just outside the southeast corner of the park (Greater Yellowstone, p 217). For great photo ops (and a good chance of seeing bison) try nearby Mormon Row.

For some R&R take it easy on the beaches of Leigh Lake, Bradley Lake, or the north end of Colter Bay. For alfresco dining pack a lunch out to the picnic spots at the north end of Jackson Lake, en route to Yellowstone.

When You Arrive

Visitors must purchase a park entrance permit, which is valid for seven days for entry into both Grand Teton and Yellowstone National Parks. The entrance fee is $20 per vehicle, $15 for individuals entering by motorcycle or snowmobile, and $10 for individuals entering by bicycle, skis, or on foot. An annual pass costs $40.

There is no charge to transit the park on Hwy 26/89/191 from Jackson to Moran and out the east entrance to the Togwotee Pass. There is, therefore, no park fee to access Jackson Hole Airport.

Visitors receive a free copy of the park newspaper, *Teewinot*, which details the extensive program of ranger-led activities, and a brochure containing a good orientation map.

ORIENTATION

Three main roads lead to the park: US 26/89/191 from Jackson to the south, US 26/287 from Dubois to the east, and US 89/191/287 from Yellowstone National Park to the north. The park begins 4.5mi north of Jackson.

The least-used entry is the very rough gravel Grassy Lake Rd from Ashton, Idaho, to Flagg Ranch in the Rockefeller Memorial Parkway. The road is not recommended for RVs. There is no entry station along this road, so you'll eventually find yourself in the park for free, though there is an entry station on the way north into Yellowstone Park.

Entrance Stations

The park has three entrance stations: one at Moose (south) on Teton Park Rd west of Moose Junction, another 3mi inside the park at Moran (east) on US 89/191/287 north of Moran Junction, and a third (southwest) a mile or so north of Teton Village on the Moose-Wilson road.

Main Regions

The north half of the park is dominated by Jackson Lake, and the Tetons dominate the west. The northwest is the most remote and least-visited area of the park and can only be accessed as part of a multiday backpacking trip. This is the only part of the park where you might find grizzlies.

WINTER FUN IN GRAND TETON

Moose Visitor Center is the focus of winter activities and the place to get information on ski trail, weather, road, and avalanche conditions. All park campgrounds are closed in winter, but there's limited tent camping and RV parking ($5) near the Colter Bay Visitor Center.

Teton Park Rd is plowed from Jackson Lake Junction to Signal Mountain Lodge and from Moose to the Taggart Lake Trailhead.

From late December to mid-March rangers lead 1.5mi (2-hour) snowshoe hikes several times a week from Moose Visitor Center. Snowshoes are provided, and children over eight can take part. Make reservations at ☎ 307-739-3399.

The Snake River winds through flat glacial deposits on the south side of the park. The east side is bordered by the forested hills of the Bridger-Teton National Forest and the remote trails of the Teton Wilderness. Concentrated in the southwest are the stars of the show, the main Teton peaks, at the foot of which lie a string of lakes, including Jenny, Bradley, Taggart, and Phelps.

Major Roads

US 26/89/191, contiguous along the east bank of the Snake River between Jackson and Moran Junction, constitutes the main north-south route through the park. At Moran Junction US 89/191 joins US 287 heading north along the shore of Jackson Lake to the John D Rockefeller Memorial Pkwy; US 26 joins US 287 heading east to Dubois via Togwotee Pass.

Teton Park Rd links Moose Junction to Jackson Lake Junction and US 89/191/287 via Jenny and Jackson Lakes. The 5mi Jenny Lake Scenic Drive connects North Jenny Lake and South Jenny Lake Junctions; the road is two-way to Jenny Lake Lodge and one-way south of it. Gros Ventre Rd heads east from US 26/89/191 at the south end of the park to Kelly and out of the park into the Gros Ventre Valley. Antelope Flats Rd is 1mi north of Moose Junction, east of US 26/89/191.

Moose-Wilson Rd is a partially paved route (its southernmost 3mi are gravel) that connects Teton Village to Moose. RVs and trailers are not allowed on this road inside the park.

Visitor Service Hubs

Colter Bay is home to the highest concentration of visitor services, with a visitor center, gas station, grocery store, restaurants, Laundromat, showers, campground, RV park, and marina.

Farther south, **Jackson Lake Lodge** has shops, photo developing, and restaurants. Headed down Teton Park Rd, **Signal Mountain** has accommodations, a restaurant, gas station, and groceries.

Moose is the park's south hub, with a visitor center, gas station, accommodations, restaurants, groceries, and equipment rental.

INFORMATION

The **Grand Teton National Park headquarters** (☎ 307-739-3600, fax 307-739-3438; ✉ grte_inf@nps.gov; ⓦ www.nps.gov/grte; Box 170, Moose, WY 83012) shares the building with the Moose Visitor Center. For visitor information call ☎ 307-739-3300. For weather information contact the 24-hour recorded message at ☎ 317-739-3611.

If you're not clued in yet on what to see and do, rangers offer a 30-minute "Teton Highlights" talk daily at 11am and 3pm at the Colter Bay Visitor Center auditorium.

Three park concessionaires operate various accommodations, restaurants, marinas, and activities:

Dornan's *(☎ 307-733-2522;* W *www.dornans.com)*
Grand Teton Lodge Company *(GTLC; ☎ 307-543-3100, 800-628-9988;* W *www.gtlc.com)*
Signal Mountain Lodge *(☎ 307-543-2831;* W *www.signalmtnlodge.com)*

Tourist Offices

The helpful **Jackson Hole & Greater Yellowstone Visitor Center** *(☎ 733-3316;* W *www.jacksonholechamber.com; 532 N Cache St, Jackson; open 8am-7pm daily in summer, 8am-5pm in winter)* is a useful port of call for visitors headed north to the park from Jackson.

Visitor Centers

The **Grand Teton Natural History Association** *(☎ 307-739-3403)* sells books and maps at all park visitor centers:

Colter Bay Visitor Center *(☎ 307-739-3594; open 8am-5pm most of May, 8am-8pm daily Jun-early Sep, 8am-5pm Sep)* is on US 89/191/287, 6mi north of Jackson Lake Lodge.

Flagg Ranch Information Station *(☎ 307-543-2401; open 9am-5:30pm June-early Sep)* sits 2.5mi from Yellowstone's south entrance. This is not a full visitor center but provides information and backcountry and boating permits, plus rest rooms and a small bookstore.

Jenny Lake Visitor Center *(☎ 307-739-3343; open 8am-7pm daily Jun-Sep)* is on Teton Park Rd, 8mi north of Moose Junction. Facilities include a store, lockers, geology exhibits, a relief model, rest rooms, and telephones.

Moose Visitor Center *(☎ 307-739-3399; open 8am-5pm daily except Christmas Day, extended summer hours 9am-7pm June 3–Sep 2)* is on Teton Park Rd, half a mile west of Moose Junction. Backcountry, climbing, and boating permits are available here, as is information on weather, road, and avalanche conditions. Plans are on the drawing board to build a new center in the vicinity.

Ranger Stations/Backcountry Offices

There are backcountry offices at Colter Bay *(☎ 307-739-3595)* and Moose *(☎ 307-739-3309)* Visitor Centers. **Jenny Lake Ranger Station** *(☎ 307-739-3343, summer only)* offers backcountry permits and climbing information.

Policies & Regulations
BACKCOUNTRY PERMITS

Backcountry permits are required for all overnight backcountry trips in Grand Teton. Permits are free. Around a third of the backcountry sites can be reserved from January 1 to May 15 by mail *(PO Drawer 170, Moose, WY 83012, fax 307-739-3438)* or in person at Moose Visitor Center, for which there's a nonrefundable $15 fee. The remaining permits can be obtained in person a maximum of 24 hours in advance from the backcountry offices at Moose and Colter Bay Visitor Centers or Jenny Lake Ranger Station. If you don't have a reservation, your best bet is to apply early in the morning the day before your intended departure. A notice board at Moose Visitor Center indicates which backcountry sites are full that day.

Backcountry camping is restricted to camping zones. Hikers (with backcountry permits) can choose their own sites inside many of these areas, but in the most heavily used zones all sites are designated (indicated by marker posts). Fires are prohibited, except at a handful of lakeshore sites, so bring a stove. Campsites must be at least 200ft from waterways.

BOATING

All private craft must obtain a permit, which costs $10/20 seven-day/annual for motorized and $5/10 for nonmotorized craft (rafts, canoes, or kayaks). Permits are issued at the Moose and Colter Bay Visitor Centers and Buffalo Fork Ranger Station (just east of the park) and should be stuck on the port (left) side of the boat at the rear. Permits for Yellowstone are good for Grand Teton (and vice versa) but must be registered at either Moose or Colter Bay Visitor Centers.

Motorized craft (maximum 7.5 horsepower) are allowed only on Jackson and Jenny Lakes. Lakes permitting hand-propelled nonmotorized craft are Jackson, Two Ocean, Emma Matilda, Bearpaw, Leigh, String, Jenny, Bradley, Taggart, and Phelps. Sailboats, water skis, and sailboards are permitted only on Jackson Lake. Jet Skis are not allowed in the park.

Floating is prohibited within 1000ft of Jackson Lake Dam. Only hand-powered rafts, canoes, and kayaks are allowed on the Snake River. Watercraft are forbidden on other rivers.

On Jackson Lake, fires are forbidden along the east shore from Spalding Bay to Lizard Creek and otherwise permitted only below the high-water mark.

See the park's *Boating* and *Floating the Snake River* brochures.

FISHING

Anglers must carry a valid Wyoming fishing license. Fishing licenses are issued at Moose Village store, Signal Mountain Lodge, and Colter Bay Marina. Jackson Lake is closed to fishing in October. The Snake, Buffalo Fork, and Gros Ventre Rivers are closed November 1 to March 31. In general anglers are limited to six trout per day, with varying size limitations. Get a copy of the park's fishing brochure for details.

Dangers & Annoyances

Black bears and, to a much lesser extent, grizzlies are present in Grand Teton National Park. For cautionary advice see "Bear Necessities" on p 54).

Areas east of US 26/89/191, the region west of US 26/89/191 along the Snake River between Moose and Moran Junctions, and the John D Rockefeller Jr Memorial Pkwy are open to elk hunting mid-October to early December. The National Park Service (NPS) *Elk Ecology & Management* pamphlet offers more details and a map. If you must venture into these areas during hunting season, exercise caution (and don a bright orange vest).

AVOIDING THE CROWDS

Parking lots at popular trailheads and areas such as Jenny and String Lakes often fill up before 11am. Jenny Lake Campground is perennially full, and Signal Mountain

Campground fills up early in the day. The Death Canyon Trailhead parking lot fills up quickly due to vehicles parked for several days by climbers and backpackers. Cascade Canyon and the Solitude Lake hike can be humming with daytrippers in August.

You can avoid the crowds by choosing less popular campgrounds like Lizard Bay or Gros Ventre. Two Ocean and Emma Matilda Lakes, in the northwest section of the park, offer excellent hikes without the crowds.

WATCHING WILDLIFE

The following are the best places to hunker down at dusk or dawn with a spotting scope or binoculars:

✔ **Oxbow Bend** – moose, elk, sandhill cranes, ospreys, bald eagles, trumpeter swans, Canada geese, blue herons, white pelicans, and lots of mosquitoes

✔ **Willow Flats** – freshwater marsh habitat for birds, moose, elk, and beavers

✔ **Blacktail Ponds Overlook** – ospreys, eagles, and moose

✔ **Antelope Flats** – bison and pronghorns

✔ **Swan Lake** – beavers, trumpeter swans, geese

Getting Around

DRIVING

The speed limit on US 26/89/191 is 55mph; elsewhere it's generally 45mph. Gas stations are open year-round at Moose (24 hours, credit card only 8pm to 8am) and Flagg Ranch Resort and summers only at Colter Bay, Signal Mountain, and Jackson Lodge.

PUBLIC TRANSPORTATION

Grand Teton Lodge Company (GTLC; ☎ 800-628-9988) operates several buses a day in summer between Jackson, Jackson Airport, Jenny Lake Lodge, and Jackson Lake Lodge ($20 one-way). From Jackson Lake Lodge there are seven buses a day to Colter Bay ($4/7 one-way/round-trip; 15 minutes) and two buses a day to Jenny Lake ($12 round-trip; 30 minutes).

Buckboard and All-Star in Jackson offer winter taxis to Flagg Ranch. Alltrans can do hiker shuttles within the park. See p 70-71 for details about these three companies

Gray Line provides daily bus service in winter between Jackson and Flagg Ranch Resort ($35 one-way, $50 round-trip; reservations required).

ORGANIZED TOURS

GTLC runs half-day tours of Grand Teton ($30/15) and full-day tours of Yellowstone ($50/30) every other day from Jackson Lake Lodge. Make arrangements at the hotel activities desk.

Flagg Ranch offers full-day tours of Teton or Yellowstone departing at 9am. The cost is $60 per person, including lunch. Gray Line runs tours from Jackson to the park (eight hours, $45 pp, plus park entry). For details about wildlife viewing tours see p 37.

The road south from Yellowstone drops off the Yellowstone plateau at the end of the Rockefeller Parkway and offers the startling first views of the Tetons soaring above Jackson Lake. The drive continues past Lizard Creek Campground to several lovely beaches that offer some of the park's nicest picnic areas.

Jackson Lake is a natural glacial lake that has been dammed, so water levels fluctuate, dropping considerably toward the end of the summer. Mt Moran (12,605ft), named after famous landscape painter Thomas Moran, dominates the north end of the park. East of Jackson Lake, hidden among the hills, are Two Ocean and Emma Matilda Lakes. Visitor services are concentrated at Colter Bay Village.

COLTER BAY

At Colter Bay Visitor Center, the **Indian Arts Museum** *(admission free; open 8am-5pm most of May, 8am-8pm daily Jun–early Sep, 8am-5pm Sep)* displays an appealing selection of artifacts from the collection of David T Vernon. Free guided tours are offered daily in summer at 9am and 4pm. At other times visitors can leaf through the museum guidebook. The visitor center offers a decent collection of books on Native American history and lore. There are frequent craft demonstrations, and videos are shown all day on subjects ranging from wildlife to Native American art.

South of the visitor center is the marina and trailhead for hikes to **Swan Lake** and **Hermitage Point**. Just north of the visitor center is a popular picnic and **swimming area**, though you'll find countless other secluded swimming or sunbathing spots dotted around Jackson Lake.

For a nice evening or early morning stroll try the 45-minute **Lakeshore Trail**, which traces a figure eight across a causeway onto a small island. The trail goes through forest (take mosquito repellent) and dips onto the beach, or you can just mosey along the beach. The trail starts on a paved road beside Colter Bay Marina, or you can access it from the amphitheater next to the visitor center. Finish the hike at the amphitheater by 7pm or 9pm to catch the evening ranger talk.

Grand Teton Lodge Company (☎ 307-543-3111) offers guided fishing trips on Jackson Lake for $57 per hour for three people, plus full-day fly-fishing trips ($350 for two people). Regular fishing boats depart from Colter Bay Marina. GTLC also runs scenic floats for $40/20, as well as lunch and dinner trips – make bookings at the activity desks in Colter Bay and Jackson Lake Lodge.

Ranger Activities

A daily ranger-led "Fire & Ice" boat cruise runs daily at 1:30pm from Colter Bay Marina. Advance ticket purchase is recommended (☎ 307-543-2811).

Once a week rangers lead a 3.5-hour canoe trip along the Jackson Lake shoreline (reservations are required). Bring your own canoe or rent one at Colter Bay Marina. Ask at the visitor center about early morning birding walks.

Rangers also lead a daily morning walk from Colter Bay Visitor Center to Swan Lake (3mi; 3hrs) and an afternoon lakeside stroll to learn about geology.

AROUND JACKSON LAKE LODGE

Jackson Lake Lodge is worth a visit, if only for the stupendous views through its 60ft-tall windows. In cold weather the upper lobby boasts huge cozy fireplaces; in summer the fine outdoor seating area is a great place to grab a draft Snake River Lager and enjoy the views.

Rangers answer questions on the back deck of Jackson Lake Lodge daily from 6:30pm to 8pm, and there is a free talk on the history of the lodge every Sunday at 8pm.

The willow flats below the hotel balcony are one the park's best spots to catch views of moose. The nearby **Willow Flats turnout** offers views of Mt Moran, Bivouac Peak, Rolling Thunder Mountain, Eagles Rest Peak, and Ranger Peak.

A short walk from the lodge, **Christian Pond** is a good place to spot riparian birdlife. The trail to the pond crosses the main road by a bridge just south of the lodge.

About a mile north of Jackson Lake Lodge a rough dirt road branches east off the main road to a trailhead, from which it's a 1mi walk one-way (with a steep climb at the end) to **Grand View Point** (7586ft), which offers fine views of both the Tetons and Two Ocean Lake. You can also visit the viewpoint as part of the Two Ocean Lake hike (see p 136).

One of the most famous scenic spots for wildlife watching is **Oxbow Bend**, 2mi east of Jackson Lake Junction, with the reflection of Mt Moran as a stunning backdrop. Early morning and dusk are the best times to spot moose, elk, sandhill cranes, ospreys, bald eagles, trumpeter swans, Canada geese, blue herons, and white pelicans. The oxbow was created as the river's faster water eroded the outer bank while the slower inner flow deposited sediment.

Heading south on Teton Park Rd, you'll find interpretive displays along the west shoulder near **Jackson Lake Dam**. Built in 1916, the dam raises the lake level by 39ft and was paid for by Idaho farmers who still own the irrigation rights to the top 39ft of water. The dam was reinforced between 1986 and 1989 to withstand earthquakes.

South of here is the **Log Chapel of the Sacred Heart**, a pleasant picnic area.

SIGNAL MOUNTAIN SUMMIT ROAD

This 5mi paved road (no RVs) east of Teton Park Rd winds up to Signal Mountain's summit for a panoramic view of Jackson Hole. The best views aren't actually from the summit but rather three-quarters of the way up at Jackson Point Overlook, a short walk south from a parking area. William Jackson took one of his famous photos from this point in 1878. The views are best at sunrise.

The mountain's name dates from 1891, when Robert Ray Hamilton was reported lost on a hunting trip. Search parties agreed to light a fire atop Signal Mountain as soon as he was found. His body was found a week later floating in Jackson Lake.

A 6mi round-trip hiking trail leads to the summit from Signal Mountain Campground, through groves of scrumptious summertime huckleberries.

In winter Signal Mountain Rd is a good Nordic skiing route, with stunning views and an excellent 5mi downhill return run. You would need to ski 1mi south from Signal Mountain along a snowmobiling trail to get to the turnoff.

HIKING & BACKPACKING

The various intersecting trails in this region can be confusing, so pick up a free trail guide from the Colter Bay Visitor Center.

HERMITAGE POINT
Distance: 9.2mi (shorter loop 3mi)
Duration: 4 hours (shorter loop 1.75 hours)
Challenge: Easy
Elevation Change: Negligible

Try to time your return trip with dusk for the best chance of spotting moose, beavers, and trumpeter swans. You can make this an excellent and easy overnight backpacking trip by reserving backcountry campsite No 9 at Hermitage Point.

From Colter Bay Visitor Center follow the parking lot south past the marina to where the parking lot loops. The trail starts by the sign that reads "Foot Trail Only, No Road." The trail follows a former road for less than 10 minutes, turns right, then right again up to the Jackson Lake Overlook. The trail descends and passes along the left (east) side of lily-filled Heron Pond, then branches right and right again for 2.2mi to the cairn marking Hermitage Point (4.4mi, 1.75 hours). The return leg (4.8mi, two hours) loops back, taking a right to Third Creek and then left past the dragonflies and beavers of Swan Lake.

If you don't have the time for the entire Hermitage Point loop, then turn left at the southeast end of **Heron Pond** to **Swan Lake** and back for a 3mi (1.75 hour) loop.

TWO OCEAN LAKE & GRAND VIEW POINT
Distance: 6.4mi
Duration: 3.5 hours
Challenge: Easy-moderate
Elevation Change: 400ft

This hike has quite a different feel from others in the park. The Teton views are secondary to the beautiful lake and lush forest. The wildflowers are particularly stunning in July; the long grass makes long trousers a good idea. Abundant huckleberries and chokeberries make the lake prime black bear territory in summer. Set out by 8am for good birding and to fully appreciate the tranquil lake.

To reach the trailhead turn north onto the smooth gravel Pacific Creek Rd 1mi west of Moran Junction. After 2mi turn left onto the rougher Two Ocean Lake Rd for 2.5mi to the parking area.

The clear trail leads counterclockwise around the lake through lovely meadows, wildflowers, aspens, and good views of the Tetons. At the west end of the lake (1.25 hours from the trailhead) the trail branches off to the right; at the next junction, turn left to continue around the lake. Another option is to take the right branch and then a left branch for 1.3mi uphill to Grand View Point (7586ft). The second hill boasts the best views of Mt Moran, as well as Two Ocean and Emma Matilda Lakes. Return to the main lake trail the way you came.

From the lake junction take a right and continue around Two Ocean Lake – sometimes by the lakeshore, sometimes through open meadows – for about an hour to the trailhead.

HORSEBACK RIDING

Colter Bay corral offers 1.5- and 2.5-hour trail rides around Swan Lake for $25/38 (no discounts for children). There are also breakfast and dinner rides, either on horseback or (cheaper) wagon. Dinner horseback rides cost $45/29 for adults/children; dinner wagon rides cost $32/23. Make reservations at the **activities booth** *(open 7am-8pm)* next to the Colter Bay grocery store, preferably a couple of days in advance.

Jackson Lake Lodge offers guided horseback rides ($25/38 for one/two hours), as well as breakfast and dinner rides by horseback or wagon.

BOATING

Signal Mountain Marina *(☎ 307-733-5470; open 7am-7:30pm mid-May–mid-Sep)*, next to the lodge, rents all manner of floating vessels, from canoes ($9.50/60 per hour/day) to fishing boats ($20/120 per hour/day) and pontoon cruisers ($54/250 per hour/day), depending on lake levels. Reservations are accepted only for the larger boats. Kayaks should be available soon. Half-day guided fishing trips start at $165.

Busy **Colter Bay Marina** *(☎ 307-543-2811; open 8am-5pm, no rentals after 3pm)* provides fishing gear and licenses, as well as motorboat, rowboat, and canoe rentals. Don't expect anything too adventurous here, as canoes aren't allowed more than .25mi from the shore.

Grand Teton Lodge Company (GTLC) arranges daily scheduled lake cruises ($15/7.50 children under 11) from Colter Bay, including breakfast/dinner cruises to Elk Island ($28/46 for adults). GTLC operates an **activities booth** *(open 7am-8pm)* next to the Colter Bay grocery store. **Leek's Marina** *(☎ 307-543-2494)*, north of Colter Bay Junction, is a simpler affair, with a gas dock and overnight buoys.

Canoes and kayaks rented at the marinas are not supposed to be taken beyond Colter Bay or Half Moon Bay (from Colter Bay) or Dornan's Island (from Signal Mountain).

Trip Options

You'll find backcountry campsites around Jackson Lake at Deadman Point, Bearpaw Bay, Grassy Island, Little Mackinaw Bay, South Landing, Elk Island, and Warm Springs. These are often busy on summer weekends when the lake is chockablock with powerboats, sailboards, sailboats, and canoes. It's a good idea to book the sites in advance (there is a maximum three-night stay).

OARS (Outdoor Adventure River Specialists) *(☎ 209-736-4677, 800-346-6277; ⓦ www.oars.com)* offers multiday sea kayaking trips around Jackson Lake, as well as rafting. Rates are $200 for an overnighter or $680 for a five-day trip.

Moran Bay offers dramatic close-up views of Mt Moran and is probably the most popular destination from Colter or Spalding Bays. You can stop at Grassy

Island en route. Sample distances from Signal Mountain: Hermitage Point (2mi), Elk Island (3mi), Little Grassy Island (6mi); from Colter Bay to Little Mackinaw Bay is 1.5mi.

Alternatively, you can paddle from Lizard Creek Campground to backcountry trails on the northwest shore. Wilcox Point backcountry campsite (1.25mi from Lizard Creek) provides backcountry access to Webb Canyon along the Moose Basin Divide Trail (20mi). For a longer intermediate-level trip you can paddle down the twisting Snake River from Flagg Ranch to Wilcox Point or Lizard Creek.

Predominant winds are from the southwest and can be strong, especially in the afternoon, when waves can swamp canoes.

FISHING

Signal Mountain Marina offers pricey half/full-day fishing trips on Jackson Lake for up to two people for $189/365. Fish are cleaned and served at the restaurant. Colter Bay Marina charges $57 per hour (minimum two hours) for guided lake fishing, plus guided fly-fishing day trips for $350 for two people

CENTRAL TETONS
Map 10

South of Signal Mountain, Teton Park Rd passes The Potholes, an area pockmarked with depressions formed by huge blocks of melting glacial ice that were stranded by receding glaciers. Just south is the Mt Moran turnout.

JENNY LAKE SCENIC DRIVE

Seven miles south of Signal Mountain, the Jenny Lake Scenic Dr branches west to offer the park's most picturesque drive.

The **Cathedral Group turnout** boasts views of the central Teton spires, known as the Cathedral Group. Interpretive boards illustrate the tectonic slippage visible at the foot of Rockchuck Peak. **String Lake** is the most popular picnic spot, with dramatic views of the north face of Teewinot Mountain and Grand Teton from sandy beaches along its east side. The one-way road kicks in beyond String Lake, just before exclusive Jenny Lake Lodge.

Perched on the lake's glacial moraine, **Jenny Lake Overview** offers good views of the Tetons, tall Ribbon Cascade to the right of Cascade Canyon, and shuttle boats headed for Inspiration Point. Be careful not to miss the turnout, as you can't back up this one-way road.

Canoeing

String Lake is perfect for a family canoe trip or even just a splash about. The String Lake canoe-only put-in is at the end of a turnoff just before the Leigh Lake Trailhead parking lot.

Leigh Lake offers the most scenic day and overnight paddles and is particularly suited to families. To get to **Leigh Lake** requires a 120ft portage. There are six backcountry campsites on the lakeshore, of which three sites (16, 14A, and 14B) are only accessible by boat. From the portage point at the outlet of Leigh Lake to farthest campsite (16) is 3mi one-way. Leigh Lake is also a good spot for **fishing**.

JENNY LAKE

Jenny Lake is the scenic heart of the Grand Tetons and the epicenter of Teton's crowds. The lake was named after the Shoshone wife of early explorer and mountain man Beaver Dick Leigh. Jenny died of smallpox in 1876 along with her children.

The **visitor center** is worth a visit for its geological displays and 3D map of Jackson Hole. The cabin was formerly in a different location as the Crandall photo studio.

SNAKE RIVER FLOATING & RAFTING

Several outfitters run leisurely Snake River float trips ($40/25). The wildest white water flows south of the town of Jackson. For details about companies running that section of river, see the Jackson section in the Gateway Towns chapter (p 66). Most commercial float trips in Grand Teton National Park meet at the riverside pullout next to Moose Visitor Center. To book a float trip contact:

Barker-Ewing Float Trips (☎ 307-733-1800; W www.barker-ewing.com), based in Moose, offers float trips from Deadman's Bar to Moose.

Fort Jackson River Trips (☎ 307-733-2583, 800-735-8430; e info@scenicfloats.com; 135 N Cache Dr, Jackson) operates longer-than-average 14mi floats from Moose to Wilson (adults $34-40, children $23-29).

Solitude Float Trips (☎ 888-704-2800, 307-733-2871; W www.solitudefloattrips.com), in Moose, runs Deadman's Bar–Moose trips and sunrise trips ($40/25 adults/children), plus shorter 5mi floats.

Triangle X Float Trips (☎ 888-860-0005; W www.jackson-hole-river-rafting.com) offers dawn, daytime, and sunset floats ($38/$28 adults/children under 18), plus a four-hour early evening float and cookout ($48/36).

Flagg Ranch Float Trips (☎ 307-543-2861, 800-443-2311; W www.flaggranch.com) runs floats on the upper Snake River, three-hour scenic float trips ($40/26.50 adults/children under 12), and one-hour mild white-water trips through Flagg Canyon ($25/20) from mid-June to early September.

Signal Mountain Lodge (☎ 307-733-5470; W www.signalmtnlodge.com) runs scenic three-hour floats in the early morning and evening ($40/22 adults/children) from mid-May to mid-September.

You'll find boat put-ins on the Snake River near Oxbow Bend, at Pacific Creek, Deadman's Bar, Schwabacher's Landing, and Moose.

The easiest do-it-yourself float is the 5mi from just below Jackson Lake Dam to Pacific Creek Landing. Pacific Creek to Deadman's Bar and Flagg Ranch to Lizard Creek are considered intermediate floats. Anything south of Deadman's Bar is considered advanced. Deadman's Bar to the Moose landing is the most commonly offered commercial white-water trip and is considered Class II. Southgate (at Yellowstone's south entrance) to Flagg Ranch via Flagg Canyon is considered advanced Class III white water. The highest flows are in spring (early trappers didn't name the Snake the "Mad River" for nothing!). For information on Snake River flows call ☎ 800-658-571. Inner tubes and air mattresses are not allowed on the Snake River.

From the visitor center a network of trails leads clockwise around the lake for 2.5mi to Hidden Falls and then continues for a short uphill run to fine views at **Inspiration Point**. If you're on the trail in the early morning or late afternoon, branch off 15 minutes (about .5mi) from the visitor center on a short detour to **Moose Ponds** for a good chance of spotting moose. If you've made it to Inspiration Point, it's worth continuing up **Cascade Canyon** for as long as you can, as you've already done most of the hard climb. From here you can return the way you came or continue clockwise to the String Lake Trailhead to make a 6mi circle around the lake.

Alternatively, **Teton Boating Company** (☎ 307-733-2703) runs shuttles (*$7/5 adults/children aged 7-12 round-trip, $5/4 one-way; 8am-6pm, June–late Sep*) across Jenny Lake between the east shore boat dock near Jenny Lake Visitor Center and the west shore boat dock near Hidden Falls, offering quick (12-minute) access to Inspiration Point and the Cascade Canyon Trail. Shuttles run every 20 minutes, but expect long waits for return shuttles between 4pm and 6pm.

Rangers lead hikes from Jenny Lake Visitor Center daily at 8:30am to Inspiration Point (via the Jenny Lake ferry; 2.5 hours, 2mi). Numbers are limited to 25, and places are first come, first served; arrive at the visitor center by 8am to secure a token.

Canoes, kayaks, and boats with motors less than 8HP are allowed on Jenny Lake. The put-in is by the east shore boat dock and is accessed by a separate road that branches off the Lupine Meadows Trailhead road. Teton Boating Company rents small motorboats ($15 for the first hour, then $12 per hour or $75 per day). Teton Boating Company also offers hour-long scenic Jenny Lake cruises ($10/7) at 7pm. Reservations are a good idea (☎ *307-734-9227*).

Jenny Lake also offers good **fishing** and is stocked with lake, brown, brook, and Snake River cutthroat trout.

SOUTH OF JENNY LAKE

Just south of Jenny Lake, Teton Park Rd passes the turnoff to the Lupine Meadows Trailhead, for hikes to Surprise Lake and Garnet Canyon. On the east side of the road watch for **Timbered Island**, an enclave of forested glacial soils atop a sea of poorly drained sedimentary soils.

Two miles south of here, Teton Glacier turnout offers some of the best views of **Teton Glacier**, the largest in the park. The Taggart Lake Trailhead is 1.5mi farther.

Half a mile north of Moose Village, a paved road leads to a short trail and William Menor's homestead cabin on the Snake River's west bank, which today you can cross in a replica of **Menor's Ferry** (*early Jul–Aug*). The fine old photos of weathered ranchers and early visitors, plus the restored buggies and the original settlers' wagon brought over the Teton Pass in 1988, offer good insight into the lives of Jackson Hole's early settlers. Stop by the obligatory old-fashioned period **store** (*open 9am-4:30pm daily*).

The nearby **Chapel of the Transfiguration** (built 1924) offers a heavenly view of the Tetons through the altar window and Sunday services in summer.

Just beyond is the **Moose Entrance Station** and **Moose Visitor Center**, with videos and the largest selection of books in the park. The park's south hub, Moose also offers accommodations, restaurants, and shops and serves as the jumping-off point for many park activities.

HIKING & BACKPACKING

The Teton peaks are the park's real draw. Alpine hiking just doesn't get better than this.

LEIGH & BEARPAW LAKES
Distance: 7.4mi
Duration: 3.5 hours
Challenge: Easy
Elevation Change: Negligible

The Leigh Lake Trailhead is at the end of the side road off Jenny Lake Dr; don't confuse it with the String Lake Trailhead. Try to get an early start on this trail, as it's very popular, particularly with young families.

The trail quickly joins gorgeous String Lake. After 20 minutes a trail branches left across the outlet to Paintbrush Canyon (and a possible loop of String Lake). Instead, take the right branch and then turn right again to Leigh Lake. You may see people carrying their canoes over this portage area. As you continue north along Leigh Lake, your surroundings open up to fine views of Mt Moran and its Falling Ice and Skillet Glaciers. The dark central stripes in both Mt Moran and Middle Teton consist of a 1.5 billion-year-old lava-injected rock called diabase, which extends 7mi west into Idaho.

Continue past the lovely lakeside campsites 12A (group site), 12B, and 12C, which make wonderful easy overnight camping destinations for families with small children. Ten minutes farther along the trail you'll pass a lovely beach, with views of Mystic Island and, from left to right, Rockchuck Peak, Mt Woodring, Mt Moran, and Bivouac Peak.

After an hour (about 2mi) of Leigh Lake views, the trail heads into forest to a meadow junction; take the central path to the west side of Bearpaw Lake and campsites 17A and C. The trail then veers away from the lake for .5mi to Trapper Lake. Before you descend too far on the trail back to Bearpaw Lake, watch for a faint path that veers off to the left. This drops through forest and over a log bridge to campsite 17B, looping back to join the earlier junction. Return to String Lake the way you came.

Several backcountry campsites make this a great easy first backcountry trip. On Leigh Lake the most popular sites are 12B and 12C – you'll need to reserve these well in advance. Remoter sites 13 and 15 are accessible by foot on an unmaintained trail that leads north from the bridge over Leigh Lake outlet. The nicest site at Bearpaw Lake is 17B, with fine views of Rockchuck Peak. Site 17A is on the lakeshore below the path; 17C is more private but a bit uphill. Trapper Lake offers the quietest site (18A). These sites are among the few in Teton where campfires are allowed (in fire grates only).

LAKE SOLITUDE
Distance: 14.4mi with boat shuttle, 18.4mi without
Duration: 6-7 hours
Challenge: Moderate-difficult
Elevation Change: 2240ft

This hike is long, with an elevation gain of 2240ft, but is not especially tough, as the grade is quite gradual. The only steep sections are at the beginning near Inspiration Point and just before Solitude Lake. Moose and bear are frequently sighted along the trail.

It's worth shelling out $7 to take the boat shuttle, as this shaves off 4mi of slog. The first boat departs Jenny Lake at 8am, and the last boat heads back at 6pm. Bring a jacket; the boat crossing can be cold in the morning.

At Cascade Canyon dock a confusing network of trails heads off to the left, passing Hidden Falls after .2mi and switchbacking up to Inspiration Point in another .5mi. Shortly afterward, the horse trail from String Lake joins from the right.

The Cascade Canyon Trail carries on straight, past a lovely riverside beach and then a high cascade, with fine views of Grand Teton. About two hours (4.5mi) from the dock you reach a split in the valley. The left branch leads to South Fork and Hurricane Pass; instead turn right, climbing gently for 30 minutes to enter the Cascade Camping Zone (12 sites), which stretches for the next 30 minutes. From the end of the zone its about 10 minutes uphill to the lake, past a small cascade and a hitch rail, which marks the end of the line for horses. It's about three hours (7.2mi) from here back to the dock.

Lake Solitude is beautiful, but you're unlikely to enjoy much solitude. Glance northeast to the diagonal slash leading up the hillside (the trail up to Paintbrush Divide) and whisper a prayer of thanks that you are not headed up there. From here the return trip is all downhill. Camping is prohibited at the lake.

The best part is still to come, as the return hike affords full views of Mt Owen and Grand Teton. The mountains are in shade most of the afternoon. After about 2mi the trail passes a rock formation on the right known as The Wigwams. Return to the boat dock the way you came.

SURPRISE & AMPHITHEATER LAKES
Distance: 9.6mi (10.2mi with glacier overlook extension)
Duration: 5-6 hours
Challenge: Difficult
Elevation Change: 3000ft

This classic 10mi round-trip hike begins at the **Lupine Meadows Trailhead**. The route's views and accessibility make it very popular, so don't expect to have the trail to yourself. The route should be free of snow by late June. No water is available between the trailhead and the two lakes, which are almost at the top of the long climb, so make sure to bring plenty.

There are three designated campsites at Surprise Lake for those who want to stay overnight, though due to heavy use, several regeneration areas are off-limits.

The well-worn trail begins by gently winding through pine trees until it mounts a shoulder and the ascent begins in earnest. A junction with the Taggart and Bradley Lakes Trail lies atop the shoulder, 1.7mi and 40 minutes from the start. Keep right and begin to climb the series of wide switchbacks that ascend the flank of Disappointment Peak. You'll find expansive views over Taggart Lake and Jackson Hole. About 1.5 hours (3mi) from the trail-head you'll pass a signed junction with the Garnet Canyon Trail (see later in this section).

The switchbacks ease shortly before the lakes, and after 2.25 hours of solid climbing you'll finally reach the inviting green waters of **Surprise Lake**. The beauty of the pool, set in a hollow beneath jagged white rocks and cliffs, makes it an ideal place to recover from your exertion. The slightly bigger and starker **Amphitheater Lake** is just .2mi farther along the trail.

Side Trip: Extension to Teton Glacier Overlook To reach the overlook, continue following the trail around the northeast shore of Amphitheater Lake and keep right at several indistinct forks. Climb between the rocks to the top of a shoulder. The view into the next valley, which sweeps down from Grand Teton, is breathtaking. The razor-sharp spires and shat-tered ridgeline between Teewinot Mountain and Mt Owen to the north contrast with the flatlands of Jackson Hole that are visible between sheer valley walls south. The sense of vertical height is impressive and will leave more than a flutter in the hearts of vertigo sufferers. Retrace your steps to the trailhead.

GARNET CANYON
Distance: approx 12mi
Duration: 9 hours
Challenge: Very difficult
Elevation Change: 4800ft

This long hike takes you up along a climbers' route into a world of rock and ice. It can be done as a day hike but is best done as an overnighter, camping at either the Meadows or South Fork sites. You need to be well acclimatized for this hike and in good shape. Set off as early as possible, as afternoon weather systems are notoriously fickle up here.

For the first 3mi follow the Sunrise & Amphitheater Lakes hike, de-scribed earlier; at the trail junction branch to the left instead of right. From this junction the trail curves around the hillside to dramatic views of Garnet Canyon and Middle Teton (12,804ft). Just over a mile from the junction the maintained trail stops and the sometimes-indistinct climbers' path continues over boulder fields for 20 minutes to the Meadows campsite. If you aren't confident with bouldering and trail finding, this is a good place to call it a night (8.4mi round-trip, five hours).

The path splits right to Spalding Falls and the base camp for Grand Teton and left through indistinct boulder fields to switchback up to a small saddle, where you'll find a couple of campsites. From here the trail traverses a small snowfield, still here in August, and heads up the valley over a series of false saddles. There are several indistinct trails, and finding the right one involves some guesswork and bouldering. About 2mi from the meadows you'll finally reach the saddle between Middle and South Teton, with fabulous views down to Iceflow Lake and across to "The Wall" and Hurricane Pass. You'll doubtless meet groups of climbers headed up to Middle Teton.

From the saddle it's a 3.5- to four-hour return the way you came. Take great care over the rocks and snowfields as you return, as you'll be tired; this is no place to sprain an ankle or worse.

TAGGART & BRADLEY LAKES
Distance: 5.9mi
Duration: 3 hours
Challenge: Easy
Elevation Change: 560 ft

This pair of glacial lakes, named after surveyors who accompanied the 1872 Hayden Expedition, lies at the base of the Tetons in an area badly affected by wildfires but blessed with fantastic summer wildflowers. The lakes offer several easy loop options ranging from 3 to 5mi total. In summer it's best to plan an early start if you don't like the heat, since much of the trail lacks shade.

The Taggart Lake Trailhead is just off Teton Park Rd, 5mi north of Moose. Follow the trail northwest, past horse corrals, and take the first left at a junction after .2mi. After another 1.4mi turn right and climb open slopes to a point on the moraine wall overlooking **Taggart Lake**. Descend the short distance to the lakeshore and use a wooden footbridge to cross the outlet creek. The views of the Tetons from the shore are fantastic.

The trail winds around the east shore of Taggart Lake and passes a trail junction signposted for the parking area (a shortcut back if you're tired). Climb steadily away from Taggart Lake and crest the moraine wall separating Taggart and Bradley Lakes. Descend through the trees to reach the forested shores of **Bradley Lake** – a considerable contrast from the burn area around Taggart Lake. You'll reach a junction just before the trail reaches the shores of Bradley Lake. Turn right to begin the trip back to the parking area or forge ahead to explore the shores of Bradley Lake before returning to this junction. There is a campsite at Bradley Lake, but it's reserved for hikers on multiday loops of the Valley Trail.

You might want to combine your hike with the daily morning ranger-led wildflower and naturalist walks that depart from the Taggart Lake Trailhead.

AVALANCHE CANYON & LAKE TAMINAH
Distance: Approx 11mi
Duration: 6-7 hours
Challenge: Difficult
Elevation Change: 2300ft

Park at the Taggart Lake Trailhead (there's a convenient toilet here). After a couple of minutes branch right and then, 1.1mi from the trailhead, left to Taggart Lake. From Taggart Lake branch right toward Bradley Lake. As you curve around the north side of Taggart Lake, you'll lose sight of the lake. Shortly afterward is the faint turnoff left to Avalanche Canyon – if you start to climb the moraine hill to Bradley Lake, you've gone too far.

The trail heads up Avalanche Canyon, past a couple of steep sections carpeted in ferns, with views ahead to 11,490ft Mt Wister. As the trail becomes increasingly wet, you'll first hear and then see Taggart Creek. There's a good chance of spotting moose here. At the head of the valley, about 2.5 hours from the trailhead, look for the waterfalls up both branches of the valley – you are headed right to **Shoshoko Falls**.

The trail winds up a steep talus slope to the right of the falls and, once you've gained most of the elevation, swings left up a small gully to meet remote **Lake Taminah**. You can get close to the falls for great views down the valley. It's about 3.5 hours from the trailhead to this point.

Return the way you came. At the junction with the main Taggart-Bradley Lake Trail, you can head back to the trailhead, though it's worth detouring to **Bradley Lake** on the Bradley Lake Trail – this only adds an extra .7mi (30 minutes) to the hike. From Bradley Lake it's 2mi back to the trailhead.

DEATH CANYON
Distance: 8-10mi
Duration: 5 hours
Challenge: Moderate
Elevation Change: 1360ft

To reach the Death Canyon Trailhead, take the turnoff 3mi south of Moose on the Moose-Wilson road, then drive 1.6mi down the narrow dirt track. The parking area is small and often crowded with climbers' and backpackers' vehicles. The nearby White Grass Ranger Station was once an outfitters' cabin.

The trail starts off uphill for .9mi to the **Phelps Lake Overlook** (elevation 7,200ft) and then descends for .7mi through lovely aspen forest to a junction; take a right here. As you enter the towering gorge, the ascent kicks in – a relentless uphill over rocky switchbacks that quickly joins the cascading river. After about 1.5mi of hard slog the path flattens out and everyone breathes an audible sigh of relief. Devoid of the river's roar, the valley seems impressively serene.

The trail hits a junction by the lovely old patrol cabin, 3.7mi from the trailhead. The right branch climbs steeply to Static Divide, but the main trail up Death Canyon continues straight. Riverside willows here make for fine moose habitat. The trail crosses an impressive old log bridge and enters a lush forest filled with berries – prime bear territory. The campsites of the **Death Canyon Camping Area** pop up occasionally, as do views of the Death Canyon Shelf, an impressive layer of sedimentary rock atop harder granites and gneiss. You can continue along this trail as long as you wish, perhaps using one of the campsites as a picnic spot, though where the trail crosses the stream is a good turnaround point.

Retrace your steps. Back at the Phelps Lake Junction you'll face a 1.6mi hike back up the moraine hill, which somehow will seem a lot longer than it did earlier in the day.

PAINTBRUSH DIVIDE LOOP
Distance: 17.8mi
Duration: 2-3 days
Challenge: Moderate
Elevation Change: 3775ft

This overnighter is the most popular backpacking trip in the park, though some speed fanatics zip through on an epic day hike. That popularity means you'll have to either reserve campsites in advance or be somewhat flexible with your itinerary.

Day 1: String Lake Trailhead to Holly Lake (4 hours, 6.2mi, 2540ft ascent) The trail kicks off from the String Lake Trailhead, up Paintbrush Canyon to Holly Lake, just off the main trail, where you'll find two designated campsites at the lake's southeast corner. If the Holly Lake sites are booked, an alternative is to camp in the Upper Paintbrush Canyon Camping Zone.

Day 2: Holly Lake to North Fork Cascade Camping Zone (3 hours, 3.2mi, 1235ft ascent) You'll ascend steeply to join the main trail and continue uphill for an hour to Paintbrush Divide (10,645ft, 1235ft ascent) for amazing views. The trail then descends along broad switchbacks to reach Lake Solitude after another hour or so. You can take it easy and camp in the nearby North Fork Cascade Camping Zone or continue all the way down Cascade Canyon to either the String Lake Trailhead or to Jenny Lake via the shuttle boat (see the Lake Solitude hike, p 141, for details of this stretch).

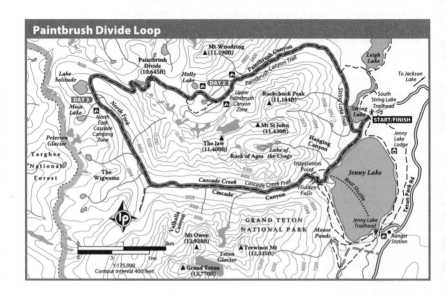

As its name suggests, this trail follows a high-altitude scenic route, dipping in and out of the neighboring Jedediah Smith Wilderness. Numerous side routes lead up the canyons or passes on either side of the trail, allowing easy access and exits.

Days 1 & 2 Day one is the same as the Paintbrush Divide Loop. Day two also follows this route as far as the junction between the North and South Forks of Cascade Canyon, where the trail branches up the South Fork to the **South Fork Cascade Camping Zone** (19 campsites). (An alternative start from Jenny Lake shaves off a day.)

Day 3: South Fork Cascade Camping Zone to Alaska Basin (3-3.5 hours, 6.1mi, 1992ft ascent) The trail takes you up to the Avalanche Divide junction and right (southwest) to Hurricane Pass (10,372ft), with unsurpassed views of Grand, South and Middle Tetons. (An excursion from the Avalanche Divide junction leads 1.6mi to the divide, a scenic overlook above Snowdrift Lake.) From the pass the trail descends into the Jedediah Smith Wilderness, past Sunset Lake, into the **Basin Lakes** of the Alaska Basin, where you'll find several popular campsites. No permits are needed here since you're outside the park, but you must camp at least 300ft from lakes and 50ft from streams.

Day 4: Alaska Basin to Marion Lake (4.5 hours, 8.2mi) The trail crosses South Fork Teton Creek on stepping stones and switchbacks up the Sheep Steps to the wide saddle of Mt Meek Pass (9726ft) to reenter the park. The trail dips for the next 3mi into the remarkable **Death Canyon Shelf** and camping zone. Past the turnoff to Death Canyon, the trail climbs to Fox Creek Pass (9,560ft) and continues southwest over a vague saddle to **Marion Lake** and its designated campsites.

Day 5: Marion Lake to Teton Village (5 hours, 9.7mi) The trail descends into the Upper Granite Canyon Camping Zone and continues past the Upper Granite Canyon patrol cabin to the junction with the Valley Trail. From here continue south to the Granite Creek Trailhead (left) or straight on to Teton Village.

Other Combinations The Teton Crest Trail can be accessed from the east by several steep canyons. The main trailheads, south to north, are Granite Canyon, Death Canyon, Taggart Lake, Lupine Meadows, Jenny Lake, and String Lake/Leigh Lake. You can hike from almost any of these canyons to the other to make a combination hike of any length. Options include:

Open Canyon to Granite Canyon – one-night 19.3mi loop from the Granite Creek Trailhead

Granite Canyon to Death Canyon – a two- to three-night 25.7mi loop via the Teton Crest Trail

Death Canyon to Open Canyon – a 24.7mi loop from the Death Canyon Trailhead

MARION LAKE & DEATH CANYON
Distance: 18mi (or 23mi loop)
Duration: 2 days
Challenge: Moderate
Elevation Change: 600ft, 4800ft descent

This overnighter starts by taking the Jackson Hole Aerial Tram ($16) to gain a welcome 2.5mi of elevation. From the tram (also known as the "Rendezvous Tram") descend to a junction at the park boundary and turn right to descend into the South Fork of Granite Canyon. Take a left at the next junction and then a right at the next two junctions to descend into the North Fork. From here it's a short climb to lovely **Marion Lake**, 6.6mi from the trailhead, where you'll find three designated campsites.

The next day takes you 2.3mi up to **Fox Creek Pass**, from which it's all downhill for 9mi, through the lovely forests of Death Canyon to the Phelps Lake Overlook and the Death Canyon Trailhead. To avoid a car shuttle, you can hike south at the junction before Phelps Lake along the Valley Trail to Teton Village (5.5mi).

You can do this hike in the opposite direction and save a few bucks (the downhill tram ride is free of charge), but you'll gain a lot more elevation.

Other Hikes

Other good options include the 12mi round-trip day hike or easy overnighter to **Marion Lake** from the Jackson Hole Aerial Tram and the day-hike loop from the top of the tram down the South Fork into **Granite Canyon** and back to Teton Village (13mi).

For an easy overnight backpacking trip see the Leigh & Bearpaw Lakes hike (p 141).

ROCK CLIMBING & MOUNTAINEERING

Garnet Canyon is the gateway to the most popular scrambles to Middle and South Teton and the technical ascent of Grand Teton. These nontechnical climbs can be handled as day hikes from bases at the Meadows, South Fork, Caves, or Moraine campsites, but you need to know what you're doing and be with someone who knows the routes.

Day climbers don't need to register, but all climbers staying overnight need a backcountry use permit (see Policies & Regulations, p 131). Call ☎ 307-739-3604 for recorded climbing information.

The **Jenny Lake Ranger Station** *(☎ 307-739-3343; open 8am-6pm Jun-Sep)* is ground zero for climbing information. A board shows availability of campsites in Garnet Canyon. Climbing guidebooks are for sale, including a series of Alpenglow Climbing Guides to the most popular climbs.

The **American Alpine Club's Climbers Ranch** *(☎ 307-733-7271; Teton Park Rd)* just south of the Teton Glacier turnout, operates an inexpensive summer **dormitory** *($8 bunks; open to climbers only, mid-June–mid-Sep)*, with cooking facilities and showers; reservations advised.

For instruction and guided climbs contact **Exum Mountain Guides** *(☎ 307-733-2297; W www.exumguides.com)* at Jenny Lake or **Jackson Hole**

Mountain Guides (☎ *307-733-4979, 800-239-7642;* W *www.jhmg.com; 165 N Glenwood St, Jackson).* Exum runs climbing schools at Hidden Falls on Jenny Lake's west shore and has a base camp at Grand Teton's Lower Saddle (11,600ft). It's also the slightly more expensive of the two.

BIKING

The are bike lanes on either side of the 3mi one-way **Jenny Lake Scenic Dr** (bicycles can ride both ways), plus there's a short bike-only section from near the Jenny Lake turnout to Jenny Lake campground.

The only other option is the **Riverside (RKO) Rd,** which parallels the scenic Snake River, offering some fine wildlife viewing opportunities. The road branches off Teton Park Rd just north of the Cottonwood Creek turnout and leads east and then north 15.5mi down a bumpy dirt track, rejoining the main road just south of the Signal Mountain Rd turnoff. You'll have to arrange a vehicle shuttle or be prepared to cycle the 12mi south back to Cottonwood Creek along busy Teton Park Rd.

THE EASTERN SLOPES
Map 9

Highway 26/89/191 traverses the park's east flank for about 25mi from the Moran Junction to the park's south gate past sagebrush flats and the occasional ranch – always with the Tetons diverting the eye westward. The area holds reflections of Jackson Hole's early homesteaders, whose hardscrabble lives are best symbolized by the valley's characteristic buck and rail fences.

MORAN TO BLACKTAIL BUTTE

Ranchers Pierce and Margaret Cunningham, an early major supporter of Grand Teton National Park, homesteaded at **Cunningham Cabin** in 1890, 6mi south of Moran Junction; a short trail elucidates local homesteading.

Four miles south of here, the **Snake River Overlook** offers good panoramas of the Tetons and opportunities for wildlife watching, though forest growth means the photo ops aren't as good as when Ansel Adams immortalized the shot.

A better place for photos is **Schwabacher's Landing**, a popular rafting put-in 4mi farther south. The views of the Tetons reflected in the meandering river rank as some of the park's most sublime. The landing is accessed via a short dirt road.

East of Blacktail Butte, an unpaved road connects Antelope Flats Rd to the north with Gros Ventre Rd to the south (when not washed out), passing **Mormon Row**, a series of pioneer barns and cabins. A nearby bison herd, the Teton backdrop, and gorgeous post-dawn light make this area exceptionally popular with photographers. There are two barns north of the junction and two south, including one in a photogenic state of collapse.

Gros Ventre Rd leads east to the Gros Ventre Slide (see p 217 in the Greater Yellowstone chapter for details).

MOUNTAIN BIKING

Antelope Flats offers a quiet, scenic, easy ride on both paved and dirt roads, past herds of bison, Teton views, and the barns of Mormon Row. Biking tour companies like Backroads and Teton Mountain Bike Tours (see the Activities chapter, p 29) run trips here. From the highway turnout by Blacktail Butte a 13.5mi (2-hour) loop takes in Mormon Row and the settlement of Kelly, returning via Antelope Flats Rd.

Just east of the park in Bridger-Teton National Forest, **Shadow Mountain** offers a fairly strenuous 9mi round-trip loop ride (with an elevation gain of 1300ft) along a gravel road. Set off from the parking lot at the end of paved Antelope Flats Rd. Just over .5mi past the summit a single-track path heads left down the hillside to connect with the gravel road, offering an exciting downhill run.

JOHN D ROCKEFELLER JR MEMORIAL PARKWAY
Map 9

This NPS-managed parkway is a 7.5mi corridor linking Yellowstone and Grand Teton National Parks. The US Congress recognized Rockefeller's contribution to the creation of Grand Teton National Park by designating this 24,000-acre parkway in his honor in 1972. The area acts as a transition between the two national parks, combining characteristics of both, though less spectacular than either. Activities focus around historic Flagg Ranch, which was established as US Cavalry post in 1872.

ORIENTATION & INFORMATION

North-south US 89/191/287 is the main road through the parkway. The turnoff to Flagg Ranch Rd is 2mi south of Yellowstone's South Entrance Station and 15mi north of Colter Bay Village. The turnoff to Grassy Lake Rd, which leads west to Ashton, Idaho, is just north of Flagg Ranch.

The **Flagg Ranch Information Station** (☎ 307-543-2401; open 9am-6pm daily Jun-Sep) is near the Grassy Lake Rd turnoff. **Flagg Ranch Resort** (☎ 307-543-2861, 800-443-2311; Ⓦ www.flaggranch.com) offers parkway accommodations and activities. The gas station, restaurant, and cabin accommodations at Flagg Ranch are open year-round and are a popular winter launching pad north into Yellowstone National Park.

No permits are required for backcountry camping in the parkway, though campers must keep a minimum of 1mi from roads and 100ft from water sources. Fires are generally allowed, but check current regulations at the information station. No bikes or pets are permitted on trails.

GRASSY LAKE ROAD

The 52mi east-west Grassy Lake Rd links US 89/191/287 to US 20 at Ashton, Idaho, offering an infrequently used "back way" into the national parks. The road follows an old Native American trade and hunting route. Numerous lakes and streams – and endless fishing, hiking, and camping options – lie hidden in the Jedediah Smith Wilderness south of Grassy Lake Rd and in the Winegar Hole Wilderness north of it. Grassy Lake Rd is also a good mountain biking route.

Shortly after crossing the Polecat Creek Bridge, the pavement ends and the graded gravel road parallels the north bank of the Snake River. Camping along this corridor is only allowed in designated sites, which are popular with anglers, hunters, and folks headed west along the rough Reclamation Rd (USFS Rd 261) to explore the Cascade Corner in Yellowstone's lush Bechler region.

The road is open until snow conditions warrant its closure in late fall, when snowmobiles take over.

HIKING

Polecat Creek offers a pleasant stroll if you're staying overnight at Flagg Ranch. The trail leads across Grassy Lake Rd from the main parking lot, passing two turnoffs to the right and an employee-housing loop before branching right to peaceful Oxbow Meadows. From here you can take a left at the next junction over a small creek to **Huckleberry Hot Springs**. The Park Service advises against bathing here due to high radiation levels in the water (caused by naturally occurring radon), but this doesn't seem to deter local employees, who come here for post-shift alfresco soaks. You can also get to the springs from a parking lot 1mi west of Flagg Ranch, though you need to ford Polecat Creek on this route, so bring waterproof shoes. This former road led to a hot springs resort until that was torn down in 1983.

A fairly interesting hiking trail also runs beside the volcanic walls of Flagg Canyon, northeast of Flagg Ranch. Get the brochure *Flagg Ranch Area Trails* from the information station.

Along Grassy Lane Rd 2.2mi west of Flagg Ranch is the Glade Creek Trailhead, which accesses the rarely visited northwest corner of the park and its Berry Creek and Moose Creek Trails.

OTHER ACTIVITIES

At Flagg Ranch Resort, Flagg Ranch Rafting offers three-hour scenic **floats** ($40/27 adults/children) and a one-hour white-water trip ($25/20) from mid-June to early September.

Flagg Ranch runs hour-long **horseback riding** trips hourly from June to September ($25).

In winter (mid-Dec–early March) Flagg Ranch Resort rents **snowmobiles** (starting at $140/day), **cross-country skis** ($10/15 half/full day), and **snowshoes** ($7/12). Snowmobile rental includes clothing and the first tank of gas, but vehicles are only licensed for use in Yellowstone National Park. Guided **snowcoach tours** to Yellowstone ($100 per person with lunch) are also available, as are snowmobile shuttles. Winter packages include transport from Jackson. You'll find **Nordic skiing** around Polecat Creek.

MONEY

Look for 24-hour ATMs at Dornan's and Jackson Lake Lodge and other ATMs at Colter Bay grocery store and Signal Mountain.

POST & COMMUNICATIONS

You'll find post offices at Colter Bay (summer only), Kelly, Moose, and Moran Junctions.

At Moose, Dornan's gift shop has Internet access at $1 for 10 minutes.

Pay phones are common in the park. Cell phones enjoy better reception here than in Yellowstone due to the park's proximity to Jackson, though reception breaks up in the canyons of the Teton Range.

MEDICAL SERVICES

The **Grand Teton Medical Clinic** (☎ 307-543-2514, 307-733-8002; open 10am-6pm mid-May–mid-Oct) is near the Chevron station at Jackson Lake Lodge.

SHOWERS & LAUNDRY

Colter Bay Village provides public showers ($3; open 8am-9pm) and laundry service (washers $1.25). Flagg Ranch RV Park also has public showers ($3.25; open 9am-9pm) and laundry ($1 a load).

CAMPING SUPPLIES

Moosely Seconds at Dornan's rents and sells mountaineering and camping equipment. Rentals include sleeping bags ($7 per day), tents ($10), ice axes ($6), and crampons ($10), with discounted weekly rates.

SPORTS EQUIPMENT

Adventure Sports (☎ 307-733-3307; open 9am-6pm daily) at Dornan's in Moose Village, rents bikes for $8 to $9 per hour, $18 to $22 per half day, and $25 to $29 for a full day, as well as kids' bikes and trailers. It also offers a range of spares and a repair shop and is a good place to get information on local trails. Ask about biker shuttles. Adventurous boaters can also rent canoes and kayaks here for $35 per day, with discounts for weekly rental.

Also at Dornan's, **Snake River Angler** sells and rents equipment and offers fishing licenses and guided trips.

Dornan's also rents cross-country skies, snowshoes, and sleds.

YELLOWSTONE & GRAND TETON
MAP SECTION

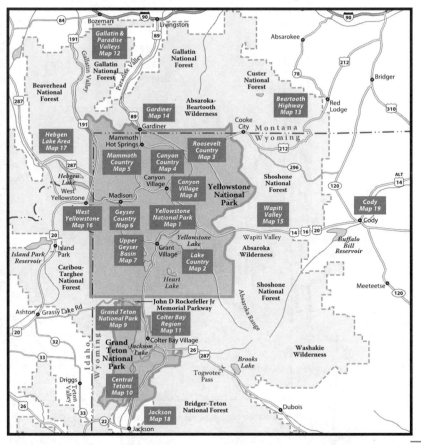

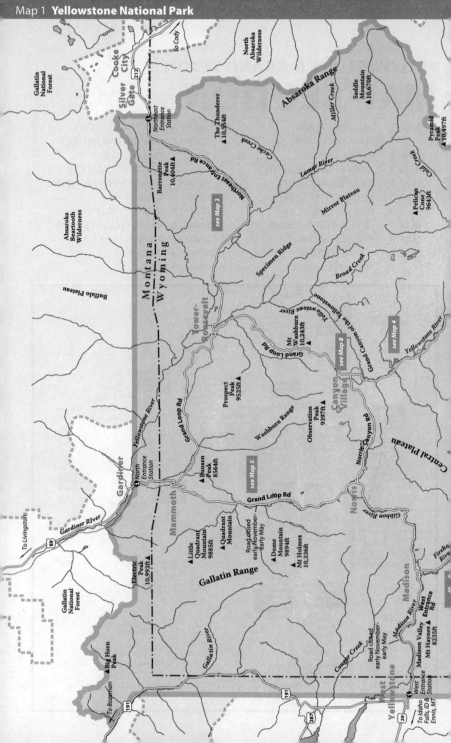

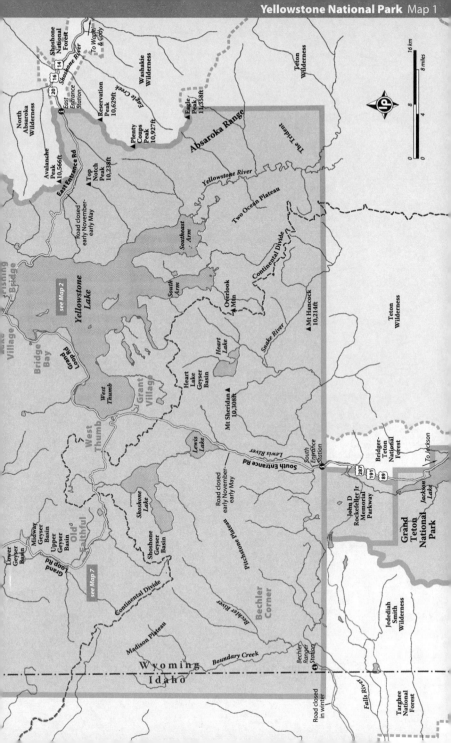

Map 2 **Lake Country**

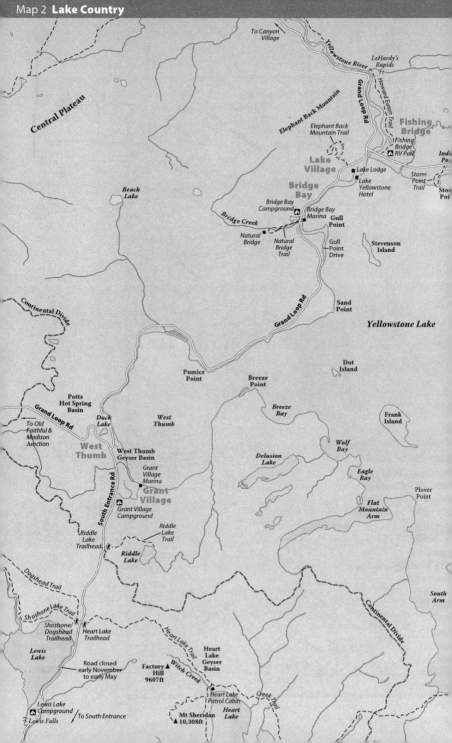

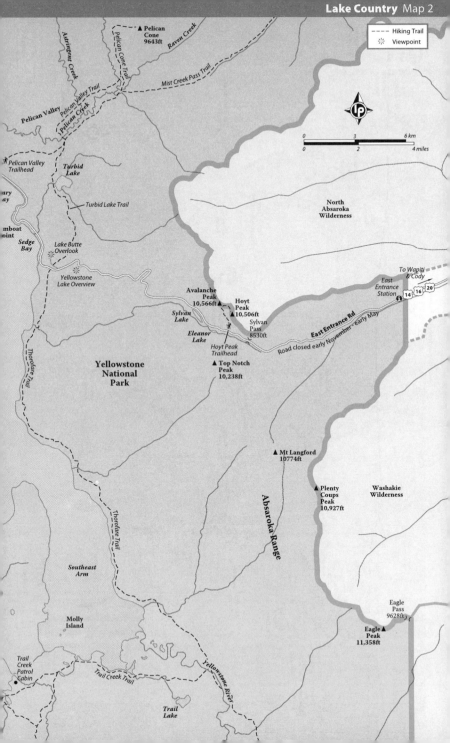

Hiking Trail
Viewpoint

Pelican Cone 9643ft

Raven Creek

Astringent Creek

Pelican Cone Trail

Mist Creek Pass Trail

Pelican Valley Trail

Pelican Creek

Pelican Valley

Pelican Creek

Pelican Valley Trailhead

Turbid Lake

Turbid Lake Trail

North Absaroka Wilderness

To Wapiti & Cody

East Entrance Station

14 16 20

Sedge Bay

Lake Butte Overlook

Yellowstone Lake Overview

Avalanche Peak 10,566ft

Hoyt Peak 10,506ft

Sylvan Lake

Sylvan Pass 8530ft

East Entrance Rd

Road closed early November–early May

Eleanor Lake

Hoyt Peak Trailhead

Thorofare Trail

Yellowstone National Park

Top Notch Peak 10,238ft

Mt Langford 10774ft

Plenty Coups Peak 10,927ft

Washakie Wilderness

Absaroka Range

Thorofare Trail

Southeast Arm

Molly Island

Eagle Pass 9628ft)

Trail Creek Patrol Cabin

Trail Creek Trail

Yellowstone River

Eagle Peak 11,358ft

Trail Lake

0   3   6 km
0   2   4 miles

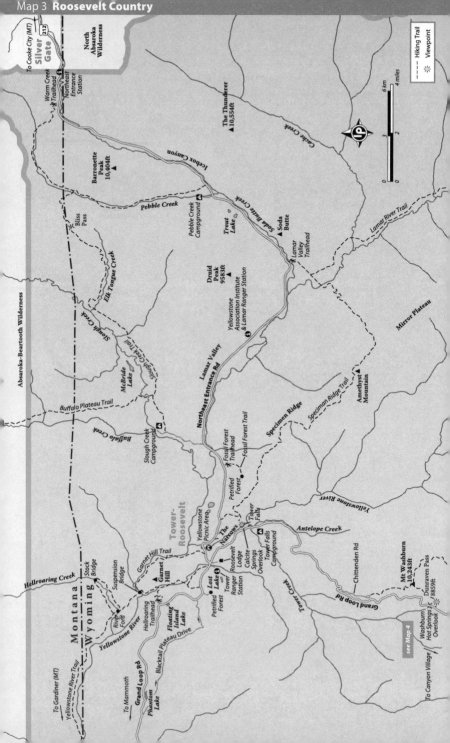

Map 3 **Roosevelt Country**

North Absaroka Wilderness

To Cooke City (MT)

Silver Gate

212

Warm Creek Trailhead

Northeast Entrance Station

The Thunderer ▲ 10,554ft

Cache Creek

Hiking Trail

Viewpoint

6 km

4 miles

Barronette Peak 10,404ft

Icebox Canyon

Pebble Creek

Bliss Pass

Pebble Creek Campground

Trout Lake

Soda Butte Creek

Soda Butte

Lamar River Trail

Elk Tongue Creek

Druid Peak 9583ft

Lamar Valley Trailhead

Slough Creek

Yellowstone Association Institute & Lamar Ranger Station

Mirror Plateau

McBride Lake

Slough Creek Trail

Absaroka-Beartooth Wilderness

Buffalo Plateau Trail

Lamar Valley

Northeast Entrance Rd

Specimen Ridge Trail

Amethyst Mountain ▲

Buffalo Creek

Slough Creek Campground

Specimen Ridge

Fossil Forest Trailhead

Fossil Forest Trail

Yellowstone River

Petrified Forest

Tower-Roosevelt

Yellowstone Picnic Area

The Narrows

Tower Falls

Antelope Creek

Hellroaring Creek

Stock Bridge

Suspension Bridge

Garnet Hill Trail

Garnet Hill ▲

Roosevelt Lodge

Calcite Springs Overlook

Tower Falls Campground

Montana

Wyoming

Yellowstone River Trail

River Ford

Hellroaring Trailhead

Yellowstone River

Lost Lake

Tower Ranger Station

Petrified Forest

Floating Island Lake

Tower Creek

Chittenden Rd

Mt Washburn 10,243ft ▲

Dunraven Pass 8859ft

To Gardiner (MT)

To Mammoth

Grand Loop Rd

Blacktail Plateau Drive

Phantom Lake

Grand Loop Rd

Washburn Hot Springs Overlook

see Map 4

To Canyon Village

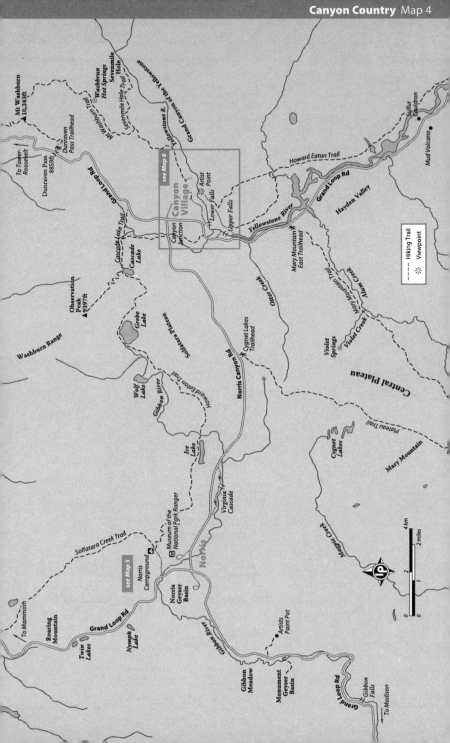

Mt Washburn
▲10,243ft

To Tower-
Roosevelt

Dunraven Pass
8859ft

Dunraven Pass Trailhead

Mt Washburn Trail

Washburn Hot Springs

Sevenmile Hole Trail

Sevenmile Hole

Yellowstone R.

Grand Canyon of the Yellowstone

Grand Loop Rd

see Map 8

Canyon Village

Artist Point

Lower Falls

Upper Falls

Canyon Junction

Howard Eaton Trail

Grand Loop Rd

Sulfur Cauldron

Mud Volcano

Yellowstone River

Hayden Valley

Mary Mountain East Trailhead

Otter Creek

Mary Mountain Trail

Alum Creek

Violet Creek

Violet Springs

Central Plateau

Cascade Lake Trail

Cascade Lake

Observation Peak
▲9397ft

Washburn Range

Grebe Lake

Solfatara Plateau

Norris Canyon Rd

Cygnet Lakes Trailhead

Plateau Trail

Cygnet Lakes

Mary Mountain

Wolf Lake

Gibbon River

Howard Eaton Trail

Ice Lake

Virginia Cascade

Maple Creek

Museum of the National Park Ranger

Solfatara Creek Trail

see Map 5

Norris Campground

Norris

Norris Geyser Basin

To Mammoth

Roaring Mountain

Grand Loop Rd

Twin Lakes

Nymph Lake

Gibbon River

Artists Paint Pot

Gibbon Meadow

Monument Geyser Basin

Grand Loop Rd

Gibbon Falls

To Madison

Hiking Trail
Viewpoint

4 km
2 miles

2

2
0
0

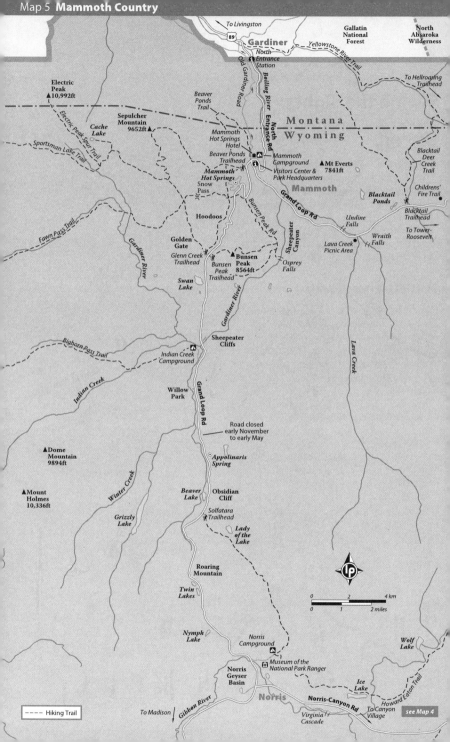

Map 5 Mammoth Country

To Livingston

89

Gardiner

To Hellroaring
Trailhead

North
Entrance
Station

Gallatin
National
Forest

North
Absaroka
Wilderness

Yellowstone River Trail

Electric
Peak
▲10,992ft

Beaver
Ponds
Trail

Montana

Wyoming

Blacktail
Deer
Creek
Trail

Electric Peak Spur Trail

Cache
Lake

Sepulcher
Mountain
9652ft ▲

Mammoth
Hot Springs
Hotel

Boiling River

North Entrance Rd

Old Gardiner Road

Beaver Ponds
Trailhead

Mammoth
Campground

Mammoth
Hot Springs

▲Mt Everts
7841ft

Childrens'
Fire Trail

Sportsman Lake Trail

Visitors Center &
Park Headquarters

Mammoth

Blacktail
Ponds

Blacktail
Trailhead

Snow
Pass

Grand Loop Rd

To Tower-
Roosevelt

Hoodoos

Undine
Falls

Gardiner River

Fawn Pass Trail

Golden
Gate

Bunsen Peak Rd

Sheepeater
Canyon

Wraith
Falls

Lava Creek
Picnic Area

Glenn Creek
Trailhead

▲Bunsen
Peak
8564ft

Bunsen
Peak
Trailhead

Osprey
Falls

Swan
Lake

Gardiner River

Lava Creek

Bighorn Pass Trail

Sheepeater
Cliffs

Indian Creek
Campground

Indian Creek

Willow
Park

Grand Loop Rd

Road closed
early November
to early May

Dome
Mountain
9894ft

Appolinaris
Spring

Winter Creek

Beaver
Lake

Obsidian
Cliff

▲Mount
Holmes
10,336ft

Grizzly
Lake

Solfatara
Trailhead

Lady
of the
Lake

Roaring
Mountain

lp

Twin
Lakes

0   2   4 km
0   1   2 miles

Nymph
Lake

Norris
Campground

Wolf
Lake

Museum of the
National Park Ranger

Norris
Geyser
Basin

Ice
Lake

Howard Eaton Trail

Norris

Norris-Canyon Rd

To Canyon
Village

To Madison

Gibbon River

Virginia
Cascade

see Map 4

- - - Hiking Trail

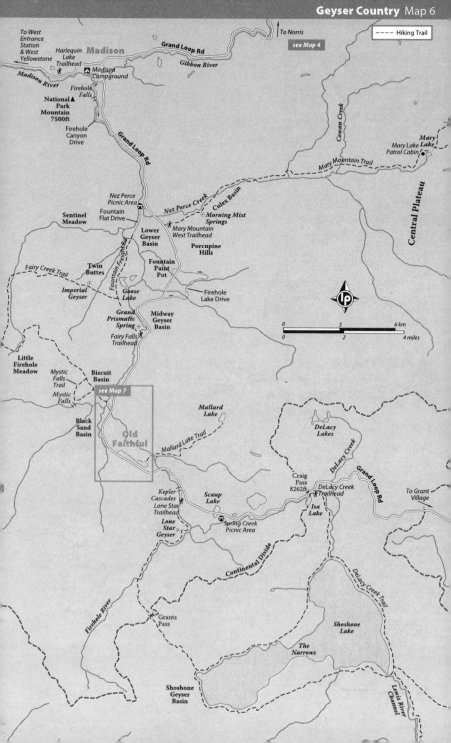

- - - - Hiking Trail

To West
Entrance
Station
& West
Yellowstone

Harlequin
Lake
Trailhead

Madison

Grand Loop Rd

Gibbon River

To Norris

see Map 4

Madison River

Madison
Campground

Firehole
Falls

National
Park
Mountain
7500ft

Firehole
Canyon
Drive

Grand Loop Rd

Cowan Creek

*Mary
Lake*

*Mary
Mary Lake Patrol Cabin*

Mary Mountain Trail

Central Plateau

Nez Perce
Picnic Area

Fountain
Flat Drive

Nez Perce Creek

Culex Basin

Morning Mist
Springs

Mary Mountain
West Trailhead

**Sentinel
Meadow**

**Lower
Geyser
Basin**

**Porcupine
Hills**

Fairy Creek Trail

**Twin
Buttes**

Fountain Freight Rd

**Fountain
Paint
Pot**

*Imperial
Geyser*

*Goose
Lake*

*Grand
Prismatic
Spring*

**Midway
Geyser
Basin**

Firehole
Lake Drive

Firehole Lake Drive

Fairy Falls
Trailhead

**Little
Firehole
Meadow**

Mystic
Falls
Trail

Biscuit
Basin

*Mystic
Falls*

see Map 7

**Black
Sand
Basin**

Old
Faithful

*Mallard
Lake*

Mallard Lake Trail

*DeLacy
Lakes*

DeLacy Creek

Grand Loop Rd

Craig
Pass
8262ft

DeLacy Creek
Trailhead

To Grant
Village

Kepler
Cascades
Lone Star
Trailhead

*Scaup
Lake*

Spring Creek
Picnic Area

*Isa
Lake*

*Lone Star
Geyser*

Firehole River

Continental Divide

DeLacy Creek Trail

Grants
Pass

*Shoshone
Lake*

*The
Narrows*

**Shoshone
Geyser
Basin**

Lewis River Channel

0   3   6 km

0   2   4 miles

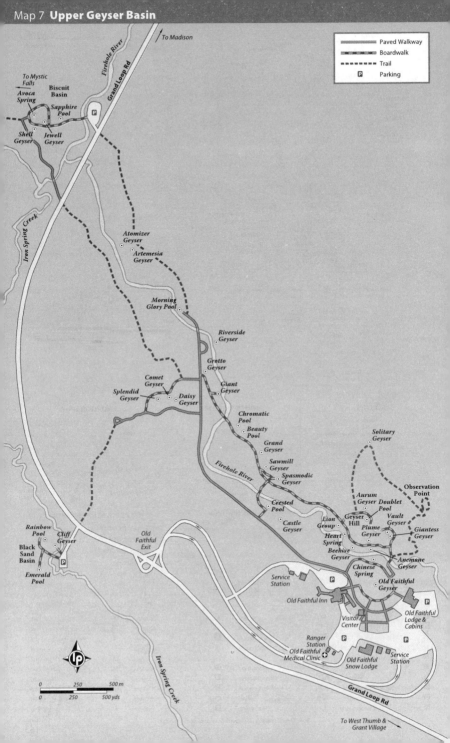

Map 7 **Upper Geyser Basin**

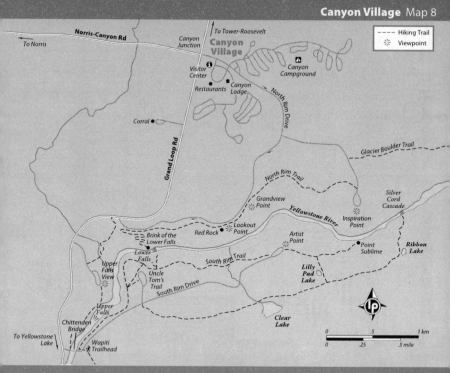

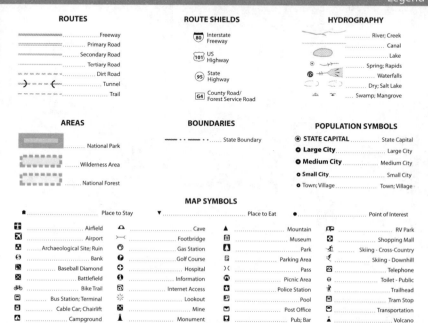

Map 9 **Grand Teton National Park**

To Dubois

Bridger-
Teton
National
Forest

State Creek

Spread Creek

Ditch Creek

Crystal Creek
Campground

Red Hills
Campground

Gros
Ventre
Wilderness

Lower
Slide
Lake

Atherton Creek
Campground

Gros Ventre Slide
Geological Area

26
89
191

Snake River

Moose
Head
Ranch

Triangle X
Ranch

Cunningham
Cabin

Shadow
Mountain
8299ft

Teton
Science
School

Kelly

National
Elk
Refuge

South Landing
Backcountry
Campsite

The
Potholes

River Rd

Raft
Launch

Snake River
Overlook

Antelope Flats

Gros Ventre Rd

Gros Ventre
Campground

Spalding
Bay

Teton Park Rd

North Jenny
Lake Junction

Schwabacher's
Landing

Mormon Row

To Jackson

Spalding Bay
Backcountry
Campsite

Grand
Teton
National
Park

Jenny Lake
Scenic Drive

Timbered Island

Glacier View
Turnout

Moose-
Blacktail
Ponds
Overlook

Moose
Junction

Blacktail
Butte

26
89
191

Leigh
Lake

Mt Moran
12,605ft

Jenny
Lake

see Map 10

Moose
Entrance
Station

Moose
Visitor
Center

Jackson Hole
Airport

Thor Peak
12,028ft

Leigh Canyon

Mt Woodring
11,590ft

Paintbrush Canyon

Mt St John
11,430ft

Cascade Canyon

Teewinot
Mountain
12,325ft

Garnet Canyon

Mt Wister
11,490ft

Buck Mountain
11,938ft

Phelps
Lake

Jackson Hole
Golf & Tennis
Club

Teton Range

Mt Owen
12,928ft

Grand Teton
13,770ft

Middle Teton
12,804ft

South Teton
12,514ft

Mt Hunt
10,783ft

Moose-Wilson Rd

Entrance
Station

Alaska
Basin

Jackson Hole
Mtn Resort

Jackson Hole
Aerial Tram

Teton
Village

Granite
Basin

Jedediah
Smith
Wilderness

Teton Canyon

Rendezvous Peak
10,927ft

Bridger-
Teton
National
Forest

To Jackson

South Leigh Creek

Grand Targhee
Ski & Summer
Resort

Caribou-
Targhee
National
Forest

To Driggs, ID

Jedediah
Smith
Wilderness

6 km
4 mile

Map 10 **Central Tetons**

Hiking Trail
Glacier

Cirque Lake

Bearpaw Lake

Leigh Canyon

Leigh Lake

Jenny Lake Scenic Drive

Jedediah Smith Wilderness

Granite Basin

Mt Woodring
▲11,590ft

Paintbrush Divide
10,645ft

Holly Lake

Paintbrush Canyon Trail

Paintbrush Canyon

Rockchuck Peak
11,144ft

String Lake Trail

To Jackson Lake

Lake Solitude

Mica Lake

▲ Mt St John
11,430ft

String Lake

Hanging Canyon

Jenny Lake Lodge

Targhee National Forest

South Leigh Lakes

Peterson Glacier

The Wigwams

Lake of the Crags

Inspiration Point ▲

Jenny Lake

Jenny Lake Campground

Cascade Canyon Trail

Hidden Falls

Jenny Lake Visitor Center

Table Mountain Trail

Cascade Canyon

Teton Crest Trail

Teton Canyon Campground

Teton Canyon

Mt Owen ▲
12,928ft

Teewinot Mountain
▲12,325ft

Moose Ponds

Exum Mountain Guides

Table Mountain
11,106ft

Grand Teton ▲
13,770ft

Middle Teton
12,804ft▲

Teton Glacier

Delta Lake

Lupine Meadows Trailhead
Glacier Falls

Timbered Island

Hurricane Pass
10,372ft

Icefloe Lake

Ampitheater Lake

Surprise Lake

Garnet Canyon

American Alpine Club's Climbers Ranch

Battleship Mountain
10,679ft

South Teton
12,514ft▲

Bradley Lake

Alaska Basin

Sunset Lake

Snowdrift Lake

Shoshoko Falls

Avalanche Canyon Trail

Taggart Lake

Jedediah Smith Wilderness

The Wall

Veiled Peak ▲
11,330ft

Lake Taminah

Mt Wister
11,490ft

Avalanche Canyon

Taggart Lake Trailhead

▲ Buck Mountain
11,938ft

Grand Teton National Park

Cottonwood Creek

Mt Meek ▲
10,681ft

Alaska Basin

Mt Jedediah Smith
10,610ft

▲ Static Peak
11,303ft

Mt Bannon ▲
10,966ft

Death Canyon Shelf

Teton Crest Trail

Death Canyon Trail

Death Canyon

Phelps Lake Overlook

Valley Trail

Chapel of the Transfiguration

Moose Entrance Station

Menor's Ferry

Patrol Cabin

Rimrock Lake

Prospectors Mountain
▲11,241ft

Death Canyon Trailhead

Ranger Station

Fox Creek Pass
9560ft

Phelps Lake

Moose Junction

Moose Wilson Rd

Spur Ranch Log Cabins

▲ Spearhead Peak
10,131

Indian Lake

Open Canyon

Open Canyon Trail

Marion Lake

Mt Hunt ▲
10,783ft

Road Closed in Winter

Granite Canyon Trail

Upper Granite Canyon Patrol Cabin

Granite Canyon

Apres Vous Peak ▲
8426ft

Granite Canyon Trailhead

Snake River

26
89
191

Jackson Hole Airport

Jackson Hole Mtn Resort

Jackson Hole Aerial Tram

Entrance Station

Teton Village

Bridger-Teton National Forest

Gros Ventre River

Gros Ventre Road

Jedediah Smith Wilderness

Rendezvous Peak ▲
10,927ft

Gros Ventre Junction

To Jackson

To Jackson

National Elk Refuge

0   1   2 km
0   .5   1 mile

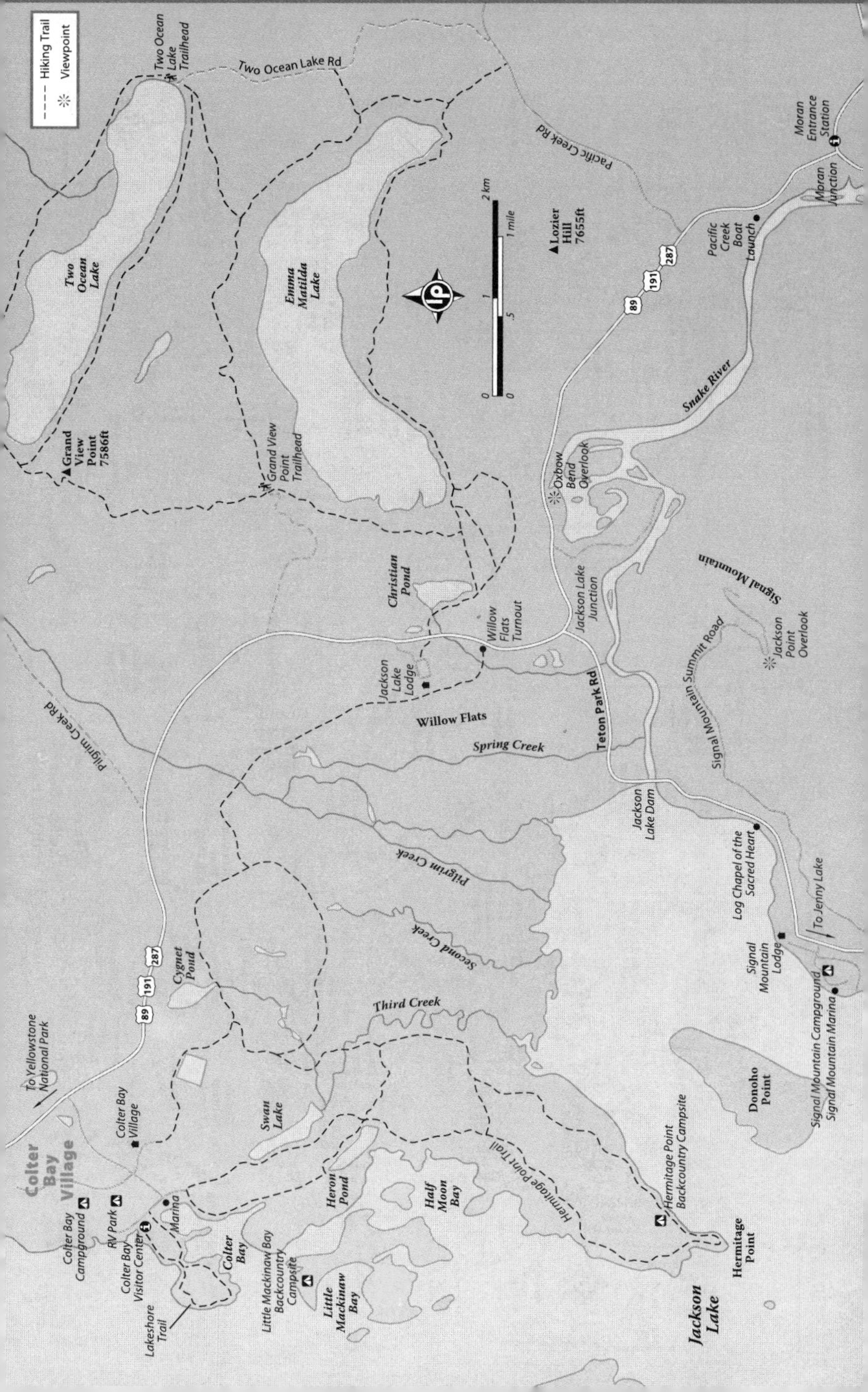

Hiking Trail
Viewpoint

Two Ocean Lake Trailhead

Two Ocean Lake Rd

Pacific Creek Rd

Moran Entrance Station

Moran Junction

Two Ocean Lake

Emma Matilda Lake

▲ Lozier Hill 7655ft

Pacific Creek Boat Launch

89 191 287

Snake River

2 km

1 mile

▲ Grand View Point 7586ft

Grand View Point Trailhead

Oxbow Bend Overlook

Christian Pond

Jackson Lake Junction

Signal Mountain

Jackson Point Overlook

Willow Flats Turnout

Pilgrim Creek Rd

Jackson Lake Lodge

Willow Flats

Spring Creek

Teton Park Rd

Signal Mountain Summit Road

Jackson Lake Dam

Log Chapel of the Sacred Heart

To Jenny Lake

Pilgrim Creek

Second Creek

Cygnet Pond

89 191 287

Third Creek

Signal Mountain Lodge

Signal Mountain Campground
Signal Mountain Marina

Donoho Point

To Yellowstone National Park

Colter Bay Village

Colter Bay Village

Colter Bay Campground

RV Park

Colter Bay Visitor Center

Marina

Lakeshore Trail

Swan Lake

Heron Pond

Half Moon Bay

Hermitage Point Trail

Hermitage Point Backcountry Campsite

Little Mackinaw Bay Backcountry Campsite

Little Mackinaw Bay

Colter Bay

Hermitage Point

Jackson Lake

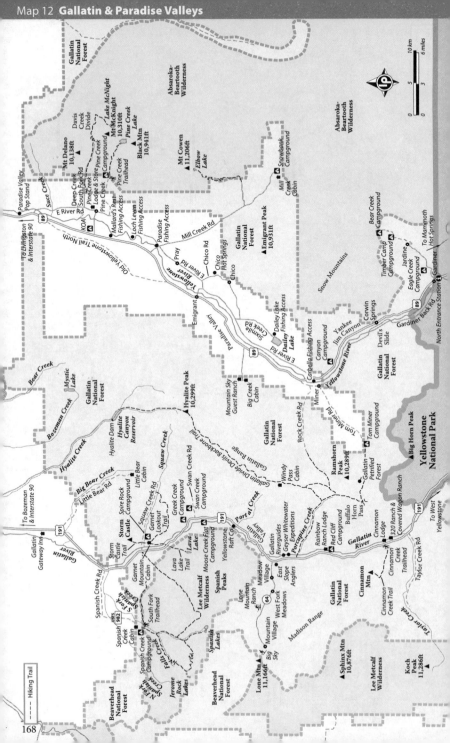

Map 12 **Gallatin & Paradise Valleys**

10 km
5
0
6 miles
3
0

Gallatin
National
Forest

Absaroka-
Beartooth
Wilderness

Absaroka-
Beartooth
Wilderness

Davis
Creek
Divide

Lake McNight

Mt McKnight
10,310ft

Pine Creek
Lake

Mt Delano 10,138ft

Black Mtn
10,941ft

Pine Creek
Campground

Mt Cowen
11,206ft

Elbow
Lake

Snowbank
Campground

Mill
Creek
Cabin

Paradise Valley
Pop Stand

Deep Creek
South Fork Rd

Pine Creek
Lodge & Store

Pine Creek
Trailhead

Pine Creek

Pine Creek

Sace Creek

E River Rd

KOA

Mallard's Rest
Fishing Access

Loch Leven
Fishing Access

Paradise
Fishing Access

Mill Creek Rd

Gallatin
National
Forest

Bear Creek
Campground

To Mammoth
Hot Springs

To Elwingston & Interstate 90

89

Old Yellowstone Trail North

Pray

E River Rd

Chico
Rd

Chico
Hot Springs

Chico

Emigrant Peak
10,931ft

Timber Camp
Campground

Jardine

Eagle Creek
Campground

To Bozeman & Interstate 90

Yellowstone River

E River Rd

Old Yellowstone Trail

Emigrant

Paradise Valley

89

Dailey Lake
Fishing Access

Snow Mountains

Dailey
Lake

Six-mile Creek Rd

Corwin
Springs

Yankee
Jim Canyon

Gardiner Back Rd

North Entrance Station

89

Gardiner

Devil's
Slide

Bear Creek

Mystic
Lake

Gallatin
National
Forest

Hyalite Peak
10,299ft

Mountain Sky
Guest Ranch

Big Creek
Cabin

Carbella Fishing Access

Canyon
Campground

Mine

Gallatin
National
Forest

Yellowstone River

Bozeman Creek

Hyalite Creek

Hyalite Dam

Hyalite
Canyon
Reservoir

Squaw Creek

Squaw Creek Rd

Gallatin Divide Devils Backbone Trail

Gallatin Range

Rock Creek Rd

Ramshorn
Peak
10,289ft

Gallatin
Petrified
Forest

Tom Miner
Campground

Tom Miner Rd

Big Horn Peak

Yellowstone
National
Park

Big Bear Creek

Little Bear Rd

Little Bear
Cabin

Spire Rock
Campground

Garnet
Lookout
Trail

Swan Creek
Campground

Swan Creek Rd

Windy
Pass
Cabin

Buffalo
Horn
Pass

Gallatin
National
Forest

To Bozeman & Interstate 90

191

Gallatin
Gateway Inn

Storm
Castle
Campground

Garnet
Mountain

Lava
Lake
Trail

Moose Creek Flat
Campground

Yellowstone
Raft Co

191

Portal Creek

Gallatin
Riverguides

Geyser Whitewater
Expeditions

Porcupine Creek

Rainbow
Ranch Lodge

Buffalo
Horn
Campground

320 Ranch &
Covered Wagon Ranch

Cinnamon
Lodge

To West
Yellowstone

191

Gallatin River

Storm
Castle
Trail

Storm
Castle
Cabin

Gallatin River

Spanish Creek Rd

S Fork

982

Spanish
Creek
Cabin

Spanish Creek

South Fork
Trailhead

Lee Metcalf
Wilderness

Lava
Lake

Spanish
Peaks

Lone
Mountain
Ranch

Meadow
Village

64

West Fork
Meadows

East
Slope
Anglers

Gallatin
National
Forest

Cinnamon
Mtn

Cinnamon
Creek
Trailhead

Cinnamon
Creek Trail

Taylor Creek Rd

Beaverhead
National
Forest

Spanish
Lakes

Falls Creek

Jerome
Rock
Lakes

S Fork Spanish Creek

Lone Mtn
11,166ft

Big
Sky

Mountain
Village

Madison Range

Sphinx Mtn
10,876ft

Lee Metcalf
Wilderness

Koch
Peak
11,236ft

Taylor Creek

Beaverhead
National
Forest

Hiking Trail

10 km
6 miles
5
3
0
0

--- Hiking Trail
☀ Viewpoint

To Interstate 90 & Billings

212
308 Washoe
To Belfry & Bridger

Red Lodge
Beartooth Ranger District
Rock Creek

64
Rock Creek Resort
Sheridan Campground
Rattin Campground
Custer National Forest

Beartooth Hwy
W Fork Rd
Red Lodge
Grizzly Peak 9416ft

Rock Creek Vista Point Overlook

Parkside Campground
Limber Pine Campground
Greenough Lake Campground
M-K Campground

Montana
Wyoming

212
Twin Lakes

Beartooth National Recreation Trail
Shoshone National Forest
Stockade Lake

Custer National Forest

Silver Run Plateau
Lake Fork Creek
Hellroaring Plateau
Rock Creek Rd

Silver Run Peak ▲12,500ft
Bear's Tooth ▲11,612ft
Mt Rearguard ▲12,204ft

Beartooth Pass West Summit 10,947ft
Gardner Lake
Long Lake
Little Bear Lake
Island Lake
Chain Lakes
Fantan Lake
Morrison Trail (4WD)

W Fork Rock Creek
Grasshopper Glacier

Beartooth High Lakes Trail
Flake Lake
Night Lake
Beauty Lake
Claw Lake
Beartooth Lake Campground
Island Lake Campground
Beartooth Lake
Top of the World Store & Motel

Sylvan Peak ▲11,943ft
Absaroka-Beartooth Wilderness
Sundance Glacier

Beartooth Plateau

Beartooth Butte
Clay Butte Overlook ☀

Alpine
East Rosebud Lake
Rainbow Lake
E Rosebud Creek

Beartooth Traverse Trail

Absaroka-Beartooth Wilderness

Lily Lake
Lake Creek Campground
Chief Joseph Hwy
To Cody

Mystic Lake
W Rosebud Creek

Granite Peak ▲12,799ft
Fossil Lake

Rock Island Lake
Vernon Lake
Fox Creek Campground

296
130-1
Beartooth Hwy
Clarks Fork Yellowstone River
Hunter Peak Campground
Chief Joseph Peak

Island Lake

Upper Aero Lake
Lower Aero Lake
Lady of the Lake
Kersey Lake
Clarks Fork Trailhead
Crazy Creek Campground
Shoshone National Forest

Grasshopper Glacier
Goose Lake
Long Lake
Round Lake
Mud Lake
Lulu Pass
Goose Lake Rd

Colter Pass 8066ft
Colter Campground
Chief Joseph Campground

Absaroka-Beartooth Wilderness

Pilot Peak ▲11,708ft

Island Lake

Soda Butte Campground
Fisher Creek

Index Peak ▲11,313ft

North Absaroka Wilderness

Custer National Forest
Stillwater River

Gallatin National Forest
212
Silver Gate
Northeast Entrance Station
Cooke City

To Tower Junction

Yellowstone National Park

Map 14 Gardiner

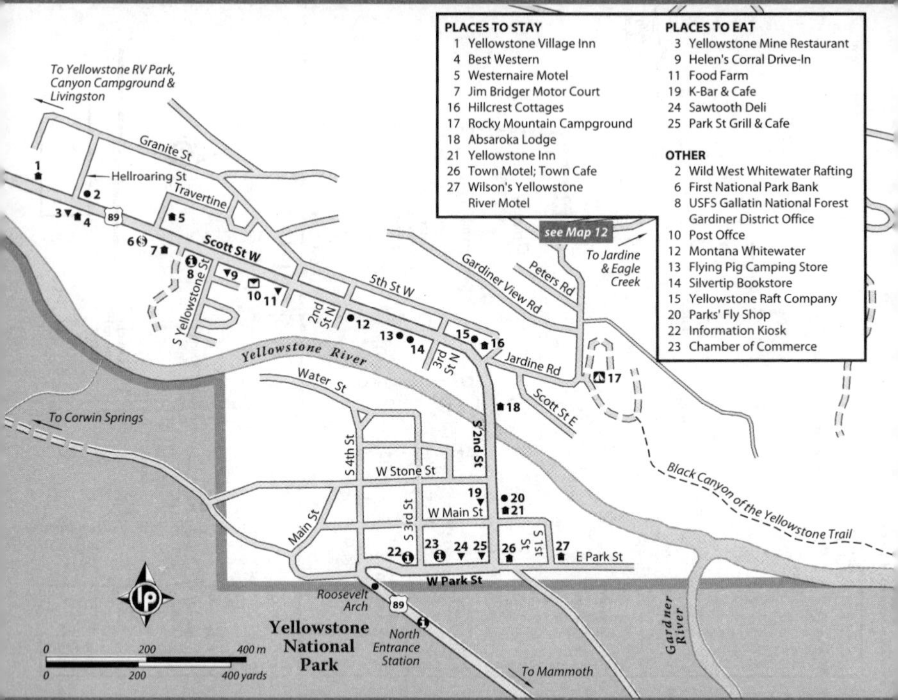

PLACES TO STAY
1 Yellowstone Village Inn
4 Best Western
5 Westernaire Motel
7 Jim Bridger Motor Court
16 Hillcrest Cottages
17 Rocky Mountain Campground
18 Absaroka Lodge
21 Yellowstone Inn
26 Town Motel; Town Cafe
27 Wilson's Yellowstone River Motel

PLACES TO EAT
3 Yellowstone Mine Restaurant
9 Helen's Corral Drive-In
11 Food Farm
19 K-Bar & Cafe
24 Sawtooth Deli
25 Park St Grill & Cafe

OTHER
2 Wild West Whitewater Rafting
6 First National Park Bank
8 USFS Gallatin National Forest Gardiner District Office
10 Post Office
12 Montana Whitewater
13 Flying Pig Camping Store
14 Silvertip Bookstore
15 Yellowstone Raft Company
20 Parks' Fly Shop
22 Information Kiosk
23 Chamber of Commerce

To Yellowstone RV Park, Canyon Campground & Livingston

Granite St
Hellroaring St
Travertine
Scott St W
89
5th St W
Gardiner View Rd
Peters Rd
To Jardine & Eagle Creek
see Map 12

Yellowstone River
2nd St N
3rd St N
Jardine Rd
Scott St E

Water St
S 4th St
2nd St S
S Yellowstone St
5th St W

To Corwin Springs

W Stone St
W Main St
Main St
S 3rd St
Black Canyon of the Yellowstone Trail

1st St S
E Park St
W Park St

Roosevelt Arch
89
North Entrance Station

Yellowstone National Park

Gardiner River

To Mammoth

0   200   400 m
0   200   400 yards

Map 15 Wapiti Valley

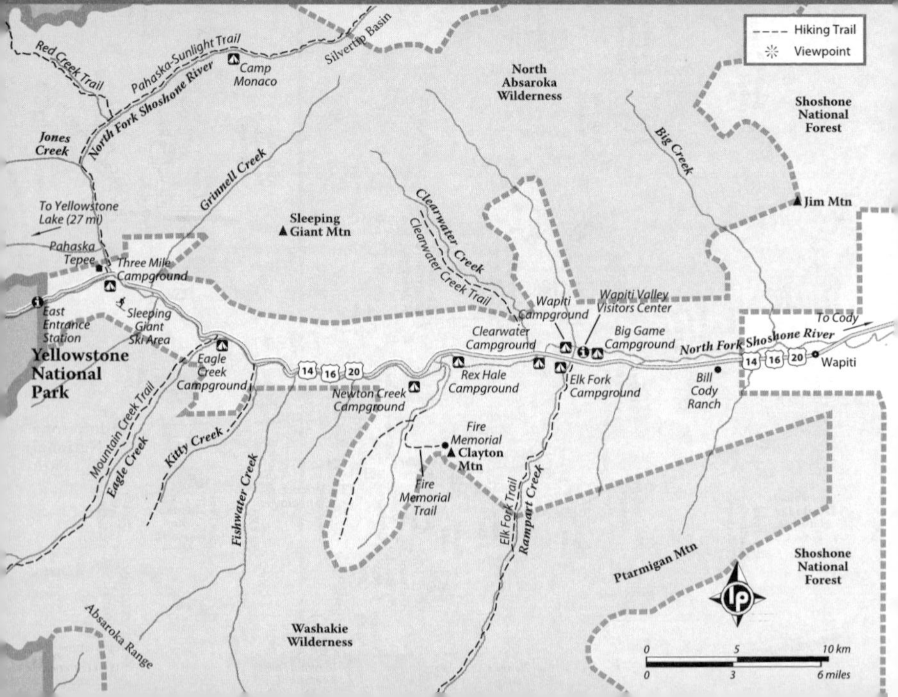

- - - Hiking Trail
☀ Viewpoint

Red Creek Trail
Pahaska-Sunlight Trail
North Fork Shoshone River
Camp Monaco
Silvertip Basin
North Absaroka Wilderness
Shoshone National Forest

Jones Creek
Grinnell Creek
Sleeping Giant Mtn
Clearwater Creek
Clearwater Creek Trail
Big Creek
Jim Mtn

To Yellowstone Lake (27 mi)
Pahaska Tepee
Three Mile Campground
East Entrance Station
Sleeping Giant Ski Area
Eagle Creek Campground
Wapiti Campground
Wapiti Valley Visitors Center
Big Game Campground
North Fork Shoshone River
To Cody

Yellowstone National Park

Mountain Creek Trail
Eagle Creek
Kitty Creek
14 16 20
Newton Creek Campground
Rex Hale Campground
Clearwater Campground
Elk Fork Campground
Bill Cody Ranch
14 16 20
Wapiti

Fishwater Creek
Fire Memorial Clayton Mtn
Fire Memorial Trail
Elk Fork Trail
Rampart Creek
Ptarmigan Mtn
Shoshone National Forest

Absaroka Range
Washakie Wilderness

0   5   10 km
0   3   6 miles

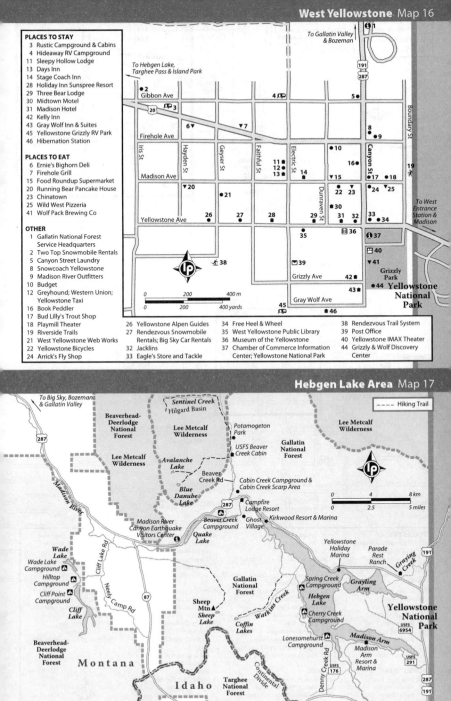

Map 18 **Jackson**

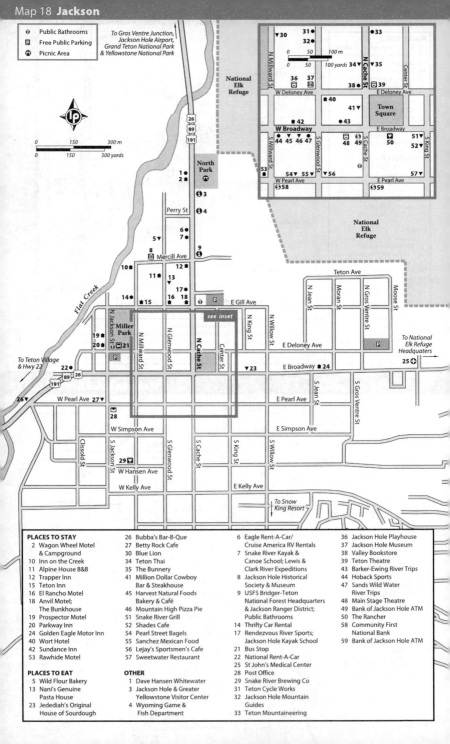

PLACES TO STAY

2 Wagon Wheel Motel
   & Campground
10 Inn on the Creek
11 Alpine House B&B
14 Trapper Inn
15 Teton Inn
16 El Rancho Motel
18 Anvil Motel;
   The Bunkhouse
19 Prospector Motel
20 Parkway Inn
24 Golden Eagle Motor Inn
40 Wort Hotel
42 Sundance Inn
53 Rawhide Motel

PLACES TO EAT

5 Wild Flour Bakery
13 Nani's Genuine
   Pasta House
23 Jedediah's Original
   House of Sourdough

26 Bubba's Bar-B-Que
27 Betty Rock Cafe
30 Blue Lion
34 Teton Thai
35 The Bunnery
41 Million Dollar Cowboy
   Bar & Steakhouse
45 Harvest Natural Foods
   Bakery & Café
46 Mountain High Pizza Pie
51 Snake River Grill
52 Shades Cafe
54 Pearl Street Bagels
55 Sanchez Mexican Food
56 Lejay's Sportsmen's Cafe
57 Sweetwater Restaurant

OTHER

1 Dave Hansen Whitewater
3 Jackson Hole & Greater
   Yellowstone Visitor Center
4 Wyoming Game &
   Fish Department

6 Eagle Rent-A-Car/
   Cruise America RV Rentals
7 Snake River Kayak &
   Canoe School; Lewis &
   Clark River Expeditions
8 Jackson Hole Historical
   Society & Museum
9 USFS Bridger-Teton
   National Forest Headquarters
   & Jackson Ranger District;
   Public Bathrooms
14 Thrifty Car Rental
17 Rendezvous River Sports;
   Jackson Hole Kayak School
21 Bus Stop
22 National Rent-A-Car
25 St John's Medical Center
28 Post Office
29 Snake River Brewing Co
31 Teton Cycle Works
32 Jackson Hole Mountain
   Guides
33 Teton Mountaineering

36 Jackson Hole Playhouse
37 Jackson Hole Museum
38 Valley Bookstore
39 Teton Theatre
43 Barker-Ewing River Trips
44 Hoback Sports
47 Sands Wild Water
   River Trips
48 Main Stage Theatre
49 Bank of Jackson Hole ATM
50 The Rancher
58 Community First
   National Bank
59 Bank of Jackson Hole ATM

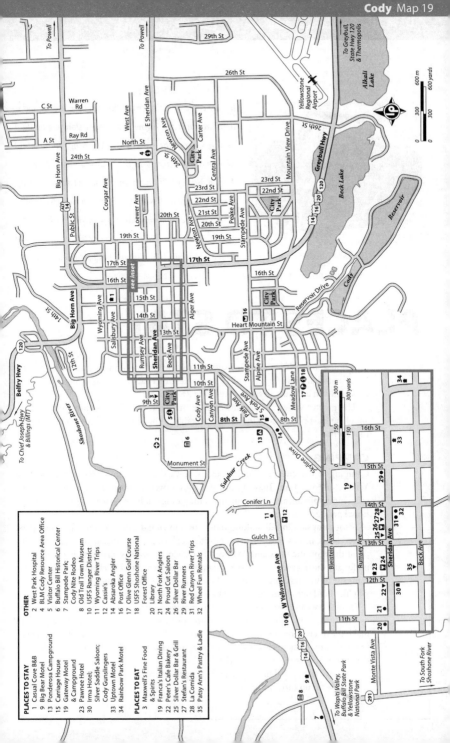

PLACES TO STAY
1 Casual Cove B&B
9 Big Bear Motel
13 Ponderosa Campground
15 Carriage House
19 Gateway Motel & Campground
23 Pawnee Hotel
30 Irma Hotel; Silver Saddle Saloon; Cody Gunslingers
33 Uptown Motel
34 Rainbow Park Motel

PLACES TO EAT
3 Maxwell's Fine Food & Spirits
19 Franca's Italian Dining
22 Peter's Cafe Bakery
25 Silver Dollar Bar & Grill
27 Stefan's Restaurant
28 La Comida
35 Patsy Ann's Pastry & Ladle

OTHER
2 West Park Hospital
4 BLM Cody Resource Area Office
5 Visitor Center
6 Buffalo Bill Historical Center
7 Stampede Park; Cody Nite Rodeo
8 Old Trail Town Museum
10 USFS Ranger District
11 Wyoming River Trips
12 Cassie's
14 Absaroka Angler
16 Post Office
17 USFS Shoshone National Forest Office
18 Olive Glenn Golf Course
20 Library
21 North Fork Anglers
24 Proud Cut Saloon
26 Silver Dollar Bar
29 River Runners
31 Red Canyon River Trips
32 Wheel Fun Rentals

It may come as no surprise that rates for accommodations are noticeably higher in the Yellowstone region than in the surrounding areas of Wyoming, Idaho, and Montana, particularly in the mad months of July and August. Still, you'll find a wide range of places to stay, from the excellent National Park Service (NPS) and Forest Service campgrounds to private RV parks, simple motels, B&Bs, and five-star luxury hotels, as well as that uniquely Western institution, the guest or dude ranch. You should be able to find something reasonably priced in most areas.

PLACES TO STAY

Yellowstone itself remains the biggest headache, with noncamping accommodations limited to a handful of pricey lodges or cookie-cutter cabins, both of which get booked up months in advance, despite there being 2175 rooms.

The greater variety of options outside the parks leads to less pressure, but you should at least phone from the road, preferably in the morning, to see what's available that night.

CAMPING

Camping is the cheapest, and in many ways the most enjoyable, approach to a Yellowstone vacation. Toasting marshmallows over an open fire, stargazing in the crisp mountain air, and taking in an evening ranger talk are essential parts of the national park experience.

Most campsites in Yellowstone and all sites in Grand Teton are on a first come, first served basis. In July and August campsites get snapped up quicker than you can pinpoint them on the map, and you need to develop a strategy. Plan on an early arrival, preferably during the week, as sites fill up fast on Fridays and weekends. Establish your campsite in the morning before you head off sightseeing, and once you have a site that you like, hold onto it and use it as a base to visit neighboring sites.

If you have a tight itinerary and will be moving around a lot, try to plan at least a few overnight stays at Yellowstone's concession (Xanterra) campgrounds, where you can make site reservations in advance. Gamblers should remember that even if you manage to score a same-day site at a Xanterra campground, you may have to move out the next day if your spot is booked that night.

If all else fails, you'll find some great Forest Service campsites outside the park, but even these fill up early in summer.

Xanterra Campgrounds

Yellowstone's concessionaire, **Xanterra** (☎ *307-344-7311*, Ⓦ *www.travelyellowstone.com),*
operates five campgrounds whose sites can be reserved in advance. You can make reservations over the phone or from other Xanterra campgrounds or facilities in the park. It's
generally possible to reserve some kind of site up to a day or two in advance. When you
make a phone booking, you must pay by credit card and then receive a booking reference
number. You'll need to show that credit card when you turn up at the campground. Xanterra doesn't take checks. Cancellations are possible 48 hours in advance.

Be careful to specify the type of site you want: tent or non-tent site, reverse-in or
pull-through site, and even the length of the site. If your site requirements change,
you'll need to change the reservation.

CAMPSITE RULES

Some rules to remember from the NPS and Forest Service:

✔ Camping in pullouts, trailheads, picnic areas, or anywhere except designated
campgrounds is illegal.

✔ Quiet hours are 8pm to 8am. No generators are allowed during this time. Some
campsites do not permit generators.

✔ Wash dishes, hair, teeth, etc, away from the spigot. Camp wastewater must be
disposed of in waste sinks, rest room sinks (no grease), or the toilet, not chucked
into your neighbor's site.

✔ Campfires must be in established grates. Never leave a fire unattended.

✔ Cutting trees or shrubs for firewood is prohibited.

✔ Don't build trenches around campsites.

✔ Checkout time is 10am.

✔ Camping in Yellowstone is limited to 14 consecutive nights.

✔ A maximum of six people and two cars are allowed at each site (some Forest Service
sites charge extra for a second car).

✔ No food, ice chests, food containers, utensils, or camp stoves may be left outside or
unattended. If you are tenting, store all food and containers in bear boxes. Don't dispose
of food in the camp area. Put it in a bag or container and dispose of it in the trash. Don't
put trash in the toilets.

✔ Pets must be physically controlled at all times. Please pick up after your pet.

✔ Bear restrictions require that only hard-sided campers (no pop-ups) can occupy sites at
Fishing Bridge in Yellowstone and certain Forest Service grounds in the upper Wapiti Valley.

National Park Service Campgrounds

Yellowstone and Grand Teton campgrounds usually have flush toilets (cheaper sites have vault toilets), drinking water, garbage disposal, fire pits (or charcoal grills), and picnic benches. Most sell boxes of firewood ($6) and kindling ($2). Sites cost $10 to $15 a night. Campgrounds usually hold a nightly campfire program in their amphitheater. Days, times, and topics are prominently posted and are listed in the park newspapers.

The process of picking a site varies with the campground but generally involves picking up a self-paying envelope, driving around the various loops until you find an available site you like, marking the site with either the tab from the envelope, some camp furniture, or the most agreeable family member, and then filling out the envelope and depositing it with the correct fee back at the entrance. Don't dally trying to find the world's best campsite – by the time you get back, the earlier one you liked may well have been snapped up. Some grounds ask you to keep the receipt tab displayed on your car windshield; others ask you to tag it to the campsite post. Rangers often come around at night to check receipts against vehicle number plates.

A "site occupied" sign can be useful to mark your turf, and these are for sale in most campsites for 50¢. In larger campgrounds such as Colter Bay in Teton and in all concession grounds in Yellowstone, you register and pay at the entrance and are computer-assigned a spot, so there's no need to mark your site.

NPS campsites accept checks but not credit cards (with the exception of Signal Mountain in Grand Teton). Golden Age and Golden Access Passports give 50% reductions on most camping fees in national parks and national forests.

When choosing a site, discerning campers scrutinize its proximity to a bathroom, trash, and water supply, whether the ground is level, and, most important, the neighbors (a scattering of kids' toys or beer cans can be a very bad sign). A campground's outer loops are usually a bit more private.

Outside the Parks

Surrounding national forest and Bureau of Land Management (BLM) campgrounds are usually less developed than national park campgrounds; some don't have drinking water and require you to pack out all trash. A few of these sites are free. Many turn off the water supply about mid-September and then either close or run the site for a while at half-price. At any rate, it's always a good idea to bring a few gallons of water when camping.

Sites can be reserved in certain Forest Service campgrounds in the Gallatin Valley, Targhee National Forest, Custer National Forest (around Red Lodge), and the Wind River Area around Pinedale through the **National Recreation Reservation Service** (☎ 1-877-444-6777, TDD 1-877-833-6777; W www.reserveusa.com). It's possible to select and reserve specific campsites online. Sites need to be booked no less than three days and no more than eight months in advance. There's an $8.65 reservation fee.

Free dispersed camping (meaning you can camp almost anywhere) is permitted in some public backcountry areas. Sometimes you can camp right from your car along a dirt road, especially in BLM and national forest areas. In other places, you must be .25mi from a developed campground and often not within .5mi of a major highway. Check with the local district ranger office.

Private campgrounds are scattered outside the park, normally close to or in a town. Most are designed with RVs in mind; tenters can camp, but fees are quite a bit higher than in public campgrounds, and sites are normally crushed together to maximize profits. Facilities can include hot showers, coin laundry, a swimming pool, full RV hookups with phone and satellite TV, a games area, playground, and convenience store.

Kampgrounds of America *(KOA;* W *www.koa.com)* is a vast national network, based in Billings, Montana, which has grounds at Billings, Bozeman, Red Lodge, Livingston, and outside West Yellowstone and Jackson Hole. Sites are at the upper end of the scale and usually range from $25 to $35, depending on facilities.

Fees listed are most often for two people per site, with a fee of $1 to $3 for each additional person. Most national forest grounds charge up to $5 for a second vehicle.

LODGING

If you aren't camping, accommodations in Yellowstone and Grand Teton are limited to concession-run park lodges and cabins. Lodges are often grand reminders of a bygone era, but the rooms have usually been renovated and are generally quite comfortable. Not all rooms are equal, and there's often a vast range of different room permutations available.

Cabins are generally remnants from the 1950s, almost always jammed in a small area to resemble anything from an affluent suburb to a military barracks. The cheaper cabins haven't been renovated for 30 years but contain a modicum of charm. The pricier cabins have modern interiors but are pretty charmless. Lodges in Grand Teton are generally more modern.

There are no TVs or radios in park accommodations (don't panic!), so bring a book. Children under 12 usually stay free.

In general, park accommodations are overpriced but not outrageously so. Lodge accommodations start around $65 for a double without bathroom and $90 for a double with bathroom. Cabins start at $40 for a double without bathroom, $56 with bathroom. Room rates listed are without tax.

Most places offer discounts in the shoulder seasons. Early bird specials of up to 40% are available for May bookings (each hotel has slightly different dates), and there are discounts of up to 20% for advance bookings in fall (late September and early October) and discounts of 25% for early winter (book before November 1 for mid-December). Check the website W www.travelyellowstone.com for occasional Internet specials.

In winter you'll save money by signing up for a joint accommodations and activities (normally snowmobile rental) package.

Reservations

Park accommodations are in great demand, and many lodges are fully booked months in advance, especially during the high season and around holidays, so reserve as soon as your plans are set. Many people book their July accommodations at least six months in advance, or at the very least by March.

The main reservation lines are **Xanterra Parks & Resorts** *(☎ 307-344-7311)* and **Grand Teton Lodge Company** *(advance reservations ☎ 307-543-3100, 800-628-9988; same-day reservations 307-543-2811).*

If you find yourself without a reservation, any of the parks' accommodations can tell you exactly what's available parkwide on the spot. If you are desperate, keep heading back to check, as cancellations open up a limited number of accommodations every day.

Make sure to let the hotel know if you plan on a late arrival – many places will give your room away if you haven't arrived or called by 6pm. Cancellation policies vary; inquire when you book.

DUDE RANCHES

Dude ranch history dates back to the late 19th century, when visiting family and friends from Eastern cities offered money to the informal accommodations supplied as a sideline by the region's ranches.

These days you can find anything from a working-ranch experience (smelly chores and 5am wakeup calls) to top-of-the-line resorts frequented by the rich and famous. Working cattle ranches are increasingly hard to find in the tourist-driven Yellowstone economy.

A few ranches offer nightly accommodations-only rates, but most require a minimum stay of three days to a week. Typical weekly rates run $150 to $200 per person per day, which includes accommodations, meals, activities, and equipment. Ranches are proud of the connections they form with their clients, many of whose families return to the same ranch generation after generation.

While the centerpiece of dude ranch vacations is horseback riding, many ranches have expanded their activity lists to include fly-fishing, hiking, mountain biking, tennis, golf, kids' programs, and cross-country skiing. Accommodations range from rustic log cabins to cushy suites with whirlpools and cable TV; meals range from steak and beans to four-course gourmet extravaganzas.

Yellowstone's dude ranches (increasingly called guest ranches) are concentrated in the Wapiti Valley near Cody, the Togwotee area near Dubois, and the Gallatin Valley. For a directory of dude ranches throughout the region, contact the **Dude Ranchers' Association** (☎ 307-587-2339; w www.duderanch.org; PO Box 2307, Cody, WY 82414). For state-specific information try the **Wyoming Dude Rancher's Association** (☎ 307-455-2084; w www.wyomingdra.com; PO Box 618, Dubois WY 82513).

Outside the Parks

Accommodations outside the parks offer much greater variety, from hostels to top-of-the-line dude ranches and fly-fishing lodges.

Forest Service cabins are an interesting option, particularly in winter, when you can snowshoe or snowmobile into a cabin equipped with woodstove, cooking utensils, and bunk beds. See the Greater Yellowstone chapter for cabins around Cooke City, Hebgen Lake, and Paradise Valley.

Houses or condominiums are available for rent in ski resort areas and can be a good value for a large group or family, as they almost always include a kitchen and living room.

Some places, especially B&Bs and some cabins, don't accept credit cards. Always ask for some kind of discount, whether it be AAA, Good Sam, seniors, off-season, shoulder season, multiday, or any other even half-credible reason you can imagine. Rates are notoriously flexible in the Yellowstone region.

Yellowstone National Park

Although competition for campsites and lodging may be fierce, there's nothing quite like falling asleep to the eerie sounds of bugling elk and howling wolves and waking to the sulfur smell of the earth erupting and bubbling around you.

CAMPING

Most of Yellowstone's campsites are in natural junctions, areas once frequented by Native Americans, as well as early trappers, explorers, and the US Army.

Camping inside the park is permitted only in 12 designated campgrounds and is limited to 14 days from June 15 to Labor Day and 30 days the rest of the year. See Policies & Regulations in the Experiencing Yellowstone chapter (p 74) for regulations on backcountry camping. Call ☎ 307-344-2114 for recorded campground information.

Some campsites ($4) are reserved for backpackers and cyclists (without vehicles) at all campgrounds except Slough Creek and Canyon. Slough Creek fills early due to popularity with anglers and wolf watchers.

Canyon is popular because of its central location. Boaters favor Grant Village and Bridge Bay; canoeists and anglers often base at Lewis Lake. The Madison Campground is closest to Old Faithful, though Grant Village isn't far off. Fishing Bridge is always full of RVs in midsummer, and reservations are essential.

Xanterra Campgrounds

Xanterra runs five of the park's 12 campgrounds ($15). They feature flush toilets, cold running water, and RV dump stations, and Xanterra accepts reservations (☎ 307-344-7311, W www.travelyellowstone.com):

Bridge Bay Campground (Map 2) *(7735ft; 429 sites; open late May–late Sept; Lake Country, along the northwest shore of Yellowstone Lake, 3mi southwest of Lake Village)* – This is an open, shadeless, and grassy area surrounded by forest. Adjacent to the Bridge Bay Marina, it appeals to those interested in fishing and boating. The vehicle sites are quite cramped. Its more desirable and remote tent-only loops (E and F) have more trees and offer lovely lake views. There are some hiker and biker sites. Showers and laundry facilities are 4mi away at Fishing Bridge.

Canyon Campground (Map 8) *(7734ft; 271 sites; open end May–early Sept; Canyon Country, near Canyon Village and the center of the park)* – Canyon offers the most tent-only sites (four out of 11 loops) and is also the most densely forested. Its high elevation makes it colder than many other campgrounds. It's a popular ground, so book at least a couple of days in advance in summer. There are pay showers and laundry on-site.

Fishing Bridge RV Park (Map 2) *(7792ft; 341 sites; RV sites $29; open mid-May–late Sept; Lake Country, along the north shore of Yellowstone Lake, 1mi east of Fishing Bridge Junction)* – Only hardshelled RVs (no pop-up camper vans) are allowed to camp here because of heavy bear activity. Rates are for up to four people and include electrical, water, and sewer hookups; all sites are back-ins. Reservations are essential in July and August. Public facilities here include a pay laundry and showers.

Grant Village Campground (Map 2) *(7770ft; 438 sites; open mid-June–end Sept; Lake Country, along the west shore of Yellowstone Lake, 22mi north of the south entrance)* – This forested campground is the only one on Yellowstone Lake and has a nearby boat launch, RV dump station, and three loops of tent-only sites. Nearby facilities include showers, laundry, and groceries. There are lovely evening and morning lakeshore strolls nearby.

Madison Campground (Map 6) *(6806ft; 280 sites; open early May–mid-Oct; Geyser Country, west of Madison Junction along the Madison River, 14mi east of the west entrance)* – In a sunny, open forest in a broad meadow above the banks of the Madison River, Madison has an RV dump station and recycling area. Tent-only sites are ideally placed along the river. Bison herds and the park's largest elk herd frequent the meadows to its west. It's a good base for fly-fishing the Madison. The nearest showers are at Old Faithful, 16mi south.

National Park Service Campgrounds

Seven campgrounds ($10 to $12) are available on a first come, first served basis. Call ☎ 307-344-2114 for recorded information:

Indian Creek Campground (Map 5) *(7300ft; 75 sites; $10; open early June–mid-Sept; Mammoth Country, 8mi south of Mammoth Junction)* – This spot is sparse and somewhat desolate, in open forest on a low rise, surrounded by moose territory. There are some hiking trails nearby, to Indian Creek or partway along the Bighorn Pass Trail (look for a handout detailing campsite trails). Generators are not allowed.

Lewis Lake Campground (Map 2) *(7779ft; 85 sites; $10; open mid-June–early Nov; Lake Country, about 10mi north of the south entrance)* – At the south end of Lewis Lake, this forested ground has a nearby boat launch that provides easy access to Lewis Lake and the Lewis River channel. Snow often remains here through June because of its high elevation and shaded location, so it may not be the best early-season campground. A few walk-in and tent-only sites are available, but generators are not allowed.

Mammoth Campground (Map 5) *(6239ft; 85 sites; $12; Mammoth Country, near the north entrance; open year-round)* – The park's most exposed campground, this is a barren, dusty, sagebrush-covered area with sparse shade. On a hairpin bend in the road below Mammoth Hot Springs, it gets a lot of road noise (the inner road sites are quietest), but its relatively low elevation makes it the warmest campground and a good choice for late-season visits. Facilities are in Gardiner, 5mi north.

Norris Campground (Map 5) *(7484ft; 116 sites; $12; open mid-May–late Sept; Mammoth Country, along the Gibbon River north of Norris Junction)* – Nestled in scenic open forest on an idyllic, sunny hill overlooking the Gibbon River and bordering meadows, this is one of the park's nicest sites. There are fishing and wildlife-viewing opportunities nearby, and Solfatara Creek Trailhead is in the campground.

Pebble Creek Campground (Map 3) *(6800ft; 36 sites; $10; open end May–late Sept; Roosevelt Country, near the northeast entrance at the lower end of Icebox Canyon)* – The park's remotest ground is surrounded on three sides by the distinctive rock faces and rugged cliffs of the Absaroka Mountains. It's along the banks of a creek in grizzly habitat and is popular with hikers and wolf watchers. The Pebble Creek hiking trail starts nearby. Generators are not allowed. Most sites are pull-through.

Slough Creek Campground (Map 3) *(6400ft; 29 sites; $10; open late May–end Oct; Roosevelt Country, 10mi northeast of Tower-Roosevelt Junction)* – This remote, peaceful site, 2.2mi up an unpaved road, is in grizzly habitat along a prime fishing stream. A couple of walk-in sites are available, and there's easy access to the Slough Creek Trail. Generators are not allowed.

Tower Falls Campground (Map 3) *(6650ft; 32 sites; $10; open mid-May–late Sept; Roosevelt Country, 3mi southeast of Tower-Roosevelt Junction)* – This small site is high above Tower Creek in an open pine forest. Generators are not allowed. There are hiking trails nearby and groceries at nearby Tower Falls.

LODGING

Of the cabin options, rustic Lake Lodge is the most peaceful, and Roosevelt Lodge offers the most authentic Western experience. Lake Yellowstone Hotel and Old Faithful Inn are the park's most atmospheric accommodations. For reservations and information call **Xanterra Parks & Resorts** (☎ *307-344-7311*, Ⓦ *www.travelyellowstone.com*).

Rooms are priced here at double occupancy, but most lodges have rooms that sleep up to six for an extra $10 per person. All Yellowstone hotel rooms are nonsmoking.

Mammoth Country
(Map 5)

Mammoth Hot Springs Hotel *(222 rooms; dbl with private/shared bathroom $90/65, suites $261, cabins with private/shared bathroom $54/86, cabins with hot tub $126; open early May–early Oct and mid-Dec–early Mar)* features a good variety of accommodations and a useful location. The cheapest rooms come with a sink and communal bathrooms down the hall.

Budget cabins have a sink but no bathroom; communal hot showers and toilet blocks are nearby. Frontier cabins come with a private bathroom and two double beds. A few of these come with a private outdoor hot tub. The cabins (closed in winter) are in single or duplex units.

Roosevelt Country
(Map 3)

For families or couples traveling together, the Roughrider cabins at **Roosevelt Lodge** *(80 rooms; Roughrider cabins $48, Frontier cabins $86 for two people; open early June–early Sept)* are among the park's great bargains, since the price is the same for cabins with one, two, or three rooms. The pleasant wood cabins come with a log-burning stove, though the one-bed cabins are a little cramped. There are no en suite bathrooms, but the three communal wash blocks have hot water and showers and are perfectly adequate.

Frontier cabins are nicely decorated and come with private bathroom, heating and two double beds. There are two handicapped cabins with private bathroom. The Frontier cabins should be booked six months in advance; the Roughriders at least a month or two. There are a limited number of outdoor grills if you want to cook your own food.

Canyon Country
(Map 8)

Canyon Lodge *(☎ 307-242 3900; 609 rooms; lodge dbl $123, Pioneer/Frontier/Western cabins $56/79/112; rooms open end May–mid-Sept, cabins close for the season a little earlier)* is a huge complex set in thick forest. The Dunraven Lodge and Cascade Lodge both offer recently built modern hotel rooms, some with forest views. Dunraven Lodge has fully accessible rooms.

The three types of cabins date from the 1950s and are laid out barracks-style, grouped into blocks of four or eight. The Pioneer cabins haven't been updated since Yogi Bear last wandered into the park and come with a shower only (no tub). The Frontiers are similar but have been renovated. Modern Western cabins come with a coffeemaker and bathtub. Cabins can sleep up to four for an extra $10 per person. There are plans to eventually replace the cabins.

Lake Country
(Map 2)

In 1895, rooms at the **Lake Yellowstone Hotel** *(296 rooms; hotel dbl $157, annex dbl $107, Frontier cabins $83; mid May–early Oct)* cost $4 a day, including all meals. Inflation has since wreaked a terrible toll.

Doubles in the stylish main lodge cost an extra $10 on the lake side but don't necessarily come with lake views. Some rooms can sleep up to six in three queen beds. Rooms in the separate annex block behind the hotel have wheelchair accessible rooms with roll-in showers. The comfortable Frontier cabins are boxed in neat suburban rows, but the exteriors and showers are in need of some work.

Lake Lodge *(186 rooms; Pioneer/Western cabins $51/112; early June–late Sept)* is the budget choice and has only cabins. The main lodge has a Laundromat, rocking chairs on the porch, and roaring fires but lacks the comfortable intimacy of the Lake Yellowstone Hotel. Western cabins are built in groups of four or six units. Some of the cabins in the A and B loops have lake views and French windows. Pioneer cabins were originally built in the 1920s as duplexes and come with a private bathroom.

The condo-like boxes in **Grant Village** *(300 rooms; motel rooms $90-101; late May–end Sept)* have been dismissed by author Alston Chase as "an inner-city project in the heart of primitive America, a wilderness ghetto," the architecture of which is "a curious mixture of Cape Cod and Star Wars." Think Ice Cube meets Martha Stewart meets Han Solo – ugghleeh.

Geyser Country
(Map 7)

The lobby of the historic **Old Faithful Inn** *(325 rooms; open mid-May–mid-Oct; dbl without bathroom $69)* is a bit of a zoo during the day, but the day-trippers quickly disappear with the sun. The hotel has a vast variety of rooms. The cheapest old wing rooms hold the most atmosphere, with original old copper-top furniture, but the bathrooms are down the hall. Beware also that you can hear every footstep through the ceiling and the radiator heat can be noisy early and late in the season. The most desirable of these rooms are on the third floor.

Families might like the two connecting rooms that can sleep five, either with private bathroom $161 or with bathroom down the hall ($132). Rates for these rooms are per room, regardless of the number of people.

The only rooms that have a view of Old Faithful are a couple of premium rooms on the front side of the east wing; these get snapped up a year in advance. Backside rooms in the east wing cost $10 less and have no view.

The west wing has comfortable rooms in the front ($163 double) or back ($120). The front rooms on the upper floor have decent views of the geyser basin. There are also mid-range ($97) and brand new high-range ($130) rooms, both of which have bathrooms and can sleep up to four.

Old Faithful Lodge *(132 cabins; cabins without/with bathroom $40/65; open mid-May–mid-Sept)* has its historical roots in Yellowstone's turn-of-the-century tent camps. The remodeled Frontier cabins come with a private bathroom. Budget cabins have sinks, but the toilets are in outside blocks and showers are only available in the main lodge.

Old Faithful Snow Lodge *(lodge rooms $134, Frontier/Western cabins $68/112; open early May–early Nov, mid-Dec–mid-Mar)* is the park's most recent accommodation (built 1999) and offers the only winter accommodations available at Old Faithful. The main lodge has a stylish lobby but bland modern hotel rooms. The Frontier cabins are fairly simple but come with bathrooms. The modern Western cabins are more spacious, with two double beds, and are warmer in winter.

Grand Teton National Park

Most campgrounds and accommodations are open early May to early October, depending on weather.

CAMPING

Camping inside the park is permitted in designated campgrounds only and is limited to 14 days (seven days at popular Jenny Lake). The National Park Service (☎ 307-739-3603 *for recorded info)* operates the park's five campgrounds ($12) on a first come, first served basis. Demand for campsites is high from early July to Labor Day, and most campgrounds fill by 11am (checkout time). Jenny Lake fills first and much earlier, by about 8am, followed by Signal Mountain. Colter Bay is a large site and fills later; Gros Ventre fills last, if at all. Signal Mountain is probably the easiest place to base because of its central location. Colter Bay and Jenny Lake have tent-only sites reserved for backpackers and cyclists.

Group sites for up to 75 people are available at Gros Ventre and Colter Bay campgrounds. Fees are $3 per person, plus a $15 reservation fee. Make (group only) reservations between January 1 and May 15 in writing to Campground Reservations, Grand Teton National Park, Moose, WY 83012.

Colter Bay Campground (Map 11) *(350 sites; open mid-May–mid-Sept; US 89/191/287, 3mi north of Jackson Lake Junction)* – This is a large, noisy campground on the east shore of Jackson Lake, with a separate RV park. A grocery store, Laundromat, and hot showers are available at nearby Colter Village. Propane is available, and there's a dumping station.

Gros Ventre Campground (Map 9) *(372 sites; open end Apr–mid-Oct; Gros Ventre Rd, 4.5mi northeast of US 26/89/191/287, 11.5mi from Moose)* – This sprawling campground has more than 100 tent-only sites surrounded by sagebrush and cottonwoods near the Gros Ventre River. It has less character but more space than the park's other campgrounds. It's closer to the Gros Ventre Mountains than to the majority of the park's attractions, and there are no Teton views, so it fills up later in the day. There's an RV dump but no hookups. Only one vehicle is allowed per site.

Jenny Lake Campground (Map 10) *(51 sites; open mid-May–late Sept; Teton Park Rd, 8mi north of Moose Junction)* – This very congenial and popular tent-only campground is convenient to many trailheads and so is almost always full. Only vehicles less than 14ft long are allowed.

Lizard Creek Campground (Map 9) *(60 sites; early June–early Sept; US 89/191/287, about 8mi north of Colter Bay Junction)* – On a forested peninsula along the north shore of Jackson Lake, this is a quiet site popular with boaters. Vehicle length limited to 30ft. It's one of the first campgrounds to close for winter.

Signal Mountain Campground (Map 11) *(86 sites; Teton Park Rd, 5mi south of Jackson Lake Junction; open mid-May–early Oct)* – This popular site has great sunset views over Jackson Lake and a nearby restaurant, bar, grocery store, and marina. Some sites are a little cramped. Vehicle size limited to 30ft, but there's a dump station for RVs.

Colter Bay RV Park (Map 11) *(reservations ☎ 307-543-2811, 800-628-9988; 112 RV sites)* has sewer, electrical, and water connections and long pull-though sites for $25 to $38. There's an extra $2 charge for vehicles over 38ft.

LODGING

Grand Teton Lodge Company *(advance reservations ☎ 307-543-3100, 800-628-9988, same-day reservations 307-543-2811, fax 307-543 3046; Ⓦ www.gtlc.com; PO Box 240 Moran, WY 83013)* operates Colter Bay Village, Jackson Lake Lodge, and Jenny Lake Lodge.

Colter Bay Village (Map 11) *(☎ 307-543-2828)*, half a mile west of Colter Bay Junction, offers two types of accommodations. **Tent cabins** *(dbl $34; open Jun–early Sept)* are very basic log and canvas structures that have all the charm of a Siberian gulag. Rooms come with bunk beds (but no bedding), a wood-burning stove, a table, picnic bench, and an outdoor barbecue. Sleeping bags/blankets can be rented for $7/1.75. At this price and level of comfort, you're better off camping. **Cabins** *(dbl with shared bathroom $34; one room with private bathroom $69-105; two-room, four-person cabins $129; open late May–late Sept)* are much more comfortable and a better deal.

Jackson Lake Lodge (Map 11) *(☎ 307-543-2811; standard rooms $124-164, lakeview rooms $225, cottages $135-200; open mid-May–early Oct)*, 1mi north of Jackson Lake Junction, on a bluff above Willow Flats, offers fine views of the Tetons and Jackson Lake. View rooms in the main lodge boast huge picture windows that frame the Tetons, though you can save yourself $100 and watch the views from the patio. The 348 cottages have been lifted straight out of the suburbs and are generally overpriced, though some cottages offer private balconies with a view. Beware that the duplex walls can be very thin. The hotel has a business center, heated outdoor pool, and a nearby medical clinic.

The timbered elegance of exclusive **Jenny Lake Lodge** (Map 10) *(☎ 307-733-4647; sngl/dbl $348/429, suites $579-$619; open early June–early Oct)*, off Teton Park Rd, is the

SECRET SITES

When Grand Teton's park service campgrounds are full, try these lesser-known first come, first served sites scattered around the edges of the park (see Map 9). You need to be pretty self-sufficient at these sites.

Hidden **Sheffield Creek Campground** *($5; open late June–Nov)* is a five-site Forest Service campground 2.5mi south of Yellowstone's south entrance and just south of Flagg Ranch, across the Snake River Bridge, then a half-mile east on a rough dirt road from a subtly signed turnoff.

Eight free, first come, first served minimally developed **campgrounds** are strung out along the unpaved **Grassy Lake (Flagg Ranch–Ashton) road**, which begins just west of the parking lot at Flagg Ranch. The first (and most popular) campground is 1.6mi along the road and has **four riverside campsites**. Each of the next **three riverside campgrounds**, in the 1.5mi stretch past Soldiers' Meadow, has two sites. The last **four campgrounds**, spaced out along the next 3.5mi, are useful for hikes into Yellowstone's southern reaches (see Grassy Lake Road, p 220, in the Greater Yellowstone chapter). All sites have toilets and trash service but no potable water. Camping is only allowed in designated sites.

Hidden, eight-site **Pacific Creek Campground** *(no fee; open mid-June–Dec)* is 12mi up gravel Pacific Creek Rd (USFS Rd 30090) from Grand Teton's Moran Ranger/Entrance Station. It's generally used as a base for backpacking trips into the Teton Wilderness.

There are several free dispersed campsites on **Shadow Mountain**, on the east edge of the valley. Don't expect water or toilets, and there's a two-day maximum stay. It's a rough drive anywhere, but you'll be rewarded with stunning dawn views of the Tetons.

only place in the park that comes close to European formality. Accommodations are in 36 log cabins that come with log furniture and a deck. Rates include breakfast, a five-course dinner, bicycle use, and guided horseback riding. The cozy main lodge has a fireplace and plenty of books and games in case of a rainy day. Reservation lines open November 1 for the following year.

Lakeside **Signal Mountain Lodge** (Map 11) (☎ *307-733-5470, 307-543-2831, fax 307-543-2569;* W *www.signalmtnlodge.com; PO Box 50 Moran, WY 83013; cabins $95-135, rooms $114-195; open mid-May–mid-Oct)*, on Teton Park Rd, 2mi southwest of Jackson Lake Junction, has three types of accommodations: cabins (one-room cabins $95-112, two-room cabins $127-135), motel rooms (standard/deluxe $114/163; lakefront rooms with kitchenette $182), and bungalows (one room $137, two rooms with kitchenette $195). Some rooms have fireplaces. There's a self-service laundry and dryers, and a TV and game room.

In Moose, Dornan's **Spur Ranch Log Cabins** (Map 10) (☎ *307-733-2522, fax 307-739-9098;* W *www.dornans.com; PO Box 39, Moose, WY 83012; one-room cabins $140-170 high season, $100-125 off-season, two-bedroom cabins $210/150 in high/low season)* are open year-round. Cabins come with a kitchen, porch, and grill and sleep up to six. High-season rates run from the end of May to the end of September. There are only 12 cabins, so make reservations at least six months in advance. In summer there is a three-night minimum (with a three night deposit), and cancellations must be made 30 days in advance (refunds minus a $25 fee).

RANCHES

Triangle X Ranch (Map 9) (☎ 307-733-2183, fax 307-733-8685; Ⓦ www.trianglex.com; 2 Triangle X Rd, Moose, WY 83012; $1300 per person per week, all-inclusive) is on the east flanks of the park. Run by the Turner family for 60 years, the ranch offers one- to three-bedroom log cabins with bathrooms, and programs run from square dancing to Dutch oven cookouts. There's a weeklong minimum stay in summer and a two-night minimum stay in winter. Rates include horse riding and all meals. The "Little Wrangler" program keeps kids under 12 busy during the day with horse riding, swimming, and crafts, and there's even a separate kids' dining hall.

The nearby **Moose Head Ranch** (Map 9) (☎ 307-733-3141; $280 per day, per person, all-inclusive; open Jun–Aug) has modern log cabins, fine food, five-day minimum stays, and lots of activities.

JOHN D ROCKEFELLER JR MEMORIAL PARKWAY
(MAP 9)

The parkway is a handy place to stay en route between Yellowstone and Grand Teton National Parks; see the Grand Teton map (Map 9). For camping options see the boxed text "Secret Sites."

Founded in 1910, **Flagg Ranch Resort** (☎ 307-543-2861, 800-443-2311, fax 307-543-2356; Ⓦ www.flaggranch.com; PO Box 187 Moran WY 83013; open mid-May–mid-Oct and mid-Dec–mid-Mar; dbl $139/145 without/with view) offers cabins with telephones, coffeemakers, and patios with rocking chairs. There are discounted packages in winter. The restaurant serves breakfast and dinner in summer and all meals in winter. Shuttles go to Jackson and the Jackson Hole Airport.

Flagg Ranch Campground (tent/RV sites $22/38; open May–early Oct) has pull-through sites, propane for sale, 24-hour showers, laundry, and a nightly campfire program. Campsites are generally available the same day, but reservations are recommended a week or more in advance for the RV sites.

Gateway Towns

The towns listed here lie no more than 5mi from the park entrances. Only Jackson (and to a lesser extent Cooke City) offer any real charm, but considering the limited accommodation options in the parks, they can be useful places to base yourself, particularly if you haven't made park reservations. You can normally find somewhere to stay if you just roll into town, but it's still a good idea to make a reservation at least a day or two in advance. The more popular hotels fill up a month or two in advance of the summer.

Prices are generally less than in the park but still higher than elsewhere in the region. Even the cheapest budget chains charge at least $70 per night. In general, summer is the peak season, and prices can as much as double; winter is also a prime season in Cooke City and West Yellowstone.

WEST YELLOWSTONE
(MAP 16)

Considering the number of motel signs, the lack of variety in accommodations here is surprising. During the off-season (October, November, and mid-March–June) the few places that remain open, including the Stagecoach Inn, Days Inn, and Kelly Inn, offer super-low rates.

Camping

The nicest tent campgrounds are **Bakers Hole Campground**, 3mi north of town on US 191, and **Lonesomehurst Campground**, 8mi west on Hwy 20, then 4mi north on Hebgen Lake Rd. Both are operated by the Forest Service, with water, flush toilets, and sites for $12. See the Greater Yellowstone chapter (p 203) for more details on other campsites and accommodations around Hebgen Lake.

Yellowstone Grizzly RV Park (☎ 406-646-4466; W www.grizzlyrv.com; RV/tent sites $38/25) is the largest (152 sites) and greenest of the RV parks in town. Facilities include showers, laundry, cable TV, and a recreation room.

Most other campgrounds are clustered on US 20 at the west end of town and charge around $18/30 for tent/RV sites. The **Hideaway RV Campground** (☎ 406-646-9049; cnr Gibbon Ave and Electric St), two blocks west of Canyon St, is one of the smaller, quieter, and cheaper options. **Rustic Campground & Cabins** (☎ 406-646-7387; 624 US 20), at the corner of Gibbon Ave, has four RV sites for every tent and five cabins with two bunk beds (cabins cost $45 per night).

Yellowstone Park KOA (☎ 406-646-7606; 6mi west of town on US 20; $31-43; open mid-May–end Sept) is a huge facility with an indoor pool, hot tub, game room, and nightly barbecue. The passing traffic on US 20 can be annoying.

Lodging

Built in 1909 as Murray's Yellowstone Hotel, the **Madison Hotel** (☎ 406-646-7745, 800-838-7745; 139 Yellowstone Ave; closed Oct-late May) has rooms in the main building for $36/42 without/with private bathroom (showers are down the hall). Corner rooms are the nicest. In back, the Madison's modern rooms run $47 to $65. The former guest list (President Hoover, Clark Gable, and Gloria Swanson, among others) makes the hotel appear more luxurious than it is.

The Madison also has several **hostel rooms** on its 2nd floor, each with three beds and a sink; beds cost $20 per person. There is no curfew and no kitchen.

Three Bear Lodge (☎ 406-646-7353, 800-646-7353; 217 Yellowstone Ave; W www.three-bear-lodge.com; main lodge $70-100 in summer, $50-85 off-season, motel dbl $55-85 in summer, $35-60 off-season) is decked out in pine logs from the lobby to the hot-tub room. There's a small outdoor pool. Pricier lodge rooms come with a Jacuzzi, and there are several family suites ($85 to $150). Prices may rise following recent remodeling.

The nearby **Midtown Motel** (☎ 406-646-7394; 24 Dunraven Ave; rooms $58-$78) is owned by the Three Bear Lodge and shares its pool and hot tub. A real gem, the **Sleepy Hollow Lodge** (☎ 406-646-7707; 124 Electric St; queen bed $61, two twin beds with kitchen $76) offers small log cabins with kitchens and is popular with anglers.

A longtime hub of West Yellowstone activity, the **Stage Coach Inn** (☎ 406-646-7381, 800-842-2882; 209 Madison Ave; motel rooms $39-49, lodge rooms $79-89 low season, $99-109 high season) has a comfortable reading area, hot tub, and a good restaurant and bar. Rooms in the lodge are very well maintained, but the motel rooms are a little grim.

The **Kelly Inn** (☎ 406-646-4544, 800-259-4672; 104 Canyon St) and **Gray Wolf Inn & Suites** (☎ 406-646-0000, 800-852-8602; W www.graywolf-inn.com; 250 Canyon St) are beside each other on Canyon St across from Grizzly Park. Both have a pool, spa, free continental breakfast, and rooms in the $65 (low season) to $100 (high season) range.

Hibernation Station (☎ 406-646-4200, 800-580-3557; 212 Gray Wolf Ave; cabins $99-159, condos $229-269) has cozy, individually decorated cabins, some with hot tubs. Discounts are available in April, May, and October to mid-December. **Holiday Inn Sunspree Resort** (☎ 800-646-7365; W www.yellowstoneholidayinn.com; 315 Yellowstone Ave) is considered the best in town.

GARDINER
(MAP 14)
Gardiner is a popular base for visits to the north part of Yellowstone, so reservations are a good idea.

Camping & RV
The woodsy Forest Service **Eagle Creek Campground** (sites $7), 2mi northeast of Gardiner on Jardine Rd, has pit toilets but no water. Farther along the dirt road, 4mi past Jardine, is **Timber Camp**. Another 2mi is **Bear Creek** campground. These two offer dispersed camping with a toilet but no water. The good news is that there's no fee. There are fine hiking options from Bear Creek Trailhead. See Map 12 for these campgrounds.

Friendly **Rocky Mountain Campground** (☎ 406-848-7251; 14 Jardine Rd; tent sites $20, RV sites $22-24, 2-/4-person cabins $22/36), overlooking the river from Jardine Rd, has a store and excellent panoramas of Yellowstone but very little shade. It also offers tent cabins.

Yellowstone RV Park (☎ 406-848-7496; RV/tent sites $31/22), at the northwest end of town, has 48 fairly cramped riverside sites with full hookups, plus showers and laundry.

Lodging
The **Yellowstone Inn** (☎ 406-848-7000; rooms with shared/private bathroom $60/98), at the corner of Main and 2nd Sts, is a picturesque Victorian B&B.

The newly remodeled **Town Motel** (☎ 406-848-7322; sngl/dbl $52/60) and slightly nicer **Wilson's Yellowstone River Motel** (☎ 406-848-7303; dbl from $55; open mid-Apr–end Oct), both on Park St, are two of the better motel-style places.

Hillcrest Cottages (☎ 406-848-7353; W www.hillcrestcottages.com; 200 Scott St; dbl $54-76, two-room cottages $70-100) features a variety of pleasant cottages, with kitchenettes, that sleep two to eight. The hotel is open May through September; opening and closing months bring discounts.

The single-story **Westernaire Motel** (☎ 406-848-7397; dbl from $65) has an old-fashioned feel with nice outdoor seating overlooking the front lawn. The equally retro **Jim Bridger Motor Court** (☎ 406-848-7371; cabins $55-65) has small cabins with either one or two beds.

The modern but surprisingly unobtrusive **Absaroka Lodge** (☎ 406-848-7414, 800-755-7414; rooms $90-$115) overlooks the river just north of the Yellowstone Bridge. All rooms boast balconies and good views of the north entrance of Yellowstone National Park.

The **Yellowstone Village Inn** (☎ 800-228-8158; dbl $75-86, suite $135-165), at the west end of Scott St, has family and kitchenette suites and an indoor pool.

Best Western (☎ 406-848-7311, dbl $95-119, family suites $175-215) offers off-season discounts of up to 50%. Choose between a mountain view or no view but a fridge and microwave. The hotel is a major center for snowmobile rentals and packages.

COOKE CITY
(MAP 13)
One-street Cooke City has a handful of motels for the relatively few visitors who stop for the night. Accommodations generally provide a more personal touch here than in the larger gateway towns like West Yellowstone and Jackson.

The Gallatin National Forest's **Soda Butte** ($9), **Colter** ($6, no water), and **Chief Joseph** ($8) campgrounds are 1.5mi, 2mi, and 4mi from town, respectively.

If it's not too cold, the **Yellowstone Yurt Hostel** (☎ 406-586-4659, 800-364-6242) offers "yurt-style" accommodations in big round tents with hot showers and cooking facilities for $14 a person. The hostel is three blocks north of the main street from the west end of town (it's well marked from the road).

High Country Motel (☎ 406-838-2272; sngl/dbl from $55/63) has a mix of cabins and motel-style rooms, some with kitchenettes (extra $10), and is open year-round. **Hoosier's Motel** (☎ 406-838-2241; dbl/tri/quad $65/70/80), across the road, offers 12 clean motel-style rooms. No pets. Other similar choices include the **Alpine Motel** (☎ 406-838-2262; open year-round) and **Elkhorn Lodge** (☎ 406-838-2332).

Antlers Lodge (☎ 406-838-2432; sngl/dbl $55/65) is a slightly ramshackle series of cabins of all shapes and sizes, some with kitchenettes. **Soda Butte Lodge** (☎ 406-838-2251; dbl $70-80, 3-bed suite $125) is the most upscale of Cooke City's hotels, though its flower is starting to fade. Rooms can be a little cramped. Facilities include a small indoor pool, hot tub, nonsmoking rooms, and a bar/restaurant.

The Gallatin National Forest Gardiner Ranger district (☎ 406-848-7375) operates a **cabin** ($25) at Round Lake that can be rented from July to mid-September and from mid-December to late March.

JACKSON
(MAP 18)
With more than 2000 in-town rooms, competition among Jackson hoteliers is fierce. Off-season rates (from October 1 until the opening of ski season in late November and after spring snowmelt in early April until Memorial Day) are up to 50% less than high-season prices quoted here. Advance reservations are essential during holiday periods.

Rates quoted here (unless noted otherwise) are for doubles with private bath, since single rates are often not available. Walk-in rates can be up to 20% less than rack rates, especially during slow periods when it pays to shop around. Check online for special seasonal package deals.

Camping
The basic, in-town **Wagon Wheel Campground** (☎ 307-733-4588, 800-323-9279; 435 N Cache Dr; $24/40 tent/full RV hookup) is cramped but popular with climbers. Grassy **Snake River KOA** (☎ 307-733-7078, 800-562-1878; $31/43 tent/full RV hookup) is 12mi south of town off US 26/89/191 near Hoback Junction. Cheaper, recommended public Forest Service campgrounds are outside of town:

Conveniently located, 12-site **Curtis Canyon Campground** ($10; open late May–Sept 30), on gravel USFS Rd 30440 (off Elk Refuge Rd), is 7mi northeast east of Jackson at 6900ft, with splendid views of the Tetons. Roadside, 10-site **Cabin Creek Campground** ($10; open late May–Sept 30) is 19mi south of Jackson and 7mi west of Hoback Junction off US 26/89 in Snake River Canyon at 5800ft.

Three miles farther along on the south side of US 26/89 is scenic, nine-site **Elbow Campground** ($15; open late May–Sept 30), 22mi south of Jackson. Two windy miles farther along toward Idaho on the southeast side of US 26/89 is the roadside, 18-site **East Table Campground** *($15; open late May–early Sept)*, 24mi south of Jackson at 5900ft. One mile farther west along the Snake River is 16-site **Station Creek Campground** *($15; open late May–Sept 30)*, 25mi south of Jackson at 5900ft.

Along the Hoback River, 8mi east of Hoback Junction and 22mi southeast of Jackson (6600ft), is the shady, 14-site **Hoback Campground** *($15; open early June–mid-Sept)*.

Five miles farther along on the east side of US 189/191 is riverside, seven-site **Kozy Campground** *($10; open late May–September 30)*, 30mi southeast of Jackson at 6500ft.

The signed turnoff for 52-site **Granite Creek Campground** *($15; open late May–Sept 30)* is 1mi north of Kozy Campground. The campground itself is 35mi from Jackson, since it's 9mi northwest of US 189/191 up (often washboard) gravel USFS Rd 30500, nestled deep in the Gros Ventre Mountains at 6900ft. There are several unmarked pullouts in the first couple of miles that lead off to the south (right) to nice free **undeveloped riverside campsites** before the bridge at the USFS Rd 30505 intersection.

For more information on campgrounds in the Jackson Ranger District call ☎ 1-800-342-CAMP.

Lodging

Budget In the basement of the Anvil Motel (see Mid-Range), **The Bunkhouse** provides $22 beds in a large 30-person coed room, offering much camaraderie but little privacy. Shared amenities include cable TV, coin laundry, and a basic kitchen. Alcohol is forbidden. Nonguests can shower here for $5.

Mid-Range Within walking distance of the town square are the friendly **Rawhide Motel** *(☎ 307-733-1216, 800-835-2999; W www.rawhidemotel.com; 75 S Millward St; $60-80)*, with two cheap cinderblock basement rooms and larger modern rooms with full baths; the **Teton Inn** *(☎ 307-733-3883, 800-429-8873; W www.jacksonlodging.com; 165 W Gill Ave; from $80)*, with quaint, cozy wood-paneled rooms; the refurbished **Golden Eagle Motor Inn** *(☎ 307-733-2042; 325 E Broadway; from $90)*; and the hospitable **Sundance Inn** *(☎ 307-733-3444, 888-478-6326; W www.sundanceinnjackson.com; 135 W Broadway; from $105)*, with an outdoor Jacuzzi, continental breakfast, homemade snacks, and gracious hosts.

The family-run **Anvil/El Rancho Motels** group *(☎ 307-733-3368, 800-234-4507; W www.anvilmotel.com; 215 N Cache Dr; dbl from $70, air-con dbl from $90)* offers smallish but clean 1950s rooms at El Rancho and larger, more modern rooms with phones and cable TV at the Anvil. Most rooms have microwaves and mini refrigerators, and all include use of an outdoor Jacuzzi.

A 15-minute walk west of downtown are the summer-only **Sagebrush Motel** *(☎ 307-733-0336, 888-219-0900; 550 W Broadway; kitchenettes from $70, cabins from $80)*, with cozy motel rooms (much quieter out back off the road) and recommended rustic kitchenette log cabins overlooking Flat Creek; and the sprawling **Virginian Lodge** *(☎ 307-733-2792, 800-262-4999; W www.virginianlodge.com; 750 W Broadway; air-con dbl from $90, kitchenettes from $120)*, with clean motel rooms and suites, all with cable TV and access to a heated outdoor pool and Jacuzzi.

North of town, overlooking the National Elk Refuge, are the comparable **Flat Creek Motel** *(☎ 307-733-5276, 800-438-9338; W www.flatcreekinn.com; 1935 N US 89; dbl with full bath from $90)* and the smaller **Elk Refuge Inn** *(☎ 307-733-3582, 800-544-3582, 1755 N US 89; dbl with full bath from $90)*, both with phones and cable TV.

More luxurious in-town options with pricier suites include the following:

The Victorian-themed **Parkway Inn** (☎ 307-733-3143, 800-247-8390; **W** www.parkwayinn.com; 125 N Jackson St; suites from $150), with antique furnishings, an indoor pool, and fitness facility.

The faux-rustic **Prospector Motel** (☎ 307-733-4858, 800-429-8835; **W** www.jacksonlodging.com; 155 N Jackson St; mini-suites from $120), with fireplaces and an outdoor Jacuzzi.

The family-owned **Trapper Inn** (☎ 307-733-2648, 888-771-2648; **W** www.trapperinn.com; 235 N Cache Dr; air-con dbl from $120), with lodgepole furniture and two shared Jacuzzis.

The sprawling Old West–style **Wagon Wheel Motel** (☎ 307-733-2357, 800-323-9279; **W** www.wagonwheelvillage.com; 435 N Cache Dr; cabins from $100), with in-room Jacuzzis, fireplaces, and kitchenettes.

Top End Contact **Snow King Resort** (☎ 307-733-5200, 800-522-5464; **W** www.snow king.com; 400 E Snow King Ave; dbl from $175, suites from $250, condos from $275) to inquire about seasonal package deals.

The classy, historic **Wort Hotel** (☎ 307-733-2190, 800-322-2727; **W** www.wort hotel.com; 50 N Glenwood St; dbl from $200) is at the center of downtown action.

Good places to splurge include the intimate, nine-room **Inn on the Creek** (☎ 307-739-1565, 800-669-9534; **W** www.innonthecreek.com; 295 N Millward St; suites from $209), with deluxe suites offering in-room fireplaces and Jacuzzis; and the Scandinavian-themed **Alpine House** (☎ 307-739-1570, 800-753-1421; **W** www.alpine house.com; 285 N Glenwood St; dbls from $155), run by former Olympic skiers, with gourmet breakfast, a shared Finnish sauna, and an outdoor Jacuzzi.

Food in Yellowstone is generally more functional than fun, though you shouldn't have difficulty finding somewhere to eat whatever your budget. The parks offer a multitude of fast-food and sandwich bars, as well as the occasional need-to-eat-something-different gourmet restaurant.

PLACES TO EAT

Outside of the parks' tourist-driven eateries, local cuisine is a stick-to-your-ribs diet of biscuits and gravy, chicken-fried steaks, turkey loaf, and mashed potatoes, interspersed with table-shaking half-pound burgers and bloody steaks. One local "delicacy" that always gets foisted (with a grin) on tourists is Rocky Mountain Oysters – deep-fried bison testicles, normally served in pairs.

If you plan on sticking to a strict vegetarian diet while traveling in Greater Yellowstone, you'll have to get used to two things: baked potatoes and grudging looks from local ranchers.

Convenient snack bars, delis, and grocery stores are never far away in the parks, but you'll find a wider selection in the gateway towns and the cheapest prices at supermarkets in larger towns like Cody and Jackson.

Taking into account the lovely locations and abundant picnic areas, picnicking is a popular option. A cooler is an invaluable piece of equipment during the heat of summer, and overpriced ice is available at most park junctions. The majority of campers bring a dual burner stove (Coleman is the most popular brand) to speed along cookouts. At the end of the day, even the blandest can of beans tastes like heaven when cooked over an open fire and under a blanket of stars.

Yellowstone National Park

Food in the park is split between campfire cuisine, cafeteria food, a couple of fast-food choices, and the more pleasant dining rooms of the park's historic inns. The park concessionaire, Xanterra, runs most dining options, so don't be surprised if you get déjà vu every time you open a menu. Most places are a pretty good value, considering the prime real estate.

The park's cafeterias are bland but convenient and economical for families. All places serve breakfast and most offer an all-you-can-eat buffet that can quickly wipe out even the best-laid hiking plans.

There's also fast food at major junctions, plus snack shops and grocery supplies in Hamilton stores. Mediocre lunches are reasonably priced but can be crowded.

Dinners are considerably more expensive but offer more culinary adventure. The Grant Village, Old Faithful Inn, and Lake Hotel dining rooms require dinner **reservations** (☎ *307-344-7311*).

CANYON COUNTRY
(MAP 8)

Don't expect too much from Canyon's restaurants; a single kitchen prepares all meals – up to 5000 per day! There are no surprises at the **cafeteria** *(entrees $6-8; open 6:30am-10am, 11:30am-3pm and 4:30pm-9:30pm, June–mid-Sept),* but it's cheap and easy, serving up trout, steak, and Santa Fe chicken. The **picnic shop** *(open 11am-9:30pm)* has deli sandwiches, baked chicken ($9.95), and hummus and pita bread ($5.25).

The **lounge dining room** has a casino/steakhouse feel to it. Lunch features the standard burgers and sandwiches, but the restaurant spreads its chicken wings for dinner, with tasty options like Parmesan and herb salmon. There's a decent soup and salad bar ($7.25). The good wine and beer list is shared with the bar (3:30pm-11pm). The breakfast menu has some lighter options, such as yogurt with fresh fruit ($3.75)

The **Hamilton Store** has an old-fashioned soda fountain, plus an ice cream and espresso stand.

GEYSER COUNTRY
(MAP 7)

All of the food options in Geyser Country are clustered around Old Faithful. The buzzing **Old Faithful Inn Dining Room** (☎ *307-344-7311; open mid-May–mid-Oct)* serves steaks ($20-23), salads ($7-8), and pasta, as well as a breakfast and lunch buffet. Make dinner reservations in the morning or preferably the day before or you'll end up eating dinner after 9:30pm. The **Pony Express Snack Shop** next door sells unappetizing prewrapped sandwiches and ice cream.

A quieter and classier option, the **Obsidian Dining Room** (☎ *307-344-7311; open early May–mid-Oct, mid-Dec–Mar)* at Old Faithful Snow Lodge creates refreshingly unexpected dishes, including sole with spinach and tarragon butter ($17) and warm goat cheese salad with pine nuts ($8.25), as well as daily dinner specials, such as elk medallions ($29).

The nearby **Geyser Grill** is a fast-food place with burgers, breakfasts, sandwiches, and beer.

Old Faithful Lodge Cafeteria *(open 11am-9pm, late May–mid-Sept)* is a good value, doling out solid standards like meatloaf and gravy ($6) and prime rib ($12-14). The Greek salad ($5) is great if you've been living off canned goods for a while. Most noteworthy are the views of Old Faithful from the side window. There's also a bakery for pretzels, cookies, and cinnamon rolls, plus espresso and ice cream stands. The cafeteria does not serve breakfast, however.

The two **Hamilton Stores** *(7:45am-8:30pm)* have snack bars that sell slices of warmish pizza ($4.50), nachos, and sandwiches.

For post-geyser or après-ski cocktails, try the **Bear Pit Bar** in the Old Faithful Inn or the **Firehole Lounge** *(open winter)* in the Old Faithful Snow Lodge.

MOUNTAINEERING The challenging Tetons attract climbers from all over the world, such as this adventurer on the Exum Ridge. [Photo: Greg Caire]

EXUM RIDGE Looking towards Middle Teton from high on the Exum Ridge (13,553ft), Grand Teton National Park. [Photo: Greg Caire]

AROUND
YELLOWSTONE & GRAND TETON

LOWER FALLS The Yellowstone River rushes down the Lower Falls into the 1000ft-deep Grand Canyon of the Yellowstone. [Photo: Gareth McCormack]

INDIAN PAINTBRUSH Wyoming's state flower blooms throughout Greater Yellowstone. [Photo: Carol Polich]

LEIGH LAKE Crossing Leigh Lake headed for Mt Moran, Grand Teton National Park [Photo: Andrew Peacock]

JACKSON LAKE Dominating the northern half of Grand Teton National Park, Jackson Lake is a popular spot for boating, swimming, fishing, or taking a family stroll. [Photo: John Elk III]

LAKE COUNTRY
(MAP 2)

Like a breath of fresh air, the stylish **Lake Hotel Dining Room** (☎ 307-344-7311; *open late May–mid-Oct*) at Lake Yellowstone Hotel combines atmosphere with inventive dishes. Lunch options include excellent salmon wraps. Dinner is an eclectic mix, from crab cakes to Asian vegetables with tofu and coconut milk ($12), plus daily specials like fettuccine with scallops and shiitake mushrooms. The hotel's **deli** (*open 10:30am-9pm*) offers fresh-made sandwiches and soup. The nearby **Lake Lodge Cafeteria** (*open from 6:30am; entrees $8*) is the less expensive option.

CHEAP EATS

It's hard to beat campfire steak 'n' beans, but try the following for a meal under $8:

✔ Cheap meals with free geyser views at the **Old Faithful Lodge Cafeteria** (YNP).

✔ **Pioneer Grill**, Jackson Lake Lodge (GTNP), for its diner-style decor and great desserts.

✔ Grab a gourmet sandwich and coffee at **Dornan's Grocery Store** (GTNP) and select one of 1700 bottles of wine for a sunset toast beside Jackson Lake.

✔ **Shades Café** or **The Bunnery** in Jackson – for a light and casual lunch.

Grant Village Restaurant (☎ 307-344-7311; *open 6:30am-10am, 11:30am-2:30pm and 5:30pm-10pm; June–mid-Sept; dinner reservations required*) has such a great steak-house smell that it's amazing there aren't grizzlies lining up for a table. Lunch is light fare like burgers and Caesar salad ($6-7); dinners include offbeat dishes such as baked trout with crabmeat stuffing and jalapeño and cream sauce ($16.75). The all-you-can-eat soup and salad bar ($4.99) will seem heaven-sent if you've been eating out of cans for a while, plus there's a good breakfast buffet ($7.75/4.95 adults/children). Grab a stool (quickly) at the tiny **Seven Stool Saloon** for a cold brew.

Head to the **Lake House** (*open 7am-10:30am and 5:30pm-9pm*) for cafeteria-style pizza and pasta and romantic sunsets over the lake. Walk down from the main parking area or gain access from the marina. It's closed for lunch.

MAMMOTH COUNTRY
(MAP 5)

Mammoth Hot Springs Dining Room (*open early May–early Oct*) has pub-style lunches, with a few surprises, such as the smoked trout bagel ($8.50) and smoked salmon cake sandwich ($7.75). Dinner is a more serious affair; if you're lucky the daily special will be the great huckleberry Brie chicken ($14.95).

Line up at the **Mammoth Terrace Grill** (*open 7:30am-9pm*) for ¼lb burgers ($2.29) and ice cream.

ROOSEVELT COUNTRY
(MAP 3)

Roosevelt Lodge Dining Room (*open early June–early Sept*) is popular for its Western-style ribs and fried chicken. The activities center offers a fun **Old West cookout** of steak, beans, and the kind of cowboy coffee you have to filter through your teeth. Kids will love it. See p 90 for details. Limited groceries are available at the small Hamilton store.

Grand Teton National Park

Dining choices in Grand Teton offer a good mix of places from formal to relaxed, with budgets to match.

COLTER BAY
(MAP 11)

Leek's Pizzeria (☎ 307-733-5470; *small pizza $11)*, at Leek's Marina north of Colter Bay Village, is open for lunch and dinner and serves pizzas, sandwiches, soups, and salads in a cozy wooden lodge environment. Admire the Tetons with a draft beer on the outdoor patio. There are open-mike nights on Mondays and live bands every two weeks.

Colter Bay Village's **John Colter Chuckwagon** *(open 7:30am-9pm)* has all-you-can-eat breakfast ($9, $6 for continental), dinner options from linguine and oysters ($10.25) to salmon and steaks ($15), and a special kids' menu. Mysteriously, the bottomless salad bowl seems to come and go.

A cheaper option next door is the breezy **John Colter Café Court Pizza & Deli** *(sandwiches $6-7; open 6am-10pm)*, with sandwiches, salads, pizza, and rotisserie chicken. Vegetarians will like the Hidden Falls sandwich, stuffed with artichoke, spinach, and red peppers.

The cheapest place to pack a picnic is the **deli** at the Colter Bay grocery store across the road.

JACKSON LAKE LODGE
(MAP 11)

Jackson Lake Lodge's **Mural Room** (☎ 307-543-3100; *dinner reservations recommended)* features "Rocky Mountain cuisine" and unbeatable views of the Tetons. You might even spot moose from your table. The entrees are eclipsed by such imaginative starters as the Wyoming roll – smoked salmon and trout wrapped in sushi rice and sesame seeds ($8.75). The murals of artist Carl Roter grace the restaurant's walls.

The more casual **Pioneer Grill** *(entrees $6-8; open 6am-10:30pm)* at Jackson Lake Lodge serves up subs, burgers, and salads diner-style. After a hard hike up Cascade Canyon, reminisce with a Mt Owen – a giant profiterole topped with ice cream, hot fudge, whipped cream, and nuts ($5.25). Box lunches are available (order before 9pm for the next day), and there's a takeout window. Exhausted hikers can have pizza delivered to their room (5pm to 9pm).

Reservations are required at the **Poolside BBQ** (☎ 307-543-2811; *adults/children $14.95/7.95; open 6pm-8pm Sun-Fri, Jul-Aug)* for all-you-can-eat barbecue buffet and live music.

The **Blue Heron** is the place to recaffeinate, with lattes and espressos served from 6am and alcohol and appetizers from 11am to midnight; occasionally you'll hit on live music. The outdoor patio is a great place for a cocktail or post-hike cold beer.

SIGNAL MOUNTAIN
(MAP 11)

Head to the **Trapper Grill** at Signal Mountain Lodge (☎ 307-543-2831) for burgers, sandwiches, and a good Western Cobb salad (smoked trout, blue cheese, avocado, and tomatoes). The **Peaks Dining Room** *(entrees $20)* next door serves heavier fare, such as pan-seasoned elk with Portobello mushrooms in red wine sauce. Outdoor patio seating, featuring sunset views over Jackson Lake, gets snapped up early. Iron stomachs can treat themselves to the breakfast buffalo sausage. Grab a Philly steak and a pint of Snake River Lager (around $12) at **Deadman's Bar**, named after the site of an unsolved murder in 1886.

Gourmands shouldn't miss the upscale **Jenny Lake Lodge Dining Room** (☎ 307-733-4647; *dinner reservations required*) for its fantastic five-course dinner ($49.95). Leave your hiking boots in the car; men are expected to wear jackets. Lunch is a more casual affair, with lighter meals (try the excellent smoked trout), but reservations are still a good idea.

MOOSE
(MAP 10)
Dornan's Chuckwagon (☎ 307-733-2415 ext 213; *breakfast and lunch entrees $7-8, dinner entrees $13-19; open noon-3pm and 5pm-9pm June–mid-Sept*), in Moose Village, is an open-air restaurant with Grand Teton views. They serve pancake and egg breakfasts, lunchtime sandwiches, and fish and steak dinners ($13-19) cooked in wood-fired Dutch ovens, plus lighter Mexican fare, weekend prime rib, and kid's meals. There's also an all-you-can-eat salad bar ($5.50). The bar has good margaritas and Snake River Lager on tap.

Get your pizza, pasta, and subs next door at the sporty **Dornan's Pizza & Pasta Company** (*pizzas $13, entrees $7-10; open noon-9pm*). Live local and national acts play occasionally, and there's a popular rooftop terrace with more of those Teton views.

Dornan's Grocery Store has the park's best quality selection, with an excellent deli, sandwich, and espresso counter and a wildly popular frozen yogurt machine. Try to pick one of the 1700 wines next-door at the **wine shop** or attend the monthly wine-tasting evenings. As their motto states, "Life is too short to drink cheap wine."

JOHN D ROCKEFELLER JR MEMORIAL PARKWAY
(MAP 9)
Your one and only choice is Flagg Ranch's **Bear's Den** (☎ 800-443-2311; *lunch entrees $7-8, dinner entrees from $17*) for sandwiches and salads at lunch and steaks and chicken potpie for dinner. The Burnt Bear Saloon serves local brews. The adjoining grocery store has a decent **deli** (*open 1:30pm-5:30pm*). See the Grand Teton map (Map 9).

Gateway Towns

The towns around the parks offer everything from Thai to Tex-Mex, with plenty of burgers and biscuits in between.

WEST YELLOWSTONE
(MAP 16)
The **Food Roundup Supermarket**, at the corner of Madison Ave and Dunraven St, is open daily 7am to 9pm year-round.

A big ol' sandwich from **Ernie's Bighorn Deli** (☎ 406-646-9467), on Hwy 20 between Geyser and Hayden Sts, is sure to fill you up for around $5. There's a good local scene and great pizza at **Wild West Pizzeria** (*14 Madison Ave; 12-inch pizza $12-15*), adjacent to Strozzi's Bar.

Wolf Pack Brewing Co (*111 Canyon St*), next to the IMAX theater, serves home-brewed beer, hearty appetizers, and sandwiches for $5-8 in a smoke-free environment.

ROCKY MOUNTAIN BREWS

The Yellowstone states of Wyoming and Montana are fast developing a reputation among beer hounds for hosting some of the country's best microbreweries.

Snake River Brewing in Jackson is the region's most popular brewpub. Flagship beers include the Austrian-style Snake River Lager, the crisp Snake River Pale Ale, the dark and creamy Snake River Zonker Stout, and numerous other brews.

The region's other main brewpub is **Spanish Peaks Brewing** in Bozeman, famed for its English-style Black Dog Ale and golden Monterey Pale Ale.

Teton Valley's **Grand Teton Brewing Company** uses local spring water to produce its Old Faithful Ale, Teton Ale, and Moose Juice Stout. Its Teton Huckleberry Wheat is one of several popular regional fruit beers.

Missoula's **Bayern Brewing** is the only German microbrewery in the Rockies, serving up Amber, Pilsner, Killarney, and Hefeweizen beers. **Big Sky Brewing**, also of Missoula, produces Montana's best-selling microbrew, Moose Drool, a creamy brown ale. The English-style Scape Goat pale ale is also excellent.

Yellowstone Valley Brewing in Billings names all its beers after fishing flies, including the amber-colored Wild Fly Ale, the dark, malty Renegade Red Ale, the clear Grizzly Wulff Wheat, and the full-flavored Black Widow Oatmeal Stout.

If you are headed along the Bearooth Hwy, drop into Red Lodge Ales en route for a brewery tour. If you are headed up to the parks in June through Idaho Falls, Idaho, check out the Mountain Brewers Beer Festival, which features more than 300 brews.

Other Yellowstone beers worth tracking down, if only to say their names out loud ("a pint of Old Stinky's, please"), are Monkey's Dunkel, Powder Hound, Trout Slayer, Custer's Last Ale and, yes, Old Stinky's.

It might be moving to the front of the Best Western Desert Inn. **Firehole Grill** (☎ 406-646-4948), on US 20 at Firehole Ave, does great barbecue and is a lively place to be on weekend nights.

For good Chinese food under $10 head to **Chinatown** (☎ 406-646-7088; 110 Madison Ave; dishes $8-10). Lunch specials ($5-6.50) come with rice and a spring roll, and they deliver for free.

Running Bear Pancake House (☎ 406-646-7703; cnr Madison and Hayden) is a family favorite for breakfast.

GARDINER
(MAP 14)

To fill up on supplies, head to the **Food Farm** (☎ 406-848-7524) across from the Super 8 Motel. For a quick lunch try the **Sawtooth Deli** (☎ 406-848-7600; 220 W Park St; open 9am-4pm daily in summer), which serves hot and cold subs and a nice selection of salads.

Helen's Corral Drive-In (☎ 406-848-7627; Scott St W; meals under $5) is an old-style malt and burger stand that's been going since 1960. Carnivores try the elk burger. The **Town Café** (☎ 406-848-7322), next to the Town Motel on Park St, is a good family-style spot with breakfast, lunch, and dinner year-round.

Their pricier upstairs loft (dinner only) has a fine view into the park and a good selection of grilled fish ($12-16).

Also open year-round is the **K-Bar & Café** (☎ 406-848-9995; cnr 2nd and Main Sts), with pizza and daily lunch specials. Locals like the **Park St Grill & Café** (☎ 406-848-7989; cnr Park and 2nd Sts) for its pasta and seafood ($12-15).

The **Yellowstone Mine Restaurant** (☎ 406-848-7336; entrees $17-23) is part of the Best Western and one of the swankiest eateries in town for steak, seafood, and salmon a l'Oscar, broiled on alder wood and topped with crab, asparagus, and hollandaise sauce ($20).

COOKE CITY
(MAP 13)

The **Beartooth Café** (☎ 406-838-2475; lunchtime sandwiches $7, dinner entrees $15-20) is a young and bright place for lunch sandwiches (such as the ⅓lb buffalo burger) served on the pleasant front deck, washed down by a fine selection of bottled local microbrews and wines. Dinner entrees like ribs, trout, and steak are more expensive. Breakfast is served weekends only.

Buns & Beds ($6 half-sandwich) is a small deli bar with a handful of seats to park those buns.

A popular place for breakfast is the homey **Bistro** (☎ 406-838-2160; breakfast $6, lunch $7, dinner entrees $15-20; open from 7am). A sandwich, soup, and fries for $6 is a good deal at lunchtime. Come nightfall the place transforms into a French restaurant with dishes like escargot in garlic butter ($10) and lamb Provençal ($21).

Prospector Restaurant (☎ 406-838-2251) in the Soda Butte Hotel is reasonably priced; lunches such as a Reuben sandwich or spinach salad run around $6. Dinner entrees are standard mountain fare – steak and trout – for $11-14, and there's a children's menu. Joan's pies sell for $3 per slice and are well worth the investment.

The **Grizzly Pad** at the north end of town is friendly and serves up honest portions of good food.

JACKSON
(MAP 18)

Jackson is home of Wyoming's most sophisticated grub. A few places are unconscionably expensive, but many offer a good value. The free, annual *Jackson Hole Dining Guide* includes menus from 60 local eateries.

Budget-conscious travelers who plan to prepare their own food should shop at **Food Town** (cheaper) or **Albertson's** (fancier) grocery stores, both at the west end of town off Broadway. A new **Smith's** market was slated to open in South Jackson in early 2003.

Budget

Wild Flour Bakery (☎ 307-734-2455; 345 N Glenwood St) supplies many local restaurants with its sweet treats. **Pearl Street Bagels** (☎ 307-739-1218; 145 W Pearl Ave) also makes good sandwiches and espresso.

Sanchez Mexican Food (☎ 307-732-2326; 65 S Glenwood St) assembles hearty tacos, tortas, and tostadas. The chop shop inside the **Million Dollar Cowboy Bar** (☎ 307-733-4790; 25 N Cache St) does credible (plenty greasy) Philly cheesesteaks.

Harvest Natural Foods Bakery & Café (☎ 307-733-5418; 130 W Broadway; everything under $7) is the best healthy-vegan-soup-and-salad option, with organic groceries, a bakery, and juice and espresso bar.

Betty Rock Cafe (☎ 307-733-0747; 325 W Pearl Ave; everything under $8; open 10am-9:30pm Mon-Fri, 10am-5pm Sat) has a superb selection of hot and cold soups, salads, sandwiches, sweets, and drinks, all made from scratch.

The Bunnery Bakery & Restaurant (☎ 307-733-5474; 130 N Cache St; breakfast $5-10, lunch $6-12, dinner $9-18; open 7am-3pm, 5pm-9pm summer only) boasts a big breakfast, lunch and veggie menu, juice bar, a shady outdoor patio, and good baked goods.

BYOB **Jedediah's Original House of Sourdough** (☎ 307-733-5671; 135 E Broadway; breakfast $3.50-7, lunch $4-$8, dinner $8-19; open 7am-2pm daily, 5:30pm-9pm summer only) is popular for cheap breakfasts (served until 2pm), big burgers, and grilled meats.

Heartily recommended **Shades Cafe** (☎ 307-733-2015; 75 S King St; everything under $7; open 7am-4pm daily) is an artsy log cabin hangout with a shady deck, serving scrumptious breakfasts, good coffee and smoothies, and foccacia sandwiches and homemade quiche after noon.

BYOB chain **Bubba's Bar-B-Que** (☎ 307-733-2288; 515 W Broadway; breakfast and lunch $5-8, dinner $8-14; open 7am-9pm daily) is popular with locals for its big biscuit breakfasts, succulent pork ribs, and decent salad bar.

Mid-Range

Tucked away in a pedestrian alley, across the street from the Teton Theatre, BYOB **Teton Thai** (☎ 307-733-0022; 135 N Cache St in Stage Stop Mall; lunch $8-10, dinner $10-12; open 11:30am-3pm and 5:30pm-9pm Tues-Sun) is Jackson's best Southeast Asian option. The imported herbs are authentic, but the entrees exhibit some Chinese twists. Stick to traditional Thai dishes like *tom kha gai* (chicken coconut soup with galanga root and kafir lime leaf).

Moderately priced **Chinatown** (☎ 307-733-8856; 850 W Broadway; lunch specials $5.50, dinner $8-13; open for lunch and dinner daily) has a huge menu of provincial specialties.

Mountain High Pizza Pie (☎ 307-733-3646; 120 W Broadway; sandwiches $6-8, pizzas $7-18; open 11am-11pm daily) has an outdoor patio and delivers good thin crust and deep dish pies.

Insomniac beef eaters rendezvous at smoky **Lejay's Sportsmen's Café** (☎ 307-733-3110; 72 S Glenwood St; breakfast under $8, lunch under $7, dinner $9-16; open 24hr daily) for cheap breakfasts and big steaks.

Sweetwater Restaurant (☎ 307-733-3553; 85 S King St; lunch $7-10, dinner $15-25; open 11:30am-3pm and 5:30pm-10pm daily), in a rustic log cabin with deck seating, crafts creative lunches like mango shrimp salad and seasonal French-influenced bistro dinners.

Intimate **Nani's Genuine Pasta House** (☎ 307-733-3888; 242 N Glenwood St; entrees $14-24; open from 5pm nightly) is Jackson's best upmarket Italian option, featuring a different regional menu each month.

One of Jackson Hole's better restaurants is in Wilson: **Nora's Fish Creek Inn** (☎ 307-733-8288; 5600 W Hwy 22; breakfast and lunch $5-10, dinner $11-20; open 6am-9:30pm daily) pulls 'em in from far and wide with big honest breakfasts and great prime rib.

Top End

The **Gun Barrel Steak & Game House** (☎ 307-733-3287, 862 W Broadway; dinner $15-25), inside the old Wyoming Wildlife Museum, does Jackson's best buffalo prime rib and pan-seared elk medallions.

The **Blue Lion** (☎ 307-733-3912; 160 N Millward St; dinner $15-28; open from 6pm nightly year-round) prepares eclectic French-influenced surf-and-turf fare like tournedos au bleu, Angus beef medallions topped with a creamy crab, artichoke and brandy–bleu cheese sauce.

The elegant **Snake River Grill** (☎ 307-733-0557; 84 E Broadway; entrees $17-28; open from 5:30pm nightly) is notable for its elaborate American haute cuisine, extensive wine list, and homemade desserts.

The 43,750 sq mi Greater Yellowstone Ecosystem encompasses seven national forests and three national wildlife refuges in three states – Wyoming, Montana, and Idaho. Conservationists consider this area an intact natural ecosystem, the largest of its kind in the world, with rivers, forests, prairies, and abundant wildlife best managed as a sustainable entity. In the 1990s the region's 12% annual population growth rate put increasing pressure on the ecosystem's finite resources.

GREATER YELLOWSTONE

For visitors, the region surrounding the parks offers almost as much scenic splendor and outdoor opportunities as the parks themselves, but without the crowds. Try to budget at least a couple of days to explore this exceptional area. The Greater Yellowstone map on p 58 ("Getting There") serves as an overview of the region.

Hebgen Lake Area
MAP 17

The mountains, lakes, and trails of the Hebgen area are largely overlooked by people making a beeline for Yellowstone, but the region offers fine recreational opportunities and shelters some wild and beautiful backcountry.

A useful road tour of the region runs west from West Yellowstone along Hwy 20 over the Targhee Pass to Henry's Lake, and then northwest along Hwy 87 to the junction with Hwy 287, near the turnoff to Cliff and Wade Lakes, to return east via Quake Lake.

CLIFF AND WADE LAKES

These hidden gems hit you out of the blue, 6mi up a dirt road that branches south 1mi west of the junction of Hwys 287 and 87. They can also be reached by an easily missed dirt road off Hwy 87. Boating and fishing are allowed on the lakes; there are some pleasant trails nearby; and the wildlife includes ospreys, bald eagles, and beaver. It's a great family spot. The lakes run along a geologic fault line and are spring fed.

Forest service campsites are at **Wade Lake**, **Cliff Point**, and **Hilltop** *(all $8)*. Cliff Point is the smallest and favorite with kayakers. Wade Lake has lakeside tent-only sites. Call the Beaverhead-Deerlodge Forestry Service (☎ 307-739-5500) for details.

BEYOND THE PARKS

NATIONAL FORESTS

The US Forest Service (USFS) is under the US Dept of Agriculture and administers the use of forests. National forests are less protected than parks, being managed under the concept of "multiple use," which includes timber cutting, watershed management, wildlife management, and recreation.

National forests have an excellent network of hiking trails, and many of the long-distance trails cross over into Yellowstone to connect with trails inside the park. Mountain bikes and pets are generally allowed on national forest trails, unlike national park trails. National forests have no entry fees.

Six national forests surround Yellowstone and are worth exploring. Call the following numbers for activities and camping information (but no reservations):

Beaverhead-Deerlodge National Forest (☎ 406-683-3900; W www.fs.fe.us/rl/b-d)

Bridger-Teton National Forest (☎ 307-739-5500; W www.fs.fed.us/r4/btnf), headquartered in Jackson, with ranger districts in Moran/Hatchet (☎ 307-543-2386), Jackson (☎ 307-739-5400), and Pinedale (☎ 307-367-4326).

Caribou-Targhee National Forest (☎ 208-524-7500; W www.fs.fed.us/r4/caribou), headquartered in Idaho Falls and St Anthony, Idaho, with ranger district offices in Ashton (☎ 208-652-7442), Idaho Falls (☎ 208-523-1412), and Driggs (☎ 208-354-2312).

Custer National Forest (☎ 406-657-6200; W www.fs.fed.us/rl/custer/; PO Box 50760, Billings, MT 59105)

Gallatin National Forest (☎ 406-522-2520; W www.fs.fed.us/rl/gallatin; PO Box 130, Bozeman, MT 59771); includes the Bozeman, Livingston (☎ 406-222-1892), Gardiner (☎ 406-848-7375), and Hebgen Lake (☎ 406-823-6961) Ranger Districts

Shoshone National Forest (☎ 307-527-6241; W www.fs.fed.us/r2/Shoshone; 808 Meadow Lane, Cody, WY 82414)

WILDERNESS AREAS

Within national forests are designated **wilderness areas**. Wilderness area restrictions limit group sizes and the length of stay and either limit or prohibit campfires. Camping must be 200ft from any water supply or occupied camp. No motorized vehicles or mechanized equipment are allowed in wilderness areas, including snowmobiles, ATVs, and mountain bikes.

The 944,060-acre Absaroka-Beartooth Wilderness, split between Custer and Gallatin National Forests, is the most visited wilderness in the region. Other wilderness areas include the Shoshone National Forest's Washakie and North Absaroka Wildernesses, Targhee National Forest's Jedediah Smith and Winegar Hole Wildernesses and the Gros Ventre, Teton, and Bridger Wildernesses of the Bridger-Teton National Forest.

QUAKE LAKE

Built atop part of the Madison landslide, the **Madison River Canyon Earthquake Area Visitors Center** (☎ *406-646-7369; admission $3*) has a working seismograph, photographs, and news clippings from the 1959 quake and a good 15-minute video that is shown every 30 minutes. Walk or drive up to the interpretive trail for a vista of the dramatic slide area and a memorial boulder inscribed with the names of 28 killed in the slide. There are several nearby remnants from the slide. A dock at Quake Lake allows boaters to glide past the surreal submerged treetops of Quake Lake.

The **Cabin Creek Scarp Area** highlights a 21ft-tall scarp that opened up along the Hebgen Lake fault line. One campsite actually straddled the fault; you can still see the picnic table above the scarp and the fire ring 21ft below.

At **Ghost Village** you can see the remains of half a dozen cabins stranded in the plain by the flood. To get here turn off the highway toward Campfire Lodge and then branch right down a dirt road. The cabins are on the other side of the river. Rangers lead a 1.5mi guided walk here Thursdays at 10am (mid-July to mid-September). Call ☎ 406-682-7220 for details.

Ten miles farther east along Hwy 287 a road leads off to a parking area and a short trail that leads down to Hebgen Lake and three partly submerged cabins destroyed by the slide.

Cabin Creek and **Beaver Creek Campgrounds** (*both $10.50*) are two scenic concession-run Forest Service campgrounds. Call the Hebgen Lake Ranger District (☎ *406-823-6961*) for information. Just across from Cabin Creek is **Campfire Lodge Resort** (☎ *406-646-7258; RV sites $16-20, cabins $40-$90*), offering cabins that sleep up to seven, plus RV sites, laundry, and showers.

THE NIGHT THE MOUNTAINS MOVED

Just before midnight on August 17, 1959, an earthquake measuring 7.5 on the Richter scale ripped the landscape of the Upper Madison Valley. As two huge fault blocks tilted and dropped, a massive 80-million-ton landslide pulverized two campgrounds and even rose halfway up the opposite valley wall.

The slip caused the lake's north shore to drop 18ft, flooding lakeshore houses and lodges. Gaps opened up in highways, and cars crashed into the gaping holes.

Hurricane force winds caused by the slide then rushed down the valley, tearing off campers' clothes and creating a huge wave on the lake. Mini tsunamis sloshed up and down the lake for the next 12 hours, pouring over the Hebgen Lake Dam, which, amazingly, held firm.

The slide had blocked the Madison River, and the waters of newborn Earthquake Lake soon started to fill, rising 9ft a day as engineers worked around the clock to cut a spillway and avoid a second catastrophic flood. In a final gesture, several hundred of Yellowstone's thermal features simultaneously erupted.

After the dust settled, it was discovered that 28 people had been killed, mostly in the Rock Creek campsite. Nineteen bodies were never found, presumably entombed under the slide. The quake had been felt in California, and water tables were affected as far away as Hawaii.

HEBGEN LAKE

Connected to Quake Lake by a scenic stretch of the Madison River, Hebgen Lake offers excellent recreational opportunities. You could easily spend a couple of days hiking, angling, and boating here. Motorboats are allowed on the lake, and you can rent boats at the **Madison Arm Resort & Marina** on the south shore and the **Yellowstone Holiday** and **Kirkwood Resort** marinas on the north shore.

Between the visitor center and the dam, **Beaver Creek Rd** turns north off the highway. The road follows Beaver Creek, through an area notorious for grizzly sightings, 3mi to the **Avalanche Lake/Blue Danube Lake Trailhead** (trail 222/152). Both Avalanche (11mi round-trip) and Blue Danube (12.5mi round-trip) Lakes make excellent day hike destinations; the trail splits 4.5mi from the trailhead.

Farther along Beaver Creek the road finishes at Potamogeton Park and the trailhead for an excellent overnight trip up Sentinel Creek to the dozen or so alpine lakes of the **Hilgard Basin** (trail 202/201). Budget a day to make the 7mi and 2700ft elevation gain to the lakes, a day to explore the basin, and a day to get back. This hike takes you into the Lee Metcalf Wilderness, so wilderness use rules apply (no camping within 200ft of the trail).

Along the northwest shore of Hebgen Lake, a couple of miles past Spring Creek Campground, is the trailhead for Watkins Creek and the 10mi round-trip day or overnight hike to **Coffin Lakes** (trail 215/209). You can take mountain bikes on this trail, which gains 1700ft in elevation.

The useful 1:63,360 USFS *Lee Metcalf Wilderness and West Yellowstone Vicinity* map marks these and many other trails in the region.

Places to Stay

On the southwest side of Hebgen Lake are three remote Forest Service campgrounds that are popular with boaters and anglers. Four miles down the tarmac road, **Lonesomehurst** *($12)* is the most accessible site and has lovely lake views, potable water, and a boat ramp. Another 2mi and 8mi, respectively, down a good dirt road are lakeshore **Cherry Creek** and **Spring Creek**, both primitive sites *(no fee)* with pit toilets but no drinking water. Reach these by turning north off Hwy 20 about halfway between Targhee Pass and West Yellowstone on Denny Creek Rd (USFS Rd 176). Call the Hebgen Lake Ranger District *(☎ 406-823-6961)* for information.

Beaver Creek Cabin *($30 per night; available year-round)* makes an excellent base for hikes. Bunk beds sleep four, and you'll find a stove and utensils, firewood, and an ax. Contact the ranger station in West Yellowstone *(☎ 406-823-6963)* for reservations.

The **Madison Arm Resort & Marina** *(☎ 406-646-9328; sites $28-40)*, 3mi north of town and 5mi west of US 191/US 287, is well suited to tenters, and there's a marina with a swimming beach and boat rentals. Lack of shade is the main drawback.

Parade Rest Ranch *(☎ 406-646-7217, 800-753-5934; ⓦ www.parade restranch.com; 7979 Grayling Creek Rd, 10mi from Yellowstone; summer rates $160 per person)* is a dude ranch northeast of Hebgen Lake. Summer rates include food, lodging in cabins, horseback riding, and fly-fishing on Graying Creek. Discounted and room-only rates are available in spring and fall.

Gallatin Valley
MAP 12

US 191 hugs the Gallatin River from its headwaters in the northwest corner of Yellowstone National Park to where it meets the Madison, Jefferson and Missouri Rivers at Three Forks. Scenically sandwiched between the Madison and Gallatin Ranges, the route is peppered with enough trailheads to keep hikers and skiers busy for years. The commercial heart of the valley is the Big Sky ski resort.

On a clear day you can see a distinct cluster of peaks (25 of which are over 10,000ft) rising sharply out of the general profile of the Gallatin Range, west of US 191. These are the **Spanish Peaks**, the valley's premier hiking and backcountry ski destination and part of the Lee Metcalf Wilderness.

BIG SKY

Valley development goes into relative hyperdrive around the turnoff to **Big Sky**, the valley's foremost destination, 18mi north of Yellowstone and 36mi south of Bozeman. As a world-class winter (and increasingly summer) resort, Big Sky attracts a cosmopolitan clientele that feels more Colorado than Montana. It's a tad more sophisticated (and expensive) than any other place in the region, save Jackson.

For information and maps contact the **Big Sky Chamber of Commerce** (☎ 406-995-3000, 800-943-4111; Ⓦ www.bigskychamber.com) at West Fork Meadows or **Big Sky Resort** (☎ 800-548-4486, Ⓦ www.bigskyresort.com).

Big Sky spreads from US 191 to the base of Lone Mountain in four parts – Gallatin Canyon, West Fork Meadows, Meadow Village, and Mountain Village. Meadow Village and West Fork Meadows have the bulk of services; all are connected by a free shuttle service in summer and winter.

Big Sky Resort is comprised of Andesite Mountain (8800ft) and Lone Mountain (11,166ft), with a 4350ft vertical drop and 3600 acres of skiable terrain, a 15-passenger tram, gondola, three high-speed detachable quads, and 13 other lifts. The north side of **Lone Mountain** has some fantastic double-diamond chutes and bowls, accessible by the tram and limited to expert skiers only. **Andesite Mountain** caters more to intermediates, and beginners will find plenty of easy terrain off the Explorer lift (next to the main parking lot) and gondola.

Lifts operate 9am to 4pm. Tickets are $58/46 full-day/half-day; children under 10 ski free. Among the many rental shops around Big Sky, **Mad Wolf Ski & Sport Shop** (☎ 406-995-4369), 100yd south of the Big Sky turnoff on US 191, tends to have the best prices, with ski rentals for around $16 per day.

A **gondola** shuttles people and bikes to the top of Big Sky's ski terrain at 10,000ft, 9:30am to 4:30pm daily (June to October) for $13 ($21 for unlimited use); buy tickets at Big Sky Sports at the base of the mountain. Serious hikers can reach the peak of Lone Mountain (11,166ft) from here, and mountain bikers can choose between a dozen great downhill rides.

Inquire about condominium, cabin, or house rentals in Big Sky through **East West Resorts** (☎ 877-845-9817; Ⓦ www.eastwestresorts.com) or **Big Sky Central**

Reservations (☎ 800-548-8846); ski packages are available throughout the winter season. Accommodations start around $150 in summer, $180 in winter.

Down near West Fork Meadows, spectacular **Lone Mountain Ranch** (☎ 406-995-4644, 800-514-4644; W www.lmranch.com) has 47mi of groomed cross-country trails and a full-service lodge; day passes cost $18. They also offer dinner sleigh rides ($69).

HIKING & BACKPACKING

Hiking trails – all open to mountain biking – head into the mountains along numerous creek drainages from both sides of US 191. Trails are marked on the useful *Lee Metcalf Wilderness* and *West Yellowstone Vicinity* Forest Service maps, available at ranger stations or local sports stores.

A favorite hike/post-hike combo is to hike up to the fire lookout at the top of the **Cinnamon Creek Trail** then have lunch or dinner at the Cinnamon Lodge, near the trailhead on US 191.

The most popular hikes are in the north half of the valley. The 6mi round-trip hike to **Lava Lake** is so popular that fires have been banned within .5mi of the lake. The trailhead is a tight turnoff at a dangerous curve in I-191. The uphill trail gains about 1600ft, crossing Cascade Creek several times to meadows and then up more switchbacks. There are good campsites on the northeast shore of the lake and decent trout fishing.

A trailhead on Squaw Creek Rd accesses several trails. The 1.5mi climb to the top of the **Storm Castle Trail** (No 92) offers great views but an unrelenting uphill climb; the last quarter mile, across loose scree, is especially strenuous and tricky.

The equally demanding 8mi round-trip **Garnet Lookout Trail** (No 85) leads off in the opposite direction, gaining 2850ft to the top of Garnet Peak, where there is a Forest Service lookout tower that can be rented as a cabin.

One of the most popular points to access the **Spanish Peaks** area is Spanish Creek Campground at the end of USFS Rd 982, about 22mi south of Bozeman. Camping is allowed at the trailhead, and there's a Forest Service cabin nearby. Most routes are overnighters or multiday loops. A popular loop leads up Falls Creek to the Jerome Rock Lakes (8mi) and then back down the South Fork. Longer loops take in the Spanish Lakes (8.5mi from the trailhead) or Mirror Lake (7.5mi) and return via Indian Ridge and Little Hellroaring Creek.

An ambitious multiday backcountry adventure is to hike the **Gallatin Divide Devils Backbone Trail**, which follows the ridgeline of the Gallatin Range.

OTHER ACTIVITIES

There are **fishing** access sites at Greek Creek, Moose Creek Flat, and Red Cliff Campgrounds, but local anglers swear that anywhere you cast a line in the beautiful Gallatin is bound to be good. Some scenes from the film *A River Runs Through It* were filmed on the Gallatin.

East Slope Anglers (☎ 406-995-4369; W www.eastslopeanglers.com), 100yd south of the Big Sky turnoff, has a store full of equipment for rent or sale and offers guided fly-fishing trips with instruction, as does **Gallatin Riverguides** (☎ 406-995-2290; W www.montanaflyfishing.com), another mile south.

Geyser Whitewater Expeditions (☎ 406-995-4989; W www.raftmontana.com), on US 191 a mile south of the Big Sky turnoff, offers **white-water rafting** trips ($41/79 for a half/full day) and **kayak trips** ($61). **Yellowstone Raft Company** (☎ 406-995-4613), 7mi north of the turnoff, has similar prices and services.

A number of outfitters offer **horseback riding** trips, including **Jake's Horses** (☎ 406-995-4630), **Diamond K Outfitters** (☎ 406-587-0448), and **Big Sky Stables** (☎ 406-995-2972). The cost is about $25 per hour, $65 for a half-day, and $125 for a full day including lunch.

PLACES TO STAY

Numerous Forest Service campgrounds snuggle up to the base of the Gallatin Range along US 191. All grounds have potable water and vault toilets and are open mid-May to mid-September. Up to 60% of sites in these grounds can be reserved in advance through the **National Recreation Reservation Service** (☎ 877-555-6777; W *www.reserveusa.com*).

Red Cliff (*$9*), 48mi south of Bozeman, has 65 sites, which means there's almost always space available. **Moose Creek Flat** (*13 sites; $9*) is on the riverside but very close to the road. **Swan Creek Campground** (*13 sites; $9*), 32mi south of Bozeman and .5mi east on paved Rd No 481, is secluded and popular, backing onto Swan Creek. A mile north, **Greek Creek Campground** (*14 sites; $9*) doubles as a fishing access site. Sites are on both sides of the highway; western riverside sites fill early. Away from the road is secluded **Spire Rock Campground** (*19 sites; $7*), 26mi south of Bozeman, then 2mi east on Squaw Creek Rd No 1321.

The Forest Service operates four cabins in the valley: **Little Bear**, **Spanish Creek**, **Garnet Mountain**, and **Windy Pass**. The last three are hike, ski, or snowmobile-in only. Most cabins are available year-round for $30 per night, sleep four and are equipped with stoves, firewood, cooking supplies, and blankets. Contact **Gallatin National Forest Bozeman Ranger Station** (☎ 406-522-2520) for booking information.

Lodges & Guest Ranches

The **Cinnamon Lodge** (☎ 406-995-4253; *cabins with kitchens $118, basic motel rooms $45*), on the Gallatin River about 10mi south of the Big Sky turnoff, gets everyone from seniors in RVs to families in minivans to groups of serious hunters and fly fishers. Its Western-feeling bar and café serves excellent Mexican food from 7am to 9pm.

320 Ranch (☎ 406-995-4283, 800-243-0320; W *www.320ranch.com; cabins from $89*), 12mi south of Big Sky by the Buffalo Horn Creek Trailhead, is a historic guest ranch with 60 log cabins, a fishing shop, hot tub, and saloon. Winter activities include sleigh rides and snowmobiling.

Covered Wagon Ranch (☎ 406-995-4237; W *www.coveredwagonranch.com; 34035 Gallatin Rd, 3mi from Yellowstone, near Taylors Fork; $180-210 per person per day, in summer; $69-89 per cabin Oct-May*) has been a dude ranch since 1925 and is less glitzy than many of the newer guest ranches.

At the valley's north end, the **Gallatin Gateway Inn** (☎ 406-763-4672; W *www .gallatingatewayinn.com; dbl $85-130*) was built by the Milwaukee Railroad in 1927 to act as the terminus for the Yellowstone line and became an elegant early gateway to the park. Gourmet food and a beautifully appointed dining room attract both tourists and locals. The bar has live music on weekends and is a favorite watering hole for Bozeman's outdoorsy 30-something crowd.

Rainbow Ranch Lodge (☎ 406-995-4132, 800-937-4132; W *www.rainbowranch.com; 12mi north of Yellowstone; rooms $135-$285*), 5mi south of the Big Sky turnoff, is a luxurious resort right on the Gallatin. The sophisticated **restaurant** (*entrees $22-36*) is a favorite splurge for valley locals, and there are barbecues three times a week.

Paradise Valley
MAP 12

With Livingston as a railroad stop, the Paradise Valley became the first travel corridor to Yellowstone National Park. Gardiner, 50mi south of Livingston and just north of the Mammoth Hot Springs entrance to Yellowstone, is still one of the park's most popular entry points. The valley is still mostly ranchland but also includes such famous residents as Peter Fonda, Jeff Bridges, Dennis Quaid, and the cultish Church Universal & Triumphant (CUT), which borders on Yellowstone National Park.

US 89 follows the Yellowstone River through this broad valley, flanked by the Gallatin Range to the west and the jagged Absaroka Range to the east. If you have time, the scenic East River Rd offers a parallel and quieter alternative to busy US 89. For a rundown on the valley's accommodations, restaurants, and services, check out W www.paradisevalleymontana.com.

CHICO HOT SPRINGS

At the mouth of Emigrant Canyon, **Chico Hot Springs** (☎ 406-333-4933; W www.chico hotsprings.com; 30mi from Yellowstone National Park) was established in 1900 as a luxurious getaway for local cattle barons. The Victorian elegance has been restored with great attention to rustic detail. It's worth a visit just to poke around and take a plunge in the large outdoor pool.

Smallish rooms in the main lodge with shared bath are $45 to $60, or $85 with private bathroom (discounted off-season). Modern high-ceilinged rooms with a porch go for $109. Motel-style Fishermen's Cabins go for $97. Chalets up the hill have mountain views, mostly sleep four to six and run from $149 to $179. Suites with private Jacuzzi are a great luxury.

Chico's activity center offers horseback riding (one-hour/half-day rides $25/65), raft trips down the Yellowstone, and dogsled treks (Thanksgiving to Easter), and rents mountain bikes and cross-country skis. There's a full spa attached.

The **Chico Inn Restaurant** (dinner with wine around $35 per person, buffet breakfast $6.95) is renowned throughout the region. The beef Wellington ($49.95 for two) gets rave reviews. The **Poolside Grill** is cheaper and more casual, with sandwiches, pizza, and ribs. The attached **saloon** has live music on weekends.

TOM MINER BASIN

Tom Miner Rd heads west of US 89, 17mi north of Gardiner and 35mi south of Livingston, into one of the prettiest pockets of land in the area. The washboard road ends 12mi west of the highway at **Tom Miner Campground** ($7), which has potable water, toilets, and 16 secluded sites.

Several trails start at the campground, including a 3mi loop (trail No 286) through the **Gallatin Petrified Forest**, where remnants of 35- to 55-million-year-old petrified wood are scattered among the Absaroka's volcanic rocks. Some of the trees were buried where they grew, but most were deposited by a great mudflow caused by nearby volcanic eruptions about 50 million years ago.

A .5mi-long interpretive trail winds around volcanic bluffs of fused ash (bear right where a sign says "Hiker Trail only") and peters out by a remarkable piece of petrified wood that is lodged in the roof of a small cave. Beyond here faint trails lead around the volcanic features. Visitors are allowed to keep one small piece of petrified wood (maximum 20 cubic inches) with a free permit available at the Gardiner, Bozeman, or Livingston ranger offices.

SOUTHERN PARADISE VALLEY

South of the Tom Miner turnoff, US 89 winds through Yankee Jim Canyon, a narrow gorge cut through folded bands of extremely old rock (mostly gneiss) that look a bit like marble cake. "Yankee Jim" George hacked out a toll road through the canyon in the 19th century and made a living from Yellowstone-bound stagecoaches until the railroad came thundering through the valley. The stretch of the Yellowstone River running through Yankee Jim Canyon is a popular white-water spot.

A couple of miles farther toward Yellowstone look for the roadside hot springs, which were once channeled into an elegant, turn of the century resort at nearby Corwin Springs. Farther south, a pullout signposted "wildlife viewing" offers fine views of the **Devil's Slide**, a superbly named salmon-pink landslide area consisting of 200-million-year-old rock.

HIKING & BACKPACKING

Paradise Valley's most popular trail is the 10mi round-trip hike to **Pine Creek Lake**. The trail starts from the Pine Creek Campground parking area and leads 1.2mi to Pine Creek Falls and then another 3.8mi to Pine Creek Lake, gaining around 3000ft en route. Budget at least four hours for the return.

Farther south, down Mill Creek Rd, is the trailhead for **Elbow Lake**, 3500ft above the trailhead at the base of 11,206ft Mt Cowen, the highest peak in the Absaroka Range. The strenuous 18mi round-trip hike (along trails No 51 and 48) is possible as a *long* day hike, but it's better to overnight at the lake.

Farther south, there are more hiking opportunities on the east side of the Gallatin Range. A popular day hike from Tom Miner Campground takes you 2.5mi up Trail Creek to meadows at **Buffalo Horn Pass**. A viewpoint five minutes' walk south offers excellent views of the Gallatin Valley; Ramshorn Peak (10,289ft) beckons to the north.

The Forest Service *Gallatin Forest East Half* map (1:126,720) provides a good overview of the valley's routes but lacks contours.

OTHER ACTIVITIES

The Yellowstone River winds past 19 **fishing** access sites along Paradise Valley, most of which have boat ramps. The Montana Department of Fishing, Wildlife & Parks runs **campsites** *(sites $5, $10 without a Montana fishing license)* at the Mallard's Rest, Loch Leven, and Dailey Lake fishing access sites. Overnight camping is permitted free of charge at the BLM Carbella and Paradise access areas, but the limited and primitive sites get snapped up quickly. All other access areas are day-use only.

Bearpaw Outfitters (☎ *406-222-6642;* Ⓦ *www.bearpawoutfittersmt.com; 136 Deep Creek Rd)* organizes **horse pack trips** in the Absaroka-Beartooth Wilderness and day rides in Yellowstone Park ($130), plus fly-fishing in Yellowstone's Slough Creek.

Try **mountain biking** along the paved East River Rd from the junction with Hwy 89 to Chico Rd and Chico Hot Springs. It's a scenic and smooth ride of 24mi. For something more rugged, try the 17mi gravel Gardiner Back Rd between Gardiner and Tom Miner Rd. This route follows the old stagecoach and railroad road from Yellowstone and takes you past the Devil's Slide and the narrows of Yankee Jim Canyon. To shorten the ride, turn off at Corwin Springs after 8mi. Combine these two routes, and you'll get a complete traverse of the valley.

PLACES TO STAY & EAT

There's a beautifully situated **KOA** (☎ *406-222-0992; tent/RV sites $17/25; open May-Oct)* between US 89 and the East River Rd, 10mi south of Livingston, with an indoor heated pool. Two miles farther south, on East River Rd, **Pine Creek Lodge & Store** *(☎ 406-222-3628; cabins $69)* has homey cabins in a peaceful location and a cozy café/restaurant (open 7am-9pm daily) with a big outside patio.

About 2mi farther south on East River Rd, Luccock Park Rd heads 3mi east to **Pine Creek Campground** *(sites $9)*, with pit toilets and hiker/biker sites. Both this and **Snowbank Campground**, 17mi south down Mill Creek Road, serve as springboards to local hikes. Call the Livingston Ranger District *(☎ 406-222-1892)* for information.

The roadside **Canyon Campground** in Yankee Jim Canyon, 16mi from Yellowstone, is waterless but does have picnic tables, fire rings, and an accessible toilet – best of all, it's free!

Mountain Sky Guest Ranch *(☎ 406-587-1244, 800-548-3392;* Ⓦ *www.mtnsky.com; 30mi from Yellowstone)* is a professionally run ranch on the west flanks of the valley, 4.5mi up Big Creek Rd. Activities include dawn horseback rides to catch the sunrise over Emigrant Peak, fishing, and tennis, a pool, sauna, and hot tub, and good kids' programs. All-inclusive weekly rates run from $2500 per person.

For a cheaper option, the Forest Service operates the year-round **Big Creek Cabin** *(reservations ☎ 406-222-1892; $30; sleeps 10),* set a half-mile from the ranch in the Gallatin National Forest, as well as **Mill Creek Cabin** *($35; sleeps four)*, on the east side of the valley.

The **Paradise Valley Pop Stand** *(☎ 406-222-2006; 2.5mi south of Livingston; closed Monday)* is a 1950s-style joint serving up malts, burgers, and homemade pie (with free coffee).

Beartooth Highway (US 212)
MAP 13

The breathtaking Beartooth Hwy connects Red Lodge to Cooke City and Yellowstone's northeast entrance along a soaring 68mi road built in 1932. An engineering feat, and the "most beautiful drive in America" according to the late journalist Charles Kuralt, this road is a destination in its own right and the most dramatic route into Yellowstone.

Covering 1474 sq mi, the Absaroka-Beartooth Wilderness stretches along Montana's border with Wyoming (a small section on its east side lies inside Wyoming) and crosses through Gallatin, Custer, and Shoshone National Forests. The wilderness area takes in two distinct mountain ranges: the Absarokas and the Beartooth Plateau (the Beartooths). The Beartooths are composed of uplifted three-billion-year-old granite, the oldest rock in the Greater Yellowstone region. Steep, forested valleys and craggy peaks characterize the Absarokas, while the Beartooths are essentially high plateaus dotted with more than 1000 lakes and tarns.

Most of the wilderness consists of high plateau above 10,000ft. Alpine tundra vegetation is the only thing that grows up here (where snow can last from October to mid-July), lending the landscape a desolate, otherworldly look. In fact, unless you are an outdoorsy type who makes frequent forays above 10,000ft, it probably *is* another world – you can't usually reach this kind of terrain by car. To really experience the surroundings, you must get out of the car, even if it's just for a few minutes to suck in the thin, cold air.

The highway has a short driving season and is usually closed between October 15 and mid to late-May. For information on weather conditions, hikes, and bear sightings pull into the **Beartooth Ranger District office** (☎ *406-446-2103),* just south of Red Lodge.

There are plans for road construction, starting in 2003, from the northeast entrance of Yellowstone National Park east to the Montana/Wyoming line. Check the website Ⓦ www.cflhd.gov/projects/wy/beartooth for developments.

THE HIGHWAY

From its starting point at Red Lodge, the highway climbs Rock Creek Canyon's classic U-shaped glaciated walls via a series of gnarled switchbacks.

A parking area at **Rock Creek Vista Point Overlook** (9160ft) has toilets and a short walk to superb views. The road continues up onto the plateau and into Wyoming.

In another 3mi the road passes **Twin Lakes**, where a parking area offers good views of the cirque and the ski lift that carries the daring to an extreme ski run. Another 1.3mi farther along is Gardner Lake. After 0.7mi, at the start of a series of switchbacks, look northwest across Rock Creek for views of the Hellroaring Plateau and the jagged **Bear's Tooth** peak, which lends the range its name. A mile later you'll crest the **Beartooth Pass West Summit** at 10,947ft.

From here the road descends past Frozen Lake, Long Lake, Little Bear Lake (the last two with excellent fishing), and the Chain Lakes (on the left) to the Island Lake and Beartooth Lake Campgrounds. Both of these offer excellent opportunities for a picnic and day hike. Between the campgrounds is the Top of the World Store, which is worth a stop for a reviving coffee (and a fishing license if you need one).

As the road descends, you'll see **Beartooth Butte**, a huge lump of the sedimentary rock that once covered the Beartooths. Two miles beyond Beartooth Lake Campground, turn right up a 2.5mi dirt road to the former fire watchtower at Clay Butte Overlook (open July and Aug; no RVs or trailers). The views from here are fantastic: Look for the effects of the 1988 Clover Mist fire and the "Reef," a snaking line of sedimentary rock that follows the entire valley, proof that this lofty region was once underwater.

A mile back on the main road is the overlook of **Index Peak** (11,313ft) and jagged **Pilot Peak** (11,708ft). Next up is the Clarks Fork Overlook (with toilets) and then a small turnout by Lake Creek Falls. Less than a mile from here, forestry road 130-1 leads 2mi north to secluded **Lily Lake**, where you'll find a canoe ramp, good fishing, and several free campsites.

The turnoff left is for Chief Joseph Scenic Hwy (see p 213), which leads to Cody and accesses Yellowstone's east entrance via Wapiti Valley. The Beartooth Hwy descends to several excellent fishing areas on the Clarks Fork and reenters Montana, crossing Colter Pass (8066ft). Not far afterwards, near Chief Joseph Campground, is **Clarks Fork Trailhead**, a fine place for a picnic. From here it's 4mi to Cooke City.

HIKING & BACKPACKING

You can gain about 3000ft of elevation by car and begin your hike from the Beartooth Hwy, but it's very important to allow a day or two to acclimatize. Also be aware that the barren terrain offers little shade, shelter, or wood. In order to protect the fragile alpine vegetation, hikers should not light campfires above the tree line. Grizzly and black bears are not common in the wilderness; hikers have a better chance of seeing bighorn sheep, mountain goats, or elk.

August is the best month to hike the Beartooths. Snow remains in many places above tree line at least until the end of July and starts to accumulate again after mid-September. Localized afternoon thunderstorms, with hail, are common in the Beartooths during June (the wettest month) and July. During early summer you'll also need lots of bug repellent and waterproof shoes to cope with swampy trails. Don't be put off; just be forewarned. With proper preparation, the plateau offers some of Greater Yellowstone's very best hiking.

From Island Lake Campground you can take a wonderful and easy hourlong stroll along the **Beartooth High Lakes Trail** to Island Lake and beyond to Night Lake and Flake Lake. All lakes are popular fishing areas. If you can arrange a shuttle, continue downhill to Beauty Lake and then left (south) to Beartooth Lake for a fine half-day hike. For a full description and map of the three-day 21mi lollipop route from Island Lake to the Beartooth High Lakes see LP's *Hiking in the Rocky Mountains* guide.

From Beartooth Lake Campground you can make a wonderful half-day 7.5mi loop via **Beauty Lake**. Branch left at the lake, up Beartooth Creek, and later bear right, passing five lakes, including Claw Lake, to the junction with the Beartooth High Lakes Trail. From here descend right to Beauty Lake and follow the trail back to Beartooth Lake. Parking is limited at the trailhead.

A longer, preferably overnight option is the 13mi **Beartooth National Recreation Trail**, accessed from the highway at either Gardner Lake or farther southwest at Hauser Lake.

The contoured USFS 1:63,360 *Absaroka Beartooth Wilderness* map ($6) covers the whole area and is adequate for most hikes. *Hiking the Beartooths* and *Easy Day Hikes in the Beartooths,* both published by Falcon Press and written by Bill Schneider, are also useful resources.

PLACES TO STAY

There are 13 basic Forest Service **campgrounds** along the Beartooth Hwy between Red Lodge and Cooke City, most charging $8 to $10. The most accessible from US 212 are **Island Lake** *($8; no water)* and **Beartooth Lake** *($10)*, both open July to mid-September. Farther south on the plateau are the **Crazy Creek** and **Fox Creek Campgrounds** *($8; open Jun–early-Sep; no water)*. These sites come under Shoshone National Forest jurisdiction *(☎ 307-527-6241)*.

Closer to Cooke City, **Chief Joseph** *($8; six sites)*, **Colter** *($6; 23 sites; no water)*, and **Soda Butte** *($8; 21 sites)* **Campgrounds** are 4mi, 2mi, and 1mi east of town, respectively. Soda Butte was

Localized afternoon thunderstorms, with hail, are common in the Beartooths.

closed for reconstruction at last report, and the others may follow suit. Call the Gardiner Ranger District (☎ 406-848-7375) for details.

Top of the World Motel (☎ 307-899-2482; rooms from $48), on the highway about 1mi east of the Island Lake turnoff, offers four basic rooms, but you are better off camping.

Wapiti Valley
MAP 15

The Buffalo Bill Scenic Byway (US 14/16/20) traces the scenic Wapiti Valley along the North Fork of the Shoshone River from Cody to the East Entrance of Yellowstone National Park, taking in what Teddy Roosevelt famously called the "most scenic 52 miles in the United States."

Hemmed in by the rugged volcanic Absaroka Range of Shoshone National Forest, the North Fork wends its way through a picturesque canyon that shifts from eroded badlands to alpine splendor. The North Absaroka Wilderness Area to the north and the Washakie Wilderness Area to the south (the latter named after a famous Shoshone chief) are home to grizzlies and black bears, deer, elk, moose, bighorn sheep, and a few bison. The valley's name comes from an Algonquin Indian word meaning "pale white rump," used to differentiate the lighter-colored elk, or *wapiti*, from darker-colored moose.

The extensive network of trails, easy access to the Lake area of Yellowstone National Park and a selection of the region's best dude ranches make the valley an excellent route into or out of the park.

Six miles west of Cody, US 14/16/20 emerges from the dramatic **Shoshone Canyon** and tunnel to views of the **Buffalo Bill Reservoir**. Past the settlement of Wapiti, Wyoming's high desert landscape and open ranchland closes in as the road enters Shoshone National Forest and becomes Buffalo Bill Cody Scenic Hwy.

The **Wapiti Valley Visitor Center** (☎ 307-587-3925; open 8am-8pm weekdays and 8:30am-5pm weekends Memorial Day–Labor Day) has a 3D map of the region, as well as information on the valley's frequent grizzly sightings.

From here on the Wapiti Valley is lined with eerie eroded volcanic buttes and hoodoos with overimaginative names (try to find the Four Bobsledders!). National forest campgrounds, trailheads, and guest ranches crop up every few miles as the scenery becomes increasingly alpine.

Two miles before the east entrance to Yellowstone is the gas station, store, restaurant, and corrals of **Pahaska Tepee Resort**, a good place to refuel. Staff lead free tours of the original lodge, built by Buffalo Bill in 1904 as a hunting lodge. Pahaska was Bill's Indian name and means "Longhair" in the Sioux language, a reference to Cody's long white hair and extravagant goatee.

HIKING & BACKPACKING

The gradual ascent of the **Elk Fork Trail** (trail No 760) up Elk Fork is particularly popular with horse packers. The trail leads 21mi up to Rampart Creek and Overlook Mountain (11,869ft), but you don't have to go the whole way. A pleasant round-trip day hike takes you 3mi up the Elk Fork to where the trail fords the river.

Explorations up Kitty Creek, Fishwater Creek or Clearwater Creek will doubtless turn up other great hikes. For details about these and other hikes in the region see

Falcon Press' *Hiking Wyoming's Teton & Washakie Wilderness Areas,* by Lee Mercer and Ralph Maughan.

OTHER ACTIVITIES

Most of the valley's guest ranches offer **horseback riding** trips to nonguests. Prices are around $20 for one hour, $30 to $35 for two hours, $45 to $65 for a half day and $90 to $100 for a full day. Most also offer overnight horse-packing trips (from $125) and cookouts two or three times a week.

The North Fork Shoshone River is a favorite of white-water **rafting** aficionados. Elk, bighorn sheep, and moose are often seen from the river. The rafting season is mid-May to mid-September in the Red Rock and Lower Canyons, and Memorial Day to late July for the North Fork. See the Cody entry (p 227) for details of rafting companies.

Four miles east of Yellowstone's east entrance, the small **Sleeping Giant Ski Area** (☎ 307-587-4044; W *www.skisleepinggiant.com*) has a base elevation of 7000ft with a maximum vertical drop of 500ft. Lift tickets are $20/10 adults/children.

North Fork Nordic Trails (☎ 307-527-7701), which connects Pahaska Tepee Resort and Sleeping Giant Ski Area, offers 25mi of groomed cross-country trails.

PLACES TO STAY

Nine Forest Service campgrounds line the Wapiti Valley, starting from 29mi west of Cody. Overflow from Yellowstone fills up the grounds in July and August, so try to arrive before late afternoon. Most are open June to late September. The following are listed from east to west. Call the Shoshone National Forest North Zone (☎ 307-577-6921) for details.

Big Game *($5)* is small but spacious and private, whereas **Wapiti** *($10)* is larger but more cramped. **Elk Fork** *($5)* is cramped and sometimes has no water but is popular as a base for hiking and horse-packing trips. Riverside **Clearwater** *($5)* has water and some groups sites. **Rex Hale** *($10)* is more exposed but has six sites with electrical hookups (sites $15). Woodsy **Newton Creek** *($10)* is pleasant but is sometimes limited to hard-sided vehicles only due to bear activity. **Eagle Creek** and **Three Mile** campgrounds (both hard-sided campers only) were being renovated at last check.

All campgrounds are along the river, offering easy access to trout fishing. Most campgrounds are open mid-May to September (a few into October), but can be closed at any time due to grizzly bear activity.

Wapiti Valley's lodges and dude ranches make a great base for exploring Yellowstone National Park or Cody. Most offer fishing, hiking, rock climbing, and guided horseback rides. Some only offer weekly rates. Luxury in proximity to the park doesn't come cheap, but you should get discounted rates before May and after September.

The historic year-round **Pahaska Tepee** (☎ 307-527-7701, 800-628-7791; W *www.pahaska.com; cabins from $90/57 peak-season/off-season*) is closest to the park and one of the best deals.

Lodges East of Yellowstone Valley (☎ 307-587-9595; W *www.yellow stone-lodging.com; PO Box 21, Wapiti, WY 82450*) provides information on the valley's numerous family-owned member dude ranches and lodges.

Chief Joseph Scenic Highway

The Clarks Fork of the Yellowstone River, Wyoming's only National Wild and Scenic River, runs along much of the Chief Joseph Scenic Hwy (Hwy 296) linking Cody (via

Hwy 120 north) with the Beartooth Hwy (US 212) and Yellowstone National Park's northeast entrance, 62mi away. It's a very scenic route that links up with the equally stunning Beartooth Hwy to make several potential loop itineraries. The highway is named for Chief Joseph of the Nez Percé tribe who came through the Clarks Fork while fleeing the US Army.

The paved highway is open year-round from Cody to the Beartooth Hwy and a short way west, though not as far as Cooke City. The Beartooth Hwy itself is closed mid-October to late May. Fall colors are particularly lovely, fishing in the region is superb, and the white water pushes the limits of even professional kayakers.

Take Hwy 120 north of Cody for 16mi to the turn left onto Hwy 296, the start of the 47mi Chief Joseph Scenic Hwy. The road heads northwest, entering Shoshone National Forest after 8mi, and climbs to a spectacular viewpoint at **Dead Indian Pass** (8048ft). Indians used to wait here and ambush game that migrated through the pass between summer pastures in the mountains and winter ranges in the plains. The pass is named for a Bannock Indian killed here in skirmishes with the Army in 1878.

As you descend from the pass, just .3mi before Dead Indian Campground a dirt road leads a couple of hundred yards to a trailhead parking lot that offers an excellent short hike to view the 1200ft deep **Clarks Fork Canyon**. The trail leads north for 2mi to a scenic overlook; watch for cairns marking the spot shortly after you first see the gorge. The views of the 1200ft granite gorge and Dead Indian Creek waterfall are breathtaking. The canyon effectively separates the 50-million-year-old volcanic rock of the Absaroka Range from the two-billion-year-old granite of the Beartooth Plateau. The trail continues for another 3mi right down to the canyon floor, but the 700ft descent and then ascent makes for a considerably more strenuous hike. To return to the trailhead, retrace your steps.

Back on the road, USFS Rd 101 branches southwest into the breathtakingly beautiful **Sunlight Basin**. If you have plenty of time, the 36mi round-trip offers some beautiful vistas, but it's a slow bumpy trip. Eight miles along the dirt road is the Sunlight Ranger Station. Beyond this are ranches framed by a wall of peaks that forms the boundary of Yellowstone National Park.

Where Hwy 296 crosses Sunlight Creek is the terrific **Sunlight Bridge**, the highest in Wyoming. You can park and cross the bridge for hair-raising views into the gorge (acrophobes beware!), though better overviews can be had .5mi north on the highway.

Just north of Crandall Creek (named after a pioneer miner who was beheaded by Indians) around Swamp Lake is a collection of half a dozen ponds that offer excellent birding (including sandhill cranes and trumpeter swans).

Hwy 296 continues northwest to the crossbar junction of US 212, where the Beartooth Hwy leads northwest to Cooke City (see the Gateway Towns chapter, p 65) and Yellowstone Park or northeast to Red Lodge and Billings.

Upper Wind River Valley

Part of the Wyoming Centennial Scenic Byway, US 26/287 climbs east from Grand Teton National Park's Moran Junction up the slopes of Bridger-Teton National Forest to Togwotee (**Toe**-ga-tee) Pass (9658ft), before dropping into the upper Wind River Valley. To the north is the 914 sq mi Teton Wilderness; to the south is the more distant Gros Ventre Wilderness. Dubois is the only town in the upper valley, east of which the landscape yields to the semiarid red sandstone Dubois badlands.

The Bridger-Teton National Forest **Buffalo Ranger District Blackrock Ranger Station** (☎ *307-543-2386, 307-739-5600)*, 8mi east of Moran Junction, has general information and free maps of the region.

MORAN JUNCTION TO TOGWOTEE PASS

About 3mi east of Moran Junction, the paved Buffalo Valley Rd forks off the main highway to offer a 4mi detour northeast up the Buffalo Fork to the Turpin Meadow Recreation Area, a popular launching pad for local outfitters. There's a Forest Service campground here and lots of dispersed camping. The road loops south as the unpaved USFS Rd 30050 to rejoin US 26/287.

Three miles from this junction, just past Togwotee Cowboy Village, a short detour to the left leads to a **scenic overlook** with fine views back to the Tetons. A second viewpoint, the **Togwotee Pass Vista View**, is 5mi farther; the actual pass is another 12mi from here. The pass, named for a Shoshone medicine man who led the US Army Corps of Engineers here in 1873, marks the Continental Divide. Just by the pass, the lovely **Wind River Lake** makes a perfect picnic spot.

Six miles downhill, the turnoff to Falls Campground offers access to pretty Brooks Lake Creek Falls, with fine views up to the breccia (lava and ash) cliffs of the Pinnacle Buttes.

Across from Falls Campground, unpaved Brooks Lake Rd (USFS Rd 515) winds uphill for 5mi to gorgeous **Brooks Lake**, a popular base for camping, canoeing, fishing, and hiking (see Activities) set at the base of dramatic Pinnacle Buttes. The road passes Pinnacle Campground before it descends to Brooks Lake Campground, a boat ramp, and trailhead. From the Brooks Lake turnoff it's 23mi to Dubois, or 31mi back to Grand Teton. For campsite information call the Wind River Ranger District (☎ *307-455-2466)*.

Jackson Hole

Early European visitors coined the term "hole" to describe a broad valley surrounded by mountains. Jackson Hole (pop 18,000) to the south of Grand Teton National Park is such a place, bounded by the Gros Ventre (**Grow**-vant; "big belly" in French) and Teton Ranges to the east and west, respectively, and the Yellowstone lava flows and Hoback and Wyoming Ranges to the north and south. The communities of Jackson, Teton Village, Kelly, Moose, Wilson and much of south Grand Teton National Park lie within the Hole.

Moose, elk, and bison roam the valley floor against the rugged backdrop of the Tetons, making Jackson Hole one of Wyoming's most breathtaking destinations. The mountains that surround the valley are part of the 3.4 million-acre Bridger-Teton National Forest, the second largest forest in the Lower 48 US states.

Downhill skiing is the main winter activity, but summertime visitors find no shortage of things to do. For details on rafting, mountain biking, and horseback riding in the valley, see the Jackson entry in the Gateway Towns chapter (p 66).

TETON VILLAGE & JACKSON HOLE MOUNTAIN RESORT

This modern year-round resort is at the foot of Rendezvous Mountain, 12mi northwest of Jackson. The resort attracts an international crowd with its long runs, deep powder, and awesome 4139ft vertical drop. After the spring snowmelt, fair weather activities include hiking, biking, white-water rafting, fly-fishing, mountain biking, and faux cowboying.

The **Jackson Hole Guest Service Center** (☎ 307-739-2753, 800-450-0477) is near the tram ticket office in the Clock Tower Building in Teton Village. Contact **Jackson Hole Mountain Resort** (☎ 307-733-2292, 888-333-7766; W www.jacksonhole.com) for a free visitors guide. The resort also has an in-town office (☎ 307-733-4005; 140 E Broadway).

Jackson Hole Aerial Tram

This scenic tram ride ($16/13/6 adults/seniors/children six and up) rises 2.5mi in 12 minutes to the top of Rendezvous Mt (10,450ft), offering great views of Jackson Hole and providing a high-altitude piggyback to Grand Teton National Park's high-country trails. Tram arrivals can either hike down the Granite Canyon Trail or choose from a series of shorter trails: the .5mi Summit Nature Loop, 3mi Cody Bowl Trail or 4.25 Rock Springs Bowl. Hikes with a resident naturalist leave at 10am and 1pm. The tram operates 9am to 5pm daily late May to late September, a bit later when demand is high.

Skiing

From the 6311ft base at Teton Village to the summit of Rendezvous Mountain, the United States' greatest continuous vertical rise makes Jackson Hole one of the world's top ski destinations. The resort's 2500 acres of ski terrain are blessed by an average of 380 inches of snow annually. The runs (10% beginner, 40% intermediate, 50% advanced) are served by six lifts, an aerial tram, two high-speed quads, and the Bridger gondola. Full-day lift tickets are $59/30 adults/children, half-day tickets (after 12:30pm) are $44/22. Ski season typically runs early December to early April. The free *Jackson Hole Mountain Map & Guide,* available at the guest service center, diagrams Teton Village.

Former Olympic skier Pepi Stiegler operates the **Jackson Hole Ski School** (☎ 307-733-4505). **Jackson Hole Nordic Center** (☎ 307-739-2629) offers 20mi of groomed track and wide skating lanes with rentals and instruction. **High Mountain Heli-Skiing** (☎ 307-733-3274; W www.skitvs.com) delivers skiers to ungroomed backcountry powder.

Several Teton Village shops rent and sell downhill gear: **Jack Dennis Outdoor Shop** (☎ 307-733-6838), **Jackson Hole Sports** (☎ 307-739-2687)], **Teton Village Sports** (☎ 307-733-2181), and **Wildernest Sports** (☎ 307-733-4297). For Nordic gear, try **Skinny Skis** (☎ 307-733-6094; 65 W Deloney Ave) in Jackson. Jackson's **Boardroom of Jackson Hole** (☎ 307-733-8327; 225 W Broadway) is the snowboarder's alternative.

Places to Stay

As in the rest of Jackson Hole, rates here vary widely and seasonally; some hotels also levy a resort fee. Quoted rates are for high-season doubles; figure up to 50% off during low season. Try **Jackson Hole Central Reservations** (☎ 307-733-4005, 800-443-6931; W www.jhsnow.com) for off-season specials and package deals.

Jackson Hole's only West Bank camping option is the full-service **Teton Village KOA Campground** (☎ 307-733-5354; tent sites/full RV hookups $28/40), 2mi north of Hwy 22 on Hwy 390.

Teton Village's only budget option is **Hostel**ˣ (☎ 307-733-3415; W www.hostelx.com; 1-2 people/3-4 people $53/67; closed during shoulder seasons). This ski lodge offers two choices: basic, four twin-bed bunk rooms or doubles with one king-size bed. Unlike most hostels, all rooms are private and include linens and daily maid service. Shared downstairs amenities include a large lounge, two TVs with VCRs, a microwave, and BBQ (but no real kitchen), free Internet access, coin laundry, and a ski waxing area.

Basic doubles with full bath and cable TV start around $125 at the **Crystal Springs Lodge** (☎ 307-733-4423; above Teton Village Sports) and **Village Center Inn** (☎ 307-733-3155, 800-735-8342).

Jackson Hole Resort Lodging (☎ 307-733-3990, 800-443-8613; Ⓦ www.jhresort lodging.com; 3200 W McCollister Dr) manages a range of Teton Village rental properties, from studio condos ($70-125 per night) to two-bedroom townhomes ($175-490), and multiple-bedroom houses (from $255).

Places to Eat

Quick-fix options include **Nick Wilson's Cowboy Cafe**, at the base of the tram, for inexpensive American breakfast and lunch standards and live aprés-ski entertainment on weekends, and **Bridger Bagels & Espresso** for soup, sandwiches, and caffeine jolts.

The **Mangy Moose Saloon** (☎ 307-733-4913; dinner $12-20; open 5pm-9pm daily) is a rockin' steak and seafood joint (with a good salad bar) that doubles as a spirited nightspot, featuring big-name live music. Downstairs, the **Rocky Mountain Oyster** (☎ 307-733-9438; breakfast & lunch under $10, pizzas $10-20; open 7am-10pm daily) dishes out cheap breakfasts, burgers, soups, sandwiches, and thin-crust, New York–style pizza.

A good value with an attractive outdoor summer deck, the **Alpenhof Bistro** (☎ 307-733-3242; lunch and dinner $10-20; open 11:30am-3pm and 6-10pm daily) specializes in wild game, seafood, and prime rib.

Just north of Vista Grande, the casual, family-friendly **Calico Italian Restaurant & Bar** (☎ 307-733-2460; Hwy 390; mains $11-19; open from 5pm daily), in a renovated 1905 church, crafts lighthearted Italian fare. Bonuses include a good wine list, rich desserts, and organic salads from the house garden. At the Inn at Jackson Hole, **Masa Sushi** (☎ 307-732-2962; combo dinners $15-25; open 5:30pm-9:30pm Tues-Sun; reservations required) serves the Teton's freshest raw fish.

GROS VENTRE SLIDE AREA

On June 23, 1925, a vast slide of 50 million cubic yards of rock, one of the world's largest recent movements of earth, plummeted 2000ft down the side of the Gros Ventre Mountains to form a 225ft high dam and huge lake atop the Gros Ventre River. Two years later the top part of the dam suddenly gave way, creating a monster wave that killed six and washed away the downstream town of Kelly.

Today the **Gros Ventre Slide Geological Area** offers a .5mi interpretive trail with views over the slide. Amazingly, some trees survived the fall, "surfing" the slide to reroot on the valley floor. The resulting Upper and Lower Slide Lakes attract anglers and boaters, and you'll find three Forest Service campgrounds.

The turnoff to the slide area is 1mi north of Kelly. Not far from the junction is the **Kelly Warm Spring**, an undeveloped pool of warm (80°F) water.

The slide area is outside Grand Teton National Park but is most easily accessed through it. See Map 9 for details.

Three nice Forest Service campgrounds (open early June to September 30) are spread out along Gros Ventre Rd beyond the Gros Ventre Slide Geological Area (18 to 23mi northeast of Jackson). Twenty-site **Atherton Creek Campground**, 5.5mi along Gros Ventre Rd at Lower Slide Lake, at the end of the paved road, has a boat dock. Five-site

Red Hills Campground is 4.5mi farther east, fronting the Gros Ventre River; 6-site **Crystal Creek Campground** is .5mi farther. All charge around $10. A 7mi round-trip day hike heads up to Grizzly Lake from near Red Hills Campground. Call the Jackson Ranger District (☎ 307-739-5400) for more information.

GRANITE HOT SPRINGS

The signed turnoff for the developed **Granite Hot Springs Swimming Pool** (☎ 307-733-6318; admission $6; open daily dusk to dawn in summer) and Granite Creek Campground (Jackson Ranger District, ☎ 307-739-5400) is 35mi southeast of Jackson on Hwy 189/191, 1mi before Kozy Campground. The route south through Hoback Canyon affords impressive views of the rocky south face of the Gros Ventre Mountains.

The campground bumps up against the **Gros Ventre Wilderness** and offers good hiking up Granite Creek. Within walking distance of the campground is the undeveloped **Granite Falls Hot Springs**, accessed from the dirt parking area just below the falls. Reaching the hot springs (on the east bank of the creek) requires an often tricky and always chilly ford, and water levels only allow for soaking from around late May until spring snowmelt submerges the pool, with winter access by snowmobile or cross-country skis. Please respect the place and enjoy one of Wyoming's best natural soaks.

Idaho's Teton Valley & Island Park

The Teton River descends the west side of the Teton Range and flows northwest into the Henry's Fork of the Snake River near Rexburg, Idaho. The valley is surrounded on three sides by the mountains of the Targhee National Forest: the Teton Range to the west, the Snake River Range to the south, and the Big Hole Mountains to the southwest. The west face of the mighty Teton Range soars above this broad, scenic valley, which is warmer, sunnier, and more peaceful than its well-known Wyoming neighbor, Jackson Hole.

TETON VALLEY

John Colter stumbled upon the Teton Valley (elevation 6200ft) in 1808 while hunting for beaver. The valley soon became known as Pierre's Hole, a favored mountain man rendezvous, where trapper Jim Bridger and his ilk gathered to trade with natives. Farming has remained the valley's mainstay since Mormon families settled here in the late 19th century, but these once-sleepy ranching towns are now a year-round mecca for outdoor adventure and summer music festivals, with fabulous skiing, hiking, mountaineering, and mountain biking. North of Driggs, however, the classic Fords and antique grain silos recall an earlier era.

Most of the valley lies in Teton County, Idaho, though a small portion (up to the Teton crest) is in Teton County, Wyoming. Known disparagingly in Jackson as the "Tetons' backside," Teton Valley locals prefer to be known as "the sunny side."

Rapidly expanding Driggs (population 1100) is the valley's tourist nerve center. The **Targhee National Forest Teton Basin Ranger District** (☎ 208-354-2312; 525 S Main St) has information on area trails and campgrounds and offers free travel planner maps. For online information visit the Teton Valley Chamber of Commerce at W www.tetonvalleychamber.com.

GRAND TARGHEE SKI & SUMMER RESORT

On the west side of the Teton Range, **Grand Targhee Ski & Summer Resort** (☎ 307-353-2300, 800-827-4433; W *www.grandtarghee.com*) is worshiped for its incredible depth of powder (more than 500 inches of snow falls each winter), its high-elevation location, and its easygoing but professional service and amenities. Base elevation is 8100ft, and four high-speed lifts to the top of Fred's Mountain (10,200ft) access 1500 acres of runs, with a total vertical drop of 2200ft in 3.2mi. The runs are suited for families and intermediate-level skiers. Full-day lift tickets are $49/32 for adults/children under 14; half-day tickets are $36/26. A round-trip bus ride and lift pass costs $59 from Jackson. Seniors get discounted rates.

Adjacent Peaked Mountain (10,230ft) is reserved for wilderness **snowcat powder skiing**. Half/full-day powder skiing costs $175/240. Grand Targhee offers a full range of rentals (ski/snowboards $23/28 per day) and instruction. Ten miles of groomed Nordic trails await ($10/5 day passes, free to lodging guests). Snowboards are welcome on all slopes, and there's a tubing slide area for the kids. The ski season is mid-November to mid-April. Other winter activities include snowshoeing, skating, and dogsledding.

Targhee, as it's often called, is a year-round resort with summer hiking, climbing, horseback riding (half-day $80), and lift-served mountain biking (single ride $12, day pass $16). Scenic chairlifts ($8) operate daily July to mid-August; three times a week at other times. A one-hour hike affords a spectacular vista of Grand Teton itself; ride the lift down for free. There's also a full spa, kids' programs and day care, bike rentals (half-day $25), a climbing wall ($6), and the novel "zip ride," a kind of cable slide ($8).

Its summer **music festival** series includes Rockin' the Tetons in mid-July, the Blues & Microbrew Fest in late July, and the Grand Targhee Bluegrass Music Festival in early August.

Places to Stay & Eat

Rates vary seasonally; check online and inquire about off-season specials and package deals. Kids under 15 stay for free. Options include:

Targhee Lodge – standard doubles from $70/90 summer/winter

Teewinot Lodge – deluxe doubles with Jacuzzi from $110/135 summer/winter

Sioux Lodge Condos – four-person studios (*from $160/200 summer/winter*) and eight-person two-bedroom units (*$195/260*)

Getting There & Away

From Driggs head 4mi east on USFS Rd 025 (toward Alta) to the Idaho-Wyoming state line and continue east 8mi to Targhee. From the second switchback en route to the resort you get the first glimpse of Grand Teton and an overlook of the Teton Basin. Sunset colors are wonderful from here.

Resort shuttles between Targhee and airports in Idaho Falls and Jackson, Wyoming, cost $30 per person for two or more people (reservations required). **Targhee Express** (☎ 800-443-6133) operates once-daily winter bus service between Jackson, Teton Village (☎ 307-733-3101), and Targhee. Round-trip fare is $14 (reservations required).

GRASSY LAKE ROAD (USFS RD 261)

This back route into the parks bumps and grinds for 52mi to Flagg Ranch in the Rockefeller Memorial Parkway. As soon as you enter Targhee National Forest, the road degenerates into gravel and then gets progressively worse – it's the kind of road you're glad you've taken once it's over, but that you wouldn't want to have to take again. Don't consider this route if you're in a hurry and take particular care if there has been heavy rain.

Sandwiched between the Winegar Hole and Jedediah Smith Wildernesses, this region is peppered by lakes, of which the most accessible are the roadside **Indian Lake** and **Loon Lake**, 1mi down a bumpy track. Farther east is the turnoff for the rough road down to stunning Lake of the Woods, site of the Boy Scouts' Loll Camp. A mile farther east is the .5mi detour south to Tilley Lake. Beyond here is the expansive **Grassy Reservoir**, which is popular for boating, fishing, and its dispersed campsites. Just after the reservoir the road enters the Rockefeller Parkway. For details of the eight free campsites farther along Grassy Lake Rd see the Rockefeller Parkway section of the Grand Teton chapter (p 150).

At the west end of Grassy Reservoir, by the dam, trailhead 9K5 is the start of the 15.5mi round-trip hike to **Union Falls**, one of the most spectacular in the park. After a mile the trail branches right, fords Cascade Creek and then branches left (right leads to the Pitchstone Plateau trail). After another 4mi the trail fords Proposition Creek and a mile later branches right onto the Union Falls Trail for another 2mi. Feathery Union Falls are the second highest in the park.

At the east end of Grassy Reservoir a pullout marks the trailhead for the 6mi round-trip hike northeast to **Beula Lake** inside Yellowstone National Park. The trail crosses the South Boundary Trail en route.

North of Yellowstone, the airports of Bozeman and Billings both offer convenient access to the park, though young and active Bozeman has more to offer visitors. As the gateway to Paradise Valley, Livingston has been entertaining Yellowstone-bound tourists for 120 years and is a must for fly-fishing enthusiasts. The interesting town of Red Lodge is the springboard to the Beartooth Hwy and is worth some time in its own right for its excellent hiking, winter sports, and scenic campsites.

EXCURSIONS

East of Yellowstone, Cody is the region's premier excursion for its artfully crafted Wild West flavor and its fine museum. From Yellowstone National Park you can visit the town in a semicircular excursion that takes in both the lovely Wapiti Valley and Chief Joseph Scenic Hwy, linking the park's east and northeast gates. See the Greater Yellowstone map (p 58) for an overview of these areas.

Bozeman

TEL 406 • POP 30,723 • ELEVATION 4800FT

This hip student town is only an hour's drive north of Yellowstone and well worth a visit. Bozeman's **Gallatin Field** airport (Ⓦ *www.gallatinfield.com*) offers flights to a number of North American destinations.

Arguably Montana's most entertaining museum, MSU's **Museum of the Rockies** (☎ *406-994-3466;* Ⓦ *www.museumoftherockies.org; cnr S 7th Ave and Kagy Blvd*) offers exceptional dinosaur reconstructions and displays on native cultures of the Northern Rockies. Known around town as "the Emerson," the nonprofit **Emerson Cultural Center** (☎ *406-587-9797; 111 S Grand Ave*) is the hub of Bozeman's art scene, with retail galleries, exhibits, and studios. The **Gallatin County Pioneer Museum** (☎ *406-582-3195; 317 W Main St*), in the old jail building, does a good job portraying local history.

The best place for all-purpose information, maps, and gear is **Barrel Mountaineering** (☎ *406-582-1335; 240 E Main St*). A community institution, independent **Country Bookshelf** (☎ *406-587-0166; 28 W Main*) hosts readings by local authors like Tim Cahill and Jim Harrison.

PLACES TO STAY & EAT

There are three Forest Service **campsites** (*$9*) southeast of town near the Hyalite Reservoir. **Bozeman KOA** (☎ *406-587-3030; tent/RV sites $24/32; 8mi west of Bozeman*), off I-90, is the only campground in the area open year-round. **Bear**

Canyon Campground (☎ 406-587-1575, tent/RV sites $12/17;; 3mi east of Bozeman; open May-Oct), off I-90 exit 313, has a heated pool, laundry facilities, and a store.

The **Bozeman Backpacker's Hostel** (☎ 406-586-4659; 405 W Olive St; bunk $14) two blocks south of Main St, is an independent hostel that serves a young, active, international clientele. In summer there's a hostel-to-hostel shuttle ($28) to Cooke City, over the Beartooth Hwy.

Budget choices include the **Rainbow Motel** (☎ 406-587-4201; 510 N 7th Ave) and **Royal 7 Budget Inn** (☎ 800-587-3103; 310 N 7th Ave), both with rooms for $45 to $70.

For around $5 you can stuff yourself on traditional Mexican fare at the **Burrito Shop** (203 N 7th Ave) or eat Asian at the **Tibetan Tea House** (122 W Lamme St). A catchall for food, beer, pool, and people-watching is **Montana Ale Works** (611 E Main St). **John Bozeman's Bistro** (☎ 406-587-4100; 125 W Main St) is Bozeman's best restaurant; expect to spend $25 per person.

Most nights bring live music to the **Zebra Lounge**, half a block north of Main on Rouse Ave S; shows start around 10pm. Student hangouts include the **Haufbrau** (22 S 8th Ave) and nearby **Molly Brown**.

Billings

TEL 406 • POP 92,988 • ELEVATION 3300FT

Montana's largest city shouldn't be a priority on a Yellowstone itinerary, but it's not a bad place to stay a night before heading to the park or catching a flight back home. Billings' **Logan International Airport** (**W** www.flybillings.com) has flights to and from Salt Lake City, Denver, Minneapolis, and Seattle.

Billings' **visitor center** (☎ 406-245-4111, 800-711-2630; 815 S 27th St) has reams of local information and will help with hotel reservations.

The **Western Heritage Center** (☎ 406-256-6809; 2822 Montana Ave), has changing exhibits and an outstanding artifact collection representing the various cultural traditions of Yellowstone Valley. The newly renovated **Yellowstone Art Center** (☎ 406-256-6804; 401 N 27th St) sits on the site of the 1916 Yellowstone County Jail. Both museums are free and are closed Monday.

PLACES TO STAY & EAT

The **Billings KOA** (☎ 406-252-3104; tent/RV sites $23/34), America's first, is in a beautiful spot next to the Yellowstone River, .5mi south of I-90.

The best motel buys downtown are at **Big 5 Motel** (☎ 406-245-6646, 888-544-9358; 2601 4th Ave N; rooms $31/36) and the **Cherry Tree Inn** (☎ 406-252-5603, 800-237-5882; 823 N Broadway; rooms $38/45).

✔ TIP

Northeast of Billings off I-94, the massive sandstone butte of **Pompey's Pillar** is where William Clark (of Lewis and Clark fame) etched his signature on July 25, 1806. Clark named the rock after Sacagawea's son, who was nicknamed "Pomp," meaning "little chief" in Shoshone. A Day of Honor will be held here on July 2006 as part of the Lewis & Clark Bicentennial commemorations. Festivities will include historical reenactments, Native American games, river floats, and the opening of a new interpretive center. For more about Lewis and Clark, see p 234.

The **Dude Rancher Lodge** (☎ 406-259-5561, 800-221-3302; 415 N 29th St; rooms $46-$70) has groovy ranch oak furniture dating back to the 1940s. Rooms at the **Billings Inn** (☎ 406-252-6800, 800-231-7782; 880 N 29th St; rooms $55/59) include a microwave, refrigerator, and breakfast.

For coffee, pastries, lunch and lively atmosphere, stop by the **McCormick Café** (2419 Montana Ave). Popular with the 30-something crowd, the **Montana Brewing Company** (113 N Broadway) brews its own beer and serves a big menu of salads, wood-fired pizzas, burgers, and appetizers.

Some locals claim that **The Rex** (☎ 406-245-7477; 2401 Montana Ave) serves the best steak in town, and others only eat beef at **Jake's** (☎ 406-259-9375; 2701 1st Ave N).

Casey's Golden Pheasant (222 N Broadway) has live jazz and blues performances nightly. A magnet for all of eastern Montana, the **Alberta Bair Theater** (☎ 406-256-6052; W www.albertabairtheater.com; 2801 3rd Ave N) is Billings' cultural jewel, with productions ranging from country music to symphony concerts.

Livingston

TEL 406 • POP 7626 • ELEVATION 4503FT

In the late 1880s the Northern Pacific Railroad laid tracks across the Yellowstone River and began building Livingston as the primary jumping-off point for Yellowstone National Park. Visited by Clark (of Lewis and Clark fame) and at one point a temporary home for one Martha Canary (otherwise known as Calamity Jane), Livingston is an excellent departure point for rafting and fly-fishing trips on the Yellowstone River.

Some of Bozeman's overflow has brought upscale restaurants, antique shops, and art galleries to Livingston's picturesque old buildings, but generally the town retains its small town feel. The saloons that Calamity Jane and Kitty O'Leary frequented remain relatively unchanged.

Livingston is at the north end of Paradise Valley, where I-90 meets US 89; the latter heads south to Gardiner and Yellowstone National Park (53mi away). Livingston's **chamber of commerce** (☎ 406-222-0850; 303 E Park St) has a very useful website (W www.yellowstone-chamber.com).

THINGS TO SEE & DO

The **Federation of Fly Fishers Fly-Fishing Museum** (☎ 406-222-9369; 215 E Lewis St) has beautiful displays of hand-tied flies, rod and reel prototypes, and aquatic habitats. On Tuesday and Thursday summer evenings they give casting lessons free of charge; equipment is provided. Built on a legacy of Goofus Bugs, Humpy Flies, Trudes, Green Drakes, and Hair Wing Rubber Legs (to name but a few), **Dan Bailey's Fly Shop** (☎ 406-222-1673, 800-356-4052; W www.dan-bailey.com; 209 W Park St) is one of the world's best fly-fishing shops.

The original Northern Pacific Railroad Depot, built in 1902, is now home to a railroad history and arts museum called the **Depot Center** (☎ 406-222-2300). From June to August, the revamped **Yellowstone Gateway Museum** (☎ 406-222-4184; 118 W Chinook St) displays local historical and archaeological treasures in an old schoolhouse. All museums cost $3 for adults, $2 for children. For more details see the website Ⓦ www.livingstonmuseums.org.

PLACES TO STAY & EAT

Central to Livingston's history, the **Murray Hotel** (☎ 406-222-1350; Ⓦ *www.murray hotel.com; 201 W Park St; rooms from $50)* balances historic charm with a rooftop hot tub. Also downtown, the **Guest House Motel** (☎ *406-222-1460, 800-222-1460, 105 W Park St; sgl/dbl $43/48)* has a restaurant and lounge.

A half-mile north of downtown is the **Parkway Motel** (☎ *406-222-3840, 1124 W Park St; dbl $42/65 in winter/summer).* The **Greystone Inn B&B** (☎ *406-222-8319, 122 S Yellowstone St; rooms $65-$95)* has elegant rooms and a hearty breakfast.

The cozy **Beartooth Bakery**, on Main St, makes wonderful cookies and brownies and has a full breakfast and lunch menu ($5 to $7). **Rumors** *(cnr 2nd and Callender Sts; breakfast and lunch under $10, dinners $10-$13)* adds a sophisticated flair to its highly touted food. **The Sport** *(114 S Main St)* has been running strong since 1909. It's a fun place to go for hot sandwiches ($6), steaks, and Mexican food (around $10).

For a first-rate wine list and reasonably priced fine dining, try Russell Chatham's **Livingston Bar & Grille** (☎ *406-222-7909; 130 N Main St),* which has a back bar that came from St Louis by wagon train around 1910 and got considerable use from Calamity Jane.

Red Lodge

TEL 406 • POP 2278 • ELEVATION 5555FT

A quaint old mining town with fun bars and more restaurants per capita than any other community in Montana, Red Lodge has long been the departure point for the Beartooth Hwy, the scenic "high road" to Yellowstone National Park (see the Greater Yellowstone chapter, page 209). With a wealth of great hiking and decent skiing nearby, plus a fun bunch of shops downtown, Red Lodge is worth spending a day in before heading to the Beartooths. The town gets its name from the red tepees of local Crow (Absoraka) Indians.

On the west bank of Rock Creek, Red Lodge is 60mi south of Billings and 80mi northeast of Cooke City and the north entrance to Yellowstone National Park. US 212 runs north-south through town as Broadway Ave, the main street, and becomes the Beartooth Hwy south of town.

The **Red Lodge Area Chamber of Commerce** (☎ *406-446-1718;* Ⓦ *www.red lodge.com; 601 N Broadway Ave),* on the north edge of town, is one of the region's best.

THINGS TO SEE & DO

Set aside a few hours for browsing the shops and galleries along Broadway Ave, making sure to stop in at **Red Lodge Ales** *(11 N Broadway Ave)* for a tasting and brewery tour (it's a small operation).

The **Carbon County Museum** (☎ *406-446-3667; 224 N Broadway)* has a terrific antique gun collection but is better known for its coverage of local rodeo lore. The old railroad depot on Eighth St, one block west of Broadway Ave, is now the **Carbon County Arts Guild Gallery**, where local artists display weavings, pottery, paintings, etc.

If you're here on the July Fourth weekend and have an interest in bucking bulls, follow locals to the fairgrounds for the **Home of Champions Rodeo**, one of the biggest amateur rodeos in Montana.

JACKSON TOWN Made of elk antlers, the Jackson Town Square arch is decorated in twinkling lights for the winter holidays. [Photo: Cheyenne Rouse]

SKIING The Yellowstone region has several world-class ski resorts at Jackson Hole (pictured here), Grand Targhee, and Big Sky. [Photo: Lee Foster]

GREATER
YELLOWSTONE

BEARTOOTH HIGHWAY A view from the Beartooth Highway, one of North America's most dramatic road trips. [Photo: Carol Polich]

WHITE-WATER RAFTING A thrilling ride on the Snake River in Jackson Hole. [Photo: John Elk III]

BEARTOOTH PLATEAU The high plateaus of the Beartooths are dotted with more than 1000 lakes and mountain pools. [Photo: Clem Lindenmayer]

CODY Original storefronts and an old wagon add to the Wild West flavor of Cody, named for the infamous "Buffalo Bill." [Photo: Emily Riddell]

Six miles southwest of downtown, **Red Lodge Mountain** (☎ 800-444-8977, 406-446-2610 for ski reports; W www.redlodgemountain.com) has a 2400ft vertical drop, serviced by eight lifts. The higher temperatures and longer days of February and March, plus a higher base elevation (7400ft) than any other Montana ski hill, give Red Lodge Mountain some of Montana's best spring skiing.

The **Red Lodge Nordic Center** (☎ 406-425-1070), 2mi west of Red Lodge on Hwy 78, is Red Lodge's top cross-country resource and a good place for beginning skiers or those who want to ski on well-maintained tracks. Numerous trails cut through the Beartooth Range, making a vast trail network well suited for cross-country and back-country skiing.

PLACES TO STAY & EAT

South of Red Lodge on US 212 are 10 Forest Service campgrounds, open May to September. The nearest are small **Sheridan** and **Rattin**, 6mi and 8mi from Red Lodge and on the east side of the road. A little farther, and with shady creekside locations, are the nicer **Parkside**, **Limber Pine**, and **Greenough Lake** grounds, 12mi south of town. All these sites are run by the concessionaire Gallatin Canyon Campgrounds, cost $9 (plus $5 per additional vehicle), and are reservable through the **National Recreation Reservation Service** (☎ 877-444-6777).

The cheapest motel is the family-owned **Eagle's Nest** (☎ 406-446-2312; 702 S Broadway Ave; sgl/dbl $38/42, "pre-remodel" rooms $26). The **Yodeler Motel** (☎ 406-446-1435; 601 S Broadway Ave; lower level sgl/dbl $45/55, upper level dbl $69), at the corner of 17th St, has upper-level rooms with balconies and in-room Jacuzzis.

A fun and elegant place to stay is the old **Pollard Hotel** (☎ 406-446-0001; 2 N Broadway Ave; dbl from $90), Red Lodge's first brick building. Its cozy lobby and restaurant are hubs of local activity. The most upscale of Red Lodge's accommodations is the **Rock Creek Resort** (☎ 406-446-1111; www.rockcreekresort.com; dbl from $95), 4.5mi south of town off US 212.

The unexciting beige exterior makes **PD McKinneys**, on the corner of 15th St and Broadway Ave, look more like an old postal building than Red Lodge's favorite breakfast spot.

Bogart's Restaurant (11 S Broadway Ave) is popular for margaritas and Mexican food, and **Red Lodge Pizza Co** (115 S Broadway) makes excellent pies and calzones. **Greenlee's**, at the Pollard Hotel, has won national acclaim for its wine list, fresh fish, and creative pasta dishes ($9 to $14).

A young, outdoorsy crowd congregates for drinking and dancing (to live bands on weekends) at the **Snowcreek Saloon** (124 S Broadway Ave), and the **Snag Bar** (107 S Broadway Ave) entertains a leather-faced crowd wearing cowboy hats and boots.

Cody
MAP 19

TEL 307 • POP 9,000 • ELEVATION 5095FT

Situated 51mi east of Yellowstone's east entrance and connected to the park by the scenic Wapiti Valley, the "Wild West" town of Cody rivals Jackson as Wyoming's premier tourist town, at least in summer. Rather than erecting new faux-Western facades, local businesses have retained or restored their original storefronts, giving Cody a veneer of greater authenticity.

The brash Wild West bluster of Cody is inextricably linked to the self-promoting vanity of William (Buffalo Bill) Cody, who gladly lent his surname to real-estate speculator George Beck's newly minted town in 1901. Early visitors were even greeted personally by Cody himself. Beck and his backers milked Cody's fame to promote settlement, attract the railroad, and lobby for a massive dam on the Shoshone River. The town's ultimate blessing turned out to be its proximity to Yellowstone National Park. **Yellowstone Regional Airport** *(☎ 307-587-5096;* W *www .flyyra.com)* is 1mi east of Cody and offers daily nonstop fights to Salt Lake City and Denver.

INFORMATION

The useful **visitor center** *(☎ 307-587-2777; 836 Sheridan Ave)* is housed in a 1927 lodgepole-pine cabin. The **Shoshone National Forest Wapiti Ranger District Office** *(☎ 307-527-6921; 203A Yellowstone Ave)* is the place to get information on the forest surrounding Wapiti Valley; for the Clarks Fork region and other areas try the **main office** *(☎ 307-527-6241; 808 Meadow Lane)*, next to the **Olive Glenn Golf Course**. Ask at either office for their useful *Recreation Guide*.

Early visitors were even greeted personally by Cody himself.

BUFFALO BILL HISTORICAL CENTER

Sometimes called (with some hyperbole) the "Smithsonian of the West," this complex of five excellent museums is a Cody must-see. Entry to the center *(☎ 307-587-4771;* W *www.bbhc.org; 720 Sheridan Ave; admission $15/13/6 adults/seniors/students, children over six $4)* is valid for two consecutive days.

The center's original collection began in 1927 with the **Buffalo Bill Museum**, which presents a wealth of fascinating, if uncritical, information on the life of William F Cody and his Wild West shows. The **Plains Indian Museum** explores Native American culture and history through its artistry. Interesting displays detail Native American ceremonies such as the Sun Dance (which honors the buffalo spirit) and explain the symbolism of tepee designs. Accounts of life on the reservation are conspicuously absent.

The **Whitney Gallery of Western Art** houses a major collection of Western artists. Most people rush politely through the **Cody Firearms Museum**. The newest addition to the complex is the **Draper Museum of Natural History**, which takes an overview of Greater Yellowstone's ecology.

OLD TRAIL TOWN MUSEUM

This unique museum *(☎ 307-587-5302; 1831 DeMaris Dr; admission $5/4 adults/children over 12)* is a collection of late-19th-century wooden buildings relocated from all over Wyoming. Butch Cassidy, Kid Curry, and the Sundance Kid used several of the buildings as hideouts, one just before an attempted bank heist in Red Lodge in 1897. Look for the bullet holes in the door of the Rivers Saloon and the grave of mountain man Jeremiah "Liver Eating" Johnson.

BUFFALO BILL STATE PARK

This state park *(day use $5)* centers on the Buffalo Bill Reservoir & Dam, 6mi west of Cody. Having acquired water rights to irrigate 266 sq mi in the Bighorn Basin, but lacking the capital to develop adequate storage, Buffalo Bill and his associates convinced the US Bureau of Reclamation to build the 328ft Shoshone Dam. Begun in 1905, it was the world's highest dam upon completion in 1910. Fishing, windsurfing, and boating are popular on the reservoir, and there are several boat launches on the north and southeast shores. The **visitor center** *(☎ 307-527-6076;* W *www.bbdvc.org)*, just west of the dramatic Shoshone Canyon, has some interpretive exhibits.

ACTIVITIES

Cody is a launch point for white-water and float trips on the North Fork of the Shoshone River. Raft and inflatable kayak trips through the Red Rock and Shoshone Canyons take two to three hours and cost $20 to $30. Half-day trips along North Fork cost $50, as do half-day scenic floats on the Clarks Fork. Wilder trips are held in June when water levels are highest. Reputable rafting companies include:

Red Canyon River Trips *(☎ 307-587-6988, 800-293-0148;*
  1374 Sheridan Ave)

Wyoming River Trips *(☎ 307-587-6661, 800-586-6661;*
  W *www.wyomingriver trips.com; 233 Yellowstone Hwy)*

River Runners *(☎ 307-527-7238, 800-535-RAFT;*
  1491 Sheridan Ave)

Butch Cassidy, Kid Curry, and the Sundance Kid used several of the buildings as a hideout.

Wheel Fun Rentals *(☎ 307-587-4779; 1390 Sheridan Ave)* rents all kinds of fun family bikes from $11 per hour, plus kayaks. Angers should make a beeline for Tim Wade's **North Fork Anglers** *(☎ 307-527-7274;* W *www.north forkanglers.com; 1107 Sheridan Ave)* for information, flies, and guided trips. Check the website for current fishing conditions. **Absaroka Angler** *(☎ 307-587-5105; 754 Yellowstone Ave)* is another option.

SPECIAL EVENTS

Cody's wildly popular **rodeo** *(☎ 307-587-5155; 421 W Yellowstone Ave)* is held 8:30 pm nightly June to August at Stampede Park. Tickets are $12/6 adults/children (free for children under 5) for grandstand seating and $14/8 for Buzzard's Roost seating, closer to the action.

The **Cowboy Poetry & Range Ballads festival** takes place the second week of April. The **Plains Indian Powwow** is held in mid-June and the **Yellowstone Jazz Festival** in mid-July. The **Cody Stampede** on July 4 weekend is the major event of the year and presents the largest rodeo action in the region.

PLACES TO STAY

Summertime rates rise by up to 50%; many places close in winter. Summer reservations are recommended, but campgrounds usually have sites available. Call **Cody Area Central Reservations** (☎ *888-468-6996; 9am-5pm weekdays*) for assistance.

The **Gateway Campground** (☎ *307-587-2561; 203 W Yellowstone Ave; tents $12, RV hookups $17*) and **Ponderosa Campground** (☎ *307-587-9203; 1815 Yellowstone Ave; tents $19, RV hookups $25*) both have somewhat cramped tent and RV sites, the latter with laundry and showers.

Along the banks of the Buffalo Bill Reservoir, 6mi west of Cody, the **North Shore Bay** and **North Fork Campgrounds** ($6 locals, $12 with out-of-state plates, no RV hookups) are exposed and shadeless but offer lovely sunsets over the lake.

Several motels begin at less than $50: the friendly **Uptown Motel** (☎ *307-587-4245; 1562 Sheridan Ave)*, **Big Bear Motel** (☎ *307-587-3117; 139 W Yellowstone Ave)*, and **Rainbow Park Motel** (☎ *307-587-6251, 800-341-8000; 1136 17th St*) charge from around $38/46.

The nonsmoking **Carriage House** (☎ *307-587-2572/3818, 800-531-2572; 1816 8th St; cabins $50-65, six-person suites $85-135*) has log cabins on attractive grounds. The slightly more expensive **Gateway Motel** (☎ *307-587-2561; 203 Yellowstone Ave*) also has cozy cabins.

The friendly, century-old **Pawnee Hotel** (☎ *307-587-2239; 1032 12th St; sgl/dbl $32/36*) is remodeled and has a nice garden. Smoky rooms with shared bathrooms are a few dollars less.

Cody also has several B&Bs; the least expensive is the three-room **Casual Cove B&B** (☎ *307-587-3622; 1431 Salisbury Ave;* W *www.casualcove.com; rooms $60-70*).

Buffalo Bill's atmospheric **Irma Hotel** (☎ *307-587-4221, 800-745-4762;* W *www.irmahotel.com; 1192 Sheridan Ave*) has charming rooms in the original hotel ($100 to $125) and the less-appealing modern annex ($65).

THE IRMA

Buffalo Bill himself built the landmark Irma Hotel in 1902 (named for his daughter), calling it "just the swellest hotel that ever was." He kept two suites and an office for his personal use, and his ghost is said to still frequent the creaking corridors. The original font lobby has since been converted into the Silver Saddle Lounge.

The hotel's most famous feature is the 50ft-long imported French cherry wood bar, in what is now the dining room. Presented to Bill by Queen Victoria, it was transported by stagecoach from Red Lodge, and, at $100,000, cost more than the hotel itself.

PLACES TO EAT

Patsy Ann's Pastry & Ladle *(☎ 307-527-6297; 1243 Beck Ave)* bakes tasty pastries and from-scratch soups and sandwiches. **Peter's Café Bakery** *(☎ 307-527-5040; 1191 Sheridan Ave)* specializes in buffalo burgers ($4.50) and has espresso and breakfasts.

Proud Cut Saloon *(☎ 307-527-6905; 1227 Sheridan Ave; mains $15-22)* is big on beef, but the lax service doesn't always cut the mustard. **Silver Dollar Bar & Grill** *(☎ 307-587-3554; 1313 Sheridan Ave)* serves up its own home-brewed pale ale to accompany its burgers.

La Comida *(☎ 307-587-9556; 1385 Sheridan Ave)* has authentic Mexican food and patio seating. **Maxwell's Fine Food & Spirits** *(☎ 307-527-7749; 937 Sheridan Ave)* is a family favorite, with a nice selection of salads, sandwiches, pizza, and bistro dinners.

The Irma *(☎ 307-587-4221)* has a popular breakfast/lunch buffet *($7),* an evening prime rib buffet *($17),* and Sunday brunch ($10). Upscale **Stefan's** *(☎ 307-587-8511; 1367 Sheridan Ave; mains $16-18)* aims to impress with contemporary American cuisine such as buffalo meatloaf and stuffed shrimp.

In a class by itself is **Franca's Italian Dining** *(☎ 307-587-5354; 1421 Rumsey Ave),* open Wednesday to Sunday in summer for dinner only (reservations required). Fixed multicourse dinners ($18 to $30) and pasta entrees ($15) are superb.

ENTERTAINMENT

The rodeo and its related events are the primary post-sunset summertime attractions. Happy hour at the Irma Hotel's **Silver Saddle Saloon** is a blast after the Gunslingers shoot their summer shtick on the porch at 6pm daily except Sunday (June to September).

Cassie's *(☎ 307-527-5500; 214 Yellowstone Ave)* is the place for heavy swilling and swingin' country and western tunes. Bobby Bridger, a descendent of mountain man Jim Bridger, performs Western ballads summer evenings at the **Old Trail Town Museum** ($12). Check the website **W** www.bbridger.com for schedules.

NPS PHOTOGRAPHS

Once a sacred gathering place for neighboring Native American tribes, Yellowstone has become one of the world's premier natural attractions, rivaled only by the African Serengeti, Amazon Basin, and Australian Outback as a wildlife watching destination. Long before Western explorers first entered Greater Yellowstone, humans made pilgrimages to its unique thermal basins and worshiped around its dramatic volcanic outcrops. Indeed, from Yellowstone sprang the very concept of a federally held and protected wilderness park. Renowned artists, writers, environmentalists, explorers, politicians, and preachers have all sought solace and found inspiration here.

GREATER
YELLOWSTONE HISTORY

First Peoples

Recent archaeological evidence unearthed near Pinedale, Wyoming, and excavations from Osprey Beach on Yellowstone Lake (forensically dated bison blood residue from chert and obsidian projectile points) suggest that human inhabitation of what is known today as the Greater Yellowstone region began soon after the Pinedale glaciation period ended, between 12,000 and 14,000 years ago.

Archaeologists divide Greater Yellowstone's first inhabitants – ice age hunter-gatherers who chased spectacular megafauna such as bear-sized beavers, enormous camels, gigantic moose, massive mastodons, and 20ft-tall bison – into two distinct cultures, Clovis and Folsom, based on the uniquely shaped stone spearheads they fashioned.

Rising global temperatures about 9000 years ago caused rapid melting of the North American ice sheet. The combination of a warmer, drier climate and overhunting by humans triggered a collapse of the ice age ecosystem, wiping out a majority of the large game species on which these cultures depended. This catastrophe was the catalyst for social diversification and cultural specialization among the early peoples of the Rocky Mountains. Late Paleo-Indian artifacts from the Cody cultural complex (6000BC) indicate continued reliance on the modern bison, but around 5500BC some peoples transitioned to hunting smaller game and foraging plants.

There's little evidence that these early inhabitants were truly at home in the Rocky Mountains' high ranges – the winter was simply too harsh. Rather, tribes from the surrounding plains established summer camps in sheltered foothill valleys, making lengthy forays into the high mountains to hunt or collect food and medicinal plants.

T I M E L I N E

9,000BC–1870s	Native American inhabitation of Greater Yellowstone.
late 1700s	First European exploration, by French fur trappers.
1803	Louisiana Purchase; France cedes Greater Yellowstone to USA.
1807-08	John Colter's winter journey into Greater Yellowstone.
1827	First written account of Greater Yellowstone is published.
1864	Montana Territory created; gold discovery at Virginia City attracts settlers.
1870	Washburn-Langford-Doane expedition leads to YNP founding legend.
1872	US President Ulysses S Grant signs the Yellowstone National Park Act on March 1.
1877	Nez Percé, led by Chief Joseph, flee US Army through Yellowstone NP.
1883	Northern Pacific Railroad spur line finished near north entrance of Yellowstone NP; Great Plains bison pronounced extinct east of Continental Divide.
1891	Congress passes Forest Reserve Act; YNP Timberland Reserve established.
1894	Lacey Act passed by Congress, prohibiting hunting in Yellowstone NP.
1903	President Theodore Roosevelt dedicates YNP North Entrance Arch.
1908	Union Pacific Railroad spur line arrives in West Yellowstone.
1916	National Park Service Act signed by President Woodrow Wilson.
1918	National Park Service (NPS) assumes management of Yellowstone NP from US Army.
1929	Congress creates Grand Teton NP; YNP's boundaries enlarged by President Hoover.
1932	Winter wildlife range near the north entrance added to YNP by President Hoover.
1941	Last bear-feeding shows at Canyon Village in YNP.
1943	President Franklin Roosevelt creates Jackson Hole National Monument.
1948	First year Yellowstone NP receives one million visitors.
1950	Jackson Hole NM becomes part of Grand Teton NP.
1967	NPS turns to "natural management" of Greater Yellowstone wildlife.
1972	50 millionth visitor to YNP; next 50 million arrive by 1992.
1988	Catastrophic wildfires sweep Greater Yellowstone region.
1992	Winter visitation of Yellowstone NP exceeds 140,000.
1995	Gray wolf reintroduction begins in YNP; Yellowstone joins the list of World Heritage Sites in Danger.
2000	New National Fire Plan implemented in response to serious wildfire season.

The human presence in Greater Yellowstone increased dramatically between 1500 and 2000 years ago, coinciding with a more favorable climate, resurgent large mammal populations, and development of the bow and arrow, which replaced the atlatl (spear-thrower). Sheep traps and *pishkum* (buffalo jumps) were the weapons of mass destruction in the Rockies and Great Plains, respectively.

The Tukudika (or Sheepeaters) – a Shoshone-Bannock people who hunted bighorn in the mountains and never acquired horses or iron tools – were the region's only permanent inhabitants before white settlement, arriving on the Yellowstone Plateau as early as 2000 years ago. Other tribes that hunted, traded, and settled seasonally in Greater Yellowstone before European exploration (and whose descendants still live in the region) include the Blackfoot, Coeur d'Alene, Crow, Flathead, Kalispel, Kiowa, Nez Percé, and Pend Oreille.

THE FLIGHT OF THE NEZ PERCÉ

Chief Joseph, circa 1884.
Courtesy of the Denver Public Library, Western History Collection, call #X-31011.

The discovery of gold in 1877 spurred the United States government to forcibly relocate the Nez Percé (Nim-i'ipuu in their language) from Oregon's Wallowa Valley. After an initial skirmish, the Nez Percé set off on what would become an epic 1100mi flight from the US Army. The route of their journey is now a national historic trail. For more info see W www.fs.fed.us/npnht.

By August 23, 1877, 700 of the Nez Percé (of whom only 250 were braves), led by Chief Joseph, crossed the Targhee Pass and entered Yellowstone Park along the Madison River. At that time only 25 tourists were visiting the park, and the Nez Percé somehow managed to bump into all of them, taking six hostage, killing one, and releasing the others near Mud Volcano. Just before reaching Pelican Creek, a band of braves diverted General Howards' men up into the Hayden and Lamar Valleys (at one point camping at Indian Pond) while the bulk of the tribe hurried up Pelican Creek and out of the park's northeast corner.

In September they progressed through Crandall Creek into the Clarks Fork of the Yellowstone with US forces pressing hard on their heels and troops led by General Sturgis blocking routes ahead; the Percé once again pulled off a brilliant escape. A group of braves diverted Sturgis' troops while the Nez Percé headed out of the valley through a gorge thought impassable by the US Army and slipped through the net.

Believing they were in Canada, the Nez Percé slowed down just a few tragic miles before the border, where US troops under General Nelson Miles finally caught up with them. After an 1100mi chase that included four battles, the 87 men, 184 women and 47 children surrendered on October 5, 1877, with Chief Joseph's words: "From where the sun now stands, I will fight no more forever." It was the end of a fight they had not sought.

The last of the Tukudika departed the region in the early 1870s for the Wind River and Bannock Reservations, just prior to formation of Yellowstone National Park. One of the region's most extraordinary modern episodes involving Native Americans was the 1877 flight of the Nez Percé, led by Chief Joseph, who fled their ancestral lands in Oregon to escape persecution by the US Army. While crossing Yellowstone, the Nez Percé briefly seized several tourists before continuing north up the Clarks Fork River. The tribe was eventually captured in Montana. Today, the National Park Service recognizes formal affiliations with 25 modern tribes.

Trappers, Traders & Tourists

The first Europeans to come in contact with Native Americans in Greater Yellowstone were French fur trappers from eastern Canada who encountered the Crow (who called the Yellowstone the Elk River) and Sioux in the late 1700s while exploring the upper Missouri River tributaries in search of beaver. These raffish French-speaking trappers gave the Tetons their name – they dubbed the three most prominent peaks *Les Trois Tetons* for their ostensible resemblance to female breasts.

The USA's Louisiana Purchase of present-day Montana, most of Wyoming, and eastern Colorado from the French in 1803 led President Thomas Jefferson to commission the famous Lewis and Clark Corps of Discovery in 1804-06. The Shoshone and Nez Percé told the expedition's leaders about a "thundering volcano to the south" that made the earth tremble. However, their published report indicates that the expedition only made it as far south as the lower Gallatin Valley and the area along the Yellowstone River, east of Livingston, Montana.

The first detailed written account of travels in Greater Yellowstone was published in a Philadelphia newspaper in 1827. Young Pennsylvanian trapper Daniel Potts' letter to the editor accurately described his trip in 1826 through the Tetons, up the Snake River, and along the shore of Yellowstone Lake around West Thumb Geyser Basin.

As knowledge of the American West grew, so did interest in its exploitable resources. Most sought after was the beaver, whose pelts were fashioned into hats favored by dapper European gentlemen. John Colter, a member of the Lewis and Clark expedition, returned to explore the Yellowstone area during the winter of 1807-08 to try his luck as a trapper. Colter sent reports about his extensive travels (and travails) to Missouri Territory governor William Lewis, who published a map of Colter's route in 1814.

After the War of 1812, renewed demand for furs propelled another generation of trappers westward. Legendary "mountain men" like Jedediah Smith, Jim Bridger, David Jackson, William Sublette, Jim Beckwourth (a free African American), and Thomas Fitzpatrick came to know the rugged Rockies' backcountry better than anyone except the Indians, with whom many of the men formed beneficial relationships. Annual summer rendezvous, attended by suppliers, Natives Americans, and even tourists, began in 1825 at the headwaters of Wyoming's Green River. The last mountain man rendezvous was in 1840, as the fur trade hit the skids and silk hats came into vogue.

The romantic image of the mountain man, however, is an exaggeration; rather than rugged individualists selling their catch to the highest bidder, most of the trappers were salaried company men who were often advanced a year's supplies. In 1823, for example, William Ashley of St Louis advertised for 100 "enterprising young men" to trap beaver in the Rocky Mountains for $200 a year. The lasting contribution of the mountain men,

LEWIS & CLARK

After President Thomas Jefferson decided to explore the western part of the country in 1803, he enlisted his young protégé and personal secretary Meriwether Lewis to lead the expedition. Lewis, then 29, had no expertise in botany, cartography, or Indian languages and was

Sacagawea

known to suffer from bouts of "hypochondriac affections" – a euphemism for schizophrenia. Lewis in turn asked his friend William Clark, already an experienced frontiersman and army veteran at the age of 33, to join him.

The ostensible purpose of the Corps of Discovery was to seek a "Northwest Passage" to the Pacific Ocean. Although a chain of "stony mountains" was known to exist in the West, the magnitude and vastness of the Rocky Mountains had been seriously underestimated – Jefferson even assumed the existence of an all-water route to the Pacific.

An entourage of 40, including 27 bachelors, Clark's African American slave, York, and a dog, set out from St Louis on May 14, 1804, pushing up the Missouri River past the spectacular White Cliffs and the Great Falls of the Missouri. (They were later joined, in North Dakota, by Sacagawea, the teenage Shoshone wife of a French trapper, who acted as an interpreter and negotiated vital assistance from the Shoshone and Nez Percé.) In August and September 1805 the expedition made an arduous crossing of the rugged Bitterroot Mountains, first via Lehmi Pass on the Continental Divide, then north over Lost Trail Pass, and finally west across Lolo Pass. Lewis and Clark continued west down the Clearwater, Snake, and Columbia Rivers to reach the Pacific Ocean on November 15, 1805. After wintering near the mouth of the Columbia River, the expedition recrossed the Bitterroots and explored several upper tributaries of the Missouri. Upon their return to St Louis on September 23, 1806, Lewis and Clark received a heroes' welcome.

Though their expedition only skirted the north edge of Greater Yellowstone near Livingston, Montana, in 1806, Lewis and Clark recorded the natural history of many familiar species. They were the first European Americans to describe and name some 170 plants and 120 animals, including bighorn sheep, grizzly bears, and prairie dogs. Despite bad weather, illness, malnutrition, rough terrain, dangerous wildlife, and hostile tribes, only one member of the expedition died (of a ruptured appendix) during the epic 2 1/2-year, 8000mi journey.

In 1808 Lewis was appointed governor of the Louisiana Territory, but he died a year later, purportedly either by suicide or murder. Clark was appointed superintendent of Indian affairs in the Louisiana Territory and governor of the Missouri Territory and died peacefully at the age of 68.

The bicentennial of Lewis & Clark's epic journey will be celebrated from 2003-2006, with traveling exhibits, historical reenactments, and other educational and cultural programs. Various communities along the route will be hosting commemorative events; check w/eb www.lewisandclark200.org or w/eb www.lewisandclark200.gov for a full schedule. The closest event to Yellowstone will be held at Pompey's Pillar, outside Billings, on July 25, 2006. See p 222 for details.

however, was their local knowledge of the terrain and pioneering of routes across the mountains, which paved the way for later emigrants and explorers.

Official Explorations

The US defeat of Mexico in the 1846-48 Mexican War yielded a bounty of new Western territory to explore. In addition, the British had recognized US sovereignty over most of Montana and Wyoming in 1846. Official exploration of these new territories was delayed by the frenzy surrounding the California gold rush of the late 1840s and through the 1850s and 1860s by domestic struggles over slavery and the subsequent American Civil War. The immediate aftermath of that war and ongoing Indian skirmishes further delayed government-sponsored territorial exploration. The US Corps of Topographical Engineers, guided by ex-trapper Jim Bridger, attempted to explore the Yellowstone Plateau from the south in 1860, but impassable snow-covered mountain passes put the kibosh on their journey.

In the fall of 1869 the private three-member Folsom-Cook-Peterson expedition headed south from Bozeman, Montana, for a month to explore the divide between the Gallatin and Yellowstone Rivers. They made it as far south as Shoshone Lake and returned in fine fettle to write a popular magazine article that refueled interest in exploration among scientists and the Eastern establishment.

Folsom, Cook, and Peterson gained enough notoriety to be invited along for the landmark 1870 Washburn-Langford-Doane expedition, bankrolled primarily by the Northern Pacific Railroad, which was seeking a route across the Montana Territory and publicity to attract investors. The 19-man party, led by former Montana tax collector Nathaniel Langford and Montana Surveyor-General Henry Washburn, was given a military escort by Lt Gustavus Doane from Fort Ellis (near present-day Bozeman). They successfully traced the route of the 1869 expedition, named many thermal features and (after deciding not to stake claims around *their* geysers) returned to the East Coast to a hero's welcome from the national media, which had finally begun to take reports of Yellowstone seriously.

One of Langford's lectures about Yellowstone caught the attention of Dr Ferdinand Hayden, director of the newly formed US Geological Survey (USGS). Hayden soon persuaded Congress, with substantial lobbying muscle from Northern Pacific supporters, to appropriate funds for the first federally funded scientific expedition of the Greater Yellowstone region.

Prospecting vs Protection

The epic California gold rush of 1848 started a new era of Western resource extraction. As the pay dirt played out west of California's Sierra Nevada, peripatetic speculators fanned out east across Nevada toward southern Idaho, Montana, and Wyoming in the late 1850s, culminating with a major gold strike at South Pass, Wyoming, in 1858.

Veins of the glittering, rich yellow stone were unearthed by prospectors all around the periphery of Greater Yellowstone after the passing of the Homestead Act of 1862: in 1863, at Alder Gulch near Virginia City, Montana (near today's Gardiner, Montana), and at Crevice Creek in 1867, just beyond the future north boundary of Yellowstone National Park. Amid newfound prosperity, the Wyoming Territory was carved out of the

General Hayden Survey Party of 1872.

Dakota Territory in 1868. The region's last significant strike occurred in 1870, at the New World Mining District near present-day Cooke City, just outside Yellowstone's northeast entrance.

In 1871 the 34-man Hayden Expedition set out from Fort Ellis with a full cavalry escort. Hayden's scientific work was fairly pedestrian, but two members of his party, landscape painter Thomas Moran and photographer William Henry Jackson, produced works of art that roused interest in the area and ultimately led to the designation of Yellowstone as a national park in 1872 – in large part because Congress was convinced that preservation of the remote, uncivilized region would do "no harm to the material interests of the people." Thus began the ongoing struggle to preserve nature while maximizing the "multiple uses" of the nation's natural resources.

The National Park Idea

Portrait artist George Catlin is credited with originally suggesting the idea of a "national park" during a 1832 trip through the wild Dakota Territory, where he decided that something had to be done by the government to shield disappearing wilderness (and native peoples) from the effects of westward expansion. A few months later Congress set aside Hot Springs, Arkansas, as the first US national reservation to save the area's vital hydrological resources.

President Abraham Lincoln's grant of Yosemite Valley to the state of California as a 10-sq-mi forest preserve in 1864 "for public use, resort, and recreation" was the next major federal act of preservation. This marked the first occasion when public land was set aside for strictly nonutilitarian purposes. Frederick Law Olmstead, pioneering landscape architect and designer of New York City's Central Park, was appointed an early Yosemite commissioner. He advised the California legislature that protecting the valley's natural beauty was essential to the "health and vigor of men." Olmstead's philosophical convictions that nature should be preserved for its own inherent qualities set the precedent for the establishment of the national park system.

In 1872, President Ulysses S Grant signed the landmark Yellowstone Act, setting aside "the tract of land in the Territories of Montana and Wyoming, lying near the headwaters of the Yellowstone River," and "all timber, mineral deposits, natural curiosities, or wonders … in their natural condition." The proclamation put a box on the map (around what was thought to be the extent of the region's thermal areas), but neglected to appropriate any management funds. Federal legislators incorrectly assumed that leases granted to private concessionaires would produce enough revenue to sustain the park until the railroad (and mass tourism) arrived. This lack of funding led early park administrators to seek private business partners, such as the railroads, to develop infrastructure and promote tourism.

The NPS's most important legacy is much greater than simply preserving a unique ecosystem. That the national park and preservation idea has spread worldwide is a testament to the pioneering thinking of early US conservationists.

The US Army & Early Stewardship

A decade of rampant squatting, wildlife poaching, wanton vandalism of thermal features, and general lawlessness in Yellowstone National Park preceded an 1882 visit by Civil War hero General Philip Sheridan. Sheridan persuaded Congress to appropriate $9000 to hire 10 protective assistants to aid the park's staffless superintendent. But park regulations still didn't allow for any substantial punishments beyond expelling trespassers. The jurisdiction of Wyoming territorial law was extended into the park in 1884, but this only created the opportunity for bribes, and chaos prevailed. The main offenders were ruffians who had helped complete the transcontinental railroad and hide-hunting poachers who had contributed to the extermination of the Great Plains bison.

US Cavalry in Yellowstone, circa 1905.

After a series of political scandals in the early 1880s involving landgrab attempts by a string of shady park superintendents (widely perceived as in the pocket of the railroad), Congress flatly refused to fund the park's civilian administration in 1886. Public opinion was divided as to whether the park should preserve the "curiosities" and "freaks and phenomena of nature" or avoid getting into "show business" entirely. A few prominent senators even insisted that the park be returned to the public domain. With no budget forthcoming, the secretary of the interior had little choice but to call in the US Cavalry to provide protection.

In the absence of park rangers, the Army patrolled the park from 1886 until the handoff to the newly created National Park Service (NPS) in 1918. At first, troops were stationed in a makeshift fort at Mammoth Hot Springs called Camp Sheridan. Construction of Fort Yellowstone (present-day park headquarters) began in 1891. By the early 1900s, mounted troops were stationed year-round throughout the backcountry. Fighting fires, building roads, protecting *desirable* wildlife (bison and elk) from poaching and predators, entertaining visitors, and preserving the park's natural features were the soldiers' primary duties. Predator control, such as poisoning of coyotes, was common, but under the Army's rule, Yellowstone's environmental status quo was largely maintained.

By 1916 the Department of the Interior was responsible for 14 parks and 21 monuments but lacked a centralized management structure. This outstanding need for coordinated policy guidance and supervision was highlighted after Congress permitted – despite writer John Muir's fierce opposition – California's damming of Yosemite's Hetch Hetchy Valley in 1913. During its formative years, NPS policies of predator eradication, habitat destruction in the name of development, and unregulated hunting outside park boundaries contributed to the development of an artificial and ultimately unsustainable ecology. Modern managers now openly admit that early efforts to exterminate predators were misguided.

Railroads, Automobiles & Mass Tourism

The Northern Pacific Railroad arrived in Livingston, Montana, in 1883, the same year Congress allocated funds to begin construction of the

President Theodore Roosevelt arrives at Cinnabar, 1903.

Grand Loop Rd in Yellowstone National Park. A spur line was extended south from Livingston to Cinnabar, just outside the park's north entrance, and the Union Pacific completed spur lines to Cody and West Yellowstone in 1901 and 1908. These concurrent developments ushered in the era of modern mass tourism in Greater Yellowstone.

The railroad's grand plans to monopolize public access to the park were thwarted by lobbying efforts of politically influential hunting groups, like Theodore Roosevelt's Boone & Crockett Club, which fervently opposed the railroad's proposals for spur lines through big-game wildlife corridors and geyser basins. Ultimately, the Army's construction of wagon roads and the arrival of the automobile would scuttle the railroad's bid for domination of concession and transportation interests.

The first aborted (illegal) attempt to enter a national park in an automobile was conducted in 1902 by a daring chap driving an 1897 Winton. HG Merry sped through Yellowstone's north entrance and made it halfway up the hill to Mammoth, where his engine died. As punishment for his infraction, he had to take the apprehending officers out for a spin.

National interest in wilderness recreation grew rapidly during the early decades of the 20th century, thanks largely to increased prosperity and higher automobile ownership. More than 80% of Yellowstone's 52,000 visitors in 1915 arrived via railroad. By 1940 nearly all of Yellowstone's half million visitors would enter the park in private automobiles.

In 1905, completion of the skeleton of what is known today as the Grand Loop Rd by the US Army Corps of Engineers established the blueprint of the standardized Yellowstone tourist experience. Lobbying by motoring clubs persuaded the NPS to admit automobiles in 1915. Constant clashes between cars and stagecoaches over right-of-way on the narrow one-way roads led to the banishment of horse-drawn wagons in 1916.

Establishment of the US Forest Service and the Yellowstone Timber Reserve (part of today's Shoshone and Bridger-Teton National Forest) in

1891, Jackson's National Elk Refuge in 1912, and Grand Teton National Park in 1929 opened up Greater Yellowstone's south flank to public visitation. East Coast philanthropist John D Rockefeller's 200,000-acre land grant in 1949 of the final pieces of Grand Teton National Park marked the tipping point in Greater Yellowstone's transition from a resource-based region to a tourist-driven economy.

Modern intensive development of a small area (about 1%) of Yellowstone National Park for tourism, however, continues to raise controversy. Fewer in-park accommodations and a significantly shorter network of roads are struggling to support bigger and bigger RVs and an ever-increasing number of visitors. The park's 370mi of narrow roads are overcrowded, and some view the more than 2000 buildings as an artificial distraction from the park's natural splendor. The NPS sees it as meeting public demand. Historian Richard White has argued that rather than being a vestige of wild America, Yellowstone is "a petting zoo with a highway running through it."

NPS PHOTOGRAPHS

A park visitor shows off her admission stickers, 1922.

Herein lies possibly the biggest challenge facing Greater Yellowstone today – is it possible for swarms of wildness- and wildlife-seekers to enjoy solitude and appreciate nature en masse? More than 90% of visitor use in YNP is concentrated in developed areas. One solution is to join the minority and explore the seldom-seen backcountry.

ROCKEFELLER, ROOSEVELT & THE TETONS

Despite the precedent set by Yellowstone, transformation of the Tetons into a national park was no foregone conclusion, as commercial ranching and hunting interests resisted attempts to transfer USFS and private lands to the NPS. At its creation in 1929, Grand Teton National Park included only the main part of the Teton Range and the lakes immediately below. Distressed at Jackson Hole's commercial development, John D Rockefeller Jr purchased more than 55 sq mi of land to donate to the park (but retained rights to all park concessions), but Congress repeatedly refused the cunning philanthropist's tax write-off until President Franklin D Roosevelt interceded.

Rockefeller's 32,000-acre bequest finally came under NPS jurisdiction when Roosevelt declared Jackson Hole a national monument in 1943. With post-WWII tourism booming in 1950, legislation conferred national park status and expanded the boundaries to include most of Jackson Hole. Today, the Rockefeller-owned Grand Teton Lodge Company is the park's major concessionaire, and the curious park is the only one outside Alaska that permits hunting and the only one with a commercial airport.

Managing Cultural Resources

Contemporary Native American oral history suggests that Greater Yellowstone was traditionally considered a place of great spiritual power. It was neutral ground, where Great Basin, Plains, and Intermountain peoples peacefully rendezvoused seasonally to hunt, trade, collect obsidian, and conduct spiritual ceremonies while visiting sacred sites like geyser basins.

Archeologists have identified more than 1000 prehistoric sites in Yellowstone National Park alone, and less than 2% of the park has been surveyed. Contemporary sites

MILLION-DOLLAR MICROBES

In 1966 microbiologist Dr Thomas Brock isolated a unique enzyme in a thermophilic microorganism called *Thermus aquaticus*, or "Taq," that he extracted from the 70°C+ Mushroom Pool in Yellowstone's Lower Geyser Basin. Coupled with the perfection of the polymerase chain reaction (PCR) process, Brock's discovery ultimately facilitated the replication of DNA for fingerprinting and genetic engineering and sparked an ongoing debate about "bioprospecting" and the commercialization of public domain resources.

The NPS continues to issue around 50 free research permits per year to scientists studying microbes. "Extremeophiles" harvested for free have generated hundreds of millions of dollars of revenue for patent holders. The Taq enzyme alone generates over $100 million a year. Until recently, no legal mechanism existed for the NPS to receive royalty payments for such scientific discoveries, but in 1997 a publicly-traded, California-based biotechnology corporation called Diversa (NASDAQ: DVSA) signed the first Cooperative Research and Development (CRADA or "benefits-sharing") agreement with the NPS. A 1999 legal challenge has held up the agreement until an environmental impact statement (EIS) is completed.

Early biothermal research: Professor Harvey of the University of Minnesota and park Naturalist Frank Thore studying algae from Mammoth Hot Springs, 1923.

NPS PHOTOGRAPHS

Not all research efforts are strictly commercial. For example, the National Aeronautic and Space Administration (NASA) is studying the biogeochemical signature of cyanobacteria found around hot springs using spectral satellite imaging. The hope is to match this signature with a similar signature on Mars, which would help to decide where to land on the red planet when attempting to confirm the existence of ancient volcanoes and hot springs.

Other startling discoveries include the DNA sequencing analysis of an organism found in a hot spring in the Hayden Valley that revealed what is considered to be the living entity most closely related to the primordial origin of life, a member of the domain *Archaea*.

Researchers estimate there are at least 18,000 active thermal features in YNP, and that as many as 99% of species present in Yellowstone's extreme environments have yet to be identified. For more on both sides of the bioprospecting debate see Ⓦ www.nps.gov/yell/nature/thermophiles/biopro.html (pro) or www.edmonds-institute.org (con).

of historical significance, such as trash pits behind old hotel sites, are also being excavated for items to add to the NPS museum collection.

Interest in "living history" programs and preservation of material evidence of past human activity were outgrowths of the Antiquities Act (1906), National Historic Preservation Act (1966), which authorized the NPS to maintain a National Register of Historic Places, and Archeological and Historic Preservation Act (1974). This new emphasis on preservation of cultural heritage arose primarily in response to the destructive effects of transcontinental highway building and other massive post-WWII federal construction projects.

While all of Greater Yellowstone is rich in cultural heritage, the majority of the region's cultural resources have been rounded up in the basement of the park's Albright Visitor Center in Mammoth, where hundreds of thousands of cultural artifacts, natural science specimens, and historic photographs and manuscripts await inspection by researchers.

Construction of a new Yellowstone Heritage and Research Center, to consolidate all of the park's historic collections, was slated to begin in Gardiner in 2003.

Managing Natural Resources

Beginning in 1959 with pioneering ecological studies of Yellowstone grizzly bears, the NPS emphasized scientific study of its natural resources. The landmark Leopold Report, published in 1963, suggested that "a national park should represent a vignette of primitive America." The report concluded that a more passive "natural regulation" regime should replace past policies biased toward hands-on resource manipulation.

Soon after the transition to natural regulation, landmark federal environmental laws such as the Wild & Scenic Rivers Act (1968), National Trails System Act (1968), National Environmental Policy Act (1969), Endangered Species Act (1973), Clean Water Act (1977), and Clean Air Act (1977) all reflected the nation's growing environmental awareness. In 1976 Yellowstone became a United Nations biosphere reserve, and in 1978 it was designated a World Heritage site.

As pilot participants in a 1996 NPS fee-retention program, Yellowstone and Grand Teton doubled their entrance fees to fund increased scientific research. The National Parks Omnibus Management Act (1998) mandated ongoing scientific research, inventorying, and monitoring of the parks' natural resources. Subsequent inventorying and monitoring conducted by the Yellowstone Center for Resources found that Greater Yellowstone is home to the following rare, threatened or endangered species: more than 100 plants, hundreds of invertebrates, at least six native fish species, several amphibians, at least 20 bird species, and 18 mammal species.

Current resource management flashpoints include the ongoing bioprospecting debate triggered by the biologically (and ultimately financially) significant 1966 discovery of the *Thermus aquaticus* microbe in a Yellowstone hot spring; questions about possible overgrazing by ungulates on the Northern Range; ongoing bear management experiments of the threatened grizzly population; the threat of mining and hydrothermal energy development adjacent to Yellowstone NP; controversies surrounding management of the park's bison herd and heated planning debates about the appropriateness and ecological impact of winter snowmobile use. Born out of the contradictions inherent in its mandate of both preservation and utilization, Yellowstone's controversies are likely to twist and turn for some time to come.

The vertical rush of an exploding geyser, the comical plop of a mud pot, and the mesmerizing blue intensity of a hot spring will remain in your mind long after you return home from Yellowstone. The park's geothermal features are the most outrageous and yet least understood of its wonders, and it's thanks to them that Yellowstone can truly be called globally unique.

GREATER
YELLOWSTONE GEOLOGY

Yellowstone is a land shaped by volcanoes and glaciers – fire and ice – on a mind-boggling scale. Through signs both subtle and eye-catching, the park's "geo-ecosystem" offers a peek into the center of the earth to the traveler armed with some background knowledge. In Yellowstone the earth is alive: breathing and belching, heaving and sighing, raging and boiling.

The Yellowstone Hot Spot

If you're already in the park, spare a moment to consider that you're standing on a thin piece of crust floating atop a huge 125mi-deep plume of molten rock. You have, quite simply, decided to set up camp atop a supervolcano, atop one of the earth's largest hot spots.

Hot spots are masses of buoyant molten rock, fueled from the earth's magma chamber, which have risen through the upper mantle close to the earth's surface. Most of these hot spots remain hidden beneath the oceans and in a few island chains like Hawaii and Iceland. As the crust of the North American plate has moved southwest an inch a year over this stationary hot spot, the hot spot has burned a chain of overlapping calderas (giant collapsed volcanic craters) across the American West, arcing from Nevada to northern Wyoming.

The Yellowstone region has been sitting atop this hot spot for about two million years now, resulting in massive supervolcanic eruptions roughly every 650,000 years. The hot spot has been stretching the earth's crust, creating mountain ranges, causing earthquakes and landslides, and even indirectly changing global climate. The last three eruptions (dated at two million, 1.3 million, and 630,000 years ago) have been centered on Island Park, Henry's Fork, and Yellowstone, respectively.

The most recent explosion formed the Yellowstone caldera, which dominates the center of the park. In an eruption 1000 times as powerful as the Mt St Helens eruption in 1980, the explosion spat out magma and expanding clouds of 1800*F liquid ash at supersonic speeds, vaporizing everything in its path. This ash billowed miles into the sky, traveling thousands of square miles in a matter of minutes. The crater roof and floor then imploded and dropped 1000 feet, creating a smoking volcanic pit 48mi by 27mi wide. Ash landed as far away as the Gulf of Mexico, and smaller fragments circled the globe many times, to cause a volcanic winter by reducing the amount of solar heat reaching Earth. In all, it is estimated that the three eruptions together expelled enough lava, ash, and debris to fill the entire Grand Canyon.

The awesome energy unleashed by the forest fires of 1988 is utterly insignificant compared to even the smallest of Yellowstone's many eruptions. Many visitors are surprised that Yellowstone is not more mountainous; the reason quite simply is that the mountains were either blown away by the explosion or sank into the caldera.

Since the explosion, at least 30 subsequent lava flows, dating from 150,000 to 70,000 years ago, have filled in and ob-

GEOLOGIC WONDERS

- ✔ **Geyser Basin** – Old Faithful, Morning Glory Pool, and other gems.
- ✔ **Grand Prismatic Spring** – The park's most beautiful geothermal feature.
- ✔ **Hebgen Lake** – Ponder the awesome earthquake of 1959.
- ✔ **Grand Teton** – Molten dikes, fault scarps, and *those peaks*!
- ✔ **Mammoth Hot Springs** – Graceful travertine terraces.
- ✔ **Petrified Forests** – Hike up Specimen Ridge in Yellowstone NP or take the interpretive walk at Tom Miner Basin in Paradise Valley.
- ✔ **Norris Geyser Basin** – The region's hottest geothermal area, featuring Echinus Geyser, the park's second most popular geyser, and Steamboat Geyser, the world's largest.
- ✔ **Mud pots** – Head to Mud Volcano, south of Canyon; Artist Paint Pots, south of Norris; or Fountain Paint Pot in the Lower Geyser Basin.
- ✔ **Sheepeater Cliffs** and **Calcite Springs** – Hexagonal basalt columns near Tower Falls.
- ✔ **Obsidian Cliff** – Dark volcanic glass from the interior of a cooled lava flow.

scured the caldera, and life has reclaimed the area, though you can still make out the caldera in places. For example, as you enter the park from Grand Teton, you enter the Yellowstone caldera by Lewis Lake. If you drive from Ashton, Idaho, to West Yellowstone, you will drive up the side of the Island Park caldera. The park's Gibbon Falls pours over the edge of the Yellowstone caldera rim.

Many of Yellowstone's rivers today follow ancient lava beds. Lakes like Shoshone Lake and Lewis Lake formed between these lava flows.

YELLOWSTONE'S THERMAL FEATURES

Fueled by the underground furnace, Yellowstone bubbles like a pot on a hot stove, with over 10,000 geothermal features – more than all other geothermal areas on the planet combined. This isn't all that surprising; magma, the earth's molten rock, is closer to the surface here than anywhere else on Earth – just 3mi to 5mi underground – and the average heat flow from the region is 40 times the global average.

But heat isn't everything. Essential to Yellowstone's thermal features is the addition of water, falling onto Yellowstone as rain or, more often, snow. This surface water may seep down as deep as 2mi before it drains through the side channels of geysers, hot springs, and underground water sources. The water that eventually comes to the surface through a hot spring or geyser may have fallen as snow or rain up to 500 years ago.

Yellowstone's geothermal features and their "plumbing" are constantly in flux. Geysers suddenly erupt or dry up; hot springs gradually appear or explode so violently that they destroy themselves. They are all a mere temporary blip in the geologic timescale. Scientists are only beginning to fathom these superficial expressions of complex underground forces. The result is a land seemingly brought alive by demonic torment or a wizard's spell and is the closest most people will ever come to magic.

Geysers

Only 3% of Yellowstone's thermal features are active geysers (from the Icelandic *geysir*, meaning "to gush or rage"), but these 250 geysers still make up 60% of the global total.

As snowmelt percolates through the hot rock beneath the park, it is superheated. This heated water, being less dense than the colder water, begins to rise, creating convection currents. The earth acts like a giant pressure cooker, keeping the water liquid even though it reaches temperatures of over 400°F. As the water rises, it dissolves silica in the surrounding rhyolite rock base. At the surface this silica is deposited as the mineral sinter (or geyserite), creating the familiar ash-colored landscape that characterizes Yellowstone's thermal basins.

What gives geysers their "oomph" is the sinter seal that is deposited in geyser chambers, which causes the buildup of gas until it eventually forces its way through. As the superheated water rushes toward the surface, the surface water overflows, the water pressure drops and the water expands more than 1500 times in a violent chain reaction as it flashes into steam, exploding into the sky. Mineral deposits continually block the internal plumbing of geysers, until an explosion blasts a new path or the water diverts to other outlets. Geysers require walls of hard rock like rhyolite (the limestone of areas like Mammoth can't stand the pressure), part of the reason why Yellowstone's geysers are concentrated in the southwest of the park.

If you are out geyser hunting, an eruption is often signaled by an overflowing cone or pool, though this can go on for hours. Yellowstone's geysers can be fountain or cone shaped. Some erupt hundreds of feet into the air; others shoot gracefully across rivers. Some erupt only every few years; others are in perpetual torment.

Geysers and hot springs are often connected in complex and delicate underground networks and affect each other in ways we have yet to understand.

Hot Springs

Hot springs occur when there is a gradual rather than explosive release of water heat. The remarkable colors are a combination of mineral content, which affects the absorption and reflection of light, and water temperature, which supports a range of algae communities. The fact that algae or thermophiles are very temperature-specific leads to beautiful concentric bands of differing colors. Blue pools are the hottest pools and absorb all color except blue. Green pools result when the blue is mixed with small amounts of yellow sulfur. The smallest springs rage away like hot oil in a deep fat fryer, and larger springs churn like giant washing machines. Still others remain completely still.

Mud Pots

Mud pots are created when rock is dissolved by the sulfuric acid in groundwater to create kaolinite, a form of clay. Mud pots are generally above the water table, higher than geysers, where less water is available. Most mud pots get their only water from rain, snow, and condensation, so the mud consistency depends on climatic conditions. Mud pots are generally quite watery in spring and thicker toward the end of the summer. The bubbling of the mud makes them appear as if they are boiling, but this is actually the release of steam and gas. The mud is often colored by minerals such as sulfur and iron, giving rise to the nickname "paint pots."

Fumaroles

These are essentially dry geysers, bursting with heat but without a major water source, whose water boils away before reaching the surface. These steam vents also give off carbon dioxide and some hydrogen sulfide (the characteristic "rotten eggs" smell), often with a hiss or roaring sound. Roaring Mountain on the Mammoth-Norris road is a huge collection of fumaroles.

Visitors at a hot spring, 1904

Travertine Terraces

The limestone rock of the Mammoth region contrasts with the silica-rich rhyolite found elsewhere in the park. Here, carbon dioxide dissolves in hot water to form carbonic acid, which then dissolves the surrounding limestone (or calcium carbonate). As this watery solution breaks the surface some carbon dioxide escapes from solution and limestone is deposited as travertine (as opposed to the geyserite), forming beautiful terraces. These terraces can grow up to an inch per day and are in constant flux.

Yellowstone Lake

One of the world's largest alpine lakes, Yellowstone Lake was formed by the Yellowstone caldera and later glacial erosion. Over time, the lake has drained west into the Pacific Ocean, north to the Arctic Ocean, and now into the Atlantic Ocean via the Gulf of Mexico.

Between 1923 and 1984 the Yellowstone caldera rose 3ft (and then started to drop). This caused the lake's north shore to rise, creating beaches, and the south shore to drop, causing inundation.

Hydrothermal explosions have further shaped the shoreline, creating the inlets of West Thumb (a caldera within a caldera), Mary Bay, and nearby Indian Pond. All the thermal features normally found in geyser basins are found beneath Yellowstone Lake. Recent underwater robotic cameras have revealed underwater geysers, 20ft-high cones, rows of thermal spires, and more than 200 vents and craters, some the size of football fields, on the lake floor. Mary Bay and the lake floor canyon west of Stephenson Island are the hottest parts of the lake, due to numerous hot springs and vents.

Other Geologic Features

GRAND CANYON OF THE YELLOWSTONE

This canyon, one of the park's premier attractions, was formed as the Yellowstone River eroded an area of faulted rhyolite that had been weakened by thermal activity (think of how a potato weakens as it is baked). The fledgling canyon was later blocked up to three times by glaciers (14,000 to 18,000 years ago), and the subsequent glacial flooding created the classic V-shaped (river-eroded) canyon. The canyon reached its present form only about 10,000 years ago.

Like many of Yellowstone's waterfalls, the Lower Falls of the Yellowstone tumble over the junction of hard lava bedrock and softer rock, in this case rhyolite and thermal areas.

PETRIFIED FORESTS

Petrified forests are found throughout the region, particularly in the Gallatin Forest and at Specimen Ridge in Yellowstone. They are mostly trees that were rapidly buried in situ by lava and mudflows. The wood cells were gradually replaced with silica derived from the volcanic ash. In many areas subsequent forests grew in the fertile volcanic soil, as quickly as 200 years after an eruption, only to have later eruptions cover them in ash and lava. In Yellowstone's Specimen Ridge, this has resulted in up to 27 petrified forests layered on top of each other. The ridge contains more than 100 types of petrified vegetation and is believed to hold the word's largest collection of petrified trees.

The petrified trees we see today are around 50 million years old and have been exposed by erosion. Studies have revealed that these trees include subtropical redwoods and oaks, which point toward moister and warmer prehistoric climatic conditions.

The Teton Fault

The Tetons are mere geologic toddlers. Surrounding ranges like the Gallatins and Beartooths were formed 55 to 80 million years ago by volcanic action, as part of the east end of the Western USA's Basin and Range region. At this time Jackson Hole was still a high plateau. The Tetons started to rise only 13 million years ago, as the earth's crust stretched apart. At that time the current peaks of the Tetons were still some 6mi underground.

The key to the Teton's breathtaking profile is the 40mi-long Teton Fault, which runs along the base of the range. Land on the east side of the fault has fallen, over millions of years, as the west block has hinged and angled upward. The east block has in fact dropped four times farther than the peaks have risen. The range was essentially created by a succession of several thousand major earthquakes and slippages. Several of these scarps are visible near Jenny Lake.

As high as the Tetons appear, this vertical distance is actually only a third of the fault's total uplift/fall. Gradual erosion of the peaks, combined with the sedimentation of the Jackson Hole valley, has diminished the Tetons by up to two-thirds.

The very tops of the Tetons consist of limestone, deposited by an ancient sea 360 million years ago. Over time these relatively soft sedimentary rocks have largely eroded, exposing more resistant granite. Freezing ice wedged and shattered this crystalline rock along its weakest joints, creating today's impressive pinnacles.

One result of the Teton's angled faulting is that the entire Jackson Hole valley tilts westward. The west half of Jackson Lake is three times deeper than the east, due to both tilting and glacial scouring. Oddly, the land west of the Teton peaks is drained to the *east*; that is, the peaks don't define the drainage systems as in most other mountain ranges.

A landscape shaped by glaciation: before and after a glacier's retreat.

Glaciation

The other major formative influence on the Yellowstone environment has been glaciation. As if supervolcanic activity weren't enough, thick sheets of ice up to 4000ft thick also periodically covered prehistoric Yellowstone and the Tetons, leaving only the highest mountain peaks visible. The most recent regional ice age, known as the Pinedale Glaciation, ended only around 13,000 years ago.

As glacial ice builds up and moves downhill, it sharpens peaks, carves out U-shaped glacial valleys, scours walls and creates moraine debris and lakes. The piedmont lakes lining the base of the Tetons were formed just in this way, as glaciers receded into lakes that were dammed behind their moraine wall, like glacial footprints. Research has shown that the Snake River once flowed south out of Jackson Lake, until blocked and diverted by these glacial moraines (it now flows east). Grand Teton's hiker favorite, the Cascade Valley, is one of several classic U-shaped glacial valleys, which contrast dramatically with the V-shaped river erosion of the Yellowstone Canyon). South of Jackson Lake, huge blocks of melting glacial ice formed the depressions known as The Potholes.

In Yellowstone's Geyser Basin, ice melted so quickly that large mounds of glacial debris were deposited to form low ranges such as the Porcupine Hills. The glacial deposits beneath today's thermal features act as water reservoirs for the various geysers and hot springs.

Today, Teton's glaciers have largely retreated, and the region's largest glaciers are now found in the Wind River Mountains, which have the largest glaciers in the Lower 48. Nor is Grand Teton the highest peak in the region – that honor goes to Gannet Peak, also in the Wind Rivers. These and other regional mountain areas, such as the Beartooth Plateau, have been extensively shaped by glaciation and are characterized by U-shaped troughs, hanging valleys, cirques, rock basins, arêtes, moraine hills, and glacial outwash plains.

Many of the features we appreciate today have been relatively recent developments. If the construction of the Tetons were compressed into a single calendar year, then Jackson Lake would appear only eight seconds before midnight on New Year's Eve. Humans would enter the scene just one second before midnight.

Everything is in flux in geologic terms, and many glacial lakes are in the slow process of silting up, a natural process that results in the creation of new meadows.

Yellowstone's Future

The Yellowstone region has been geologically stable for about 10,000 years now, but the land remains restless. Earthquakes are the most visible and violent modern proof of continued tension in the earth's crust.

In 1925 the entire mountainside flanking the Gros Ventre river collapsed, forming a dammed lake that held for two years, until the dam finally broke and tore downstream, killing six people in the settlement of Kelly.

In 1959 the Madison Canyon slide killed 28 people in the Hebgen Lake region, creating Quake Lake in the process (see "The Night the Mountain Moved" on p 202). Three hundred of Yellowstone's geysers spontaneously erupted in the wake of the quake.

In 1975 a 6.1 scale earthquake rocked the Norris geyser basin. Hundreds of other small earthquakes are recorded every year in the Yellowstone region, proof that the astonishing geologic forces of the past are still very much alive.

Yellowstone is rising or falling as much as an inch a year, moving 65ft with each slow motion "breath," particularly at Mallard Lake Dome just east of Old Faithful, and Sour Creek Dome, east of the Hayden Valley. These bulges in the earth's crust are probably due to the withdrawal of molten rock from twin magma chambers on the rim of the Yellowstone caldera.

No one knows for sure what will happen if (or when) Yellowstone's slumbering giant awakens. Such an explosion remains beyond human experience. The role of this and similar hot spots in mountain building, plate tectonics, and possibly even the extinction of the dinosaurs is the subject of continued research and speculation. The bulging of magma chambers on the rim of the Yellowstone caldera indicates that another eruption is likely – but scientists agree not for *at least* another 10,000 years. A major eruption would undoubtedly destroy the park as we know it, causing major climate change that would affect human activity around the world.

Until then, enjoy the wondrous spectacle of Yellowstone's thermal features and, as you gaze up at Old Faithful or down through a hot spring into the bowels of the earth, remember the awesome forces at work below these mere surface expressions of Yellowstone's true grandeur.

NPS PHOTOGRAPHS

The 2.5 million acres of wilderness within Yellowstone and Grand Teton National Parks constitute the biological heart of what is increasingly referred to as the Greater Yellowstone Ecosystem – the earth's largest intact temperate ecosystem.

GREATER
YELLOWSTONE ECOSYSTEM

Greater Yellowstone radiates out from its untamed core into 11.7 million acres of surrounding federal lands, including seven national forests, three national wildlife refuges, 125,000 acres of Bureau of Land Management (BLM) rangeland, and one million acres of privately held property. Transitional edges spread out north beyond Bozeman and Red Lodge, east to Cody and Lander, south past Pinedale toward Big Piney, and west to Idaho Falls and Ennis. The Greater Yellowstone Ecosystem's rapidly growing human population exceeds 300,000.

The Greater Yellowstone concept originated in the early 1960s during a pioneering study of population dynamics among Yellowstone's grizzly bears, which mapped their year-round range at more than 300 sq mi. The concept has been expanded to include buffer zones around what federal land managers identify as "an island of mountains in the high, dry plains." The ecosystem's total area has been calculated at anywhere from five to 19 million acres.

This unique biogeographic island – a moist massif surrounded by arid plains – sustains the largest free-roaming concentration of wildlife in the Lower 48 states. With the reintroduction of wolves in 1995, the ecosystem is believed to harbor its full historic complement of vertebrate species (with the exception of the black-footed ferret). Greater Yellowstone's defining characteristics are the lack of ponderosa pines, the dominance of lodgepole pines, and the range of the grizzly bear.

For Everything There Is a Season, by Frank Craighead, is a unique book that illustrates the interdependent patterns of life in the changing seasons of the Greater Yellowstone Ecosystem.

Life Zones

Two main forces determine vegetation zones in Greater Yellowstone: bedrock geology and precipitation. Elevation is the most important factor determining which plant species grow where. Although hikers will note significant variations in plant species, the overall patterns of forest composition are surprisingly consistent. Botanists generally distinguish five Rocky Mountain vegetation zones – riparian, foothills, montane, subalpine, and alpine. These zones are not strictly defined, and there is considerable overlap between them. The width and altitude of each zone increases progressively as you move from the north to the south.

Sagebrush dominates the **foothills** (4000-6000ft) of Yellowstone's arid Northern Range, which averages less than 20 inches of annual precipitation. The thin **riparian zone**, dominated by water-loving plants such as cottonwood, willow, aspen, and sedges, provides a transition between aquatic and drier upland steppe environments. **Steppe** (semiarid, sagebrush-interspersed meadows) eases the transition between dry prairies and the timbered montane zone. Here, plants take hold best on north-facing slopes, which are less exposed to the sun and hence retain moisture longer. Steppe vegetation is most often scrubby, with light woodland and sparse grasses, of which there are more than 160 species.

WILDLIFE MANAGEMENT IN THE PUBLIC EYE

How best to conserve the Greater Yellowstone Ecosystem and its native wildlife is a very contentious issue. Yellowstone National Park has traditionally been a focal point of the conservation policy-making maelstrom. Bear management is a case study. Prior to 1970 bears were considered a premier tourist attraction and were routinely lured to garbage dumps near hotels, where they were fed in front of the guests under the guard of an armed park ranger. In 1970 a comprehensive program was developed to discourage the habituation of bears to human food.

Elk management is another debated issue. Yellowstone's large population of elk traditionally migrates to lower elevations in the park's Northern Range for the winter. Past theories suggested that the concentration of animals grazing in this area damaged vegetation. As a result, a proportion of Yellowstone's ungulates (including bison and pronghorn) were routinely trapped or killed. Slaughtering thousands of fuzzy creatures on federal land eventually led to public outcry, and the practice ceased in 1968. A system of "natural regeneration" has been experimented with since then, and results have shown that the Northern Range is able to self-regulate and winter grazing does not have a significant effect on overall biodiversity.

One of the main obstacles to sound management is that decisions are often driven by public and political pressure rather than by scientific information. A case in point is bison management. The park's current management scheme caps the bison population at 3000, based largely on local pressure from ranchers to control the herd and protect neighboring livestock. Given that the total number of bison in the USA fell to less than 800 animals around the 1890s (from an estimated population of 65 to 80 million before the arrival of European Americans), the issue of genetic diversity in surviving animals is a major worry. Yellowstone's current herds are thought to have descended from between eight and 50 individuals. Current management plans restrict the free movement of bison – herds are discouraged from wandering beyond park boundaries and outside creatures are not allowed in. Annual culling based on number and disease tends to remove animals with certain characteristics, leading to fears that unnatural selection could be compounding the problem of low genetic diversity.

In the **montane zone** (6000-9500ft), snowfields linger later in the season and result in short, cool summers. These conditions limit the number of species but still support botanically diverse pine and fir forests on warmer south-facing slopes, where winter snow melts more quickly. Numerous shrub and berry species thrive in the damp montane understory.

The untamed **subalpine zone** (7500-11,00ft) is where trails break out into sweeping vistas speckled with twisted old trees and scattered pockets of forest. This rugged zone is dominated by so-called fir-spruce forest, where snow depths are the greatest. While powerful winds and biting frost limit forest development, stupendous wildflower displays erupt after the spring snowmelt.

Only the hardiest hikers ascend into the rugged **alpine zone** (above 9000-10,000ft), which takes in all rocky outcrops and exposed areas above the tree line. Despite a short frost-free period, alpine meadows support a myriad of wildflowers, which are at their most magnificent in June and August. Arctic-type "tundra" vegetation supplants stunted trees, commonly known as "krummholz," which can survive only in sheltered southern exposures. The Beartooth Plateau, where more than 200 plant species have been documented, sustains one of the country's largest expanses of alpine tundra.

Changing of the Seasons

Every time you sidle up to the bar, you'll hear a different story about the region's weather. Year-round resident pundits insist that Greater Yellowstone only has three seasons – July, August, and winter. Impatient hunters often ask, "If it's called 'tourist season,' why can't we shoot 'em?"

SPRING

The first tentative signs of spring appear during cold but clear and sunny late-February days, when shiny pairs of ravens perched in "ghost trees" start preening each other. Call-and-response hoots of great horned owls and the arrival of mountain bluebirds also signal that the vernal equinox (March 21) is just around the corner, even though snow still blankets much of the landscape.

Great horned owl

The first green leaves of stinging nettles appear as snowmelt begins in the lowlands. Spring has truly sprung when fluffy white male willow catkins appear in riparian zones. The majority of precipitation arrives during the May-June "monsoon."

As the snow line recedes around Jackson Hole, elk strike out northward from the refuge in search of fresh green forage. Paired sandhill cranes begin their elaborate courtship dances while red-breasted robins probe thawing stream banks for earthworms. The nests of overwintering eagles begin to host eggs in April, as northward migrating hawks become more conspicuous and ground squirrels emerge as if on cue from nine months of hibernation. Ravenous grizzly bears exit their dens with cubs in tow just as winter-killed ungulate carcasses begin to thaw.

Bison begin dropping calves in April as early wildflowers burst into bloom on warm, southeast-facing slopes. Cow moose begin calving in May, and cutthroat trout migrate upstream toward their summer spawning grounds. Waterfall watching is at its best during May and June, when rivers are at maximum flow.

SUMMER

As the days lengthen, the alpenglow lingers, and nighttime temperatures increase, it often feels as though *everything* is in bloom. Elk, deer, pronghorn, and coyotes are all dropping babies as the summer solstice (June 21), the longest day of the year, approaches. Bull elk sport antlers in full velvet as prodigious stonefly hatches coincide with the opening of angling season. Spring has truly yielded to summer once grasshoppers, mosquitoes, and biting flies abound. The wildflower bloom peaks mid-July in Yellowstone National Park and a bit later at higher elevations around Grand Teton National Park.

AUTUMN

Bison and then elk start rutting (mating) in late July and consummate their relationships before the first major snowfalls in October. Wild berries are everywhere in August, especially along watercourses at lower elevations, and mosquitoes and other winged nasties abate. Fall colors begin to appear as early as August in riparian areas around Jackson, and linger until snowfall in alpine zones. All the while, chipmunks furiously scramble about, caching winter seed and nut stashes.

WINTER

No matter what the altitude, winter in Greater Yellowstone is characterized by deep snow, short days, and bitter cold. Hints of winter appear as early as the autumnal equinox (September 23) – snowfall has been recorded every single day of the year somewhere within Greater Yellowstone. The long, dark six- to seven-month period sets in for good by November. Occasionally a warm westerly chinook wind blows in over the Rockies and raises temperatures to 40°F, melting the snowpack. More often the windchill factor sends the mercury well below zero. While many animals bed down for the winter, humans come out of hibernation on infrequent sunny days for cross-country skiing, geyser gazing, and snowmobiling. Yellowstone National Park's average annual snowfall is 150 inches, with up to 200 to 400 inches at higher elevations.

Animals Great & Small

Greater Yellowstone is arguably one of the world's premier wildlife-viewing areas, especially for larger mammals. Threatened species include the lynx, bald eagle, and grizzly bear. Endangered species are the whooping crane and a reintroduced gray wolf population. Featured below are some species visitors are most likely to see – or would *most like* to see.

LARGE MAMMALS

The prospect of seeing "charismatic megafauna" is one of the region's biggest draws. Yellowstone National Park alone harbors 60 resident mammal species, including seven native species of ungulates (hoofed mammals). Much of the wildlife mentioned below also ranges beyond the parks' boundaries into surrounding buffer zones.

Bears

The **black bear** roams montane and subalpine forests throughout Greater Yellowstone. It's an adaptable, primarily vegetarian forager that sporadically hunts smaller animals. About half of black bears are black in color; the anomalies are brown or cinnamon. Black bears are somewhat smaller than grizzlies and have more tapered muzzles, larger ears and smaller claws. Although they are generally more tolerant of humans and less aggressive than grizzlies, black bears should always be treated as dangerous.

Like grizzlies, black bears hibernate in a den over the winter, conserving energy by reducing their metabolism. During the tourist season, they are often spotted in Yellowstone National Park around Tower and Mammoth. Increasingly, they are being poached for their gall bladders and other internal organs used in Chinese traditional medicine.

The endangered **grizzly bear** (aka brown bear) once ranged across the western US. Today its population in the Lower 48 has been reduced to less than 1200, with 400 to 600 grizzles inhabiting the Greater Yellowstone region. Federal delisting of the grizzly as a threatened species and the implementation of an ecosystemwide conservation strategy are among the region's hottest topics.

Male grizzlies reach up to 8ft in length (from nose to tail) and 3.5ft high at the shoulder (when on all fours) and can weigh more than 700lb at maturity. Although some grizzlies are almost black, their coats are typically pale brown to cinnamon, with "grizzled," white-tipped guard hairs (the long, coarse hairs that protect the shorter, fine fur of the undercoat). They can be distinguished from black bears by their concave (dish-shaped) facial profile, smaller and more rounded ears, prominent shoulder hump and long, nonretractable claws.

Omnivorous opportunists and notorious berry eaters, grizzlies have an amazing sense of smell – acute enough to detect food miles away. Grizzlies enjoy a wide range of food sources, which varies seasonally. After bears emerge from hibernation between early March and late May, they feed mostly on roots and winter-killed carrion, turning to elk calves and then spawning cutthroat trout in late June. A feast of army cutworm moths lures bears to higher elevations in early September. Fall signals the buildup to hibernation, and consumption of whitebark nuts and the raiding of squirrels' pinecone stashes become obsessions. Before hibernation, bears can eat up to 100,000 berries in a single day. Scientists are concerned that falling levels of cutthroat trout in Yellowstone Lake and the spread of blister rust fungus, which kills whitebark pines, will have an increasingly detrimental effect on grizzly food supplies in the park.

Grizzly bear
and cubs

Male grizzlies generally live alone, require over 800 sq miles of territory, and can live for up to 30 years. Females have one to four cubs every three years and are fiercely protective of their cubs, which stay by their mothers' side for two years.

Grizzlies are most active at dawn and dusk in open meadows and grasslands near whitebark and lodgepole pines. They can become extremely agitated and aggressive if approached or surprised, but otherwise they do not

Coyote

normally attack humans. However, they viciously defend carcasses, thus trails are often closed when a grizzly is feeding nearby on a bison, elk or moose. For tips on what to do if you encounter a bear, see "Bear Necessities" on p 54.

Foxes & Dogs

The cagey **coyote** (locally known as "kye-OAT") is actually a small opportunistic wolf species that devours anything from carrion to berries and insects. Its slender, reddish-gray form soon becomes familiar to hikers. Coyotes form small packs to hunt larger prey such as elk calves or livestock, for which ranchers detest them. While wide-scale coyote eradication programs have had no lasting impact, reintroduction of wolves (which fill a similar ecological niche) is estimated to have reduced the region's coyote population by 50%.

The small, nimble **red fox** grows to 3.5ft, weighs up to 15lb and has a brilliant red coat. Foxes have catlike pupils, whereas wolves and coyotes have round pupils. Foxes favor meadows and forest edges and are primarily nocturnal. Although widely distributed, the red fox is not as abundant as the coyote, perhaps because the latter is such a strong competitor.

Red fox

The **gray wolf** (aka timber wolf) was once the Rocky Mountains' main predator, but relentless persecution reduced its territory to a narrow belt stretching from Canada to the northern Rockies. Its successful reintroduction continues to spark much controversy. Wolves look rather like a large, blackish German shepherd and roam in close-knit packs of five to eight animals ruled by a dominant "alpha" male and female pair. The alpha pair are the only members of a pack to breed (normally in February), but the entire pack cares for the pups. Between four and six pups are born in April or May, and denning lasts into August.

Wolves eat meat only and, in Greater Yellowstone, tend to focus their predation skills on elk. Packs communicate via facial expressions, scent markings, and long, mournful howls that can be heard from miles away.

Packs currently roam the Greater Yellowstone region as far afield as the Washakie Wilderness, Spanish Peaks, Beartooth Mountains, and the Teton and Gros Ventre National Forests. In Yellowstone itself packs go by the names Mollie (the upper Lamar Valley), Druid (Lamar Valley), Chief Joseph (the northeast corner), Leopold (southeast of Mammoth), and Nez Percé (the central plateau).

Ungulates

Greater Yellowstone's most abundant large mammal, **elk** (aka wapiti or red deer in Europe) can weigh 700lb and stand up to 5ft tall at the shoulder. Their summer coats are golden-brown, and the males (bulls) have a darker throat mane. Each year bulls grow

Elk

CALL OF THE WILD

Gray wolves, the ultimate symbol of wilderness (literally "where wild beasts roam"), have long been a barometer of wildlife-management policy in Greater Yellowstone. Revered by Native Americans, they were systematically exterminated in the West by the 1920s, listed as endangered species in 1973, then reintroduced into Central Idaho and Greater Yellowstone in 1995. The flourishing wolves have since successfully and rapidly dispersed. Packs now den in Grand Teton National Park and are frequently seen feasting on carcasses at the National Elk Refuge near Jackson Hole in winter.

Wolves ranged widely throughout North America in pre-Columbian times. They flourished in the West until the late 19th century, when homesteaders' livestock replaced bison herds in the Great Plains ecology. Poaching and predator control greatly reduced their population in the early 1900s. The creation of the National Park Service (NPS) in 1916 paradoxically led to the wolf's extinction within a few years, under misguided predator-control policies that allowed big game populations to increase to unsustainable levels.

Recognizing the need for a sustainable control regime, federal agencies worked more than 20 years on plans to reintroduce gray wolves. Ranchers were predictably suspicious, claiming that the alpha-predator would diminish game populations and that adequate compensation for wolf-killed livestock was unlikely. They also argued that wolves had already returned to the region, though some reported sightings may have been mistaken. The gray wolf, 26 to 34in high at the shoulder, 5 to 6ft long (from nose to tail), and 70 to 120lb, is more imposing than the smaller coyote, but inexperienced viewers could easily confuse the two from a distance.

Federal wildlife managers proposed a compromise, revising the wolves' status from "endangered" to "threatened," thereby granting ranchers the right to shoot wolves caught attacking livestock. In February 1995, 14 captured Canadian wolves were released into acclimation pens in Yellowstone's Lamar Valley. According to the Yellowstone Wolf Project, as of March 2002, 24 packs totaling 216 animals were denning in Greater Yellowstone. The organization Defenders of Wildlife has reimbursed ranchers $232,000 for depredations since 1987.

Idaho and Montana have drafted wolf conservation and management plans, and the Wyoming Game and Fish Commission hopes to have a plan ready by February 2003. Federal delisting of wolves as an endangered species could happen by the end of 2003. Check the Yellowstone Wolf Tracker (W www.wolftracker.com) for updates.

---

impressive, multipoint antlers (up to 5ft long, weighing up to 30lb) for the fall rut (mating season), when they round up harems of up to 60 breeding hinds and unleash resonant, bugling calls to warn off other males. Although elk populations were decimated in the 19th century, their numbers have largely recovered – beyond sustainable levels in areas say some. Elk are cautious and elusive, and prized by trophy hunters. Elk graze along forest edges; the largest herd in Yellowstone National Park beds down in the meadows west of Madison Campground. September to mid-October is the rutting season. Irresistibly cute calves drop in May to late June. A spring 2002 count estimated 30,000 elk in Yellowstone National Park and 17,000 in Jackson Hole. In winter, large herds migrate south to the National Elk Refuge in Jackson Hole.

Bison

Vast herds of **American bison** (commonly called "buffalo"), North America's largest land mammal, once grazed the eastern Great Plains as well as the western Great Basin, often migrating to Greater Yellowstone's high plateaus during summer. Greater Yellowstone is the only region where bison have roamed wild since primitive times. By 1902 there were only 23 wild bison living in the Yellowstone region. The park's current population was effectively bred back from the brink of extinction. Today, numerous herds exist throughout the Greater Yellowstone Ecosystem (an increasing number on private ranches), with three distinct herds ranging in Yellowstone National Park and another in Grand Teton National Park.

A truly majestic animal, full-grown male (bull) bison may stand more than 6ft high, have a total length of 12ft, and weigh in at 2000lb. Bison have a thick, shaggy light brown coat and a high, rounded back. Both sexes have short black horns that curve upward.

Despite their docile, hulking appearance and "aloof" manner, bison are surprisingly agile. They become increasingly uneasy when approached. A raised tail indicates one of two subsequent events: a charge or discharge. Statistically speaking, bison are

BISON & BRUCELLOSIS

A national symbol long revered by Native Americans, Yellowstone's hybrid mountain-plains bison are some of the USA's last free-roaming herds. Despite protection within national parks, their existence is threatened. Recent harsh winters forced bison to stray north outside the parks toward Gardiner, Montana, and west toward West Yellowstone, Montana, to forage.

During the 1996-97 winter, Montana ranchers slaughtered more than 1100 (one-third of the herd), ostensibly to prevent the spread of brucellosis, a bacterium that causes domestic cows to abort their calves. Brucellosis spreads from the region's abundant elk population to the bison, which are themselves unaffected by the bacteria. Whether or not brucellosis can actually spread from bison to cattle is questionable, as scientific studies are inconclusive. But public outrage soared upon viewing footage of the slaughter, filmed by the Missoula, Montana-based group Cold Mountain, Cold Rivers.

No policy to halt continuing bison slaughter has been implemented, but a long-term management plan is being considered that would allow bison to move outside the park into designated safe foraging areas, limit the maximum number of bison inside the park or vaccinate bison against brucellosis. Yellowstone's bison specialists doubt that brucellosis can be eradicated, however, due to the overpopulation of elk.

Snowmobiling also affects winter bison movement and is being studied as part of the equation. For updates on this volatile issue, contact the West Yellowstone-based Buffalo Field Campaign (☎ 406-646-0070; Ⓦ www.wildrockies.org/buffalo).

much more dangerous than bears. Every year several visitors are gored and seriously injured, sometimes even killed.

Bison roam three main areas of Yellowstone National Park: Lamar Valley, Pelican Valley at the north end of Yellowstone Lake, and along the Mary Mountain corridor between Hayden Valley and Lower Geyser Basin beside the Firehole River. August is rutting season – keep your distance to avoid becoming an unwilling rodeo clown. The bacterial disease brucellosis is one of the ecosystem's hottest issues. A new joint management plan calls for intense monitoring of the bison population, with goals of reducing the herd to 3000 animals and maintaining Montana's "brucellosis class-free" status.

Like bison, the **North American pronghorn** (often mistakenly called "antelope," though not related to true African antelope) is essentially a Great Plains herd animal, but a declining population also inhabits Greater Yellowstone sage tracts. Pronghorn have a tan coat with a white underbelly and rump patch. The tips of its horns are "pronged," curling backward to form a half-hook. The fastest animal in North America, the pronghorn can run up to 45mph, but its inability to jump fences is an often fatal weakness on the ranch-covered Northern Range.

The **mule deer** is a stocky, gray-brown animal with a white rump patch and white, black-tipped tail. Its name comes from its large donkeylike ears. A male (buck) typically reaches 5.5ft in length, stands 3.5ft at the shoulder, and grows 3.5ft antlers. Rutting bucks lock antlers, each trying to push the rival's head below its own. The mule deer's distinctive gait involves jumping with all four feet leaving and hitting the ground simultaneously. They are common in forests and grasslands, numbering up to 2500 during summer in Yellowstone National Park.

Mule deer

The less-common **white-tailed deer** were originally rare in Greater Yellowstone, but the clearing of forest by settlers enabled this adaptable species to spread throughout the region. The white-tailed deer is similar in form to, but somewhat sleeker than, the closely-related mule deer and can be identified by its conventional gait, smaller ears, and reddish-brown coat with distinctive white patches on its neck, snout, underbelly, and underside of its tail, which it raises while running.

The largest of the world's deer species, **moose** stand up to 7.5ft at the shoulder, can reach 10ft in length, and weigh as much as 1000lb. They have a brownish-black coat and a thick, black horselike muzzle. The male (bull) produces massive, cupped palmate antlers, each weighing up to 50lb, which are shed after the fall rut. Moose mainly browse aspen and willows, but also feed on aquatic plants. They are superb swimmers and can dive to depths of 20ft. Moose may become aggressive if cornered or defending

Moose

calves and may strike out with powerful blows from their front hooves. They favor marshy meadows and lakeshores with protective forest cover and are estimated to number around 1000 in Yellowstone National Park.

Arguably the animal that best symbolizes the Rocky Mountains, **bighorn sheep** are robust, muscular beasts, colored grayish brown with a white muzzle tip, underbelly, and rump patch. Males (rams) grow up to 6ft long, stand almost 4ft at the shoulder, and weigh more than 300lb. Their ideal habitat is alpine meadows or subalpine forests fringed by rocky ridges, which allow them to easily escape predators. Rams have thick, curled horns (weighing up to 40lb), which they use during the fall rut (from mid-September to late October) in fierce head-butting bouts with rivals. Discreet hikers can often closely observe bighorn herds around ridges or alpine valleys. The national parks, especially Glacier and Yellowstone, are some of the best places to spot bighorns, although they inhabit most wilderness areas in the northern Rockies.

The nonnative **mountain goat** is found from the Canadian border through the Idaho-Montana Rockies. Sure-footed and confident in even the most precipitous terrain, the mountain goat is highly adapted to the harsh environment of the upper subalpine and alpine zones. It has a shaggy, snow-white coat that includes a thin "missionary" beard and narrow, almost straight, black horns. Mountain goats can reach 5ft, stand 4ft at the shoulder, and weigh up to 300lb. Beware where you pee: Goats crave salt and will gnaw down vegetation (and anything in their way) in order slake their hankering.

Mountain goat

Cats

The solitary, nocturnal **bobcat** is a handsome feline – a scaled-up version of the domestic tabby – with a brown-spotted, yellowish-tan coat and a cropped tail. It mainly eats birds and rodents, but when easier prey is scarce, it may take small deer or adult pronghorn. Bobcats are thought to be widespread in the region, and it's not unusual to see one darting across a forest meadow or into a willow thicket.

North America's largest cat, the **cougar** (aka mountain lion) prefers remote, forested areas of the montane zone. With a size and shape similar to that of a smallish (African) lioness, the cougar may reach 7.5ft from nose to tail and can weigh up to 170lb. Even backcountry biologists who study it rarely encounter this solitary and highly elusive creature. It typically preys on mule deer, elk, and small mammals, and in summer it follows these animals as they migrate to higher ground. Curiously known to "stalk" humans without harmful intent, cougars have occasionally made predatory – but very rarely fatal – attacks on humans.

Cougar

In 1999 a female cougar with three cubs set up den on Millar Butte, in full view of Elk Refuge Rd, just south of Grand Teton National Park, and stayed there for six weeks. Around 15,000 people visited the area to see the cougar family during its brief stay.

The seldom-seen, solitary **lynx** is only slightly larger than the bobcat but has a silvery-gray coat and prominent black tufts on the tips of its ears. Males often have a slight mane and a biblike white underside. Their range extends from Canada through the Idaho-Montana Rockies, with two isolated populations in Utah's Uinta Mountains and Wyoming's Bighorn Mountains. Its preferred habitat is dense conifer forest. The entire predatory focus of the lynx is on the snowshoe hare. In 2000 the lynx was listed as a threatened species in the Lower 48. In 2001 ground and aerial snow-tracking surveys began on the east side of Yellowstone Lake, and in April 2001, DNA samples collected from hair snares confirmed the presence of a female lynx.

SMALLER MAMMALS
Rodents

A frequent inhabitant of montane and alpine streams, the **beaver** is a large, amphibious, paddle-tailed hydrologic engineer, gnawing down whole forests in order to dam up mountain waterways. They build island-like mounded dens (lodges) that protect their colonies from predators and winter cold. Busy beaver activity sustains open valley meadows that trees would otherwise recolonize.

It's difficult to distinguish the common species of **chipmunk** (least, Uinta, and yellow pine). All three are reddish-gray to ginger and have several longitudinal black and white stripes. Lightning fast, chipmunks can afford to be daring in their pursuit of a meal. Seemingly no campsite is without a resident chatterer ready to raid unsecured food.

The aptly named **yellow-bellied marmot** is a large alpine rodent that establishes extensive burrow systems in boulder-strewn terrain. Marmots fatten up on grasses and forbs during the frenetic summer months, then hibernate for up to eight months. Sentinels keep watch over feeding colonies and blast loud warning whistles at intruders.

Chipmunk

The bushy-tailed **red squirrel** has a brownish-red coat, a white underbelly, and light eye rings. It's especially common in the montane zone, feeding largely on conifer seeds. Red squirrels work feverishly to collect seed cones for winter, knocking them off the trees (sometimes hitting passing hikers) and burying them in secret caches. Strongly territorial, they furiously berate intruders with shrill chattering. Also entertaining are their fall mating antics, when courting pairs dart around like dervishes.

Greater Yellowstone also harbors numerous other small native mammal species, including gophers, ground squirrels, mice, voles, and wood rats.

Pikas, Rabbits & Hares

The precocious **pika** somewhat resembles a hamster. It inhabits alpine talus fields (often in close association with marmots) and communicates

Pika

using a distinctive high-pitched bleat. The pika energetically collects flowers and grasses, which it lays on rocks to dry before stacking them into bundles as winter fodder. Pikas are tolerant of humans and often crash picnics. Like rabbits, pikas eat their own feces.

White-tailed jackrabbits, desert cottontail, and mountain cottontail rabbits are all common in lower-elevation sagebrush and grasslands.

The ubiquitous **snowshoe hare** favors high tundra meadows and sports a reddish-brown summer coat, which turns snowy white in the fall as camouflage. Prolific breeders, hares are the main prey of the lynx.

Mustelids

About the size of a small dog, the **badger** avoids forested areas, mainly inhabiting stream environs, tundra meadows, or open foothills. Its coat is yellowish-gray with fainter side stripes and a long white stripe running back from between its eyes. This expert excavator builds large burrows (which later provide shelter to other species) and chiefly feeds on gophers, ground squirrels, marmots, and pikas, which it ferrets out of their burrows. The badger's search for food sometimes brings it into campsites.

Once extensively trapped for its soft pelt, the chestnut-colored **pine marten** (aka American sable) is a playful, weasel-like animal that prefers old-growth coniferous forests. It preys primarily on small mammals and sometimes ventures into the alpine zone to hunt marmots or pikas.

The largest member of the weasel family, the wily **wolverine** is typically 30-40in long and weights 30-60lb. Its coat is dark brown with a yellow-white racing stripe across its forehead and along each side. Confident in any terrain, this agile nocturnal animal is an enviable climber, digger, and swimmer. Despite its modest stature, wolverines can be incredibly vicious – reports of wolverines killing young elk and deer and seriously injuring bears are not uncommon.

Racoons

Racoon

The rascally **raccoon** frequents forest lakes in the montane zone, but (as a nonhibernator) it cannot thrive in higher areas with a harsh winter. Its fur is brownish-black and gray with a paler underbelly and characteristic black patches around each eye. The raccoon has an acute sense of touch in its front paws, which it uses to feel out hidden food sources. No joke: It will eat *anything*.

BIRDS

Boasting 316 recorded winged species (of which 148 are nesting), Greater Yellowstone is one of North America's most varied bird-watching habitats. The American Bird Conservancy recently recognized Yellowstone National Park as a "globally important bird area." Serious birders should pick up a copy of *Birds of Yellowstone* by Yellowstone National Park wildlife biologist Terry McEneaney.

Noteworthy large birds include common black ravens, resurgent peregrine falcons, reclusive sandhill cranes, honking Canadian geese, and American white pelicans. Smaller birds like pesky black-billed magpies and yellow-headed blackbirds are common sights.

Birds of Prey

This group of birds (aka raptors) includes eagles, falcons, hawks, and harriers. Sweeping across lakes, forests, or plains in search of fish or small game, they are some of the most interesting and "watchable" birds.

The iconic, recovering **bald eagle** is a large raptor, with a wingspan up to 8ft. It has brown plumage and a distinctive "bald" white head. Bald eagle pairs mate for life, building their nest close to water. The size of the nest grows with each breeding season to become a truly massive structure up to 12ft in diameter. The bald eagle often takes fish (or harasses an osprey until it drops its catch), but also preys on other birds or smaller mammals. Nesting eagles are extremely sensitive to human disturbance.

Bald eagle

The true "king of the Rockies," the gracious **golden eagle** is sometimes spotted riding thermals high above craggy ridges. This majestic mountain bird was venerated by Native Americans, who fashioned headdresses from its golden-brown plumage. The golden eagle is only marginally smaller than the bald eagle and typically nests on rocky cliff ledges that afford a bird's-eye view of potential prey and predators. The golden eagle's diet is also more varied, and it will swoop down on anything from fish and rodents to deer fawns.

The hooting **great horned owl** is mottled gray-brown and has prominent, "horned" ear tufts and a white throat. It's found throughout the Rockies, although its camouflage is so effective that few hikers even notice when they pass one. A largely nocturnal hunter, it preys mostly on rodents, but also feasts on grouse and other birds. It has a deep, resonant call.

The large, black **turkey vulture** (aka buzzard) is a clumsy creature, but once airborne it's a superb glider with a wingspan up to 6ft. Although its featherless red face should be enough to scare animals to death, the turkey vulture is a sporadic predator. It takes the occasional small rodent but prefers carrion.

The fish-eating **osprey** haunts larger lakes and rivers, nesting in shoreline treetops. Its upper wings and body are dark

Osprey

brown, and its underside is white on the body and inner wings and speckled brown-white on the outer wings. This well-adapted hunter has efficient water-shedding feathers and clamplike feet with two pairs of opposing toes to better grasp slippery, wriggling fish.

Waterfowl

A vast number of waterfowl are (at least partial) Greater Yellowstone inhabitants. Many migrate to the region only for the warmer months, arriving in May and departing for their wintering grounds in mid-September. They include species of coot, crane, gulls, and teals.

The spectacular native **Rocky Mountain trumpeter swan**, North America's largest wild fowl, is hardy enough to winter here, primarily on the Henry's Fork and Red Rock Lakes region west of the park. In 1932 only 69 swans remained alive in the Lower 48 states, all of them in Greater Yellowstone. Since then numbers have climbed to around 2500, but their numbers are declining. It has proven difficult to wean them from winter feeding, and cantankerous **Canadian trumpeter** populations continue to crowd them out.

Although not a true waterfowl, the flighty **American dipper** is amazingly well-adapted to life in subalpine streams. This otherwise unspectacular, small gray bird is often seen darting in and out of icy waters, feeding on fish fry or aquatic insects. It has oily, insulating feathers, strong claws to keep its footing in a swift current, and even "flies" underwater.

The majestic **great blue heron** is a large, gray-blue wading bird common around mountain lakes, marshes, and rivers. Often mistaken for a crane, it quietly stalks in the shallows, waiting to pluck out fish, frogs, or invertebrates. The bird's long neck is kept fully recoiled while it roosts, and its gangly legs are outstretched awkwardly in flight.

The **common loon** is quite prevalent, and its beautiful mournful wail echoes across tranquil backcountry lakes. Up to 35in long, it has a black-green head with speckled upper body and white underparts. The loon's dense body mass enables it to dive to depths of 150ft but also necessitates a long runway for takeoff, which limits it to larger lakes.

The small **snow goose** has either white or bluish-white plumage and black wing tips. In one of North America's great natural events, in early spring (from April) enormous flocks of snow geese overfly the Rockies on their way to nesting grounds on the arctic tundra. In the fall (from mid-September) the geese return south to overwinter along the Mexico/US border, completing their epic 12,000mi journey.

The attractive **western grebe** is found on deeper lakes. It's recognizable by its mellow, lilting call, a distinctive long, slender neck with a white front and black back, and a yellow, pointed beak. Its other plumage is whitish brown. In a complex courtship ritual, pairing

Great blue heron

Western grebe

western grebes flit and "dance" together across the water, then build a floating nest moored to underwater plants.

Smaller Birds

The boisterous **Clark's nutcracker**, a member of the crow family, is light gray with black wings and a white tail. It patrols subalpine forests, feeding largely on conifer nuts, which it breaks open with its long, black beak.

The diminutive **mountain chickadee** is a titmouse species and year-round resident of subalpine forests, where it gorges on insects. It has a black cap and throat bib, and its onomatopoeic name describes its distinctive call, "chick-a-dee-dee-dee."

Clark's nutcracker

The **red-naped sapsucker** is a woodpecker species with a black back, white stripes above and below each eye, and a red chin and forehead. It bores into tree bark (preferably aspen or willow), discharging gooey sap that traps insects, both of which it devours. Despite the damage it causes to the trees, the bird's activity helps control the even more destructive bark beetle and other noxious insects.

The striking **Steller's jay** has lustrous-blue plumage, except for its black crest (the longest of any North American bird), head, and nape. Its grating "ack-ack-ack" call is also distinctive, if less attractive. Although its diet consists of pine nuts, berries, and insects, it's also an incorrigible scavenger and frequently raids camps for unattended scraps.

FISH

Yellowstone Lake is at the heart of one of North America's most significant aquatic wildernesses, which is home to 21 gilled species. There are 2650mi of running water, with more than 220 lakes and at least a thousand streams covering 5% of the park's surface area. Fish provide critical forage for bears, waterfowl, otters, and raptors throughout the ecosystem.

Steller's jay

When Yellowstone became a national park, 40% of its waters were fishless. Introduction of nonnative species and stocking of some 310 million fish drastically altered the aquatic environment. Today 40 of the park's lakes are fishable. In 2001, NPS fishing regulations changed to require the release of all native sport fish caught in park waters. Terminal fishing tackle must be lead free, and no live bait is allowed. The grand irony here is that fish are the only wildlife that humans are allowed to prey upon in national parks – imagine catch-and-release elk or bison hunting! **Fish-watching** is an increasingly popular pastime around the outlet of Yellowstone Lake at Fishing Bridge and LeHardy's Rapids, where cutthroats spawn in spring.

Current major threats to Yellowstone's near-pristine aquatic ecosystem include the illegal introduction of predatory **lake trout** into Yellowstone Lake, increased cutthroat mortalities from parasitic whirling disease, and the invasion of **New Zealand mud snails**, which crowd out native aquatic insects.

There are three main native sport fish: two subspecies of cutthroat trout – the nearly extinct **westslope cutthroat trout** of the Gallatin and Madison river systems and the **Yellowstone** of the Yellowstone River system; the rare and protected **fluvial or riverine Arctic grayling**, which is barely hanging on in the Gibbon River drainage; and the slender silver **mountain whitefish**.

Nongame fish are much less studied (by anglers and biologists alike) than sport fish, but they are no less integral to the aquatic environment. Greater Yellowstone is home to at least nine nongame fish: five **minnows** (longnose dace, speckled dace, redside shiner, Utah chub, and a redside shiner–speckled dace

hybrid); three **suckers** (longnose, mountain, and Utah) and the **mottled sculpin**, which resembles a small catfish and provides forage for trout.

Six nonnative species live in the Yellowstone area: tasty **rainbow trout**, big **brown trout**, diminutive **brook trout**, tyrannical **lake trout** (the biggest culprits in the decline of the native cutthroat), lead-colored **lake chub** and a **cutthroat-rainbow trout hybrid**.

Brown trout

REPTILES & AMPHIBIANS

Cold-blooded and water-loving creatures are easily overlooked in Greater Yellowstone. Prehistoric glacial activity and current cool, dry climatic conditions are considered the main causes of their scarcity. Although none of the ecosystem's 24 species are listed as endangered, several are thought to be declining in the western US.

Reptiles

The poisonous **prairie rattlesnake** is most often found around rocky outcrops in river valleys below 7000ft; its bite is rarely fatal

to adults. The big **bull snake** is the region's largest snake, found below 6000ft along river corridors. The **valley garter snake** ranges west of the Continental Divide and is typically seen near water. The aquatic **wandering garter snake** is the region's widest-ranging serpent, found at up to 10,000ft. The secretive **rubber boa** is also found near water, where rocks and logs provide shelter. The slim **yellowbelly racer** is most often seen slithering around Lander and Cody.

The rare **short-horned lizard**, which squirts blood from its eyes when attacked, inhabits the Wind River Range and sagebrush lowlands around the Snake River. The **northern**

Prairie rattlesnake

sagebrush lizard inhabits arid sage tracts around the ecosystem's eastern fringes.

Amphibians

Once common throughout Greater Yellowstone, the **boreal toad** is now much rarer than the regions' other amphibians. Adults can range far from wetlands and defend themselves by secreting an irritating fluid from behind their eyes. The common **boreal chorus frog** is seldom seen, owing to its small size and secretive habits. You're more likely to hear its conspicuous call, which resembles a thumb running along the teeth of a plastic comb.

The abundant **Columbia spotted frog** is the region's best-known amphibian, found in abundance near most bodies of water. The uncommon **northern leopard frog** is most often associated with beaver and cattail ponds below 9000ft. The widespread **blotched tiger salamander** breeds in fishless ponds and lakes, with a large population in Yellowstone's Lamar Valley.

INSECTS

Except for mosquitoes and a few of the 128 conspicuous butterfly species, Greater Yellowstone's daunting variety of 12,000 insects largely escapes the attention of most visitors (but not fly fishers). Although invertebrates are known to be extremely sensitive to environmental change (and therefore serve as key indicators of ecosystem health), few ecosystemwide inventories have been conducted.

Columbia spotted frog

Plant Life

Seven distinct floras from the surrounding mountains, deserts, montane forests, arctic tundra, and great plains converge in Greater Yellowstone. Yellowstone National Park's herbarium has inventoried 1717 species (counting 190 nonnative species), including nonvascular plants such as mosses, fungi, liverworts and 186 species of lichen. Seven percent of these species are considered rare.

Aquatic plants and grasses thrive in the marshes, rivers and lakes. A large community of unique algae and cyanobacteria, along with plants like the yellow monkey flower, flourishes in and around thermal features. Yellowstone's sparsely vegetated Northern Range supports grasses, sagebrush, and Rocky Mountain juniper. Lower-elevation mixed sagebrush and grasslands are carpeted by wildflowers, grasses, and shrubs and enjoy relatively warm, dry weather.

Plants of Yellowstone and Grand Teton National Parks, by Richard J Shaw (Wheelwright Press, 2000), is a well-illustrated introduction to the region's rich vegetation.

TREES

While flowers rise and fade with ephemeral beauty, trees maintain their majesty for centuries and are thus an ideal study for the budding nature enthusiast. With a few simple tips in hand it's possible to identify prominent species and appreciate the full sweep of trees cloaking the landscape. The harsher climatic conditions at higher elevations strongly favor coniferous species. With the exception of aspen, eight conifers dominate Greater Yellowstone's forests, which make up 60% of the region's total vegetation. Pines are especially well represented, with two-, three-, and five-needle species.

Douglas fir cone

In Yellowstone National Park, Douglas firs, quaking aspens, shrubs, and berry bushes blanket the mixed forests from 6000 to 7000ft between Mammoth Hot Springs and Roosevelt Junction. Lodgepole pine forests, which range from 7600 to 8400ft, cover 60% of the park's broad plateaus. At elevations above 8400ft the forests are predominantly Engelmann spruces and subalpine firs, interspersed with lodgepole pines, which shade out the spruces and firs. Above the tree line (10,000ft) is alpine tundra that supports lichen, sedges, grasses, and delicate wildflowers like alpine buttercup and phlox.

A beautiful, subalpine poplar species, **quaking aspen** has radiant silver-white bark and rounded leaves that "tremble" in the mountain breezes. Aspen foliage turns a striking orange-gold for just a few weeks in fall. As a regeneration species, it tends to reproduce by sending out root runners rather than by seeding. A stand of aspen is likely to consist mainly of clones from an original parent tree.

Not a true fir at all, **Douglas fir** is a tall, adaptable, and extremely widespread "false hemlock," whose natural habitat ranges from the foothills to the subalpine zone and from very dry to quite moist locations. Douglas fir has flattened, irregularly arranged needles, 4-inch-long cones with distinctive three-toothed bracts protruding between the scales, and thick, corky bark that protects it from fire.

Firs bear a superficial resemblance to spruces, but can be easily differentiated by their flat, blunt needles and cones that point upward on their upper branches. Easily the Rockies' most abundant and widespread fir species, the **subalpine fir** is usually found in close association with the Engelmann, or blue, spruce. Subalpine fir has characteristic silvery-gray bark with horizontal blister scars that often become cracked on older trees.

Lodgepole pine forests extend well into the montane zone. Lodgepole are dependent on periodic forest fires (without which they gradually lose ground to more shade-tolerant tree species). Lodgepole cones are coated in resin that melts in high temperatures, ensuring its seeds disperse only when fire has prepared a fertile bed of ash. Lodgepoles sport needles in bunches of two

Lodgepole pine

and straight, narrow "polelike" trunks that make for dense stands in recently regenerated forests.

The five-needle **limber pine** is essentially a subalpine tree and is always found on exposed outcrops at or near the tree line. As the name implies, limber pines have branches that bend rather than break under the force of gales or heavy snowpack. Found in subalpine zones, the closely related **whitebark pine** looks similar to limber pine, but has smaller, almost round cones that remain purple until maturity. Its seeds provide crucial autumnal forage for grizzly bears. Large individuals of this species stand near Dunraven Pass in Yellowstone and South Cascade Canyon in Grand Teton National Park.

Engelmann spruce is a towering, cold-tolerant conifer capable of withstanding winter temperatures of -50°F. It tends to dominate subalpine forests. Like other spruce species, Engelmann has round, slightly pointed needles and pendant cones that hang off the branch. Its resonant wood is used to make piano sounding boards.

Blue spruce (aka Colorado spruce) shares many of its characteristics with the Engelmann spruce, but its needles are slightly longer, tightly clustered, and have a striking silvery-white or "blue" tinge when young. It's not found in Yellowstone National Park, but is common along Grand Teton's Snake River as it courses toward Jackson Hole.

Black cottonwood is the largest broadleaved tree in the two parks. The slender **narrow-leaf cottonwood** species, which looks more like a willow, has more narrow, lance-shaped leaves.

Engelmann spruce

SHRUBS

The term "shrub" is a somewhat arbitrary label that designates a woody plant with many stems. These small woody plants may grow as heaths, form thickets, or stand as single bushes on slopes and in meadows.

Shrubby cinquefoil grows in meadows from the foothills to the tundra, sometimes in association with sagebrush. Throughout summer, this multibranched bush (up to 4ft high) is covered in yellow, buttercup-like flowers with five petals. Both livestock and native mammals, such as deer and bighorn sheep, browse the foliage only when no other food is available, so nibbled cinquefoil bushes are a useful indication of overgrazing.

Several dozen species of small willows are found in Greater Yellowstone, but their diversity often makes precise taxonomical classification impossible. Willows can be identified by their distinctive fluffy-silky "catkin" flowers, which resemble small bottlebrushes. **Dwarf willows**, such as the tiny arctic willow, only reach a few inches in height and creep along heat-storing alpine rocks to form "mats". **Shrub willows**, including the common

Blueberry

gray-leafed willow, form thickets along subalpine and alpine stream basins.

The scrumptious **blueberry** genus includes species locally known as bilberry, cranberry, grouseberry, huckleberry, and whortleberry. Almost all produce small, round fruits of bright red to deep purple that sustain bears and other wildlife throughout the Rockies. One of the most common species is the dwarf blueberry, which typically grows among lodgepole pines. Its low mats emit an enticingly fruity fragrance.

Junipers are aromatic, cedarlike conifers that generally thrive in dry, well-drained areas. Rocky Mountain juniper can approach the size of a small tree, and older shrubs (which may reach 1500 years) are typically gnarled and knotted. Birds feed on juniper "berries," allowing the seed to sprout by removing its fleshy covering.

The collective name for several strongly aromatic species of the wormwood genus, **sagebrush** thrives on foothills and drier montane meadows. Native ungulates and livestock shun the bitter foliage, so overgrazing tends to favor the spread of sagebrush. Hikers, on the other hand, enjoy the rich fragrance of a sagebrush meadow in the wake of afternoon thundershowers.

The **thimbleberry** (aka salmonberry) is a typical understory shrub found in moist, semishaded sites. It has thornless canes and vinelike leaves. Each August it produces a small cluster of edible red berries with a fleshy seedy texture and bitter taste not unlike raspberries.

WILDFLOWERS

A breathtaking variety of native (and exotic) wildflowers are found throughout Greater Yellowstone. Blooms peak from June to July, although some species (like gentians) tend to be at their best in August.

There are more than a dozen species of **gentian** (usually pronounced "jen-shun") in Greater Yellowstone. Most have trumpetlike flowers that are at least partially blue or purple. They tend to bloom much later than most other Rockies wildflowers. Found above 10,000ft, the pretty **arctic gentian** has trumpeted, greenish-white flowers with purple stripes and prefers moist, open sites like alpine bogs.

Columbines come in variants of blue, red, white, and yellow and are typically found at the edges of small, shaded clearings up to 9000ft. The especially attractive **Colorado columbine** has blue-white flowers with delicate long spurs, resembling a bird in flight. The nectar in the spur tips attracts butterflies and hummingbirds.

Fireweed is a perennial that grows as a single stem up to 6ft tall, crowned by clusters of pink, four-petal flowers about an inch

Columbine

in diameter. As its name suggests, fireweed is a vigorous opportunist that colonizes recently burned areas.

The **globeflower** has dish-shaped flowers with five creamy (sometimes pinkish) sepals around a yellow center. It favors swampy alpine meadows and associates with its near twin the marsh marigold.

Succulent shoots of **Indian hellebore** (aka corn lily) emerge from melting snowbanks in early summer and quickly develop into proud, 7ft-high stalks with large leathery leaves crowned by maizelike flower tassels. This plant, found mainly on moist, subalpine slopes, contains poisonous alkaloids – Native Americans used it as an insecticide.

Scores of species of semiparasitic **Indian paintbrush** are present in Greater Yellowstone. They generally have a tightly packed flower head, vaguely reminiscent of a small artichoke. Most are reddish in color, but yellow and white varieties are also fairly common. Indian paintbrushes often tap neighbors' roots for nourishment and hybridize readily to produce many variations, making it difficult for botanists to identify individual species.

Many species of **lupine** are found throughout the ecosystem, generally favoring dry, open slopes from the foothills to the alpine zone. Lupines have palmate leaves and produce purplish-blue flowers that set into seedpods (some of which are poisonous).

The delicate, yellow **glacier lily** (aka dogtooth violet or fawn lily) is a perennial subalpine to alpine species that thrives where winter snow lingers. In early summer the bulb produces several bright yellow flowers with six upward-curled petals. These lilies often blanket entire tundra slopes, which bears eagerly dig over to extract the edible bulbs.

Another member of the lily family, **beargrass** is limited to the southern part of Yellowstone National Park and the northern reaches of the Tetons. It's a hardy perennial found in well-drained montane and subalpine clearings. Fragrant white star-like flowers cluster around a central 4ft-high stalk. The waxy, blade-like leaves are favored tender spring forage among grizzly bears.

Lupine

LICHENS, FUNGI & MOSSES

Of all the lesser-known groupings of plants (mosses, fungi, liverworts, etc), lichens are worthy of pause. Arising from an odd symbiotic relationship between algae and fungi and growing at a rate best measured in millimeters per century, lichens are truly remarkable life-forms. Although 364 species have been identified in Yellowstone National Park, lichens are so poorly known that many species await discovery in Greater Yellowstone.

A few lichens are a familiar and unavoidable part of the Greater Yellowstone experience. Take for example the ubiquitous

wolf lichen, neon-yellow strands that festoon nearly every conifer trunk in the region. Look closely and notice how the lichens stop abruptly at a line that's several feet off the ground – this is the height of the winter snowpack. This is the only species of lichen that's known to be poisonous and was formerly mixed into bait set out to poison wolves, hence its name.

The **tree hair lichen** (also called "edible horsehair") colonizes conifers. This species looks so much like clumpy knots of brown hair that a Native American myth describes how it originated when trickster Coyote snarled his braid of hair in a tree and had to cut it loose. The Nez Percé used it to soothe stomachaches, and it remains the most widely used edible lichen in North America.

Fire & the Ecoystem

Each year tens of thousands of acres go up in flames in Greater Yellowstone. Some of these wildfires burn hot and fast, while others creep along, but all naturally ignited blazes are now considered an integral part of the ecosystem's life cycles. Land managers are increasingly experimenting with proscribed burns after decades of "Smoky the Bear" style fire suppression and prevention. Low-intensity wildfires allowed to burn at regular intervals clean out accumulated brush on the forest floor and deposit nutrient-rich ash in the soil that stimulates plant growth. In the absence of fire, conifer seedlings thrive. The resulting dense forest canopies produce a shady understory and biological desert that provides little sustenance for wildlife.

In 1972 the NPS switched to a more realistic "let-burn" policy in a sizable chunk of the backcountry, which acknowledged the importance of a natural fire regime but failed to recognize that what remained was not a natural ecosystem but an unsustainable, artificial one. Smaller prescribed burns might have restored the natural balance over time, but several hundred lightning strikes in one day during the dry, windy summer of 1988 ignited major infernos that threatened historic structures and blackened 793,880 acres. Only early September snows fully extinguished the fires that began in May.

The 1988 fires were more a public relations disaster than an environmental catastrophe. Only a third of the park's surface burned, and not even half of that was full-blown canopy fire – though many scorched areas are still visible from trails and along the Grand Loop Rd. Only a few large mammals, mostly elk, died. Small mammals, on the other hand, perished in large numbers because they were unable to outrun the fires and proved more vulnerable to predators in the fires' aftermath due to reduced habitat. Tourism operators in gateway communities, which suffered short-term losses from decreased visitation, unfairly criticized the essentially sound NPS policy of allowing natural fires to burn.

Since 1988, ecological (and economic) developments have been encouraging. In many of the burned areas, the open understory has flourished, with new grasses, wildflowers, shrubs and tree seedlings providing more diverse wildlife habitat. This developing mosaic may lack the appeal of pure stands of coniferous forest, but an increasing number of discriminating visitors are finding the recovering post-fire Yellowstone region an equally interesting or even more rewarding experience.

Stresses on the System

Greater Yellowstone faces innumerable vexing challenges. Perhaps the biggest is how to accommodate the swelling numbers of residents and visitors. Another is what to do about the invasion of exotic species like lake trout that are decimating native populations such as cutthroat trout, upon which threatened keystone inhabitants like grizzlies depend. Yet another conundrum is management of the ecosystem's widely wandering bison herds.

Current flashpoints cropping up on private lands in the ecosystem's buffer zones include threats to resume mining (some of which were thwarted by the Clinton administration's 1996 authorization of a buyout of the New World Mine near Cooke City) and negotiated land swaps in Paradise Valley to head off massive logging proposals. Possible road expansion projects within the national parks are another potential environmental boondoggle.

History has shown that Greater Yellowstone is not an ecological island. The age-old tensions surrounding the development versus preservation and passive management versus manipulation debates are heating up again as we enter a new century.

General Yellowstone Information

Yellowstone National Park ☎ 307-344-7381; TDD 307-344-2386
  W www.nps.gov/yell/
Albright Visitor Center ☎ 307-344-2263
Old Faithful Visitor Center ☎ 307-545-2750
Lake Clinic ☎ 307-242-7241
Mammoth Clinic ☎ 307-344-7965
Old Faithful Clinic ☎ 307-545-7325

General Grand Teton Information

Grand Teton National Park ☎ 307-739-3600; TDD 307-739-3400, 307-739-3544
  W www.nps.gov/grte/
Recorded Backcountry & River Information ☎ 307-739-3602
Visitor Information ☎ 307-739-3600
Weather ☎ 307-739-3611
Lost & Found ☎ 307-739-3450
Road Construction & Fire Information ☎ 307-739-3300
Emergency Park Dispatch ☎ 307-739-3300
Grand Teton Medical Clinic, Jackson Lake Lodge ☎ 307-543-2514
Colter Bay Visitor Center ☎ 307-739-3594

APPENDIX

Yellowstone Accommodations & Dining

Xanterra (lodging, activities or dining)
  ☎ 307-344-7311; TDD 307-344-5395
  W www.travelyellowstone.com
Xanterra Same-Day Accommodation Reservations ☎ 307-344-7901
Dining Reservations ☎ 307-344-7901
Camping Information ☎ 307-344-2114
Lost and Found ☎ 307-344-2109

Grand Teton Accommodations & Dining

Recorded Campground Information ☎ 307-739-3603
Grand Teton Lodge Co ☎ 800-628-9988, 307-543-2811
Dornan's ☎ 307-733-2415
  W www.dornans.com

Grand Teton Lodge Company ☎ 307-543-2811
  W www.gtlc.com
Signal Mountain Lodge ☎ 307-543-2831
  W www.signalmtnlodge.com
Flagg Ranch ☎ 800-443-2311
  W www.flaggranch.com

Grand Teton Activities

Recorded Climbing Information ☎ 307-739-3604
Activity Reservations ☎ 307-543-2811
Signal Mountain Marina ☎ 307-733-5470
Colter Bay Marina ☎ 307-543-2811
Leek's Marina ☎ 307-543-2494

Useful Organizations

Grand Teton Natural History Association ☎ 307-739-3606
  W www.grandtetonpark.org
Greater Yellowstone Coalition ☎ 406-586-1593
  W www.greateryellowstone.org
Teton Science School ☎ 307-733-4765
  W www.tetonscience.org
Yellowstone Association ☎ 307-344-2289
  W www.yellowstoneassociation.org
Yellowstone Institute ☎ 307-344-2294
  W www.yellowstoneassociation.org/institute
Yellowstone Journal W www.yellowstonepark.com
Yellowstone Net News W www.yellowstone.net/newspaper

Greater Yellowstone

NATIONAL FORESTS
Bridger-Teton Natonal Forest ☎ (307) 739-5500
  W www.fs.fed.us/r4/btnf
Caribou-Targhee National Forest ☎ 208-524-7500
  W www.fs.fed.us/r4/caribou
Custer National Forest ☎ 406-657-6200
  W www.fs.fed.us/rl/custer
Gallatin National Forest ☎ 406-587-6701
  W www.fs.fed.us/rl/gallatin
Shoshone National Forest ☎ 307-527-6241
  W www.fs.fed.us/r2/shoshone
National Recreation Reservation Service
  W www.reserveusa.com

TOURISM ORGANISATIONS
Travel Montana ☎ 406-841-2870, 800-VISIT-MT
  W www.visitmt.com
Yellowstone County ☎ 800-736-5276
  W www.yellowstone.visitmt.com
Custer Country ☎ 800-346-1876
  W www.custer.visit.mt.com
Wyoming Division of Tourism ☎ 307-777-7777, 800-225-5996
  W www.wyomingtourism.org
Wyoming State W www.state.wy.us.
Wyoming's Yellowstone Country ☎ 307-587-2297, 800-786-6772
  W www.yellowstonecountry.org
Cody Wind River Visitors Council ☎ 800-645-6233
  W www.wind-river.org
Idaho Travel Council ☎ 208-334-2470, 800-635-7820
  W www.visitid.org

CHAMBERS OF COMMERCE & COMMUNITIES
Big Sky W www.bigskychamber.com
Bozeman ☎ 800-228-4224
  W www.bozemanchamber.com
Cody ☎ 307-587-2777
  W www.codychamber.org
Cooke City ☎ 406-838-2495
  W www.cookecitychamber.com
Gardiner ☎ 406-848-7971
  W www.gardinerchamber.com
Jackson Hole ☎ 307-733-3316
  W www.jacksonholechamber.com
Jackson Hole Visitor Information Center ☎ 866-500-3654
  W www.dojacksonhole.com
Livingston W www.yellowstone-chamber.com
Paradise Valley W www.paradisevalleymontana.com
Red Lodge W www.redlodge.com
Teton Valley ☎ 208-354-2500
  W www.tetonvalleychamber.com.
West Yellowstone ☎ 406-646-7701
  W www.westyellowstonechamber.com

Winter Recreation

Travel Montana W www.wintermt.com
Backcountry Avalanche Hazard & Weather Forecast W www.jhavalanche.org
Mountain Weather W www.mountainweather.com
Snow King Resort ☎ 800-522-KING
  W www.snowking.com
Jackson Hole Mountain Resort ☎ 307-733-2292
  W www.jacksonhole.com

Red Lodge Mountain ☎ 800-444-8977
   W www.redlodgemountain.com
Grand Targhee Ski & Summer Resort ☎ 307-353-2300
   W www.grandtarghee.com
Big Sky Resort ☎ 800-548-4486
   W www.bigskyresort.com

Airlines

Northwest W www.nwa.com
Horizon-Alaska W www.horizonair.com
Delta-Skywest W www.delta.com
United-Skywest W www.united.com
Big Sky Airlines W www.bigskyair.com
American Airlines W www.aa.com
Skywest W www.skywest.com

Maps

Yellowstone National Park, National Geographic/Trails Illustrated
Grand Teton National Park, National Geographic/Trails Illustrated
Hiking Map & Guide: Yellowstone National Park, Earthwalk Press
Hiking Map & Guide, Grand Teton National Park, Earthwalk Press
USGS Map Index phone ☎ 888-ASK-USGS (275-8747)
   W http://mapping.usgs.gov

Books

Lonely Planet's *Rocky Mountains* by Mason Florence, Marisa Gierlich, and Andrew
   Dean Nystrom.

A River Runs Through It by Norman Maclean.
   Chicago: University of Chicago Press, 2001.
Death in Yellowstone by Lee H Whittlesey. Lanham, MD: Roberts Rinehart, 1995.
Downriver: A Yellowstone Journey by Dean Krakel.
   San Francisco: Sierra Club Books, 1987 (out of print).
Teewinot: A Year in the Teton Range by Jack Turner.
   New York: St Martin's Press, 2000.
Walking Down the Wild: A Journey Through the Yellowstone Rockies by Gary
   Ferguson. New York: HarperCollins, 1995.

HISTORY/GEOLOGY/ECOSYSTEM

Birds of Yellowstone by Terry McEneaney. Lanham, MD: Roberts Rinehart, 1988.
For Everything There Is a Season by Frank Craighead. Guilford,
   CT: Falcon Publishing Company, 1994.
Greater Yellowstone by Jim Reese and Rick Reese. Lanham,
   MD: National Book Network, 1991.
Indians in Yellowstone National Park by Joel C Janetski.
   Salt Lake City: University of Utah Press, 2002.

Journal of a Trapper by Osborne Russell. Santa Barbara,
   CA: The Narrative Press, 2001.
Plants of Yellowstone & Grand Teton National Parks by Richard J Shaw.
   San Francisco: Wheelwright Press, 2000.
Scats & Tracks of the Rocky Mountains by James Halfpenny. Guilford,
   CT: Falcon Publishing Company, 2001.
Yellowstone: A Visitor's Companion by George Wuerthner. Mechanicsburg,
   PA: Stackpole Books, 1992.
Yellowstone & Grand Teton: Wildlife Watchers Guide by Todd Wilkinson and
   Michael Francis. Chanhassen, MN: Creative Publishing International Inc, 1999
Wildflowers of Grand Teton & Yellowstone National Parks by Richard J Shaw.
   San Francisco: Wheelwright Press, 1991 (out of print).
Windows into the Earth by Robert B Smith and Lee J Siegel.
   New York: Oxford University Press, 2000.

ACTIVITIES

Lonely Planet's *Hiking in the Rocky Mountains* by Clem Lindenmayer, Helen
   Fairbairn and Gareth McCormack.
Lonely Planet's *Travel With Children* by Cathy Lanigan.

A Climber's Guide to the Teton Range by Leigh N Ortenburger and Reynold G
   Jackson. Seattle: Mountaineers Books, 1996.
Best Easy Day Hikes: The Beartooths by Bill Schneider. Guilford,
   CT: Falcon Publishing Company, 1998.
Cross-Country Skiing Yellowstone Country by Ken and Dena Olsen and Steve and
   Hazel Scharosch. Guilford, CT: Falcon Publishing Company, 1994.
Exploring the Yellowstone Backcountry by Orville E Bach.
   San Francisco: Sierra Club Books, 1992.
Fly-Fishing the Henry's Fork by Mike Lawson & Gary LaFontaine. Guilford,
   CT: The Lyons Press, 2002
Hiking Grand Teton National Park by Bill Schneider. Guilford,
   CT: Falcon Publishing Company, 1999.
Hiking the Beartooths by Bill Schneider. Guilford,
   CT: Falcon Publishing Company, 2001.
Hiking Wyoming's Teton & Washakie Wilderness Areas by Lee Mercer and Ralph
   Maughan. Guilford, CT: Falcon Publishing Company, 2000.
Hiking Yellowstone National Park by Bill Schneider.
   Guilford, CT: Falcon Publishing Company, 1997.
Jackson Hole Hikes by Rebecca Woods. Wilson, WY:
   White Willow Publishing, 1996.
Mountain Biking in & Around Jackson Hole, Wyoming by the Adventure Cycling
   Association, Missoula, MT.
National Geographic Photography Guide for Kids by Neil Johnson. Washington
   DC: National Geographic, 2001.
Photographer's Guide to Yellowstone and the Tetons by Joseph K Lange.
   Mechanicsburg, PA: Stackpole Books, 2000.
Teton Classics: Fifty Selected Climbs in Grand Teton National Park by Richard
   Rossiter. Evergreen, CO: Chockstone Press, 1997.

The Book: Guide to Mountain Biking in the Jackson Hole Area by Brian Prax and
  Mark Schultheis. Prax Photography & Productions, 2001.
The Yellowstone Fly-Fishing Guide by Craig Matthews and Clayton Molinero.
  Guilford, CT: The Lyons Press, 1997.
Yellowstone Trails: A Hiking Guide by Mark C Marschall.
  Yellowstone National Park, WY: Yellowstone Association, 1999.

Films

Shane (1953) dir George Steven; starring Alan Ladd
Mountain Men (1980) dir Richard Lang; starring Charlton Heston and Brian Keith
Little Big Man (1970), dir Arthur Penn; starring Dustin Hoffman
A River Runs Through It (1992) dir Robert Redford; starring Brad Pitt and
  Craig Scheffer
The Horse Whisperer (1998) dir Robert Redford; starring Robert Redford & Kristin
  Scott Thomas

Bookstores

Yellowstone Association ☎ 307-344-2293
  Ⓦ www.yellowstoneassociation.org operates bookstores at the park's visitor centers,
  information stations, and at Norris Geyser Basin.
Grand Teton Natural History Association ☎ 307-739-3403)
  Ⓦ www.grandtetonpark.org sells books and maps at all park visitor centers.
The Book Peddler ☎ 406-646-9358
  106 Canyon St
  West Yellowstone, MT
Cody Newsstand ☎ 307-587-0030
  1121 13th St
  Cody, WY
Country Bookshelf ☎ 406-587-0166
  28 W Main
  Bozeman, MT
Moose Rack ☎ 406-995-4521
  48025 Gallatin Rd
  Big Sky, MT
Red Lodge Books ☎ 406-446-2742
  16 N Broadway
  Red Lodge, MT
Silvertip Bookstore ☎ 406-848-2225
  501 Scott Street W
  Gardiner, MT
Thomas Books ☎ 406-245-6754
  209 N 29th St
  Billings, MT
Valley Bookstore ☎ 307-733-4533
  125 N Cache
  Jackson, WY

LONELY PLANET

You already know that Lonely Planet produces more than this one guidebook, but you might not be aware of the other products we have on this region. Here is a selection of titles which you may want to check out as well:

Rocky Mountains
ISBN 1 86450 327 0
US$24.99 • UK£14.99

Hiking in the Rocky Mountains
ISBN 1 74059 333 2
US$19.99 • UK£12.99

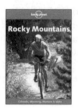

Yosemite National Park
ISBN 1 74104 117 1
US$19.99 • UK£14.99

USA
ISBN 1 86450 308 4
US$24.99 • UK£14.99

Available wherever books are sold.

INDEX

CLIMATE CHARTS

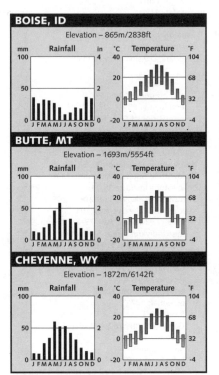

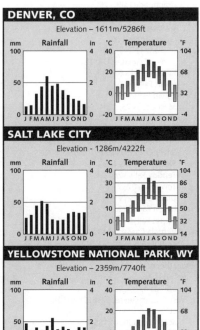

BOISE, ID
Elevation – 865m/2838ft

BUTTE, MT
Elevation – 1693m/5554ft

CHEYENNE, WY
Elevation – 1872m/6142ft

DENVER, CO
Elevation – 1611m/5286ft

SALT LAKE CITY
Elevation - 1286m/4222ft

YELLOWSTONE NATIONAL PARK, WY
Elevation – 2359m/7740ft

LONELY PLANET OFFICES

Australia
Locked Bag 1, Footscray, Victoria 3011
☎ 03 8379 8000 fax 03 8379 8111
email talk2us@lonelyplanet.com.au

USA
150 Linden Street, Oakland, California 94607
☎ 510 893 8555, TOLL FREE 800 275 8555
fax 510 893 8572
email info@lonelyplanet.com

UK
10a Spring Place, London NW5 3BH
☎ 020 7428 4800 fax 020 7428 4828
email go@lonelyplanet.co.uk

France
1 rue du Dahomey, 75011 Paris
☎ 01 55 25 33 00 fax 01 55 25 33 01
email bip@lonelyplanet.fr
www.lonelyplanet.fr

World Wide Web: www.lonelyplanet.com or AOL keyword: lp
Lonely Planet Images: lpi@lonelyplanet.com.au